As inequality deepens and morphs globally, it is urgent to understand the actors and driving forces behind it. This book offers a comprehensive understanding of how elite interests and organization impact inequality, the state, and the economy in Latin America, but also of how elites change in response to current shifts in capitalism and geopolitics. Bringing together brilliant young scholars with established influential academics, it provides a welcome addition to a booming literature on Latin American elites. It is essential for anyone keen on understanding the potential for building more just, egalitarian, and sustainable societies, in Latin America and beyond.

– **Benedicte Bull,** *Professor, Centre for Development and the Environment, University of Oslo*

The Political Economy of Elites in Latin America

Recent years have seen renewed interest in elites around the world, and their interconnection with power, privilege, social stratification, and social change. The contributors to this edited volume explore the many facets of the role of elites in the political economy of Latin America: their position within society, their impact upon the economy, and their influence within governing institutions.

The book demonstrates that in Latin America, as in many other parts of the world, structural change and movements toward more just, inclusive, and sustainable societies seem impossible without the involvement of elites at some level. This raises important questions: Under what conditions do elites push for reform? How do elites react to societal and economic challenges and changes? To what extent can popular classes successfully pressure elites? Bringing together a selection of case studies covering different Latin American countries, the book focuses on three key themes to address these questions: first, it explores how elites react to economic and societal challenges with some chapters looking at moments of change, as well as measures taken by individual elites to alter the status quo. Second, it seeks to understand the interrelation between external and domestic factors that engender elite action including global markets, geopolitics, state institutions, social forces, and the internal structure of elite groups. Third, it reflects upon methodological questions of studying elites in Latin America, laying bare the potential pitfalls and offering possible routes to further inquiry.

This book will be vital reading for researchers in political economy, development economics, economic sociology, and Latin American studies more broadly.

Jan Ickler is a researcher and Ph.D. candidate at the University of Kassel and coordinator at the Center for Advanced Latin American Studies (CALAS). He is focusing his doctoral research on the role of economic elites in Latin America's political economy. He studied philosophy, political sciences, and sociology and obtained his Master's degree in political economy.

Rebeca Ramos Padrón is a postdoctoral researcher within the CALAS-Laboratory Project Confronting Inequalities in Latin America: Perspectives on Wealth and Power. Previously, Ramos was a DAAD fellow as a visiting professor in the

Department of Political Science at the University of Kassel. For over 20 years, she worked as a professor in the Chair of Sociology at the University of Havana (UH), serving as its vice-director for 7 years. Ramos completed her Ph.D. in sociology at the UH and her MA in International Social Work at the University of Gothenburg, Sweden. Member of the UNESCO Chair on Sustainable Human Development-UH and consultant for UN-HABITAT-Cuba. She has published on issues related to social policy systems, employment, and labor market insertion from a perspective of social inequalities, socio-ecological transformation, and human development in Cuba and Latin America.

Global Challenges in Political Economy

Taxation and Inequality in Latin America
New Perspectives on Political Economy and Tax Regimes
Edited by Philip Fehling and Hans-Jürgen Burchardt

The Political Economy of Extractivism
Global Perspectives on the Seduction of Rent
Edited by Hannes Warnecke-Berger and Jan Ickler

Global Rentier Capitalism
Theory and Development
Edited by *Balihar Sanghera*

For more information about this series, please visit: www.routledge.com/Global-Challenges-in-Political-Economy/book-series/GCPE

The Political Economy of Elites in Latin America

Edited by Jan Ickler and Rebeca Ramos Padrón

Section Editors

Thomas Chiasson-LeBel, Aaron Schneider and Mariana Heredia

Routledge
Taylor & Francis Group
LONDON AND NEW YORK

CALAS
MARIA SIBYLLA MERIAN CENTER

First published 2025
by Routledge
4 Park Square, Milton Park, Abingdon, Oxon OX14 4RN

and by Routledge
605 Third Avenue, New York, NY 10158

Routledge is an imprint of the Taylor & Francis Group, an informa business

British Library Cataloguing-in-Publication Data
A catalogue record for this book is available from the British Library

ISBN: 9781032636726 (hbk)
ISBN: 9781032636757 (pbk)
ISBN: 9781032636764 (ebk)

DOI: 10.4324/9781032636764

Typeset in Times New Roman
by Newgen Publishing UK

Contents

Illustrations

Figures

Tables

Contributors

Ximena Alvarenga Fournier is a Costa Rican with a degree in political science from the University of Costa Rica (UCR) and a Master's degree in Virtual Learning Environments from the National Technical University (UTN, Costa Rica). She currently teaches at the School of Political Science at the UCR and is an associate researcher at the Institute of Social Research (IIS-UCR). She works on projects related to cultural management, e-learning mediation, and virtualization of training programs.

Jonathan Báez Valencia is an economist and research professor at the Universidad Central del Ecuador. He holds a Master's degree in Sociology from FLACSO, Ecuador. His research interests include inequalities, elites and economic groups, fiscal policy, and labor economics.

Thomas Chiasson-LeBel is an assistant professor in the Department of Economics and Social Innovation at the Université de l'Ontario français and an active member of the Extractivism and Society Research Cluster. He writes on economic elites, state theory, extractivism, and theories of development.

Gustavo Fuchs is a doctoral student at the University of Texas at Austin. He holds a Master's degree in Communication Studies from FLACSO Ecuador and a Master's in Law (LLM) from the University of Nottingham. He has worked as a researcher for the Inter-American Institute of Human Rights (IIHR) and as an associate professor at the University of Costa Rica, the National University of Costa Rica, and FLACSO Costa Rica. His research has focused on media studies, religion, human rights, and political communication.

Mariana Heredia is a sociologist who graduated from the University of Buenos Aires and completed Master's and doctoral studies at the Ecole des Hautes Etudes en Sciences Sociales in Paris. She is currently an independent researcher at the National Council for Scientific and Technical Research. She is a regular professor and director of the Master's in economic sociology at the Interdisciplinary School of High Social Studies of the University of San Martín.

Jan Ickler is a researcher and Ph.D. candidate at the University of Kassel and coordinator at the Center for Advanced Latin American Studies (CALAS). He is focusing his doctoral research on the role of economic elites in Latin America's political economy. He studied philosophy, political sciences, and sociology and obtained his Master's degree in political economy.

Juan Pablo Jiménez holds a Bachelor's degree in Economics from the University of Buenos Aires (Argentina), a Master's degree in Public Policy from Columbia University (U.S.A.), and a Master's degree in Economics from the Di Tella Institute (Argentina). He is Professor of Public Finance at the Latin American Faculty of Social Sciences (FLACSO). He is also a researcher at the Center for the Implementation of Public Policies promoting Equity and Growth (CIPPEC) and the Vice President of the Ibero-American Association for Local Financing (AIFIL). Jiménez was the Office Director of the Economic Commission for Latin America and the Caribbean (ECLAC) in Uruguay and the coordinator of the Fiscal Area of the Economic Development Division of ECLAC in Santiago, Chile.

Fernando Ignacio Leiva is a full professor at the Department of Latin American & Latino Studies at the University of California, Santa Cruz | UCSC. He holds a Ph.D. in Economics from the University Massachusetts Amherst.

Fernando Lorenzo graduated in economics at the University of the Republic of Uruguay. Diplome d'Etudes Approfondies (DEA) en Economie et Finances Internationales, Universidad Paris IX-Dauphine. Ph.D. in economics, Universidad Carlos III de Madrid. Former Minister of Economy and Finance in Uruguay. Senior researcher at the Centre for Economic Research (CINVE). President of the South American Network of Applied Economics.

James Mahon teaches courses on political economy, comparative politics, Latin American politics, U.S.–Latin America foreign relations, and Cuba. He has authored various works on taxation and financial flows in Latin America, political economy, and comparative social inquiry. His current research examines fiscal politics and the reform of the state in Latin America.

Martí Medina-Hernández is an interdisciplinary social scientist with training in sociology, political science, and quantitative methods. Before joining the Ph.D. program in Network Science at CEU, he worked analyzing the transnationalization of the Mexican corporate network and investigating the relationship between sexual networks and sexual orientation expression. He has a wide range of interests that span several areas, such as corruption, corporate elites, sexual networks, 4E cognition, and complex social systems in general.

Gabriel Ondetti is the Clif and Gail Smart Professor of Political Science and Director of the Master of International Affairs program at Missouri State University. His research focuses mainly on the politics of land reform and taxation in Latin America. Ondetti has also taken a strong interest in the dynamics of social protest. His second book, *Property Threats and the Politics of Anti-Statism: The Historical Roots of Contemporary Tax Systems in Latin America*, was published by Cambridge University Press in 2021.

Rebeca Ramos Padrón is a postdoctoral researcher within the CALAS-Laboratory Project Confronting Inequalities in Latin America: Perspectives on Wealth and Power. Previously, Ramos was a DAAD fellow as a visiting professor in the Department of Political Science at the University of Kassel. For over 20 years, she worked as a professor in the Chair of Sociology at the University of Havana (UH), serving as its vice-director for 7 years. Ramos completed her Ph.D. in sociology at the UH and her MA in International Social Work at the University of Gothenburg, Sweden.

Fabio Resmini is an assistant professor in the Department of Social Sciences at the Pontificia Universidad Católica del Perú in Lima. He was a Post-Doctoral Fellow at the Center for Inter-American Policy and Research (CIPR) at Tulane University (2022–23) and received his Ph.D. in political science at the University of British Columbia in Vancouver, Canada in 2022. His research interests include political parties, political economy, and democracy, with a regional focus on Latin America. His work has appeared in the pages of Comparative Political Studies and Comparative Politics.

Francisco Robles-Rivera is a researcher at the Institute of Social Research and professor at the School of Communication at the University of Costa Rica. Holds a Ph.D. in political science from the Freie University Berlin. CALAS fellow at the Confronting Inequalities Lab. He coordinates the Research Network for Latin American Elites Studies (Red Elites América Latina – REAL) and the working group "Elites" of the Consejo Latinoamericano de Ciencias Sociales (CLACSO).

Alejandra Salas Porras currently works at the Faculty of Social and Political Sciences, Universidad Nacional Autónoma de México. Alejandra does research in political sociology and political economy, as well as in corporate and political elites in Mexico. Her current project is "Transnational projection of Mexican and Latin American State elites."

Aaron Schneider is a professor of international studies at the University of Denver. His work focuses on the intersection of wealth and power, and he has conducted research in Latin America, India, and sub-Saharan Africa. In particular, he emphasizes the study of public finance as a window into the political economy of development and democracy. The way governments secure contributions from key social groups and how states decide what to do with the money tells a story about the nature of national political communities – who is in, who is out, and who will enjoy what benefits of membership.

Eduardo Silva received his doctorate from the University of California-San Diego in 1991. Before joining the Tulane faculty, he was professor of political science at the University of Missouri-St. Louis, where he also served as department chair and graduate director. His research focuses on Latin American politics, and he has published extensively on the political economy of state–society relations, sustainable development with a focus on forest policy, and mass mobilization.

He has conducted extensive field research in Chile, Costa Rica, Mexico, and Venezuela. He also has expertise in the Andean countries and Argentina.

Rose J. Spalding is a professor of political science and a Vincent DePaul Professor at DePaul University. She is also an affiliated faculty member in the Latin American and Latino Studies Department and in the Peace, Justice and Conflict Studies Program. She teaches courses on Latin American Politics, Latin American–U.S. Relations, Latin American Political Economy, States, Markets and Societies, Inequality in American Society, and Civic Engagement, among others. Her areas of specialization are Latin American Politics, Resource Conflicts, Elite Studies, Social Movements, Environmental Politics, and Civic Engagement.

Gustavo Viñales Guillama is a certified public accountant from the School of Economics and Administration of the Universidad de la República. Master's degree in Public Finance and Financial and Tax Administration, with specialization in tax administration, from the National University of Distance Education (UNED) of Spain. He has been teaching continuously since 1992 at the School of Economics and Administration of the UdelaR. He is Professor of the Postgraduate Specialization and Master's degree in Taxation of the UdelaR. He is an associate researcher and coordinator of the Fiscal and Tax Laboratory of the Center for Economic Research (CINVE).

Acknowledgments

This edited volume is the result of extensive and fruitful discussions on the relationship between elites and inequality in Latin America. Mariana Heredia, Thomas Chiasson-LeBel, Aaron Schneider, and the editors came together during the COVID-19 pandemic to transform these theoretical and methodological debates into a cohesive book.

In 2021 and 2022 the Maria Sibylla Merian Center for Advanced Latin American Studies (CALAS) hosted a research phase on "Confronting Social Inequalities: Perspectives on Wealth and Power" during which parts and individual contributions of this book were designed, written, and edited. The researchers gathered at the CALAS headquarters in Guadalajara, Mexico, during this time.

As editors, we are grateful to have worked with such incredible people and thank all contributors for their patience, perseverance, and passion. We owe a debt of gratitude to Mariana, Thomas, and Aaron for their work in arranging the three different parts of this book. Finally, we are thankful to CALAS for its support and funding, particularly to the directorate under Hans-Jürgen Burchardt and the management in the form of Jochen Kemner. We also extend our thanks to Routledge and its editorial staff. A special thanks goes to Samuel Withers for copyediting many chapters of this volume.

1 Introduction

The Political Economy of Elites in Latin America[1]

Jan Ickler and Rebeca Ramos Padrón

1.1 Challenges

Latin America[2] is confronted with a myriad of political, economic, and social challenges, many of which have been exacerbated by recurrent economic and political crises, such as the COVID-19 pandemic. In this complex landscape, political responses are urgent. However, formulating, enacting, and advancing these solutions is daunting, given the deeply entrenched institutional setting, which is often inefficient, non-transparent, and prone to partisan influence. In addition, political and economic reforms in the region are highly contested, and different social actors mobilize diverse resources and establish direct and often opaque channels with the state to secure their interests. They include social movements, political parties, governments, business leaders, and companies, among others. These actors are characterized by varying levels of influence and access to local, national, and regional political and economic governance, as well as within contexts of limited sociopolitical participation and fragile democracies.

One of the major historical challenges in Latin America has been the reduction of inequality and poverty. Since the colonial period, the region has been characterized by persistent social inequalities, income disparities, and unequal wealth distribution, accompanied by dynamics of exclusion and marginalization (Astorga 2016; Williamson 2011; Goinheix 2009). Although the recent period of the so-called pink tide brought about a notable reduction in income inequality and poverty, the disproportionate concentration of income, property, and power in the hands of the wealthiest remains an unresolved issue for the region (Lustig et al. 2011; Bértola and Williamson 2017).[3]

This reality is observable in studies that expose the wide income gap between the wealthiest 1% and the remaining population share: data from the World Inequality Database (WID [World Inequality Database] 2022) signals that the wealthiest 1% in the region account for 24% of all income and 44% of all personal wealth (Bivens and Kandra 2022; Ruíz 2020). Further studies suggest that the recent decline in inequality has only been a temporary phenomenon linked to the increase in the state budget due to the commodity boom, enabling the transfer of economic resources to the poor and extremely poor (Burchardt, Dietz, and Warnecke-Berger 2021). At the same time, the population with the highest incomes and wealth could maintain and/

DOI: 10.4324/9781032636764-1

or increase their fortunes (Burchardt and Ickler 2023). The interplay of these socio-economic factors underscores the multifaceted nature of Latin America's inequalities, demanding a more thorough discussion of the region's underlying economic and sociopolitical dynamics of the development paths.

Consequently, another significant challenge lies in transitioning from a resource-dependent development model to an economically and socio-ecologically sustainable one. This shift is crucial to transcend the region's historical dependence on natural resources and primary commodities since its integration into international markets. This dominance is characterized by the extraction and export of non-renewable resources such as minerals, hydrocarbons, and gas (Burchardt and Dietz 2014; Bulmer-Thomas 2003), as well as the large-scale export of agricultural products such as soy, palm oil, and biofuels. This has resulted in a defined set of characteristics deemed 'typical' for extractivist economies.[4] Specialization in extractive sectors tends to lead to recurrent boom and bust cycles, making economies highly vulnerable to global commodity price fluctuations. This instability extends beyond the economic realm: the dominance of extractive activities not only undermines the competitiveness of other sectors, thus perpetuating structural heterogeneity (Warnecke-Berger and Ickler 2023; Amin and Pearce 1976), but also reinforcing the control exerted by elites and state classes over natural resource extraction, exportation, and financialization (Göbel, Góngora-Mera, and Ulloa 2014; Elsenhans 1992). This perpetuates the prevalence of rent-seeking behavior in nature-dependent societies and facilitates the consolidation of extractivist enclaves and clientelist networks. Extractivism is a dirty business that impedes livelihoods, fosters further fragmentation and repolarization of the production structure, rapidly depletes natural reserves, and exacerbates the global dynamics of climate change (Engels and Dietz 2017). At the same time, looking at the trajectory of the past pink tide era with its renewed neo-extractivist impulses and the emerging global demand for critical natural resources, a structural shift away from this development model seems unlikely.

Another significant challenge for Latin America today, closely related to the first two mentioned above, is to enhance the quality of the region's democratic systems. Notably, a significant portion of the population is excluded from formal decision-making processes, limiting the representativeness of governance structures (Oxhorn 2022); the access to – often inefficient – state institutions is unequally distributed (Wright 2023, 170f.); recent trends indicate a decline in the Electoral Democracy Index for the region, signaling a deterioration of democratic standards (Valdés Ugalde 2023, 108). Furthermore, Latin American parliaments lack mobility and transparency in decision-making, hindering accountability and fostering opacity in governance practices (Garcia Montero and Rodriguez 2020). The legates of military dictatorships and authoritarian governments continue to influence contemporary political dynamics, perpetuating political cleavages; instances of past and present (political) violence cloud the political arena, further hampering efforts to consolidate democratic institutions. The political culture of populism, an overarching phenomenon in Latin America, results in political pendulum swings (Doyle 2011; de

La Torre 2010). A stark polarization of the political landscape, entrenched clientelism, and dubious practices during electoral campaigns make reforms difficult (Justesen and Manzetti 2023).

Amid social inequality, economic decline, and political stagnation, understanding the relational dynamics, structures, and reproduction mechanisms of key social actors within Latin American societies is imperative. Here, the pivotal role of elites emerges, intricately interconnecting these factors. Elites reflect the stratification of individual societies, characterized by the concentration of wealth and power on top. They also possess an enormous economic weight in the economies of Latin America. Lastly, personal and informal networks facilitate elites' access to the state and politics; clientelism, rent-seeking, and revolving doors are ubiquitous (Castellani 2018; Menaldo 2016; Solimano 2014). However, elites are not only expressions of such dynamics; they are also central, but not omnipotent, actors who can promote, limit, or block structural change. In this way, elites fulfill a double role and are one crucial puzzle piece for understanding Latin American societies' past, present, and future.

In recent years, there has been a significant resurgence of interest in studying elites in Latin America, marking a departure from a prolonged period of relative silence on the subject (Cárdenas 2020). This contemporary research on elites in Latin America is not just a rehash of 'classical' elite sociology frameworks but a fresh exploration with new theoretical and methodological perspectives. However, there is a noticeable dearth of comprehensive studies delving into the interconnections between elites, the economy, and the state. Furthermore, studies often remain confined to individual cases and micro-level analyses of specific elites. In contrast, this book seeks to understand elites' embeddedness in economic and political structures and the external and internal factors that undergird elite action.[5] This involves identifying the politico-economic spaces in which elites maneuver, such as markets, geopolitics, and state institutions, but also investigating the constellation of social forces and the internal structure of divergent elite groups.

While studies on inequality have predominantly concentrated mainly on people with low or extremely low incomes, this book demonstrates an apparent effort to explore the intricacies of the mechanisms of social, political, cultural, and economic reproduction of wealth. Therefore, the chapters presented here discuss the reproduction of wealth, Latin American elites, and inequality from a political economy perspective. Furthermore, the volume aims to provide a regional perspective through cross-country comparisons. This book examines the relations between elites and the state by presenting case studies of Argentina, Brazil, Bolivia, Mexico, Guatemala, Panama, and Chile. It also uncovers the interactions of corporate groups and global elites within contexts influenced by international and domestic economic dynamics. The remainder of this introduction presents the state of research regarding elites in Latin America. It establishes an overview of this book's theoretical and methodological program, introducing the contributions resembled in this volume.

1.2 Elites in Latin America: Institutions, Economy, and Struggle

Elites in Latin America have been studied from various theoretical perspectives and by pursuing multiple research strategies. From the old classics, which portray a rather functionalist conception of elites (Lipset 1971), up to refined quantitative studies of members of parliament in different countries of the region (Gonzales-Bustamante 2023), scholars have sought to identify the main dynamics that explain the composition, the resources, the strategies, and the impact of elites. Historians have focused on different phases of elite domination, their circulation, and trajectories from colonization onward (Gilbert 2017). They have paid particular attention to how educational, political, and economic institutions have given continuity to colonial legacies still present in Latin American societies and how their designs, norms, and networks serve as an opportunity for the reproduction of inequality (Adelman 1999).

A central topic in elite research is the proper definition of elites. It is the answer to the question: Who belongs to the elite? While myriad definitions exist, they each have certain shortcomings. Higley and Best, with a focus on political elites, give this definition of elites: "[...]individuals and small, relatively cohesive, and stable groups with disproportionate power to affect national and supranational political outcomes on a continuing basis" (Best and Higley 2018, 3). Research in this functionalist literature, thus, analyzes the formation of differentiated elites, such as educational elites, economic elites, and political elites, by focusing on formal positions. More critical approaches that emphasize elite resources and unified interest concern themselves with a relatively coherent and homogenous 'power elite' and its historical development (Hartmann 2007; Mills 1956). Apart from this, the existence of a transnational elite is discussed, which either appears in the form of a transnational capitalist class or is interpreted as a cosmopolitan elite (Davidson, Poor, and Williams 2009). Anthropological studies, in turn, have tackled the everyday practices of elites, including consumption patterns and lifestyles, often devoted to carving out dynamics of segregation and distinction (Cerón-Anaya 2019; Shore and Nugent 2002).

Historically, whereas in the colonial era and subsequently in many Latin American countries, it has been primarily land-bound elites (large landowners, caudillos, etc.) who wielded their economic power, in the last century, these elites have been transformed into entrepreneurs and financiers (Bulmer-Thomas 2003). This means that other forms of income and wealth have been added to land rent. Generally, elites portrayed a notable ability to adapt to different conditions and a certain degree of circulation. For Bull, Castellacci, and Kasahara (2014) as well as Schneider (2013), for example, this is reflected in the growing importance of large corporations. Also known as *multilatinas*, these conglomerates often operate in different sectors and are responsible for a large proportion of income and production in Latin America. Often family-owned and with far-reaching networks in politics and society, they shape the current economic structure of various countries. Here, the relationship between the specific insertion of Latin America into the international economy and the role of international elites is important (overview: North and Clark 2018).

Contrarily, the literature on democratic transition in Latin America focuses on the internal conditions in Latin American societies, portraying the ways elites have been influencing the democratization process (Collier 1999; O'Donnell and Schmitter 1986). In the 1980s, elite fractions opposed the autocratic systems to ensure against arbitrary state power and exploit new economic opportunities (Ansell and Samuel 2014). In this literature, different patterns of elite disunity led to divergent transition trajectories (Gill 2000, 51; Stepan 1986) and influenced the possibilities for inter-elite pacts. The focus on strategic elite interactions reveals an actor-centered approach, which seeks to explain patterns and forms of democratization by analyzing elites as quasi-rational actors who – determined by their self-interest in stabilizing their rule – choose their political actions by employing a set of given resources crystallized in political and economic institutions.

Often, elites in Latin America are analyzed as oligarchies enjoying paramount political power without much contestation. Here, an actor-centric approach seeks to explain the growing influence of elites and corporations on public decision-making processes in the Latin American region (Crabtree and Durand 2017; Hellman, Jones and Kaufmann, 2000; Hellman and Kaufman, 2001). The 'state capture by elites-thesis' often assumes a mere instrumentalist view of the state, being conquered by elite interests (Katz 2013; Lust 2020). Against this elitist reading of Latin American societies, intuitionalist approaches seek to understand the quality of conditions that enable and constrain elite action (Robinson 2012). Drawing from institutional economics and historical institutionalism, weak institutions are central to explaining development failures and elite performance (Acemoglu and Robinson 2013). Political settlement literature represents another institutionalist strand of elite research for which political settlements are an "[...] interdependent combination of a structure of power and institutions at the level of a society that is mutually 'compatible' and also 'sustainable' in terms of economic and political viability" (Khan 2010, 20). The political settlement is a configuration in which institutional structure and power distribution are compatible, thereby conducing to economic and political stability. In his original 2010 work, Khan indicates that political settlements can modify the institutional structure according to the interests of the powerful groups. If specific political alliances emerge, they can alter the institutional settings, producing unknown consequences. The objective here is to identify critical junctures in which power balances shift, ruling fractions undertake institutional reforms, and political settlements begin to change. The new constellation, as a function of its longevity and stability, represents a new political settlement, which endures over a new combination of institutional structure and distribution of 'organizational power.'

All these approaches have put a particular emphasis on the dynamics of elite circulation and elite struggle. Well-established and declining elites engage in complex networks of alliances and competition among themselves and occasionally with other social actors and the state, seeking to advance their economic interests internationally and nationally. Simultaneously, new elite groups may emerge, capitalizing on changing market dynamics and technological advancements to carve out their niche in the global economy.

Elite responses to economic shifts and trends generally reflect their strategic maneuvers to maintain and expand their economic and political influence in an increasingly globalized world. By capitalizing on emerging opportunities and forging alliances, elites strive to consolidate their power and control over resources, contributing to the particular configuration of the region's economic development and entrenching the existing social inequalities. This volume seeks to contribute to this research by presenting an approach to elites in Latin America rooted in political economy.

1.3 Content of the Book

A political economy approach to studying elites entails examining several dynamics: on the one hand, it investigates the configuration of power at the global, national, and local level; it aims to understand the economic dynamics in given contexts and their effects on the production, appropriation, and use of economic and political resources. On the other hand, it examines social actors with the capacities to influence and shape the social structure of their societies position themselves; it delves into the relationships among elites, their rivalries, and their capacities to form networks and alliances; it does not portray elites as all-powerful, monolithic entities but instead considers their relational positions vis-à-vis other social actors.

Furthermore, a political economy approach to elites stresses the centrality of understanding the interactions between elites and the national state and the implications of global phenomena. From a critical and contemporary point of view, it also challenges the limitations of traditional theories on elites, enhancing our understanding of how elites in Latin America navigate and shape socioeconomic and political landscapes. The following section of this introduction presents the book's structure and locates the individual chapters in this research program.

1.3.1 Part I: Elites in the Political Economy of Latin America

The first part of this volume dissects precisely this interplay between economic dynamics in Latin America and the position of economic elites. Using a combination of political economy and sociology, it explores the particularities and the most significant changes in the region's political economy. It scrutinizes these changes in relational dynamics with other elite factions and their interactions with the broader spectrum of social classes and groups within societies. This part also presents comparative studies between countries within the Latin American region – namely, Brazil, Mexico, Ecuador, and Bolivia. The authors question standard approaches that generalize elites as a compact group of economic actors with privileges that persist over time. The authors propose the existence of a heterogeneous elite, combining old and new factions, some with traditional local power resources and others more global.

As *Aaron Schneider's* chapter about two major economic sectors in Brazil illustrates, traditional sectors such as agriculture – especially in Latin America, which has a long history of excessive inequality in land ownership – exhibit a dynamic where internationally competitive elites tend to choose accommodative intra-elite relations with declining elite factions. Schneider portrays these elites as establishing economic and political ties at the expense of fostering relationships with popular class factions.

Gabriel Ondetti contributes a comparative analysis of the public sectors in Brazil and Mexico. The chapter sheds light on the relationship between elites, states, and development patterns, thus embedding elites in the general economic structure of societies. Ondetti argues that the ideology and organization of economic elites have determined the differences in the size of the public sectors in both countries.

Eduardo Silva and Fabio Resmini answer a similar question concerning Bolivia and Ecuador. The authors seek to understand how and why elites in both countries changed their preferences regarding economic policy during the pink tide. The chapter portrays how economic elites react and adapt to radical changes proposed by the governments. Silva and Resmini also consider the economic, social, and political resources elites utilize in both cases.

In the last chapter of Part I, *Alejandra Salas Porras and Martí Hernandez* analyze the relationship between Mexican elites and global corporate networks. Their chapter concerns the reorganization of Mexican economic elites after the crisis of import substitution in Mexico. Using network analysis, the authors can show the complex process of interaction and integration into global power networks, highlighting four different paths of how this integration took place.

1.3.2 Part II: Elites and the State in Latin America

The second part of this volume engages with the relationship between economic elites and the state. Thus, the authors of this part propose to delve deeper into how elites react in different cases to economic and social challenges. By doing so, they also discuss the autonomy of Latin American states from elites' influence and the State Capture thesis (Crabtree and Durand 2017; Cannon 2016). Given that the positions of economic and political elites have decisive power over the shape, scale, and outcome of development strategies (Amsden et al. 2012; Mahoney and Thelen 2010), this power might not be uncontested. This means identifying ruptures and moments of change and concrete strategies of individual elites to alter, stabilize, or give continuity to the status quo and shape the institutional environment in which they operate.

Fernando Leiva discusses the elite capture of the state framework in the Chilean case. By contrasting classical institutionalist frameworks with critical cultural and political economy, Leiva analyzes how Chilean elites have been capable of securing hegemony. To explain this outcome, Leiva introduces the concept of rentier capitalism and its underlying political and economic mechanisms.

Rose Spalding takes another route by analyzing concrete shifts in the relationship between elites and the Nicaraguan state. She focuses on the negations and alliance-building practices and how they have changed. In doing so, Spalding mainly focuses on the influence of dramatic shifts on the internal structure as well as the strategies of elites.

Thomas Chiasson-LeBel takes up this debate by discussing the state's autonomy concerning Bolivia and Ecuador. Incorporating the recent experiences of center-left governments in the two Andean countries, the chapter explains the changing positions of the economic elite vis-à-vis the state. Chiasson-Lebel also goes on to portray the internal division of elites when negotiating alliances with governments.

1.1.3 Part III: Elites, Wealth, and Power

The third part of this book analyzes the interrelation between power and wealth in the region. This entails discussing power theoretically by analyzing the power resources elites use to pursue their interests. Power is discussed here in terms of structural and instrumental power, highlighting multiple ways in which the capacities of elites can be analyzed (Fairfield 2015). However, as power does not only reside in the economic realm, the chapters also scrutinize elites' possibilities to influence public discourse.

In Chapter 9, *Mariana Heredia* is researching the structural and instrumental power of elites in Argentina. The author discusses power and analyzes the role of a mobilized society in restraining the elites' capabilities. The chapter not only traces the socioeconomic shifts in Argentina in the last 50 years but also captures the changing composition of elites.

Francisco Robles Riviera, Ximena Alvarenga Fournier, and Gustavo Fuchs present a study examining five cases in Central America. By employing a content analysis of elite discourse in social media, they trace how elites have been capable of influencing public opinion. By doing so, they shed light on how elites in these countries have influenced the political answers to the COVID-19 pandemic.

The two last contributions of this book tackle the region's marked disparities in the concentration of wealth resulting from limited Latin American tax systems and lacking instruments that effectively tax high incomes and extreme wealth (Burchardt and Fehling 2023). According to Zucman and Piketty (2016, 53), tax revenue loss for the states of Latin America amounts to 21 billion US dollars. In this context, and within the framework of this volume, economic elites play a central role, as they are not only the essential actors with the most significant access to wealth but also the leading players in the game of hiding wealth and fortunes. By employing diverse tax evasion practices, they condemn Latin American economies to more significant difficulties. This book's last part focuses on the problems of finding, measuring, and attributing this wealth, as well as the mechanisms to control and redistribute it.

Juan Pablo Jiménez, Fernando Lorenzo, James Mahon, and Gustavo Viñales examine the relationship between wealth concentration and the role of direct taxes and the absence of coherent records on corporate and real estate ownership structures as a fundamental reason for the weak distributive impact of the current tax structures in the region.

For his part, *Jonathan Báez* addresses the issue of tax havens in general and discusses the tax evasion mechanisms used by the wealthy in Ecuador. His main contribution is his analysis of the beneficiaries of nearly a thousand trusts in Ecuador to find companies in tax havens and estimate the resources these economic groups failed to contribute to national income.

Notes

1 This book project developed from the research phase on Inequality and Elites hosted by the *Center for Advanced Latin American Studies* (CALAS), www.calas.lat.
2 When referring to Latin America in this book, the term also encompasses the Caribbean region. This inclusion recognizes the historical, cultural, and economic ties that bind Latin America and the Caribbean, acknowledging the shared experiences and interconnected dynamics of these regions.
3 The term 'pink tide' refers to the electoral success of left and center-left governments (Levitsky 2011).
4 In this context, natural resource-driven development model and extractivism are used interchangeably. For a discussion of different terminology, see Warnecke-Berger, Hannes, and Jan Ickler (2023).
5 We are leaning toward a definition of elites based in political economy. Consequently, we focus on which actors under what conditions produce, appropriate, and distribute economic goods. For more on elite definitions, see later in this chapter.

References

Acemoglu, Daron, and James A. Robinson. 2013. *Why Nations Fail: The Origins of Power, Prosperity, and Poverty*. London: Profile Books.

Adelman, Jeremy, ed. 1999. *Colonial Legacies: The Problem of Persistence in Latin American History*. Hoboken: Taylor and Francis.

Amin, Samir, and Brian Pearce. 1976. *Unequal Development: An Essay on the Social Formations of Peripheral Capitalism*. Marxist theory and contemporary capitalism. New York: Monthly Review Press.

Amsden, Alice H., Alisa DiCaprio, and James A. Robinson, eds. 2012. *The Role of Elites in Economic Development*. Oxford: Oxford University Press.

Ansell, Ben W. and David J. Samuels. 2014. *Inequality and Democratization: An Elite-Competition Approach*. Cambridge: Cambridge University Press.

Astorga Junquera, Pablo. 2016. "The Haves and the Have Nots in Latin America in the 20th Century." *Revista de Economía Mundial* 43, 47–68.

Bértola, Luis, and Jeffrey Williamson. 2017. *Has Latin American Inequality Changed Direction?*. Cham: Springer International Publishing.

Best, Heinrich, and John Higley. 2018. "Introduction: The Palgrave Handbook of Political Elites." In *The Palgrave Handbook of Political Elites*, edited by Best, Heinrich, and John Higley, 1–6. London: Palgrave Macmillan UK.

Bivens, Josh, and Jori Kandra. 2022. "CEO pay has skyrocketed 1,460% since 1978. CEOs were paid 399 times as much as a typical worker in 2021". En: Economic Policy Review. 4 Octouber, 2022. Washington, DC. www.epi.org/publication/ceo-pay-in-2021/ (May 1, 2024).

Bull, Benedicte, Fulvio Castellacci, and Yuri Kasahara. 2014. *Business Groups and Transnational Capitalism in Central America: Economic and Political Strategies*. Basingstoke: Palgrave Macmillan.

Bulmer-Thomas, Victor. 2003. *The economic history of Latin America since independence*. Cambridge, New York: Cambridge University Press.

Burchardt, Hans-Jürgen, and Jan Ickler. 2023. "Riqueza, elites, impuestos – Viejos desafíos para un nuevo «giro a la izquierda»". *Nueva Sociedad* 303, 78–87.

Burchardt, Hans-Jürgen, and Kristina Dietz. 2014. "(Neo-)Extractivism – A New Challenge for Development Theory from Latin America." *Third World Quarterly* 35 (3), 468–486.

Burchardt, Hans-Jürgen, Kristina Dietz, and Hannes Warnecke-Berger. 2021. "Dependency, Rent, and the Failure of Neo-Extractivism." In *Dependent Capitalisms in Contemporary Latin America and Europe*, edited by Stefano Palestini, and Aldo Madariaga, 207–229. London, New York: Palgrave Macmillan.

Burchardt, Hans-Jürgen, and Phillip Fehling, eds. 2023. *Taxation and Inequality in Latin America: New Perspectives on Political Economy and Tax Regimes*. New York: Routledge.

Cannon, Barry. 2016. *The Right in Latin America. Elite Power, Hegemony and the Struggle for the State*. Milton Park: Taylor and Francis.

Cárdenas, Julián. 2020. "Élites en América Latina: una introducción." *Revista Española de Sociología* 29 (3), 459–465.

Castellani, Ana. 2018. "Lobbies y puertas giratorias – Los riesgos de la captura de la decisión pública" *Nueva Sociedad* 276, 48–61.

Cerón-Anaya, Hugo. 2019. *Privilege at Play: Class, Race, Gender, and Golf in Mexico*. Oxford: Oxford University Press.

Collier, Ruth Berins. 1999. *Paths toward Democracy. The Working Class and Elites in Western Europe and South America*. Cambridge: Cambridge University Press.

Crabtree, John, and Francisco Durand. 2017. *Peru: Elite Power and Political Capture*. London: Zed Books.

Davidson, Roei., Nathaniel Poor, and Ann Williams. 2009. "Stratification and Global Elite Theory: A Cross-Cultural and Longitudinal Analysis of Public Opinion." *International Journal of Public Opinion Research* 21 (2): 165–186.

de La Torre, Carlos. 2010. *Populist Seduction in Latin America*. Athens: Ohio University Press.

Doyle, David. 2011. "The Legitimacy of Political Institutions." *Comparative Political Studies* 44 (11): 1447–1473.

Elsenhans, Hartmut. 1992. *Equality and Development*. Dhaka: Centre for Social Studies.

Engels, Bettina, and Kristina Dietz. 2017. *Contested Extractivism, Society and the State*. London: Palgrave Macmillan UK.

Fairfield, Tasha. 2015. *Private Wealth and Public Revenue*. Cambridge: Cambridge University Press.

García Montero, Mercedes, and Cecilia Graciela Rodríguez. 2020. "Political Paths and Gender in Latin America. An Analysis of the Trajectories of Legislative Elites." In *Politics and Political Elites in Latin America*, edited by Alcántara, Manuel, Mercedes García Montero, and Cristina Rivas Pérez, 173–200. Cham: Springer Publishing.

Gilbert, Dennis L. 2017. *The Oligarchy and the Old Regime in Latin America, 1880–1970*. New York, London: Rowman & Littlefield.

Gill, Graeme. 2000. *The Dynamics of Democratization. Elites, Civil Society and the Transition Process*. London: Macmillan Education.

Göbel, Barbara, Manuel Góngora-Mera, and Astrid Ulloa. 2014. "Las interdependencias entre la valorización global de la naturaleza y las desigualdades sociales: abordajes multidisciplinarios." In *Desigualdades socioambientales en América Latina*, edited by Göbel, Barbara, Manuel Góngora-Mera, and Astrid Ulloa, 13–47. Bogotá: Editorial UNAL.

Goinheix, Sebastián, coord. 2009. *Conflictos y expresiones de la desigualdad y la exclusión en América Latina* (Martínez-Amador, David and María G. Carvajal Santillán, eds.). Argentina: Elaleph.com.

González-Bustamante, Bastian. 2023. "Ministerial Stability during Presidential Approval crises: The Moderating Effect of Ministers' Attributes on Dismissals in Brazil and Chile." *The British Journal of Politics and International Relations* 25 (4), 655–675.

Hartmann, Michael. 2007. *The Sociology of Elites*. New York, London: Routledge.

Hellman, Joel and Daniel Kaufmann. 2001. "Confronting the Challenge of State Capture in Transition Economies." *Finance and Development* 38 (3), 31–35.

Hellman, Joel, Geraint Jones, and Daniel Kaufmann. 2000. "Seize the State, Seize the Day: State Capture, Corruption, and Influence in Transition Economies," *World Bank Policy Research Working Paper No. 2444*. Washington: World Bank.

Justesen, Mogens Kamp, and Luigi Manzetti. 2023. "Poverty, Partisanship, and Vote Buying in Latin America." *Latin American Politics and Society* 65 (3), 1–19.

Katz, Claudio. 2013. Clases, Estados e Idiologias impreiales. Revista HERRAMIENTA, No.52. www.herramienta.com.ar/?id=1897

Khan, Mushtaq. 2010. "Political Settlements and the Governance of Growth-enhancing Institutions. Draft Paper." *Research Paper Series on Growth-Enhancing Governance*. London: SOAS; University of London.

Levitsky, Steven. 2011. *The Resurgence of the Latin American Left*. Baltimore: Johns Hopkins University Press.

Lipset, Seymour Martin. 1971. *Elites y desarrollo en América Latina*. Buenos Aires: Paidós.

Lust, Jan. 2020. Una crítica al concepto de la captura del estado. *MiNGA* 3 (4), 105–116.

Lustig, Nora, Luis Felipe Lopez-Calva, and Eduardo Ortiz-Juarez. 2011. "The Decline in Inequality in Latin America: How Much, since When and Why." *SSRN Journal*. DOI: 10.2139/ssrn.2113476

Mahoney, James, and Kathleen Ann Thelen. 2010. A Theory of Gradual Institutional Change. In *Explaining Institutional Change: Ambiguity, Agency, and Power* (pp. 1–37). Cambridge University Press.

Menaldo, Victor. 2016. "Democracy, Elite Bias, and Redistribution in Latin America." *Political Science Quarterly* 131 (3), 541–569.

Mills, C. Wright. 1956. *The Power Elite*. Oxford University Press.

North, Liisa L., and Timothy D. Clark. 2018. *Dominant Elites in Latin America*. Cham: Springer International Publishing.

O'Donnell, Guillermo, Schmitter, Philippe C., and Laurence Whitehead, eds. 1986. *Transitions from Authoritarian Rule: Prospects for Democracy*. Baltimore: The Johns Hopkins University Press.

Oxhorn, Philip. 2022. *Sustaining Civil Society: Economic Change, Democracy, and the Social Construction of Citizenship in Latin America*. University Park, PA: Penn State University Press.

Robinson, James A. 2012. "Elites and Institutional Persistence." In *The role of Elites in Economic Development*, edited by Amsden, Alice H., Alisa DiCaprio, and James A. Robinson, 29–50. Oxford: Oxford University Press.

Ruíz, Susana. 2020. "¿Quién paga la cuenta? Gravar la riqueza para enfrentar la crisis de la COVID-19 en América Latina y el Caribe." *OXFAM Internacional: Informes y publicaciones*. 27 julio, 2020. www.oxfam.org/es/informes/quien-paga-la-cuenta-gravar-la-riqueza-para-enfrentar-la-crisis-de-la-covid-19-en-america (March 14, 2024).

Schneider, Ben Ross. 2013. *Hierarchical Capitalism in Latin America: Business, Labor, and the Challenges of Equitable Development.* Cambridge studies in comparative politics. Cambridge: Cambridge University Press.

Shore, Cris, and Stephen L. Nugent, eds. 2002. *Elite Cultures: Anthropological Perspectives.* London, New York: Routledge.

Solimano, Andrés. 2014. *Economic elites, Crises, and Democracy. Alternatives beyond Neoliberal Capitalism.* Oxford: Oxford University Press.

Stepan, Alfred. 1986. "Paths toward Redemocratization: Theoretical and Comparative Considerations." In *Transitions from Authoritarian Rule: Comparative Perspectives*, edited by O'Donnell, Guillermo, Philippe C. Schmitter, and Laurence Whitehead, 64–84. Baltimore: Johns Hopkins University Press, 1986.

Valdés Ugalde, Francisco. 2023. *Democracy in Latin America: The Failure of Inclusion and the Emergence of Autocratization.* Berlin, Boston: De Gruyter.

Warnecke-Berger, Hannes, and Jan Ickler, eds. 2023. *The Political Economy of Extractivism: Global Perspectives on the Seduction of Rent.* Abingdon, Oxon, New York: Routledge.

WID (World Inequality Database). 2022. *World Inequality Report 2022.* WID.

Williamson, Jeffrey G. 2011. *Trade and Poverty: When the Third World Fell behind.* Cambridge: MIT Press.

Wright, Thomas C. 2023. *Democracy in Latin America: A History since Independence.* New York, London: Rowman & Littlefield.

Zucman, Gabriel, and Thomas Piketty. 2016. *The Hidden Wealth of Nations: The Scourge of Tax Havens.* Chicago, London: The University of Chicago Press.

Part I

Elites in the Political Economy of Latin America

2 Brazilian Agribusiness and Aviation

Intra-Elite Competition and Accommodation, Cross-Class Exclusion and Incorporation

Aaron Schneider

2.1 Introduction

Over the last 30 years, the international economy has been characterized by globalization, an increasingly integrated production, distribution, and consumption pattern through global value chains (GVC) (Gereffi 2018; Kaplinsky 2013). For Brazil and other developing countries, globalization has shifted the relative importance of different elite factions, with those adapted to international competition rising in prominence while others decline. Rising elites face a choice to accommodate declining elites or compete to displace them. Rising elites also relate to popular actors by incorporating them into dynamic, internationally competitive sectors or excluding them. These relations between elite factions and across upper and lower classes shape critical outcomes in terms of growth, distribution, sovereignty, and political inclusion.[1]

To make sense of these dynamics, this chapter explores intra-elite relations and relations with popular class factions in two sectors: agriculture and aviation. Both sectors adapted well to international integration over the last three decades but were subject to very different intra- and inter-class dynamics. To understand developmental and democratic outcomes, we must study the relational dynamics between rising and falling elite factions and popular sectors.

To summarize the argument, global integration raises the profile of elites adapted to new international insertions while decreasing the profile of elites poorly adapted to international competition. Yet, the politics of relations between rising and falling elite factions can produce competitive or accommodationist tendencies. In turn, intra-elite relations interact with relations to popular sectors, in which dynamic elites can either incorporate popular sectors or attempt to exclude them (Collier and Berins Collier 1991). Dynamic elites who incorporate popular sectors tend to produce more democratic and distributive outcomes. As a corollary, dynamic elites and popular sectors offer a social base in favor of greater strategic action from the state, including investments in research and development, human capital, infrastructure, and strategic action concerning international capital, thereby contributing to long-term development (Armijo and Katada 2014). By contrast, where rising elites accommodate declining elites, this elite pact uses the state to repress lower classes, offering more constraints and fewer incentives (Selwyn 2016). This

DOI: 10.4324/9781032636764-3

is unlikely to contribute to democracy or distribution, and it offers only short-term development by concentrating surplus and sharing it among rising and declining elite factions. The failure to invest in long-term strategies of international competitiveness forces local elites into a submissive relation to international capital (Katz 2015).

In Brazil, over the last three decades, aviation has been a sector in which dynamic, internationally competitive elites have been compelled to incorporate popular sectors whose skills, networks, and organizations operate within the production process to give lower classes leverage. They use this leverage to demand state support for competitiveness and a share of profits from dynamic factions of capital. Even when rising elites attempted to abandon their lower-class compatriots and submit to international capital, it was the relationship with lower classes that preserved a degree of sovereignty, developmentalism, and distribution in the operation of the sector. By contrast, agriculture has been a sector in which dynamic, internationally competitive elites have chosen to accommodate declining elite factions while excluding popular sectors, whose participation in GVC has been limited and possesses limited points of leverage to influence elite behavior. The result has been a lucrative agricultural sector that remains corrupt, environmentally destructive, and highly unequal, with limited strategic international insertion.

This chapter will explore intra-class and cross-class relations in two sectors in Brazil. It first outlines the relational approach taken here. To define the relational approach, the chapter considers varied institutional and political approaches to elites and democracy and development, arguing that other approaches have failed to consider institutions as political relations between and among class factions. Next, the chapter explores some of the evidence from agriculture and aviation, two sectors in which Brazil is competitive internationally but class relations between and among elites and other actors contrast.

2.2 Elitist Theories of Development and Democracy

Most approaches to elites (and popular sectors) attempt to characterize their core attributes with respect to outcomes such as development and democracy. This section will review some of the most typical of these approaches while making the case for a relational approach, in which elite factions are not necessarily imbued with core attributes but rather adopt behaviors and practices depending on their relations with other groups. It is, therefore, preferable to lay out a framework in which we can characterize the relations among and between class factions, in which explanatory power is drawn from these relations.

Some of the best-known theories of democratization focus on the attributes of elites. Modernization theory posited that democracy was associated with wealth, presumably requiring a certain level of development (Lipset 1959; Przeworski et al. 2000). More detailed causal analysis argued that less inequality was associated with democratization (Boix 2003; Acemoglu and Robinson 2006) while others emphasized middle-class size (Ansell and Samuels 2014) and values (Almond and Verba 1963). However, such deterministic predictions offered inconsistent evidence and could not explain backtracking, so the focus turned to the character of elites.

Some elites inherently, or could be convinced to, behave with tolerance, and favor democratic mechanisms of settling differences rather than outright conflict (Dahl 1982). Such approaches gave labels to describe elite position with respect to democratization: "hard-liners" and "soft-liners" (O'Donnell and Schmitter 1986), while others found that certain elites underwent "transformation" such that they no longer viewed politics as "zero-sum" (Higley and Burton 1998) or were "authoritarian" in personality and social composition (Fromm 1957; Adorno 1950).

Still others brought in popular sectors as an external pressure on elite decision-making. For Acemoglu and Robinson, the threat of violence from below forced authoritarians to "concede, repress, or democratize" (2006). Similarly, game theoretic approaches attempted to map elite and mass moves in sequences that occasionally produced democratic institutions, though they preserved the conceit that democratization "is often an enterprise undertaken by elites and for elites" (Albertus and Menaldo 2018, 3). In short, elite theories of democracy tend to presume that elites have inherent characteristics leading them to offer democracy to societies or not.

The same conceit characterizes elite theories of development, in which elites provide development and other classes are merely recipients or inputs. Classical approaches presumed that capitalism required first a dynamic class who accumulated wealth in an initial stage to subsequently invest and employ workers in industry – "previous accumulation" (Smith 1776, 117) or "primitive accumulation" (Marx 1990). Similarly, modernization theory presumed a "big push" of investment by those holding excess capital, i.e. elites (Rostow 1960). For growth theory, labor market inflexibility appears as a problem to be overcome,

> if there are too many restrictions on the freedom of employers to fire and to hire, or if the permissible hours of work are too tightly regulated, [...] or if trade unions have too much power [...] or if statutory health and safety regulations are too stringent.
>
> (Solow 2008)

Meanwhile, Washington Consensus approaches mimicked the "market fundamentals" approach (Williamson 1990) and attempts to modify a post-Washington Consensus approach presumed elites would drive development once states resolved market failures, "the government should see itself as complementary to markets, undertaking those actions that make markets fulfill their functions better – as well as correcting market failures" (Stiglitz 2007, 22). Workers remained primarily inputs to production, "growth accounting also attributes a substantial portion of growth in developing countries to human capital accumulation" or as potential obstacles if they "impose inflationary wage and other demands" (Stiglitz 2007, 25; 29).

Even more statist approaches continued to place decisive action in the hands of elites, framed as state elites, economic elites, or as Evans put it, the "embeddedness" of one in the other (1995). Drawing on economic and historical analyses, developmentalist approaches emphasized the need to alter comparative advantage such that elites invested in industry instead of primary production, eventually achieving international competitiveness (Gerschenkron 1962). Within the most influential work on East Asian development states, state elites provided incentives, encouraged innovation, and offered guarantees to economic elites, guiding them into industrial activities and toward more complex activities, "governing the market" (Wade 2004), "collaboration between big business and the state" (Johnson 1982), and "government imposes strict performance standards on those industries and companies that it aids" (Amsden 1989). Labor, once again, was an afterthought or, at best, an input to be disciplined (Chang 2002).

Even the institutionalist turn continues an elite focus. While it is the preference of political and economic elites to establish "extractive institutions" that preserve their power and concentrate wealth in their hands, they can be pressed by challengers or popular sectors to establish "inclusive institutions," such as secure property rights, law, and order, relatively open markets, state support to markets (public goods provision, regulation, contract enforcement), and education and opportunity for a sizeable portion of citizens (Acemoglu and Robinson 2012, 70–121).

Other institutional approaches are similarly elite-focused. For North, Wallis, and Weingast (2013), development depends on elites consenting to constrain their "use of violence to gather wealth and resources" (North, Wallis, and Weingast 2013, 1). "Open access orders" promote development through "open access and competition: political competition to maintain open access in the economy and economic competition to maintain open access in the polity" (North, Wallis, and Weingast 2013, 16). Varying degrees of less open access and competition afflict developing countries, as elites have not been convinced to abstain from violence or personalized institutions to capture the rents from economic activity.

Institutional approaches explained stagnation but could not explain why elites failed to alter their institutions, something that the political settlements approach tackled (Kelsall 2022; Khan 2018). Political settlements are "the elite bargain that structures the distribution of rents and personalized institutional arrangements between members of the dominant coalition" (Pritchett, Werker, and Sen 2017, 19). In a return to attempts to characterize elites as inherently "pro-growth" (Hickey, Sen and Bukenya 2015; Mehta and Walton 2014) or "rent-seeking" or "extractivist" (Bebbington et al. 2017), political settlements approaches turned attention to surveys of elites and a search for behaviors such as an orientation to exports and attempts to out-compete other firms, in short a search for "magicians" (Pritchett, Sen, and Werker 2017, 22).

2.3 A Relational and Class Factions Approach

The approach offered here argues for a relational approach, considering both varied factions among elites and lower-class groups, focusing especially on the relations among them. Essentially, one could argue that the specific characteristics of actors can be read and understood through "connections, ties, transactions, and other kinds of relations among entities" rather than as intrinsic features (Jackson and Nexon 1999, 2). Elites adopt their behaviors and take on their characteristics not because of inherent traits but because of their relations with other elites and popular sectors, and vice versa.

The most well-known relational approach is probably that found in Marx, who understood capital as a social relation that attained meaning when related to labor within a specific productive relation at a particular historical moment, "capital is not a thing, but rather a definite social production relation, belonging to a definite historical formation of society, which is manifested in a thing and lends this thing a specific social character" (Marx 1990, 814). Capital is only capital when it is deployed to purchase labor power (as in wages) or the means of production (such as machines); otherwise, capital is something else.

In the current framework, the important relations are horizontal among different elite factions and vertical between elite and popular sector actors. Among elites, the important factions are rising elites atop sectors dynamic because they compete to capture expanding rents from globally integrated forms of world production, while declining elite factions depend on existing comparative advantages or fail to compete at all. Relations among rising and declining factions of the elite can be either competitive or accommodating, in which competition indicates that dynamic elites are achieving dominance and driving structural transformation; accommodation indicates that dynamic elites either coexist with or submit to declining elites, utilizing corruption, coercion, or other practices that secure surplus without driving structural transformation, what some understand as "passive revolution" (Gramsci 1971) or "modernization from above" (Trimberger 1978).

Intra-elite relations interact with vertical relations between upper and lower classes. Popular sectors are either incorporated into dynamic, globally integrated value chains or are excluded. Where they are included, as in a greater demand for their labor and skills, they gain a degree of leverage within the production process and politically. They can threaten to withdraw their compliance and force concessions from dynamic factions of capital, forcing a "cross-class alliance" of the type some associate with "social democracy and development" (Reuschemeyer, Stephens, and Stephens 1992).

Coincident with the combinations of various class factions, various behaviors follow with respect to democracy, development, and international relations. Where lower classes are included and dynamic elites competitive, they can combine to pursue things like overcoming resistance from declining elites. They can also ally to secure state support for strategic actions with respect to foreign capital. Further, leverage within the production process allows lower classes to claim a greater share of the surplus, and leverage within politics allows them to press the state for more distributive public policies and more democratic practices (Boito Jr. 2018).

By contrast, where popular sectors are excluded from dynamic sectors, they must exert leverage from outside the production process; they have fewer mechanisms to claim surplus from production and less political weight to demand distributive policies and democratic practices. Excluded lower classes are also

Table 2.1 Relational Approach

Vertical relations: inclusive↔exclusive	Horizontal relations: competition↔accommodation		
	Upper class	International capital Dynamic elites Developmental state elites	Declining elites Coercive political elites
	Lower class	Middle-class Workers/peasants	Lower middle-class Precariat

Source: Own elaboration.

less useful to dynamic elites as allies when it comes to overcoming the resistance of declining elites, coinciding with, and perhaps even requiring, repressive and undemocratic authority to cement accommodation between rising and declining elites (Reuschemeyer, Stephens and Stephens 1992; Moore 1966).

This relational approach does not assume the intrinsic characteristics of elite or popular sector factions, nor does it assume the outcome of their interactions. In fact, it is possible, even likely, that relations among actors will change, producing shifting and dynamic outcomes for development and democracy. The figure below displays a table to indicate the possible relations (see Table 2.1). The important labels describe the relations among actors, competition/accommodation and inclusion/exclusion, as the relation gives the actors their character, shaping their behaviors and generating outcomes of interest.

By looking at the horizontal and vertical relations, various scenarios, actor characteristics, and democracy and development outcomes follow. Accommodating horizontal relations between rising and declining elites tends to combine with exclusionary vertical relations between upper- and lower-class groups. To exclude lower classes from upper-class accommodative relations requires aid from coercive political elites, such as unaccountable bureaucratic, police, military, and judicial authorities. To the degree lower classes are included, it is on the basis of neofascist appeals, finding ways to include groups identified as dominant, such as middle classes drawn from dominant racial identities, attracted to issues such as traditional values or fear of outsiders, to distract from the fact of an upper-class economic agenda (Saad Filho and Morais 2018).[2] Upper-class accommodation also tends to require acceptance of the international strategies of declining elites, settling for existing comparative advantages, and submission to international capital (Aiyar et al. 2013; Lin and Treichel 2012). Upper-class accommodation is, therefore, an attempt at modernization without structural change, avoiding shifts in international relations and avoiding change in the relations among domestic social classes.

By contrast, competitive horizontal relations indicate that rising elites compete to displace declining elites. To build political support, competitive horizontal relations tend to be associated with inclusive vertical relations, mobilizing lower-class groups on the basis of more progressive distributive and productive relations and more democratic political processes. Further, assistance with global competition requires economic statecraft from developmental state elites (Norris 2016), acting strategically to insert rising elites in GVC and engage in more complex and lucrative activities to expand national share of rents (Vigevani and Cepaluni 2016). This, too, requires lower-class support to overcome the resistance of declining elites comfortable to accept existing comparative advantages. Competitive horizontal relations and inclusive vertical relations are associated with more development and democracy; accommodating horizontal relations and exclusionary vertical relations is associated with less development and less democracy.

It is worth mentioning that this approach is fully relational in the sense that one could begin with vertical relations and the outcomes would be the same, though the causal mechanism, interestingly, is different. Where lower classes mobilize and force inclusive vertical relations, they claim a greater portion of the surplus in production. If rising elites wish to maintain their profits, this forces them to innovate to increase the size of the surplus, driving competition with declining elites, who prefer to capture surplus by repressing wages, cutting social policies, and preventing distribution to lower classes. An additional rising elite source of profit exists in altering comparative advantage, for which they require assistance from developmental state elites, who can act strategically to help capture a greater share of international rents. To strengthen the hand of developmental political elites, democratic institutions take advantage of lower-class mobilization to provide a base of support to resist declining elite demands to utilize the coercive power of the state to repress lower classes.

The sections below will trace these horizontal and vertical relations in Brazilian agriculture and aviation. To foreshadow the argument, agribusiness tends to be characterized by accommodation between rising and declining elites, exclusionary relations between upper- and lower classes, and therefore less development and democracy. By contrast, aviation tends to be characterized by competition between rising and declining elites, inclusive relations between upper- and lower classes, and therefore more development and democracy. In each sector, as will be seen, there have been moments and periods in which relations change, but there are social relations that pressure toward a return to the dominant pattern.

2.4 Agribusiness: Elite Accommodation, Lower-class Exclusion

Brazilian agribusiness provides a useful case of upper-class accommodation, in which rising elites coexist with declining elites, producing a sector with modern production technologies alongside backward and coercive practices. This upper-class alliance coincides with exclusion of lower classes, and the result is that elites are quick to embrace anti-democratic practices and submit to international capital. Lower classes resist, but their leverage within production processes is limited, and elites and their representatives have found ways to minimize leverage outside within politics or elsewhere.

The most lucrative and internationally expansive sector within agribusiness is animal protein, led by international giant JBS. Brazil enjoys low production costs, especially low-cost land and labor, and an ample supply of raw materials, namely animal feed, holding the largest commercial cattle stock in the world, with

232 million head in 2018. Public subsidy allowed JBS to buy its competitors domestically until it was practically a monopoly producer within the Brazilian market, subsequently absorbing foreign competitors and turning JBS into the world's largest purveyor of animal protein (Sierra 2016).[3]

The international insertion of JBS invites competing modernizing and oligarchic interpretations. JBS executives claimed their strategies were driven by a desire to upgrade. First, by absorbing technology and management expertise from international competitors, including research and development facilities; second, to gain knowledge of the tastes of consumers in different markets; and third, to learn compliance with phytosanitary and other regulations operating in developed country markets (Interview, JBS US headquarters 2016).

On the other hand, JBS acquisitions were hardly moving Brazilian producers to the front of the technology frontier. In the words of brother-owner Wesley Batista, "Meat processing is the same all over the world. Killing cows is the same" (as quoted in Dieguez 2015). The government Institute for Policy and Economic Analysis (IPEA) observed that "selling cows will not impact the collective welfare or modernize national industry" (Mansueto Almeida as cited by Dieguez 2015). Further, even the regulations noted as elements of the learning process were also simply trade barriers leapfrogged by purchasing Northern producers.

Among the more unsavory elements accommodated within JBS were abuses, including land grabbing and concentration, environmental degradation, corruption, financialization, and labor violations. Cattle producers consistently seek ever larger areas of land for pasture, particularly in undeveloped regions, and therefore available at lower prices.[4] Their expansion attracts domestic and international actors speculating in land, further driving land grabbing and concentration of holdings (Wilkinson, Reydon, and DiSabbato 2012; Dávalos et al. 2014).[5]

It is in penetrating the Amazon that much of the environmental degradation associated with cattle farming occurs.[6] According to the 2009 Greenpeace study, "'JBS' cattle supply chain includes significant supplies from within the Amazon rainforest. The company sources from suppliers whose ranches are grossly in breach of deforestation limits and who actively continue to clear remaining forest within ranch boundaries" (Greenpeace 2009, 97). In fact, the cattle sector in the Brazilian Amazon is responsible for 14% of annual deforestation worldwide, and 62% of Brazilian greenhouse gas emissions.[7] More than 750,000 square kilometers of Amazon rainforest have been destroyed since the 1980s, with about 60% replaced by cattle pasture, as cattle are the most extensive use of large areas of land (Greenpeace 2015, 12).

Additional retrograde practices appear in the form of corruption. Some corruption seeks to evade the few regulations that exist to control the sector, as in the case of monthly bribes to food safety inspectors.[8] Other forms of corruption seek to overturn or reverse regulation entirely, as revealed by the Batista brothers themselves.[9,10] Though they both served time in jail, the business press viewed it as normal.[11]

Part of international insertion for Brazilian agribusiness has been the increasing coincidence of interests with finance capital and, ultimately, international capital.

Certain purchases of failing competitors appeared to satisfy financial rather than productive objectives (Dieguez 2015). As domestic financial interests are already well-entwined with international finance, agribusiness financialization submits JBS to international capital (Sierra 2016). One indicator appears in efforts to weaken regulations limiting foreign access to Brazilian land and agribusiness firms, something the agribusiness lobby achieved under the Bolsonaro government (Federal Brazilian Law No. 5709/71, regulatory Decree No 74.965/74) and liberalized the use of mostly imported herbicides and pesticides, cynically nicknaming the bill the "Safer Food Law" (Persichetti 2020, 18–19; Mano 2019).

Another core characteristic of agribusiness in Brazil has been the exclusion of lower classes. Demand for labor is low, working conditions poor, wages stagnant, investment in human capital almost non-existent, and these exclusionary practices persist and worsen despite a 4.5% annual increase in productivity (Morães 2007). While agribusiness accounts for 46% of exports, it uses only 20% of the labor force, and two-thirds of its workers are kept in informal status, denied the benefits of formal contracts and driving down wages (Rennó Castro 2020, 16). Regarding human capital, 60% of agribusiness workers lack a high school education, compared to a national average of 43% (Rennó Castro 2020, 11–12). Most striking, "since 2003, over 21 thousand workers have been freed from slavery in the Brazilian Amazon; 70% of those cases were related to the cattle sector" (Greenpeace 2015, 14). JBS itself was fined millions for use of slaves in its facilities in Rondônia and Mato Grosso and purchased inputs produced by subcontractors using slave labor.[12]

Popular sectors have resisted, but their leverage within the production process is limited. In those cases in which working classes and popular sectors have attempted to block encroachment and production by agribusiness, the most retrograde elements of the agribusiness elite turn to violence, using both local police and paramilitary criminal forces. The most famous assassination was probably the 1988 killing of Chico Mendes, organizer among rubber tappers, environmental defender, and activist on behalf of the indigenous,[13] though there was also the assassination of Sister Dorothy Stang and, more recently, journalist Dom Phillips.[14] Additional massacres of workers often target Landless Workers Movement (MST) leaders and activists, including what appear to be staged killings by federal police[15] as well as execution-style murders by criminals.[16]

Popular sectors are forced to mobilize at the margins of agribusiness, attempting to induce state action on their behalf or operate outside the agribusiness sector entirely. Among the most important social movements in all of Latin America, the MST has articulated an alternative to agribusiness rooted in "food sovereignty through agro-ecological production and the promotion of popular agrarian reforms."[17] At the core of the MST strategy is an article within the Brazilian constitution granting usufruct rights to those occupying unproductive land, which has grown in area through land speculation. On reclaimed land, the MST establishes cooperatives and puts in place ecological, communally held food production, as well as public services such as housing, education, and health. In total, the MST has secured land title for approximately 136 thousand families since 1995, though the rate of titling depends on who holds the presidency.[18]

In part, the tenuous political impact can be traced to agribusiness dominance within national institutions. For decades, agribusiness interests have articulated their support within Congress through the Bancada Rural (Lucchese et al. 2018). The Bancada Rural generally draws from parties of the Center and Right, though they claim members across the political spectrum, and while their representatives dominate in more commodity-exporting states, they enjoy a presence in almost every region of the country.[19] With members across parties filling almost a third of the Congress, they have been known as "supra-party/trans-party" (Macedo and Becker, n.d., 65), fluctuating in size from 227 in 2002 to 241 in 2015 to a 2020 peak of 327 Senators and Deputies (Camargo 2009; Siminonatto and Costa 2012; Persichetti 2020; www.camara.leg.br/). Since 1995, every agricultural minister, including one, has come from the ranks of the Bancada Rural.[20]

Agribusiness, as exemplified by animal protein giant JBS, displays the most modern and the most retrograde elements of Brazilian capital, with lead firms positioning themselves strategically to capitalize on public subsidy, concentrate domestic control, and absorb international rivals. Global expansion has increased the weight of financial interests, both domestic and international, and modernized production using the technology, know-how, innovation systems, and market access available in foreign markets. Yet, even as they compete internationally, agribusiness uses retrograde practices such as land grabbing, slave labor, environmental degradation, and corruption. With the limited need for easily replaced unskilled labor, agribusiness has excluded lower-class interests, and most of the resistance they face comes at the margins, from landless, indigenous, and popular movements dependent on support from Left political parties. To protect their combination of modern and retrograde practices, agribusiness maintains access to national politics, securing large caucuses in Congress and privileged access to the executive, including virtually constant control of the agriculture ministry.

2.5 Aviation: Elite Competition, Lower-Class Inclusion

In contrast to agribusiness, the aviation sector in Brazil is characterized by a rising elite forced to modernize by competing with rival elite factions, as lower classes organizing at the point of production block accommodation to declining elites and submission to international capital. The leverage of lower and middle classes has more than once preserved developmental state elite assistance for strategic international insertion. As a result, the sector has survived multiple potential collapses, workers are better trained and working conditions better, and the sector boasts an ecosystem of innovative firms and activities clustered around Embraer, originally a state-owned company, now privatized but with significant ongoing state participation.

The aviation sector has to be understood as a cutting-edge technology sector whose very existence would be impossible without strategic action to alter comparative advantage, especially for a developing country like Brazil (Porter 1990). Aircraft require constantly advancing technology and know-how, as well as frequent infusions of large sums of capital, and successful design and production of a new model requires years of investment, development, and testing. If initial costs can be borne, there is a period of monopoly rent, as competing firms take time to catch up to technological advances. Yet, these rents quickly dissipate once other producers master new technologies, and entire sectors can disappear if a new pipeline of investment, development, and testing is not already undertaken (Gomes 2012, 149). This kind of boom-and-bust business cycle is prohibitive for many elite factions, especially in developing countries, and Brazil is among the few countries in the world to have mastered aviation technology such that they can certify their commercial planes around the world.

The origins of Brazilian aviation lie in part in World War II, when the US relocated parts of its military aviation assembly to Brazil. Production dropped off precipitously after 1945, and a series of enterprises failed in the 1950s and 1960s. Finally, the government convinced technicians from MIT and German aeronautical engineers to help the airforce establish the General Command of Science and Technology (CTA by its Portuguese acronym), along with subordinate institutes, the Aeronautic Technological Institute (ITA by its Portuguese acronym) and the Institute of Research and Development (IPD by its Portuguese acronym). These entities trained engineers and invested in research and development – developmental state elites essentially played the role of modernizing the bourgeoisie. Eventually, these investments in human capital, infrastructure, and technology resulted in the IPD 65/04 Bandeirante, launching Embraer in 1969 as a state-owned enterprise. Ongoing action from developmental state elites spurred growth during the 1970s through subsidies, tax incentives, guaranteed purchases, tariffs, and quotas to manage international competition and sustain profit margins.

Responses to episodes of downturn further demonstrate the ongoing role of developmental state elites. As Bandeirante sales began to falter and other firms caught up to Brazilian technology, state elites negotiated international partnerships to secure capital and new technologies, first from US-based Piper Aircraft in 1974 and then in 1979 for the AMX military aircraft with Aermacchi of Italy (Bartels 2009). Resulting investments and technological improvements sustained a new boom cycle in the 1980s, though the decade-end global downturn from the war in Iraq and a bad bet on a partnership with an Argentine producer produced serious financial problems starting in the 1990s (Barbieri Ferreira 2009). This downturn coincided with the Brazilian debt crisis, and developmental state elites found themselves weakened in comparison to neoliberal political elites and declining economic elites willing to accept existing comparative advantages, embodied in the financial sector (Medeiros and Trebat 2021). Both favored privatizing the company to the highest bidder (Silva 2008).

In response, middle-class engineers and lower-class metal workers used their leverage within the production process to rebalance political forces. News of privatization had sparked protest, resistance, and the largest and widest ranging strike in Embraer's history. It was led by metalworkers, a faction of the working-class that had already achieved victories and mobilized in the automobile sector, playing a central role in "social movement unionism" that reshaped shop floor unions in the 1970s as well as the democratization struggle of the 1980s (Seidman and Seidman

1994). The Association of Engineers joined the metalworkers, bridging working- and middle-class actors. Together, they forced several limits on the terms of privatization, including securing a portion of shares for the workers of the company, with workers and their unions purchasing slightly over 10%.[21] In addition, developmental state elites retained a "golden share" of company shares,[22] giving the state a veto over certain corporate decisions, even after privatization. In particular, the state veto was to be used to protect the "military, economic, and social functions" of the company.[23] Finally, regulations limited foreign ownership to 40%, preserving space for dynamic Brazilian elites alongside international capital (Ferreira 2009, 135–136). To complete the privatization, the state absorbed $700mi in debt and rolled over $350mi and added US$500mi in cash, as well as promising ongoing government support to research and development and exports.

New flexibility to form low-risk private partnerships generated a host of spin-off enterprises led by former Embraer engineers and employees. Embraer transformed from producer to designer of aircraft, system assembler, and coordinator of a new cohort of smaller enterprises in the sector (Vertesy and Szirmai 2010, 28; Gomes 2012). In effect, the state created its own dynamic elite of suppliers, design firms, and aftermarket parts producers (Vinhões 2022). The resulting restructuring worked to resuscitate the company and the sector, producing an extended boom in which Brazilian aeronautics rose to the top three in the world. Embraer's production profile could not challenge the jumbo jets of Boeing and Airbus, but the technologies Embraer developed for mid-size jets were leaders in the sector, matched only by Bombardier of Canada. The cycle of innovations came exactly as the airline industry in the US and Europe turned to a hub and spokes model of jumbo jets serving major regional airports (Boeing and Airbus), and regional jets distributing passengers to smaller airports (Embraer and Bombardier). As a result, the highly successful ERJ series (135/140/145) earned approximately $55bi with more than 2000 jets produced, mostly for export markets (Gomes 2012). The graph below shows the sharp increase in sales, exports, and employees occurring after 1994, reversing what appeared to be sharp declines from 1990–1994 (see Figure 2.1). In comparing Embraer to the much larger Canadian firm, Bombardier, observers noted "the minnow has recently been more profitable than the giant" (Goldstein 2003, 16).

Despite this productive success, dynamic elite factions remained relatively weak and declining elites expanded their influence. A comparison of the São José dos Campos Embraer cluster to the Montreal Bombardier cluster showed only 30 Brazilian firms as compared to 250 Canadian, and 13,000 total employees as compared to 40,000 (Goldstein 2003). With each subsequent downturn, financial interests acted as the declining elite within Embraer, expanding their influence, forcing accommodation from dynamic elites, and seeking to submit to international capital. For example, in 2006, the company swapped old shares for shares in "New Embraer" and assigned additional external controls and incentives to satisfy shareholders. The swap pleased international capital, as indicated by "investment grade" evaluations from Moody's and Standard & Poor's (Moraes 2017, 24), raising the value of shares by 22.5%, but the new shares were open to purchase by international capital, increasing their control of the company (DIEESE 2018).

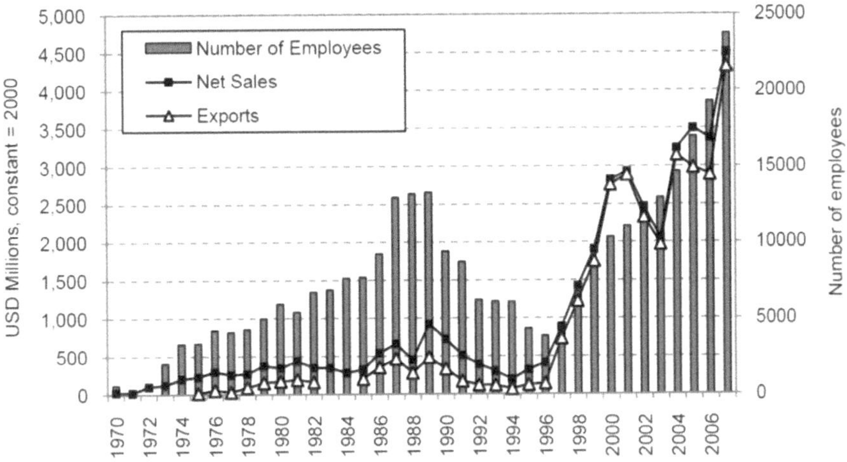

Figure 2.1 Historical evolution of Embraer' sales, employment, and exports.

Source: Vertesy and Szirmai (2010, 22).

Financial elite influence was blocked by the mobilization of lower classes, who forced new action from developmental state elites. In the face of the 2009 financial crisis, Embraer dismissed more than four thousand workers,[24] but metalworkers mobilized and won support from the Workers' Party government, securing new investments and diversifying into new sectors. Embraer opened service, maintenance, and training facilities in the US, Europe, and China.[25] Embraer also diversified into military, executive, and aircraft servicing, as well as financial strategies, including derivatives markets and government bonds (Moraes 2017, 27). The new resources, along with continued government support, allowed Embraer to produce the next line of commercial jets, EMB-170/175/190/195, reaching the size of 120 passengers, toward the lower end of competition with the larger jets produced by Boeing and Airbus. At the same time, Embraer was developing its smaller jets into executive jet models, the Phenom 100 and SIVAM EMB-145 AEW&C.

While the combination of working-class mobilization and developmental elite action seemed to stave off the 2009 crisis, economic downturn from 2013 forward opened a new opportunity for financial elites to gain control. By 2015, the value of the company began to falter, and orders and backlog declined. By late December 2017, reports were surfacing of an offer from Boeing to purchase 80% of Embraer shares for $4.2bi. For the deal to go through, the Brazilian government would have to give up its golden share and sell the remaining 20% after ten years. A 2014 parliamentary coup removed the Workers' Party president and gave control to neoliberal state elites, who promptly agreed to the sale, eager to submit to international capital. The main observer in the BNDES articulated the perspective of financial elites, "Embraer is no longer a maker of planes anyway. It designs, markets, and coordinates a production process, but where that production happens matters not."[26] Embraer shares increased by 5% overnight and steadily climbed by an additional 20% by the time the sale was officially announced. One analyst offered an observation fitting for the financial sector, "Money is money."[27]

As soon as the dismantling of Embraer began to take shape, the workers and engineers in the company and across the sector resisted. In response to salary cuts and threats to offshore production in 2014, they had mounted their biggest labor action since privatization.[28] Five years later, on the eve of the decision to release the government's golden share and in response to company efforts to trim worker benefits, the union of metalworkers mounted another strike. The election of Bolsonaro in 2018 had put neoliberal political elites and declining financial elites in charge. In the opinion of metalworker leader Herbert Claros, however, worker mobilization saved the company, as Boeing canceled its offer to purchase the company: "We were right all along. Just as in the case of privatization – when the workers rise, we preserve the sovereignty of Embraer and the potential for Brazil in the world."[29]

At the time of this writing, Embraer faces another downturn, the legacy of the pandemic slowdown, and a commercial aviation sector in which only Boeing, Airbus, and Embraer survive. As the smallest of the three, neoliberal elites within the state foresee its collapse, "Big companies will tie purchase of jumbo jets to sale of the regional jets, and we won't compete. It's the way the market works," said one BNDES observer.[30] Yet, the return of the Workers' Party in the presidential election of 2022 could herald a return of developmental elites to the heart of policymaking. Buttressed by an organized working class with leverage at the point of production, there may yet be a chance to insert Brazilian producers strategically in GVC and pursue a competitive advantage in aviation.

2.6 Conclusion

The contrast between agribusiness and aviation offers an opportunity to consider the importance of relations among and between different class factions. In agribusiness, rising elites accommodate declining elites, producing a mix of modern and retrograde practices with respect to lower classes and submitting to international capital by accepting existing comparative advantage. Among the retrograde practices are efforts to expand accumulation by repressing wages, even to the point of employing slave labor and exploiting the environment, trampling indigenous rights, and absorbing the lands of small farmers. As lower classes provide limited inputs to this model of accumulation they have little leverage within the production process, and their attempts to pressure the state are constrained by the dominance of agribusiness interests in Congress and key ministries.

By contrast, in aviation, rising elites would appear to compete directly with declining elites, pursuing modernization with the help of developmental state elites and inserting strategically into GVC by pursuing competitive advantage. At various moments, especially moments of downturn, declining economic elites, embodied in financial sectors, gain a degree of power over dynamic factions of capital, and developmental state elites cede to neoliberal political elites. While the preference of declining economic elites and neoliberal political elites is to submit to international capital and repress lower classes, lower- and middle-class resistance at the point of production strengthens the hand of developmental state elites and returns dynamic elites to a medium-term strategy of pursuing competitive advantage with respect to international capital.

Several observations emerge from this comparison. First, the relational approach is far superior to attempts to characterize elites according to intrinsic characteristics. Rising elites rise because they enter a competitive relationship with declining elites and include lower- and middle classes in a cross-class alliance. This alliance provides a base for developmental state elites to overcome neoliberal rivals and support dynamism with industrial policies and distribution to lower classes while inserting dynamic sectors strategically in the international system. The characteristics of economic and political elites and non-elite social groups emerge from their mutual relations, not because they are inherently one thing or another.

It is also notable that dynamic elites in developing countries like Brazil occupy a relatively weak position. Only with cross-class support from lower classes can rising elites resist the pressure of declining elites, and only with the assistance of developmental state elites can rising elites insert strategically into the international system. Still, the temptation to accommodate declining elites always exists, especially at moments of downturn, and the temptation to accept existing comparative advantages and submit to international capital is always encouraged by global great powers. Further, the temptation to exclude lower classes also grows during moments of downturn, when the threat of lower-class mobilization appears more dangerous to rising elites than accommodating declining elites or submitting to international capital.

This weakness of rising elites is a chronic condition for developing countries in an uneven international capitalist system. Leading factions of capital from already developed poles of the international economy operate with certain advantages. Developed societies are much less unequal and governed by much more capable states; they can afford to be more inclusive of lower- and middle classes, who therefore pose less of a threat to elites. Further, more capable states can insert economic actors more strategically in the international system to maintain competitive advantages. While declining profit rates occasionally lead elites from advanced countries to open space in the international system for rising elites from developing countries, there is always the possibility and temptation to return developing countries to a submissive position of accepting existing comparative advantages. In developing countries, the weakness of rising elites in relation to rival elite factions and lower classes leads them to accept submission to international capital over and over again.

Notes

1 Elites here are economic and political actors in dominant positions within the production process and the state. There is significant overlap with the concept of classes, as

command over the surplus is an important part of elite status, and the chapter will refer to the class identity of elites and popular sectors as upper and lower class.

2 Fascism is a strategy to "make reaction popular" (Moore 1966).

3 JBS purchased the biggest producers in Argentina and the US (www.marketwatch.com/story/brazils-jbs-buys-swift-foods-for-14-bln, June 14, 2023), "a case of the guppy swallowing the whale" (Interview, US executive of JBS 2016).

4 The sequence is common in environmental reserves, indigenous reservations, and much of the Amazon. Once timber has been cleared, cattle producers enter, more intensive grain, soy, and sugarcane users drive up prices and forcing cattle producers deeper into areas defined as frontier, restarting the cycle.

5 The Gini index for land distribution in Brazil rose from 0.856 to 0.872 between 1996 and 2006 (www.brasildefato.com.br/2018/07/26/no-brasil-2-mil-latifundios-ocupam-area-maior-que-4-milhoes-de-propriedades-rurais/, (June 14, 2023).

6 These practices are connected, "Rampant slave labor and land-grabbing (such as the theft of indigenous lands) often goes hand-in-hand with environmental destruction" (Greenpeace 2015, 12).

7 Despite a voluntary "Cattle Agreement," JBS has been fined R$ 264 million for purchasing cattle from farms practicing deforestation (https://reporterbrasil.org.br/2017/03/jbs-compra-gado-de-areas-desmatadas-ilegalmente-e-leva-multa-de-r24-milhoes/, June 14, 2023).

8 To provide the specific and disgusting details, JBS mixed rotten meat, meat doctored with carcinogenic chemical substances, and low-quality meat into exports www.bbc.com/news/world-latin-america-40377203 (June 14, 2023).

9 See: Lauro, Jardin. 2017. "Dono da JBS grava Temer dando aval para compra de silêncio de Cunha." *O Globo*, June 17, 2017. www1.folha.uol.com.br/poder/2017/05/1884947-senador-aecio-neves-psdb-mg-pediu-r-2-milhoes-a-joesley-diz-jbs.shtml (June 14, 2023).

10 See: Ladeira, Pedro. 2017. "Aécio Neves pediu R$ 2 milhões a Joesley, dizem executivos da JBS." Folha de S.Paulo, April 4, 2017. www1.folha.uol.com.br/poder/2017/05/1884947-senador-aecio-neves-psdb-mg-pediu-r-2-milhoes-a-joesley-diz-jbs.shtml (June 14, 2023).

11 See: Marques, Felipe, and James Attwood. 2021. "Brazil's Batista Brothers Are Out of Jail And Worth $6 Billion." Bloomberg, July 15, 2021. www.bloomberg.com/news/articles/2021-07-15/brazil-s-batista-brothers-are-out-of-jail-and-worth-6-billion?leadSource=uverify%20wall (June 14, 2023).

12 See: Aranha, Ana. 2017. "JBS comprou de fazendas flagradas com trabalho escravo e desmatamento ilegal." Repórter Brasil, June 7, 2017. https://reporterbrasil.org.br/2017/06/jbs-comprou-de-fazendas-flagradas-com-trabalho-escravo-e-desmatamento-ilegal/ (June 14, 2023).

13 See: Shoumatoff, Alex. 2013. "Murder in The Rain Forest." *Vanity Fair*. November 4, 2013. www.theguardian.com/world/2022/jul/22/three-charged-brazil-murder-dom-phillips-bruno-pereira (June 14, 2023).

14 See: Vinher, Katharine. 2022. "Three charged in Brazil with murder of Dom Phillips and Bruno Pereira." *The Guardian*. July 22, 2022. www.theguardian.com/world/2022/jul/22/three-charged-brazil-murder-dom-phillips-bruno-pereira (June 14, 2023).

15 See: Business & Human Rights Resource Centre. 2017. "Brazil: Pau D'Arco is the second largest slaughter for land conflicts in 20 years; company comments." July 12, 2017. www.business-humanrights.org/en/latest-news/brazil-ten-rural-workers-killed-in-farm-massacre-in-the-amazon-as-a-result-of-land-conflicts/ (June 14, 2023).

16 See: Friends of the MST. 2018. "Two MST leaders brutally assassinated in the northeast of Brazil." December 10, 2018. www.mstbrazil.org/news/two-mst-leaders-brutally-assassinated-northeast-brazil (June 14, 2023).
17 See: Friends of the MST. 2020. "In times of pandemics, peasants are united to feed the people!." March 25, 2020. www.mstbrazil.org/news/times-pandemics-peasants-are-united-feed-people (June 14, 2023).
18 See: Ghiraldelli, Gabriela. 2022. "Fatos Primeiro: Bolsonaro acerta sobre números de titulação de terras, mas omite dados de reforma agraria." CNN Brasil, July 21, 2022. www.cnnbrasil.com.br/politica/fatos-primeiro-bolsonaro-acerta-sobre-numeros-de-titulacao-de-terras-mas-omite-dados-de-reforma-agraria/ (June 14, 2023).
19 Rural interests operate in the national Congress through political parties advancing the interests of large landholders or as a caucus, currently known as the Frente Parlamentar da Agropecuária (FPA) (Siminonatto and Costa 2012, 12).
20 See: Frente Parlamentar de Ageropecuária 2023. Homepage. https://fpagropecuaria.org.br/ (June 14, 2023).
21 See: Vale, Da Folha. 1994. "Ações da Embraer têm alta de 59% em 7 dias." *Folha de S. Paulo*, December 10, 1994. www1.folha.uol.com.br/fsp/1994/12/10/dinheiro/20.html (June 14, 2023).
22 See: Reuters.1994. "For Sale: Brazil's Embraer." *New York Times*, April 14, 1994. www.nytimes.com/1994/04/14/business/for-sale-brazil-s-embraer.html (June 14, 2023).
23 See: Ottoboni, Júlio. 2018. "Os verdadeiros controladores da Embraer." A Embraer É Nossa, April 3, 2018. http://embraernossa.com.br/2018/04/03/10-os-verdadeiros-controladores-da-embraer/ (June 14, 2023).
24 See: Redação ConJur. 2009. "TST decide que demissão na Embraer não foi abusive." Consultor Jurídico, August 10, 2009. www.conjur.com.br/2009-ago-10/tst-decide-demissao-massa-embraer-nao-foi-abusiva (June 14, 2023).
25 See: Vinholes, Thiago. 2016. "Embraer encerra produção de aviões na China." Airway, June 1, 2016. https://airway.uol.com.br/embraer-encerra-producao-do-legacy-na-china/ (June 14, 2023).
26 Interview with BNDES executive in the aerospace sector, Rio de Janeiro (October 6, 2018).
27 Interview with analyst of the aeronautics sector for Itaú bank, São Paulo (November 6, 2018).
28 O Globo. 2014. "Operários da Embraer fazem greve por reajuste salarial em São José, SP." *O Globo*, October 10, 2014. https://g1.globo.com/sp/vale-do-paraiba-regiao/noticia/2014/10/operarios-da-embraer-fazem-greve-por-reajuste-salarial-em-sao-jose-sp.html (June 14, 2023).
29 Interview Conlutas Headquarters, São Jose dos Campos, (June 10, 2022).
30 Interview with BNDES executive, Rio de Janeiro (June 8, 2022).

References

Acemoglu, Darren, and James Robinson. 2006. *Economic Origins of Dictatorship and Democracy*. New York: Cambridge University Press.

———. 2012. *Why Nations Fail: The Origins of Power, Prosperity, and Poverty*. New York: Random House.

Adorno, Theodor W. 1950. "The Authoritarian Personality" *Studies in Prejudice Series, Volume 1*. New York: Harper and Row.

Aiyar, Shekhar, Romain Duval, Damien Puy, Yiqun Wu, and Longmei Zhang. 2013. *Growth Slowdowns and the Middle-Income Trap.* IMF Working Paper, 13–71. Washington: International Monetary Fund.

Albertus, Michael, and Victor Menaldo. 2018. *Authoritarianism and the Origins of Democracy.* New York: Cambridge University Press.

Almond, Gabriel, and Sidney Verba. 1963. *The Civic Culture.* Princeton: Princeton University Press.

Amsden, Alice. 1989. *Asia's Next Giant: South Korea and Late Industrialisation.* New York: Oxford University Press.

Ansell, Chris, and David Samuels. 2014. *Inequality and Democratization.* Berkeley: University of California Press.

Armijo, Leslie, and Saori Katada, eds. 2014. *The Financial Statecraft of Emerging Powers: Shield and Sword in Asia and Latin America.* New York: Palgrave Macmillan.

Barbieri Ferreira, Marcos José. 2009. *Tese: Dinâmica da Inovação e Mudanças Estruturais: Um Estudo de Caso da Indústria Aeronáutica Mundial e a Inserção Brasileira.* Campinas: Universidade Estadual de Campinas.

Bartels, Walter. 2009. "A Questão Tecnologia Aeronáutica no Brasil." *Seminário Estrateégia de Defesa Nacional e a Indústria de Defesa.* Sao Jose dos Campos: Associação da Indústrias Aeroespaciais do Brasil.

Bebbington, Anthony, Denise Humphreys Bebbington, Abdul-Gafaru Abdulai, Marja Hinfelaar, and Cynthia Sanborn. 2017. *Political Settlements and the Governance of Extractive Industry: A Comparative Analysis of the Longue Duree in Africa and Latin America.* Manchester: Effective States and Inclusive Development Research Centre (ESID); The University of Manchester.

Boito Junior, Armando. 2018. *Reforma e Crise Política no Brasil.* Campinas: Editora UNESP.

Boix, Carlos. 2003. *Democracy and Distribution.* Princeton: Princeton University Press.

Camargo, Orson José Roberto. 2009. *Elite Política Brasileira e a Renegociação das Dívidas do Crédito Rural: O caso da bancada ruralista..* Phd-Thesis. Campinas: Instituto de Filosofia e Ciências Humanas, Universidade Estadual de Campinas.

Chang, Ha-Joon. 2002. *Kicking away the Ladder? Economic Development in Historical Perspective.* London: Anthem.

Collier, David and Ruth Berins Collier. 1991. *Shaping the Political Arena.* Princeton: Princeton University Press.

Dahl, Robert. 1982. *Dilemmas of Pluralist Democracy.* New Haven: Yale University Press.

Dávalos, Liliana M., Jennifer S. Holmes, Nelly Rodríguez, and Dolors Armenteras. 2014. "Demand for Beef Is Unrelated to Pasture Expansion in Northwestern Amazonia." *Biological Conservation* 170, 64–73.

DIEESE. 2018. *Embraer a Boeing: Combinação de Negócios ou Venda para a gigante norte-americana?* São Paulo: DIEESE.

Dieguez, Consuleo. 2015. "O Estouro da Boiada: Como o BNDES Ajudou a Transformar a Friboi na Maior Empresa de Carnes do Mundo." *Revista Piauí* 101, https://piaui.folha.uol.com.br/materia/o-estouro-da-boiada/ (January 23, 2024).

Evans, Peter. 1995. *Embedded Autonomy: States and Industrial Transformation.* Princeton, NJ: Princeton University Press.

Fromm, Erich. 1957. "Die autoritäre Persönlichkeit" *Deutsche Universitätszeitung* 12 (9), 3–4.

Gereffi, Gary. 2018. *Global Value Chains and Development.* New York: Cambridge University Press.

Gerschenkron, Alexander. 1962. *Economic Backwardness in Historical Perspective: A Book of Essays*. Cambridge, MA: Belknap Press of Harvard University Press.
Goldstein, Andrea. 2003. High-tech clusters in the north and in the south: comparison between Montreal and São José dos Campos. *Presented at* EADI Workshop Clusters and Global Value Chains, Novara, Italy.
Gomes, Sérgio Bittencourt Varella. 2012. *A indústria aeronáutica no Brasil: evolução recente e perspectivas*. Rio de Janeiro: BNDES.
Gramsci, Antonio. 1971. *Selections from the Prison Notebooks*. New York: International Publishers Co.
Greenpeace. 2009. *Slaughtering the Amazon*. Greenpeace: São Paulo.
———. 2015. *Grilling Away the Amazon*. Greenpeace: São Paulo.
Hickey, Sam, Kunal Sen, and Badru Bukenya. 2015. *Politics of Inclusive Development*. Oxford: Oxford University Press.
Higley, John, and Michael Burton. 1998. "Elite Settlements and the Taming of Politics." *Government & Opposition* 33 (1): 98–115.
Jackson, Patrick Thaddeus, and Daniel H. Nexon. 1999. "Relations before States: Substance, Process and the Study of World Politics." *European Journal of International Relations* 5 (3), 291–332
Johnson, Chalmers. 1982. *MITI and the Japanese Miracle*. Stanford: Stanford University Press.
Kaplinsky, Raphael. 2013. *Globalization, Poverty and Inequality*. Oxford: Wiley.
Katz, Claudio. 2015. "Dualities of Latin America" *Latin American Perspectives* 42 (4), 10–42.
Kelsall, Tim, Nicolai Schulz, William D. Ferguson, Mattheus Von Mau, Sam Hickey, Brian Levy. 2022. *Political Settlements and Development*. Oxford: Oxford University Press.
Khan, Mushtaq H. 2018. "Political Settlements and the Analysis of Institutions." *African Affairs* 117 (469): 636–55.
Lin, Justin, and Volker Treichel. 2012. *Learning from China's Rise to Escape the Middle-Income Trap: A New Structuralist Economics Approach to Latin America*. Washington: World Bank.
Lipset, Seymor Martin. 1959. "Some Social Requisites of Democracy." *The American Political Science Review* 53 (1), 69–105.
Lucchese, Giovani da Silva, Felipe Esteves Oliveski, Sandra Beatriz Vicenzi Fernandez. 2018. "A bancada ruralista e a política pública ambiental brasileira", Revista Observatorio de la Economía Latinoamericana, (septiembre 2018).
Macedo, Rayane B., and Simone Becker. "Contornos das biografias de agentes envolvidos no tramite da PEC 215." *Nanduty* (n.d.): 60–87.
Mano, Ana. 2019. *Brazil clears new pesticides as government aims to speed approvals*. Reuters. 17 September 2019.
Marx, Karl. *Capital: A Critique of Political Economy*. London: Penguin, 1990.
Medeiros, Carlos Aguiar, and Nicholas Trebat. 2021. "The Failures of Neoliberalism in Brazil." *Journal of Economic Issues* 55 (2), 408–415.
Mehta, Pratap Bhanu, and Michael Walton. 2014. "Ideas, interests and the politics of development change in India: capitalism, inclusion and the state." *Global Development Institute Working Paper Series* esid-036-14. GDI, The University of Manchester.
Moore Jr., Barrington. 1966. *The Social Origins of Dictatorship and Development: Lord and Peasant in the Modern World*. Boston: Beacon Press.
Moraes, Livia de Cassia. 2017. Nas asas do capital: Embraer, financeirização e implicações sobre os trabalhadores. *Caderno CRH* 30 (79), 13–31.

Morães, Márcia Azanha Ferraz Dias. 2007. "O mercado de trabalho da agroindústria canavieira: desafios e oportunidades." *Economia Aplicada* 11 (4), 605–619.

Norris, William J. 2016. *Chinese Economic Statecraft*. Ithaca: Cornell University Press.

North, Douglass, John Joseph Wallis, and Barry R. Weingast. 2013. *Violence and Social Orders*. New York: Cambridge University Press.

O'Donnell, Guillermo, and Philippe C. Schmitter. 1986. *Transitions from Authoritarian Rule, Vol. 4: Tentative Conclusions about Uncertain Democracies*. Baltimore: The Johns Hopkins University Press.

Persichetti, Simonetta. 2020. "O Brasil Agrario: O Conservadorismo e a Direita na Bancada Ruralista." *Em tese*, 17 (1).

Porter, Michael E. 1990. *The Competitive Advantage of Nations*. New York: The Free Press

Pritchett, Lant, Kumal Sen, and Eric Werker. 2017. *Deals and Development*. Oxford: Oxford University Press.

Przeworski, Adam, Michael E. Alvarez, and Jose Antonio Cheibub. 2000. *Democracy and Development*. New York: Cambridge University Press.

Rennó Castro, Nicole, et al. 2020. "The Brazilian agribusiness labor market: measurement, characterization and analysis of income differentials O mercado de trabalho do agronegócio brasileiro: mensuração, caracterização e análise de diferenciais de rendimento." *Revista de Economia e Sociologia Rural* 58 (1), 1–20.

Reuschemeyer, Dietrich, John Stephens, and Evelyn Huber Stephens. 1992. *Capitalist Development and Democracy*. Chicago: University of Chicago Press.

Rostow, Walt W. 1960. *The Stages of Economic Growth: A Non-Communist Manifesto*. New York: Cambridge University Press

Saad Filho, Alfredo, and Lecio Morais. 2018. *Brazil: Neoliberalism vs. Democracy*. London: Pluto Press.

Seidman, Ann, and Robert B. Seidman. 1994. "Transforming the Colonial State: Controlling the Bureaucratic Bourgeoisie." In *State and Law in the Development Process. International Political Economy Series*, 170–195. London: Palgrave Macmillan. https://doi.org/10.1007/978-1-349-23615-2_10

Selwyn, Benjamin. 2016. "A Theory and Practice of Labour-based Development." *Third World Quarterly* 37 (6), 1–18.

Sierra, Jazmin. 2016. *Global Champions Are Made at Home: The Brazilian Development Bank and Domestic MNCs*. Paper Presented at American Political Science Association Annual Meeting, San Francisco.

Silva, Ozires. 2008. *A Decolagem de um Grande Sonho*. São Paulo: Elsevier Editora.

Siminonatto, Ivete, and Carolina Rodrigues Costa. 2012. "Ruralista, Como os Dominantes Dominam: O Caso da Bancada." *Temporalis, Brasilia* (24), 215–237, jul./dez.

Smith, Adam. 1776. *The Wealth of Nations*. Chicago, IL: University of Chicago Press.

Solow, Robert. 2008. "What is Labor-market Flexibility? What is it Good For? Keynes Lecture" *Proceedings of the British Academy* 97, 189–211.

Stiglitz, Joseph. 2007. *Making Globalisation Work*. New York: W. W. Norton.

Trimberger, Ellen Kay. 1978. *Revolution from Above: Military Bureaucrats and Development in Japan, Turkey, Egypt, and Peru*. New York: Transaction Books.

Vertesy, Daniel and Szirmai, A. 2010. "Brazilian aerospace manufacturing in comparative perspective: a Brazil/USA comparison of output and productivity." *Working Paper, n. 2010-032*. Maastricht: United Nations University.

Vigevani, Tullo, and Gabriel Cepaluni. 2016. *A política externa brasileira: a busca da autonomia de Sarney a Lula*. São Paulo: Editora UNESP.

Vinhões, Thiago. 2022. "Embraer não é a única" *O Globo*. 7/26/2022.

Wade, Robert. 2004. *Governing the Market*. 2nd ed. Princeton, NJ: Princeton University Press.

Williamson, John, ed. 1990. *Latin American Readjustment: How Much has Happened?* Washington, DC: Peterson Institute for International Economics.

Wilkinson, John, Bastiaan Reydon, and Alberto Di Sabbato. 2012. "Concentration and Foreign Ownership of Land in Brazil in the Context of Global Land Grabbing." *Canadian Journal of Development Studies/Revue canadienne d'études du développement* 33 (4), 417–38.

3 Economic Elites and Public Sector Size in Brazil and Mexico

Gabriel Ondetti

3.1 Introduction

Latin American countries differ greatly with regard to the size of their public sectors. While some have revenues and spending of well over 30% of gross domestic product (GDP), in others, the public sector is half that size or less. This variance has not received much scholarly attention. To the extent that it has been studied, it has generally been attributed to the impact of economic variables, such as development level, trade openness, and dependence on agriculture (Cetrángolo and Gómez Sabaini 2007; Rossignolo 2017), although some studies also suggest a role for political factors, including government ideology and regime type (Martín-Mayoral and Uribe 2010; Stein and Caro 2013).

Little attention has been devoted to the notion that variance in public sector size among Latin American countries may be rooted in differences in how economic elites think or act politically.[1] To be sure, some studies stress the influence of elites on taxation (Schneider 2012; Flores-Macías 2014; Fairfield 2015). However, they generally focus exclusively on direct taxes, which in most cases account for less than a third of total revenues. The exception is Schneider (2012), which examines overall taxation but looks at the increment in that variable over a specific period rather than its absolute level. Similarly, studies of public spending have focused on particular types, especially social spending, and make little reference to elites (Huber and Stephens 2012; Martín-Mayoral and Fernández Sastre 2017).

In contrast, this chapter demonstrates that historically constructed differences in elite ideology and political organization can impact public sector size.[2] It does so through a comparative analysis of Brazil and Mexico. The case selection reflects a "most-similar case" research design in which the cases resemble each other on a number of key independent variables while differing on the dependent variable (Przeworksi and Teune 1970, 32–34; Gerring 2007, 131–134). The main advantage of this design is that it controls for the variables on which the cases are similar, allowing the researcher to focus on others that may not be as well established in the literature.[3] Brazil and Mexico resemble each other with regard to several variables commonly said to influence public sector size, including development level, political regime type, and some aspects of constitutional structure.[4] Yet, they differ markedly in terms of the magnitude of public revenues and spending.[5] With regard

DOI: 10.4324/9781032636764-4

to both measures, Brazil has among the largest public sectors in Latin America, while Mexico ranks much lower. Empirically, the study relies mainly on quantitative data from international institutions and existing scholarly analyses of the economic and political development of the two countries.

The chapter argues that Mexico's public sector is smaller because major attempts at redistribution, especially during the 1930s, prompted a conservative backlash that became institutionalized in a growing network of organizations devoted to restricting state control of the economy. This antistatist bloc, consisting mainly of business associations and a political party, has posed an enduring obstacle to public sector growth. In contrast, the lack of major redistributive threats in Brazil has meant that economic elites in that country never developed a similarly strong aversion to statism or a set of organizations dedicated to halting its growth. While both countries shifted from import substitution industrialization to more liberal development approaches during the 1980s and 1990s, this underlying difference in elite ideology and political organization has persisted.

These arguments are developed in four sections. The first compares the magnitude of the Brazilian and Mexican public sectors. The second assesses how well existing theories explain the contrast between these countries. The third elaborates on the alternative account outlined above. The fourth concludes the chapter by summarizing its findings and discussing their wider validity.

3.2 Comparing the Brazilian and Mexican Public Sectors

Brazil has a much larger public sector than Mexico in terms of both taxation and spending. That difference is longstanding, dating back to about the 1940s. Although Brazil's fiscal system effects little redistribution compared to those of many developed countries, studies suggest that it is more redistributive than Mexico's.

Table 3.1 reports the average total public revenues and spending relative to GDP for Mexico and Brazil between 2015 and 2019. All levels of government are included. The revenue figures are broken down by tax and non-tax sources. As the table suggests, the gaps between the two countries are large. In percentage terms, they are comparable, for example, to those between the United States and the Nordic countries, often seen as representing contrasting varieties of capitalism within the developed world (Hall and Soskice 2001).[6]

Table 3.1 Public Sector Size in Brazil and Mexico, 2015–2019

Country/ Region	*Total Revenues/GDP*	*Breakdown of Total Revenues*		*Total Spending/GDP*
		Tax Revenues/ GDP	*Non-Tax Revenues (GDP)*	
Brazil	33.4	32.6	0.8	38.3
Mexico	19.3	16.3	3.0	26.4

Sources: OECD Revenue Statistics in Latin America and the Caribbean (2018–2021); IMF World Economic Outlook Database.

Brazil collects more revenue relative to GDP in every major tax category, but the differences are especially large with regard to consumption and social security taxes (OECD Revenue Statistics in Latin America and the Caribbean 2018–2021). Spending data by policy area is not available at subnational levels for Mexico, but central government figures published by the United Nations Economic Commission for Latin America and the Caribbean (ECLAC) show that the gap is particularly wide with regard to social protection (CEPALSTAT database). Relative to GDP, Brazil spends roughly three times as much in this area as Mexico.

The contrast between the two countries is not new. Accurately tracking the historical trajectory of overall revenue and spending is difficult, but it is more feasible with regard to tax revenues specifically. Figure 3.1 examines the evolution of total tax revenues relative to GDP between 1900 and 2019. Brazil had much heavier taxation at the outset due to its greater post-independence stability, but World War I devastated its largely trade-based tax system. During the 1920s and 1930s, the two countries had roughly similar tax burdens. Nevertheless, this convergence was reversed beginning in the 1940s. For three decades, Mexico's tax burden stagnated, while Brazil's grew robustly. By 1970, Brazil's tax revenues, at 25% of GDP, were more than double Mexico's. Since then, the gap has narrowed somewhat, but Brazil's revenues are still about double Mexico's relative to GDP.

Considering non-tax revenues alters the picture only for recent decades. Since the late 1970s, when Mexico experienced an oil boom, taxation has been complemented by large non-tax revenues from the state oil company Mexican Petroleum (PEMEX). Hence, the difference in fiscal capacity between Mexico and Brazil has been smaller than would appear by focusing on taxes. However,

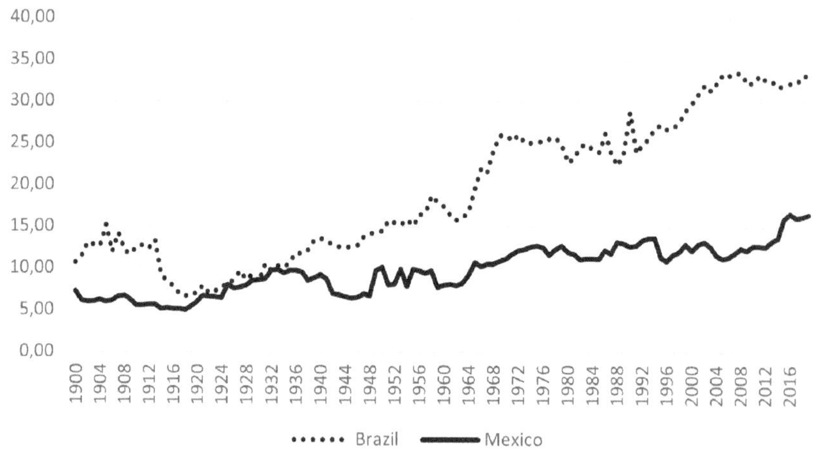

Figure 3.1 Total tax revenues/GDP in Brazil and Mexico, in percent, 1900–2019.

Source: ECLAC, OECD.

as Table 3.1 demonstrates, non-tax revenues fall far short of compensating for the difference in taxation. Moreover, the gap in tax revenues that emerged between the two countries after World War II was not substantially compensated by oil revenues, which were modest until the 1970s.[7] Mexico's fiscal poverty during this period is illustrated by scattered spending figures. For example, its current spending relative to GDP was only 51.3% of Brazil's in 1960 and 65.1% in 1970 (ECLAC 1979, 104).

Brazil's heavy taxation and spending does not mean its fiscal system is highly redistributive. At least by developed country standards, it is not. This is partly because the tax system relies heavily on relatively regressive taxes. In addition, although there are some strongly redistributive spending programs, such as conditional cash transfers, others deliver their benefits mainly to better-off people. Nevertheless, fiscal incidence studies suggest that Brazil's system is significantly more redistributive than Mexico's (Hanni et al. 2015; Lustig 2017).

3.3 Existing Theory and the Cases

Existing scholarship offers a variety of explanations for differences in public sector size. While they may work well in other contexts, none of these explanations offers a convincing account of the gap between Brazil and Mexico.

Much of the literature emphasizes economic conditions. Easily the best-established theory is that economic development increases public sector size by fomenting demands for public goods (Pessino and Fenochietto 2010). Trade openness is also commonly viewed as promoting public sector growth, mainly by creating pressure for social protection from external shocks (Ram 2009). Finally, dependence on agriculture is said to inhibit state expansion because of the difficulty of taxing geographically scattered farmers (Piancastelli 2001).

Institutional variables also receive considerable attention. Democracies are viewed as favoring bigger government due to their permeability to demands for redistribution (Boix 2001). Other arguments emphasize the design of democratic institutions. Presidentialism is reputed to favor smaller government because its division of powers inhibits rent-seeking (Persson and Tabellini 2003). Majoritarian electoral systems are also viewed as having this effect because they tend to result in right-leaning governing coalitions, whereas proportional representation favors left-leaning ones (Iversen and Soskice 2006). Finally, federalism has traditionally been said to hinder public sector growth by allowing taxpayers to shop around for the lowest taxes (Brennan and Buchanan 1980). However, some works maintain that it has the opposite effect if subnational governments have substantial spending authority but depend on central government transfers for revenue (Rodden 2003).[8]

Finally, students of public sector size have sometimes argued that government ideology matters. In particular, they contend that the public sector will be larger in countries where the state is more often controlled by left-leaning parties, mainly because of the premium the latter place on redistribution (Cameron 1978).

A handful of studies specifically on Latin America examine some of the same variables. They generally agree that economic development favors public sector growth (Cetrángolo and Gómez Sabaini 2007; Martín-Mayoral and Uribe 2010). Some also find that dependence on agriculture inhibits it (Cetrángolo and Gómez Sabaini 2007; Martín-Mayoral and Uribe 2010) and that trade openness promotes it (Cetrángolo and Gómez Sabaini 2007; Rossignolo 2017). In addition, there is some support for the positive effect of democracy (Martín-Mayoral and Uribe 2010), unbalanced federalism (Stein 1999), and left-party control of government (Stein and Caro 2013).

Latin Americanists have also made distinctive contributions to this area, especially by using qualitative methods, which are rare. Schneider's (2012) study of Central America argues that tax revenues grew more rapidly in the 1990s and 2000s in countries where the leaders of emerging transnational economic sectors achieved more cohesion and political dominance. In such cases, these groups invested in state-building in order to consolidate their influence and advance their economic interests.[9]

Despite its diversity, the scholarship on public sector size sheds little light on the gap between Brazil and Mexico. The economic variables, as Table 3.2 suggests, are particularly unhelpful. Development cannot explain the contrast because, as noted earlier, the countries are similarly developed. With regard to agricultural dependence and trade openness, the correlations are the opposite of what the theory predicts. Mexico has a smaller farm sector and a more open economy but boasts a smaller public sector. These trends are longstanding. Since the 1980s, Mexico and Brazil have had comparable development levels (World Bank database). Before that time, moreover, Mexico tended to be more prosperous (Astorga et al. 2005, 788). Data going back to the 1960s show that Brazil was more agriculture-dependent and less trade-dependent than Mexico for all but a handful of years (World Bank database).

The institutional explanations are also, on balance, unconvincing in this context. With regard to regime type, Mexico and Brazil have both widely been considered democracies in recent decades, but Mexico has fewer cumulative years of democratic governance over the course of its history, largely due to the dominance of the Institutional Revolutionary Party (PRI) between the 1930s and the mid-1990s (Ondetti 2021, 32). While this difference suggests that Mexico's smaller public sector may be due to a historical lack of democracy, other evidence contradicts that idea. Most importantly, Brazil's public sector has grown robustly under both democratic and authoritarian regimes. For example, as Figure 3.1 suggests, the

Table 3.2 Key Economic Variables, 2015–2019

Country	*Per capita GDP (US Dollars)*	*Agriculture/GDP (%)*	*Trade/GDP (%)*
Brazil	9,141.68	4.5	26.1
Mexico	9,513.25	3.3	76.6

Source: World Bank database; IMF World Economic Outlook database.

period of fastest sustained growth in Brazil's tax burden was under military rule during the 1960s.

Brazil's strong public sector growth under authoritarianism and Mexico's dearth of democratic experience cast doubt on explanations highlighting specific variations of democracy. In addition, these explanations face other objections. Both countries have presidential systems so that variable is irrelevant. Moreover, neither has a pure majoritarian electoral system. Mexico has a hybrid system, but its party system, which possesses a clear left, right, and center, is what one would expect under proportional representation. With regard to federalism, the traditional view suggests that Brazil, which has a more decentralized version of federalism than Mexico, should have a smaller public sector, but that is not the case. The emphasis on fiscally unbalanced federalism does no better because the imbalance between subnational taxation and spending is greater in Mexico (Ondetti 2021, 35).

With regard to government ideology, there is no clear pattern in either country. In Mexico, of the governments that followed the PRI's defeat in 2000, the one that raised tax revenues most was that of Enrique Peña Nieto (2012–2018), a centrist PRI politician. However, overall revenue and spending increased faster under the center-right National Action Party (PAN). Despite leading the nominally left-leaning Movement of National Regeneration (MORENA), current President Andrés Manuel López Obrador has rejected tax increases and practiced fiscal austerity (Pérez 2022). In Brazil, although recent conservative governments have sought to contain spending, the fastest public sector growth since the 1985 democratic transition occurred under the center-right governments of the 1990s and early 2000s rather than those of the left-leaning Workers' Party (PT), which ruled from 2003 to 2016.

While compelling for the period and cases it examines, Schneider's (2012) elite-focused argument also has trouble explaining the difference between Brazil and Mexico. Its emphasis on elite cohesion as a driver of public sector growth is contradicted by the fact that, as discussed later, Mexican elites are more politically united than their Brazilian counterparts, yet Mexico's state apparatus is smaller. In the long term, as this chapter suggests, elite cohesion in the Latin American context tends to discourage public sector expansion.

3.4 Explaining the Brazil–Mexico Contrast

Thus, although there is a rich body of scholarship on the determinants of public sector size, it sheds little light on the contrast between Brazil and Mexico. How, then, can we solve this puzzle? The argument developed here emphasizes how instances of state-led redistribution can indirectly affect this variable by influencing the ideology and organization of economic elites. In particular, it suggests that especially acute threats can inadvertently give rise to intense antistatist attitudes that become embedded in the entities that represent elites politically, including peak business associations and pro-business parties, endowing them with a strong sense of collective purpose and identity. The result is a political bloc whose breadth, cohesion, and ideological commitment to limiting state intervention in the economy pose a significant obstacle to public sector growth.[10] Particularly important in forging such blocs are episodes of widespread expropriation of private property (e.g., land reform and nationalization of non-agricultural assets, such factories, mines, or oil production facilities), which can readily engender beliefs among the elite that the state poses, or may come to pose, an existential threat.[11]

This emphasis on historically constructed differences in elite ideology and organization is new to the study of public sector size but it echoes themes from other literatures. In emphasizing the enduring, self-perpetuating impact of historical episodes of redistribution, it illustrates the concept of path dependence, especially those versions that acknowledge the role of ideology and norms in institutional persistence (Mahoney 2000; Pierson 2000). Relatedly, it supports Levitsky et al.'s (2016) theory of party-building in Latin America, which stresses the role of political conflict in forging enduring parties. Finally, it corroborates Fairfield's (2015) emphasis on the negative impact of elite organizations on attempts to increase taxation.

More specifically, the argument developed below suggests that Mexico's public sector is smaller than Brazil's because redistributive reforms featuring major property threats produced an economic elite more committed to limiting state intervention and better organized to oppose it. Reforms undertaken under Lázaro Cárdenas (1934–1940) were particularly important because of their magnitude and the fact that they mobilized a powerful antistatist network that would influence politics for decades to come, opposing statist policies and constructing an expanding coalition of like-minded actors. In contrast, the public sector grew larger in Brazil because the lack of similar threats, either during the 1930s or in any subsequent decade, meant that elites never developed the same wariness of state intervention or the organizations to oppose it.

Evidence for the argument is provided below in three subsections. The first focuses on differences in the extent of threats to elite interests between the two cases, the second on the impact of threat or its relative absence on organization and ideology, and the third on the consequences of the latter variables for public sector growth.

3.4.1 Differences in Threat Level

Both countries have seen recurrent waves of social reformism that provoked concern among economic elites and other conservatives. In Mexico, the most important occurred under Cárdenas, who implemented both the first major land reform and the first major nationalization (of the oil industry) in Latin America and also sought to promote unionization and labor rights (Hamilton 1982). Although subsequent governments would generally be more conservative, bouts of reformism also occurred under Adolfo López Mateos (1958–1964) and, especially, Luis Echeverría (1970–1976). López Mateos advanced a profit-sharing program for workers, created a social security system for civil servants, and proposed a progressive tax reform. Echeverría substantially expanded social spending and the public enterprise sector.

In Brazil, the most important reforms occurred under Getúlio Vargas (1930–1945 and 1951–1954), who promoted union organization, founded the social security system, and established a relatively worker-friendly labor code as a part of a broader expansion of the state's economic role (Malloy 1979). Subsequent episodes occurred, most notably under João Goulart (1961–1964) and Luiz Inácio Lula da Silva (2003–2010). The former promoted rural unionization and limits on profit remittances by multinational corporations and sought to implement a substantial land reform. The latter focused mainly on income distribution through targeted social programs and minimum wage increases. His successor, Dilma Rousseff (2011–2016), also a member of the left-leaning PT, pursued a similar strategy.

Despite these surface similarities, the two countries differ in that reformism has been much farther-reaching in Mexico, especially with regard to property. Cárdenas, in particular, expropriated about a fifth of Mexico's farmland, including some of its most valuable estates (Hamilton 1982). He also seized important non-agriculture holdings, including the US- and British-owned oil companies. Although Cárdenas was not an avowed socialist, these policies, combined with his alliances with the Communist Party and organized workers and peasants, convinced many that Mexico was headed for socialism (Contreras 1989; López Portillo 1995). Among later governments, the most crucial property threat occurred under José López Portillo (1976–1982), who was not a prominent social reformer but nationalized the banking sector in response to capital flight.

In contrast, neither Vargas nor any of his successors mounted a similarly serious challenge to property rights. Vargas nominally endorsed land reform but did little to advance it (Ribeiro 2008). Goulart did promote a substantial land reform but failed to secure legislative approval for it. Neither engaged in significant expropriation of non-farm assets. The PT had traditionally endorsed massive land reform and renationalization of privatized firms, but Lula and Rousseff eschewed both in favor of fiscal redistribution. Somewhat surprisingly, it was the center-right Fernando Henrique Cardoso government (1995–2002) that implemented the most significant property reform by expropriating some 10 million hectares of farmland (Ondetti 2016). However, relative to total land, this reform was far smaller than Cárdenas' and had no counterpart outside agriculture.

3.4.2 Threats, Elite Ideology, and Organization

The greater intensity of redistributive threats in Mexico cultivated a more antistatist culture among the country's elite and a greater willingness to engage in political organization-building at the national, cross-sectoral level. In comparison, Brazilian elites have been more tolerant of state intervention and less disposed to organize against it. This contrast has persisted despite policy reforms that have shifted the structure of the economy over time in both countries.

In Mexico, repeated bouts of resistance to progressive reforms since the 1910–1920 revolution gradually forged a network of conservative organizations that cuts across regions and economic sectors. In 1929, business leaders responded to a labor reform proposal by creating the Employers' Confederation of the Mexican

Republic (COPARMEX), the country's first encompassing (or multisector) business association. A decade later they combined with social conservatives to found the PAN, which opposed Cárdenas' socioeconomic reforms and attempts to curtail Catholic Church influence. The Mexican Business Council (CMN), an elitist group representing the country's largest firms, arose in 1962 out of concerns with López Mateos' reformist impulses. Similarly, the creation of the Business Coordinating Council (CCE) in 1975 reflected business concern with Echeverría's efforts to forge a more interventionist state. Joining together national sectoral associations, as well as COPARMEX and CMN, the CCE is one of Latin America's most encompassing business associations (Schneider 2004). Finally, López Portillo's 1982 bank nationalization prompted many businesspeople to join the PAN, helping transform it from a largely symbolic opposition to the one-party regime to a real contender for power (Mizrahi 2003).

However, the incremental character of this process masks the profound influence of the deep, largely property-based reforms under Cárdenas, which spurred the rise of a powerful antistatist network that would set the tone for business–state relations for decades to come. The Cárdenas era was a watershed. The 1917 constitution, drafted during the revolution, had laid the legal foundation for a redistributive, nationalist state with robust control over natural resources. For years, however, implementation of these provisions was tentative. Cárdenas changed that by aggressively advancing labor rights and seizing property on a large scale (Hamilton 1982). He also sought to transform public schools by advocating a more progressive, secular brand of education. To push his agenda forward, he stoked popular mobilization and built an alliance with Mexico's Communist Party.

The reform wave met with intense resistance from business elites and social conservatives (Hamilton 1982; Contreras 1989). At the forefront were the industrialists of the northern city of Monterrey, then Mexico's major manufacturing center. In the heat of their conflict with the state, the so-called Monterrey Group forged a unique collective identity combining regional pride with defense of free enterprise (Saragoza 1988). To curry wider business support for their cause, they revived and expanded COPARMEX. The Monterrey elite were joined by other anti-reform groups, including the PAN, the fascist Gold Shirts, and a rural movement called the National Synarchist Union (Unión Nacional Sinarquista o Movimiento Nacional Sinarquista (UNS)).

By the late 1930s, Cárdenas had been forced to attenuate his reformism, and that trend would be deepened by subsequent presidents. Policies moved in a notably conservative, pro-business direction until López Mateos. However, the organizations and social networks created to block earlier reforms did not simply dissolve. Big business, in particular, hung together in a loose but powerful alliance including the Monterrey Group, COPARMEX, and sectoral groups representing commerce, finance, and industry. The PRI managed to co-opt some smaller manufacturing firms represented by the state-sponsored National Chamber of Manufacturing (CANACINTRA), which favored aggressive pro-industrialization policies and accepted the PRI's paternalistic ties to labor. However, big business was skeptical of state-led development and derided CANACINTRA as "communist" for endorsing it uncritically (López Portillo 1995; Gauss 2010).

Subsequent developments in elite organization cannot be understood without underscoring the role of this preexisting antistatist network. The changes to the state's role championed by López Mateos and Echeverría were modest by the standards of other middle-income Latin American countries (Ondetti 2021, 129). The reason they prompted enduring changes in business organization is that they aggravated an existing sense of hostility toward the state. This dynamic is particularly clear with regard to the CCE, whose creation was spearheaded by the private sector's so-called radical faction, consisting of COPARMEX, the Monterrey Group, and the Confederation of National Chambers of Commerce (CONCANACO) (Luna Ledesma 1992).[12]

Largely the same network was behind the PAN's revival a few years later. Many of the businesspeople who joined the party were from Monterrey and other parts of northern Mexico and were affiliated with COPARMEX (Mizrahi 2003). For example, the party's most prominent leader during the 1980s, Manuel Clouthier, was a former COPARMEX and CCE president who was from the northwestern state of Sinaloa and attended Monterrey Tech, a prestigious private university created by the Monterrey Group.

Thus, tight elite organization in Mexico reflects a path-dependent process of incremental strengthening driven by antistatist attitudes inadvertently stimulated by post-revolution reformers, especially Cárdenas. Because they occurred in the context of an elite already deeply wary of interventionism, each subsequent attempt to substantially expand the state's role prompted a potent counterreaction that both blunted the reform (as highlighted below) and further bolstered elite organization. Of course, Mexico has undergone major economic transformations since the 1930s. The industrial sector generally expanded under ISI policies until the early 1980s. Subsequently, the adoption of liberalizing policies exposed it to greater competition, causing some firms and subsectors to decay and others to boom. Nevertheless, because it is rooted in shared ideas, rather than particular economic structures, the political cohesion of Mexican elites has survived these changes.

In Brazil, a very different causal process has unfolded. The nonoccurrence of major redistributive threats has contributed to an elite culture that is less antistatist. Lacking their Mexican counterparts' reflexive wariness of state intervention, Brazilian elites have been largely content to focus their political capital on deriving particularistic benefits from it, rather than opposing it tout court. This attitude has discouraged sustained class-wide political organization.

Scholars have long noted the comparatively relaxed attitude of Brazil's economic elites toward state intervention. In an early work on Brazilian interest groups, Schmitter (1971) questions the notion that business "[…] must have some sort of 'natural' ideological antagonism toward government participation and interference in economic life." Drawing on field research, he argues that "[…] on balance one would have to admit that industrialists' associations, in particular, did *not* see things this way." Furthermore, he underscores the "opportunism" of Brazil's business associations, which "deprives them of ideological consistency and militancy, and leads them to operate out of pure empiricism and pragmatism" (362).

Subsequent works have expressed similar views. Both Diniz and Boschi (1978) and Evans (1979) emphasize the willingness of business elites to work with state enterprises and allow them to assume important economic roles. Sikkink (1991), in a study of mid-twentieth-century developmentalism in Argentina and Brazil, underscores the greater consensus (spanning the public and private sectors) in the latter country on the positive role of state intervention. Finally, in a work directly comparing Mexico and Brazil, Graham (1982) underscores the greater assertiveness of Mexican business in opposing attempts to expand the state's economic role.

This attitude is a product of the historical lack of serious redistributive threats in Brazil (Schmitter 1971; Ondetti 2021). Business owners are less worried about state intervention because it has not menaced their core interests, particularly their interest in preserving their property. Their unconcern is reflected in a dearth of broad political organization (Weyland 1996; Schneider 2004). There are no encompassing associations in Brazil comparable to the CCE, CMN, or COPARMEX. The broadest business organizations represent specific sectors, such as industry and commerce. Most are state-sponsored corporatist entities that benefit from obligatory dues payment. Despite their considerable financial resources, these groups are often considered ineffective, and business leaders frequently prefer to lobby through narrower associations or personal contacts (Schneider 2004). There is also no longstanding pro-business party in Brazil comparable to the PAN. Although non-left parties have tended to dominate elections, they are generally centrist or clientelistic ones, rather than programmatic right parties with strong ties to organized business (Montero 2014).

To be sure, broad elite organization has not been altogether lacking in Brazilian history. Encompassing business groups have arisen during periods of particular risk or uncertainty, including the leftist Goulart presidency and the democratic transition of the late 1980s, which included a major constitutional reform (Kingstone 1999; Schneider 2004). Vargas' social reforms helped give rise to a party, the National Democratic Union (UDN), with a liberalizing agenda and links to some businesses. Another right-leaning party, the Liberal Front Party (Partido da Frente Liberal, PFL) (now known as Brazil Union), arose during the 1980s transition. However, all these initiatives eventually disappeared or faded into irrelevance, giving way to the particularism that has traditionally marked elite political activity.

Admittedly, there is an exception to the rule of fragmented elite organization in contemporary Brazil: commercial agriculture. Since the 1990s, farm elites have developed an interlocking set of organizations with no rival among other sectors. The key actor is the Parliamentary Front for Agriculture (FPA), a legislative caucus that is among the most powerful actors in the country's Congress (Bruno 2017). The FPA collaborates with other entities, including the Agricultural Thought Institute, a think tank, and the National Confederation of Agriculture, the corporatist group for agriculture (Pompeia 2020). This coalition has acted with considerable unity on a variety of issues.

However, far from contradicting the importance of threats, this exception reinforces it, since agriculture has suffered more significant property rights challenges than other sectors. Although Brazil has never implemented a major land reform, efforts in this area intensified during the democratic transition and eventually gave rise to significant expropriation activity, especially under Cardoso. Fear and resentment of land reform stimulated a sustained process of organization-building among large producers, endowing them with the capacity to act collectively not only on this issue but also on others, including environmental protection and indigenous land titling (Bruno 2017).

Like Mexico, Brazil has experienced major changes in its economic structure, due partly to shifts in development strategy. Manufacturing output expanded robustly from the 1930s until the mid-1980s but has contracted relative to total GDP since then (World Bank database). Its role has been taken up mainly by service industries. These transformations have contributed to shifts in associational influence. For example, manufacturers' associations like the state industrial federations of São Paulo and Rio de Janeiro wield less clout than they did at the apex of Brazil's industrialization. However, they have not changed the overall character of business organization, which remains more decentralized than in Mexico.

3.4.3 Consequences of Elite Ideology and Organization for Public Sector Size

The contrasts in elite ideology and organization discussed above largely explain the striking difference in public sector size between Brazil and Mexico. Mexico's public sector is smaller than Brazil's because economic elites in that country have been more motivated and better organized to resist its expansion.

As Figure 3.1 suggests, the large contemporary gap in public sector size between these countries emerged initially between the 1940s and the 1960s. While in the 1930s, the Brazilian and Mexican states were of roughly comparable size, by 1970, there was a yawning gap between them. This divergence is curious, given that both countries were nominally pursuing the same state-led industrialization strategy promoted by ECLAC and that both had introduced Bismarckian social security systems by World War II. It can only be understood if we appreciate the impact of differences in how elites viewed state intervention and how they organized, or failed to organize, to restrict its growth.

As argued above, the Cárdenas reforms induced an elite countermobilization that congealed into an informal coalition of larger businesses wary of state intervention. Although PRI authorities after Cárdenas were cognizant of the state's low revenues and society's numerous unmet needs, their efforts to placate this coalition restricted public sector growth (Ondetti 2021, 120–122). The governments of the 1940s and 1950s were focused on rebuilding business confidence in the state and thus attentive to concerns about limiting intervention. They repeatedly sought to raise additional revenue, but their efforts encountered stiff resistance and ultimately had little impact. Consumption taxes and social security offer good illustrations since their slow expansion is a major reason why Mexico's public sector growth fell behind Brazil's.[13]

With regard to consumption taxation, perhaps the most ambitious initiative was by President Miguel Alemán (1946–1952), who in 1948 introduced a national sales tax. The Mercantile Revenue Tax was intended to replace some existing federal and state levies with the purpose of both raising revenue and streamlining the tax system (Martínez de Navarrete 1973, 48–49; Aboites Aguilar 2003, 210–212). State governments willing to renounce some of their own taxes would gain a share of its revenues. However, the tax did little to achieve these goals since the rate applied was low and several large states rejected the offer. It would only become a truly national tax in the 1970s, and the rate would remain low.[14]

A key source of resistance to the tax came from business leaders, who raised concerns about its impact on consumption. In an attempt to secure their acquiescence, in 1947 the government asked the CONCANACO to organize an elaborate meeting, dubbed the First National Convention of Taxpayers, in which authorities would dialogue with business (López Portillo 1995, 289–290; Aboites Aguilar 2003, 197). Despite these efforts to solicit their input, business leaders protested bitterly about the tax, as well as an accompanying measure increasing penalties for evasion. Their opposition may have contributed to the adoption of a rate below the already modest one originally proposed (Aboites Aguilar 2003, 212).

Social security also faced strong resistance. The Cárdenas government drafted a social security bill including pensions, healthcare, and other provisions but shelved it due to the climate of business unrest following the 1938 oil expropriation (Dion 2010, 65–66). The more conservative Ávila Camacho was able to pass a similar bill in 1942, but the law gave the executive authority to determine what groups of workers would be covered. With the partial exception of CANACINTRA, businesses steadfastly opposed the system's expansion due to both the required employer contributions and concerns about how authorities would use the revenue (López Portillo 1995, 308; Dion 2010, 73, 80–81). Because of these objections, along with the declining influence of organized labor, social security's key support base, the system grew slowly thereafter.

López Mateos and Echeverría sought to break with this pattern by asserting a stronger state role in economic and social development. However, they failed in this quest, especially with regard to taxation. Both presidents attempted to raise revenue and increase progressivity but achieved only limited change (Elizondo 1994; Aboites Aguilar and Unda Gutiérrez 2011). Scholars, as well as policymakers who participated in these efforts, attribute the failures mainly to officials' fears of aggravating already tense relations with a suspicious private sector (Solís 1988; Elizondo 1994; Ortiz Mena 1998). As a result, planned reforms were diluted or abandoned.

In Brazil, in contrast, elites' relatively benign view of the state and their lack of class-wide organization facilitated the consolidation of a large public sector during the era of state-led development. Consumption taxes and social security are, again, useful examples. Revenues from consumption taxes grew steadily during the post-World War II era, driven by piecemeal changes in both national and subnational levies (Varsano 1996). Beginning in the late 1950s, they tended to stagnate, due to growing macroeconomic problems. However, they rebounded strikingly in the mid-1960s, mainly as a result of the military regime's sweeping reform, which boosted revenue across all major tax categories (Oliveira 1991). With regard to consumption taxation, the major change was the introduction of Latin America's first value-added tax (VAT), which would become a mainstay of Brazil's fiscal system (Varsano 1996, 9).[15]

The social security system, which Vargas had largely created during the 1930s, also grew thereafter in terms of coverage and revenue (Malloy 1979). Even the conservative military regime substantially expanded it. Although the main beneficiaries were relatively well-off formal sector employees, the regime also introduced a non-contributory program for farm workers. By the mid-1970s, Brazil's social security revenues were about 60% higher than Mexico's and its spending 80% higher (Mesa-Lago 1990, 26). Brazil, it is worth noting in passing, was also more statist than Mexico in other areas. For example, the state played a more important role in capital formation through its public enterprises and development bank, and its effective trade protection was higher (Graham 1982).

These policies elicited comparatively little concerted opposition from economic elites. The literatures on taxation and business politics during these decades reveal very limited evidence of organized resistance to revenue increases, even the mid-1960s reform, which increased revenue by roughly 6% of GDP (Schmitter 1971; Diniz and Boschi 1978; Evans 1979; Oliveira 1991; Varsano 1996). Likewise, there appears to have been little business–state conflict over social security expansion (Malloy 1979; Delgado 2007). In fact, as Schmitter (1971, 368) notes, a remarkable aspect of Brazilian politics during this period is how the public sector grew without provoking sharp conflicts. Graham (1982) makes a similar point in comparing Brazil to Mexico, arguing that the latter's private sector was more autonomous and active in checking the state's expansion.

The differences in elite ideology and organization between these countries have continued to influence public sector growth since the crisis of state-led development in the early 1980s and the subsequent shift toward economic and political liberalization. Consequently, the gap established in the immediate post-World War II period has persisted.

In Mexico, business cohesion and the revival of the PAN have helped prevent the emergence of a substantial welfare state, despite the transition to democracy during the 1990s and the region-wide trend of social policy expansion in recent decades. The PAN held the presidency for the first dozen years (2000–2012) after the end of PRI hegemony. Although its governments made efforts to raise taxes and expand the social safety net, they were modest relative to those of other Latin American countries, reflecting the party's liberal economic views and close ties to business (Ondetti 2021, ch. 4). The somewhat more progressive PRI government that followed from 2012 to 2018 made a more ambitious attempt to raise tax revenues. However, its 2013 reform faced strong business resistance led by the CCE and achieved modest change (Unda Gutiérrez 2021). It was only after oil prices plummeted in late 2014 that tax revenues began to surge, reflecting a need to compensate for lower PEMEX earnings. However, total revenue remained constant at about 20% of GDP.

Brazil's public sector growth trajectory in recent decades has been different. Although deep macroeconomic problems pushed authorities to adopt certain neoliberal reforms during the 1990s, the public sector continued expanding robustly in fiscal terms. For example, the tax burden, which at 24% of GDP was already the heaviest in Latin America when the military relinquished power in 1985, had risen to 33% of GDP by 2007 (see Figure 3.1).

The proximate causes of this trend were the democratic constitution adopted in 1988, which created new social spending commitments, and the stabilization of the currency in 1994, which facilitated tax collection (Melo et al. 2010). However, a key underlying factor was the lack of strong antistatist actors. Brazil's more conservative parties, such as the PFL/Brazil Union, have supported liberalizing reforms during periods of crisis but have otherwise tended to prioritize access to patronage, which requires spending (Weyland 1996; Montero 2014). Business has remained politically fragmented and only tepidly committed to market-based policies (Kingstone 1999; Ondetti 2021). Although multisector initiatives arose to protect key business interests (e.g., property rights) in the 1987–1988 constituent assembly, they largely neglected fiscal questions and faded once the constitution was ratified. Another coalition emerged during the mid-1990s to lobby for tax reform, but it was loosely organized, boasted few resources, and had little policy impact (Ferreira 2002).

Admittedly, resistance to public sector growth has stiffened in recent years, contributing to the stabilization of tax revenues at about a third of GDP. Anti-tax mobilizations involving business associations and conservative parties contributed to the 2007 defeat of a "temporary" financial transaction tax that had been renewed repeatedly since the mid-1990s, the legislative removal of President Rousseff (who sought to revive the tax) on charges of fiscal irregularities, and the approval under interim President Michel Temer (2016–2018) of a constitutional amendment capping public spending in inflation-adjusted terms for at least a decade.

Nevertheless, there is little reason to believe that Brazil is poised to reduce the weight of the public sector in its economy. Even Jair Bolsonaro (2019–2022), the most economically liberal president in two decades, did not achieve major changes in this sense. Although he did pass a reform to moderate pension outlays, he also carved out exceptions to the spending cap to launch populist cash transfer initiatives and failed to substantially advance proposed structural reforms, such as privatization (Ferrari Filho and Terra 2023). Moreover, tax revenues reached a historic peak during his term. While various factors contributed to Bolsonaro's failure to transform Brazil's development model, the lack of a powerful antistatist coalition in Congress and civil society undoubtedly played a role. The return of the PT's Lula to the presidency in 2023 means that liberalizing reform will be off the political agenda until at least 2027. In fact, Lula has already won approval of a law permanently weakening the spending cap (Tiossi 2023).

3.5 Conclusions

Existing theories cannot account for the striking difference in public sector size between Brazil and Mexico. Standard variables like economic development, trade openness, federalism, and democracy provide little, if any, explanatory leverage.

However, this chapter has argued that the gap can be understood by highlighting the impact of historical episodes of major redistribution on the ideology and organization of economic elites. Mexico's public sector is smaller than Brazil's because post-revolution reforms spurred the rise of a strong antistatist coalition anchored by business associations and the PAN. This coalition has thwarted the emergence of a more interventionist state. In Brazil, the lack of comparable reforms meant that elites have not embraced antistatist views to the same extent and have not organized as effectively to block public sector expansion. Consequently, taxation and public spending have reached higher levels.

While this chapter deals with only two cases, there are a priori reasons to believe that the argument may shed light on other Latin American countries. For example, there is a correlation between the occurrence of a major expropriation-based land reform at some point in a country's history and the existence today of strong encompassing business associations, suggesting that acute redistributive threats can help spur private sector organization. Countries that experienced such a reform, such as Chile, Guatemala, and Peru, generally have influential multisector business associations, while those that did not, such as Argentina, Ecuador, and Uruguay, lack such actors (Schneider 2004).

Furthermore, there is at least some evidence that high levels of elite organization tend, other things being equal, to hinder public sector growth. Chile, Guatemala, and Peru all have comparatively small public sectors, and the influence of organized business has generally been seen as discouraging state intervention (Fairfield 2015; Durand 2016; Ondetti 2021). Meanwhile, Argentina, Ecuador, and Uruguay, where business boasts less encompassing organization, have much higher taxation and spending.

While this chapter has emphasized the non-economic causes of differences in public sector size, it must be acknowledged that ongoing economic changes could eventually erode the ideas underpinning differences in elite organization, facilitating the emergence of new trends in public sector growth. Across much of the world, for example, advances in information technology are transforming the character of business assets and the nature of state intervention in the economy. To the extent that Mexico and Brazil partake in them, these transformations could potentially shift the concerns of economic elites in ways that destabilize longstanding patterns of political activity and give rise to new cleavages.

Notes

1 Economic elites are defined here as owners of substantial capital, regardless of the sector they are involved in, and top managers of large private enterprises.
2 The chapter does not offer a wide-ranging analysis of elite ideology but rather focuses on attitudes toward state intervention in the economy, as discussed further below.
3 Its main disadvantage is that, as with small-N research in general, it offers less external validity (i.e., generalizability of the findings) than statistical approaches.
4 See Section 3.2 for a discussion of how the cases compare on these variables.
5 See Section 3.1 for comparative data.

6 For 2015–2019, Brazil's revenues were 73.1% higher and it's spending 45.1% higher than Mexico's. On average, the Nordic countries had 65.5% higher revenues and 40.5% spending than the United States.
7 PEMEX's contribution to federal revenues increased from 3.9% in 1972 to 38.1% in 1982 (Chávez 2005, 74).
8 Such an imbalance may force national authorities to tax heavily to pay for the free spending of their subnational counterparts.
9 Ondetti (2021) also elaborates an elite-focused theory of taxation level, some of the key themes of which are echoed in this chapter.
10 Consistent with the discussion in Section 3.1, public sector growth is understood here mainly in terms of fiscal revenues and spending.
11 This theoretical argument is developed extensively in Ondetti (2021). The importance of threats in stimulating enduring business organization in Latin America is also underscored by Durand and Silva (1998), albeit with less emphasis on property threat.
12 Monterrey firms alone voluntarily contributed a third of the CCE's funding in its early years (Schneider 2004, 83).
13 The difference between Brazil and Mexico was generally smaller in other areas, such as income taxation.
14 The general rate increased from 3% to 4% during the 32 years of its existence.
15 Brazil's VAT is unusual in that it is a state rather than central government tax. Mexico would not adopt its own VAT until 1980.

References

Aboites Aguilar, Luis. 2003. *Excepciones y Privilegios: Modernización Tributaria y Centralización en México 1922–1972*. Mexico City: El Colegio de México.

Aboites Aguilar, Luis, and Mónica Unda Gutierrez. 2011. *El Fracaso de la Reforma Fiscal de 1961*. Mexico City: El Colegio de México.

Astorga, Pablo, Ame R. Berges, and Valpy Fitzgerald. 2005. "The Standard of Living in Latin America during the Twentieth Century." *Economic History Review* 58 (4), 765–796.

Boix, Carles. 2001. "Democracy, Development, and the Public Sector." *American Journal of Political Science* 45 (1), 1–17.

Brennan, Geoffrey, and James M. Buchanan. 1980. *The Power to Tax: Analytical Foundations of a Fiscal Constitution*. New York: Cambridge University Press.

Bruno, Regina. 2017. "Bancada ruralista, conservadorismo e representação de interesses no Brasil contemporâneo." In *Questões Agrárias, Agrícolas e Rurais: Conjunturas e Políticas Públicas*, edited by Maluf, Renato, and Georges Flexor, 155–168. Rio de Janeiro: E-Papers..

Cameron, David R. 1978. "The Expansion of the Public Economy: A Comparative Analysis." *American Political Science Review* 72 (4), 1243–1261.

Cetrángolo, Oscar, and Juan Carlos Gómez Sabaini. 2007. *La tributación directa en América Latina y los desafíos a la imposición sobre la renta*. Santiago: ECLAC.

Chávez, Marcos. 2005. "Las Finanzas Públicas en México, 1970–2000. Crónica del Fracaso de la Política Fiscal." In *Penuria Sin Fin: Historia de los Impuesto en México Siglos XVIII–XX*, edited by Aguilar, Luis Aboites, and Luis Jáuregui, 211–302. Mexico City: Instituto Mora..

Contreras, Ariel José. 1989. *México 1940: Industrialización y Crisis Política*. Mexico City: Siglo Veintiuno Editores.

Delgado, Ignacio Godinho. 2007. "O Empresariado Industrial e a Gênese das Políticas Sociais Modernas no Brasil." *Locus: Revista de História* 13 (2), 135–160.

Diniz, Eli and Renato Raul Boschi. 1978. *Empresariado Nacional e Estado no Brasil.* Rio de Janeiro: Forense-Universitária.

Dion, Michelle. 2010. *Workers and Welfare: Comparative Institutional Change in Twentieth-Century Mexico.* Pittsburgh: University of Pittsburgh Press.

Durand, Francisco. 2016. *Extractives Industries and Political Capture: Effects on Institutions, Equality, and the Environment.* Lima: Oxfam.

Durand, Francisco, and Eduardo Silva. 1998. "Organized Business and Politics in Latin America." In *Organized Business, Economic Change, and Democracy in Latin America*, edited by Durand, Francisco, and Eduardo Silva, 1–50. Miami: North-South Center Press.

ECLAC. 1979. *Statistical Yearbook for Latin America.* Santiago: ECLAC.

Elizondo, Carlos. 1994. "In Search of Revenue: Tax Reform in Mexico under the Administrations of Echeverría and Salinas." *Journal of Latin American Studies* 26 (1), 159–190.

Evans, Peter. 1979. *Dependent Development: The Alliance of Multinational, State, and Local Capital in Brazil.* Princeton: Princeton University Press.

Fairfield, Tasha. 2015. *Private Wealth and Public Revenue in Latin America: Business Power and Tax Politics.* New York: Cambridge University Press.

Ferrari Filho, Fernando, and Fábrio Henrique Bittes Terra. 2023. "The Political Economy of Bolsonaro's Government (2019–2022) and Lula da Silva's Third Term (2023–2026)." *Investigación Económica* 82 (324), 27–50.

Ferreira, Roberto Nogueira. 2002. *A Reforma Essencial: Uma Análise, sob a Ótica Empresarial, das Propostas e dos Bastidores da Reforma Tributária.* São Paulo: Geração Editorial.

Flores-Macías, Gustavo A. 2014. "Financing Security through Elite Taxation: The Case of Colombia's Democratic Security Taxes." *Studies in Comparative International Development* 49 (4), 477–500.

Gauss, Susan M. 2010. *Made in Mexico: Regions, Nation, and the State in the Rise of Mexican Industrialism, 1920s–1940s.* University Park: Pennsylvania State University Press.

Gerring, John. 2007. *Case Study Research: Principles and Practices.* New York: Cambridge University Press.

Graham, Douglas H. 1982. "Mexican and Brazilian Economic Development: Legacies, Patterns, and Performance." In *Brazil and Mexico: Patterns in Late Development*, edited by Hewlett, Sylvia Ann, and Richard S. Weinert, 13–56. Philadelphia: Institute for the Study of Human Issues..

Hall, Peter A., and David Soskice. 2001. *Varieties of Capitalism: The Institutional Foundations of Comparative Advantage.* Oxford: Oxford University Press.

Hamilton, Nora. 1982. *The Limits of State Autonomy: Post-Revolutionary Mexico.* Princeton: Princeton University Press.

Hanni, Michael, Ricardo Martner, and Andrea Podestá. 2015. "El potencial redistributivo de la fiscalidad en América Latina." *Revista CEPAL* 116, 7–26.

Huber, Evelyne, and John D. Stephens. 2012. *Democracy and the Left: Social Policy and Inequality in Latin America.* Chicago: University of Chicago Pres.

Iversen, Torben, and David Soskice. 2006. "Electoral Institutions and the Politics of Coalitions: Why Some Democracies Redistribute More than Others." *American Political Science Review* 100 (2), 165–181.

Kingstone, Peter R. 1999. *Crafting Coalitions for Reform: Business Preferences, Political Institutions, and Neoliberal Reform in Brazil.* University Park: Pennsylvania State University.

Levitsky, Steven, James Loxton, Brandon Van Dyck, and Jorge I. Domínguez. 2016. *Challenges of Party-Building in Latin America.* New York: Cambridge University Press.

López Portillo, Felícitas. 1995. *Estado e Ideología Empresarial en el Gobierno Alemanista.* Mexico City: Universidad Nacional Autónoma de México.

Luna Ledesma, Matilde. 1992. *Los Empresarios y el Cambio Político: México, 1970–1987.* Mexico City: Ediciones Era.

Lustig, Nora. 2017. "El impacto del sistema tributario y el gasto social en la distribución del ingreso y la pobreza en América Latina. Una aplicación del marco metodológico del proyecto Compromiso con la Equidad." *El Trimestre Económico* 84 (3), 493–568.

Mahoney, James. 2000. "Path Dependence in Historical Sociology." *Theory and Society* 29 (4), 507–548.

Malloy, James M. 1979. *The Politics of Social Security in Brazil.* Pittsburgh: University of Pittsburgh Press.

Martín-Mayoral, Fernando, and Carlos Andrés Uribe. 2010. "Determinantes económicos e institucionales del esfuerzo fiscal en América Latina." *Investigación Económica* 69 (273), 85–113.

Martín-Mayoral, Fernando, and Juan Fernández Sastre. 2017. "Determinants of Social Spending in Latin America During and After the Washington Consensus: A Dynamic Panel Error-Correction Model Analysis." *Latin American Economic Review* 26 (10), 1–32.

Martínez de Navarrete, Ifigenia. 1973. "La evolución del sistema tributario de México y las reformas 1972–73." *Revista de Análisis Económico y Social* 23 (1), 48–55.

Melo, Marcus André, Carlos Pereira, and Saulo Souza. 2010. *The Political Economy of Fiscal Reform in Brazil: The Rationale for the Suboptimal Equilibrium.* Washington, DC: IDB.

Mesa-Lago, Carmelo. 1990. *Ascent to Bankruptcy: Financing Social Security in Latin America.* Pittsburgh: University of Pittsburgh Press.

Mizrahi, Yemile. 2003. *From Martyrdom to Power: The Partido Acción Nacional in Mexico.* Notre Dame: University of Notre Dame Press.

Montero, Alfred P. 2014. "Brazil: Explaining the Rise and Decline of the Conservatives." In *The Resilience of the Latin American Right*, edited by Luna, Juan Pablo, and Cristóbal Rovira Kaltwasser, 294–318. Baltimore: John Hopkins University Press.

Oliveira, Fabrício Augusto de. 1991. *A Reforma Tributária de 1966 e a Acumulação de Capital no Brasil.* Rio de Janeiro: Oficina de Livros.

Ondetti, Gabriel. 2016. "The Social Function of Property, Land Rights and Social Welfare in Brazil." *Land Use Policy* 50, 29–37.

_____. 2021. *Property Threats and the Politics of Anti-Statism: The Historical Roots of Contemporary Tax Systems in Latin America.* New York: Cambridge University Press.

Ortiz Mena, Antonio. 1998. *El Desarrollo Estabilizador: Reflexiones Sobre una Época.* Mexico City: Fondo de Cultura Económica.

Pérez, David Marcial. 2022. "La reforma fiscal se aleja de la agenda de López Obrador." *El País*, October 22. https://elpais.com/mexico/2021-10-22/la-reforma-fiscal-se-aleja-de-la-agenda-de-lopez-obrador.html (June 22, 2023).

Persson, Torsten, and Guido Tabellini. 2003. *The Economic Effects of Constitutions.* Cambridge: The MIT Press.

Pessino, Carola, and Ricardo Fenochietto. 2010. "Determining Countries' Tax Effort." *Hacienda Pública Española/Revista de Economía Pública* 195 (4), 65–87.

Piancastelli, Marcelo. 2001. *Measuring the Tax Effort of Developed and Developing Countries: Cross Country Panel Data Analysis – 1985/95*. Rio de Janeiro: IPEA.

Pierson, Paul. 2000. "Increasing Returns, Path Dependence, and the Study of Politics." *American Political Science Review* 94 (2), 251–267.

Pompeia, Caio. 2020. "Concertação e poder: O agronegócio como fenômeno político no Brasil." *Revista Brasileira de Ciências Sociais* 35 (104), 1–17.

Przeworski, Adam, and Henry Teune. 1970. *The Logic of Comparative Social Inquiry*. New York: Wiley-Interscience.

Ram, Rati. 2009. "Openness, Country Size and Government Size: Additional Evidence from a Large Cross-Country Panel." *Journal of Public Economics* 93 (1–2), 213–218.

Ribeiro, Vanderlei Vazelesk. 2008. *Cuestiones Agrarias en el Varguismo y el Peronismo: Una Mirada Histórica*. Buenos Aires: Universidad Nacional de Quilmes.

Rodden, Jonathan. 2003. "Reviving Leviathan: Fiscal Federalism and the Growth of Government." *International Organization* 57 (4), 695–729.

Rossignolo, Darío Alejandro. 2017. "El esfuerzo fiscal en los países de América Latina y el Caribe." *Revista Finanzas y Política Económica* 9 (2), 215–247.

Saragoza, Alex M. 1988. *The Monterrey Elite and the Mexican State, 1880–1940*. Austin: University of Texas Press.

Schmitter, Philippe C. 1971. *Interest Conflict and Political Change in Brazil*. Stanford: Stanford University Press.

Schneider, Aaron. 2012. *State-Building and Tax Regimes in Central America*. New York: Cambridge University Press.

Schneider, Ben Ross. 2004. *Business Politics and the State in Twentieth-Century Latin America*. New York: Cambridge University Press.

Sikkink, Kathryn. 1991. *Ideas and Institutions: Developmentalism in Brazil and Argentina*. Ithaca: Cornell University Press.

Solís, Leopoldo. 1988. *Intento de la Reforma Económica de México*. Mexico City: El Colegio Nacional.

Stein, Ernesto. 1999. "Fiscal Decentralization and Government Size in Latin America." *Journal of Applied Economics* 2, 357–391.

Stein, Ernesto, and Lorena Caro. 2013. *Ideology and Tax Revenues in Latin America*. Washington, DC: IDB.

Tiossi, Saulo. 2023. "Novo marco fiscal aprovado pelo Congresso põe fim ao teto de gastos." *CNN Brasil*, August 22.

Unda Gutiérrez, Mónica. 2021. "The Superfluous Congress: Executive Dominance and Business Lobbying in Mexico's 2013 Tax Reform." *Mexican Studies* 37 (1), 93–122.

Varsano, Ricardo. 1996. *A evolução do sistema tributário brasileiro ao longo do século: anotações e reflexões para futuras reformas*. Brasília: IPEA.

Weyland, Kurt. 1996. *Democracy without Equity: Failures of Reform in Brazil*. Pittsburgh: University of Pittsburgh Press.

4 Economic Elites and Development with Equity in Bolivia and Ecuador

Eduardo Silva and Fabio Resmini

4.1 Introduction

From the 1980s to 2020, in the context of democratic regimes, Latin America wavered between neoclassical development models and more mixed-economy models with greater social equity. Economic elites in the region generally held strong preferences in favor of the former and opposed shifts to less laissez-faire macroeconomic models. However, after the elections of left-wing parties in government, business and agrarian elites acquiesced to mixed-economy models and social equity goals that the new progressive governments pursued. What explains this change of stance?

We argue that economic elites[1] accommodated the new development model because of critical changes in the balance of power between them and left-wing governments. The commodity boom, the crisis of pro-market parties, and the fragmentation within the pro-business associational space caused a decline in the economic, political, and social resources possessed by economic elites. This momentary disadvantage forced them to at least acquiesce to a more mixed-economy approach to development with equity, even without wholeheartedly supporting it.

Our argument is based on analyzing four decades of state-business relations in Bolivia and Ecuador. We begin by examining how the Latin American debt crisis of the 1980s and its management shaped business support for radical market-oriented adjustments. After two decades of economic instability and widespread backlash to mounting socio-economic exclusion, left governments pursued a more mixed-economy development model with greater social equity. Following initial resistance, a fragile modus vivendi was established between business elites and the left governments of Ecuador and Bolivia in the context of the commodity boom. When the commodity boom ended, business elites aggressively turned away from state-led development with equity and the governments that supported it. Our two cases then diverge in the way in which the cooperative phase between economic elites and left governments came to an end. While in Ecuador, the rupture was a combination of poor macroeconomic conditions and a split within the pro-state-led development party, in the case of Bolivia, it was mainly due to the unraveling of the socio-political coalition that supported the government of Evo Morales.

DOI: 10.4324/9781032636764-5

4.2 Neo-Classical Economics versus Mixed Economies with Social Equity

As Gustavo Flores-Macías (2012) observes, the key differences between the neoclassical and the mixed-economy development models revolve around the state's role in the economy. His indicators use the neoclassical model as a benchmark for contrast. The model postulates that free markets – decentralized decision-making in response to the incentive for private gain – yield the greatest output and, thus, the greatest total wealth. The function of government is to leave the market alone. Mixed-economy models, by contrast, argue that free markets produce unstable, uneven economic growth accompanied by high levels of social inequality. States use government policy to correct the market's shortcomings.

The first set of indicators encompasses trade, financial, and monetary liberalization. While the neoclassical model emphasized reforms to liberalize trade, capital flows, and monetary policy – such as ceding control of monetary policy to independent central banks and eliminating restrictions on investment and price controls – mixed-economy models re-regulated the financial sector, re-introduced protectionism to boost domestic production, and variously reinstated price control and subsidies to consumption.

A second indicator involves differences regarding privatization and nationalization of key industries. Privatization of state enterprises was a hallmark of the neoclassical model under the assumption that the private sector produces goods and services more efficiently than the state with lower prices and better quality. Privatization also reduced the state's fiscal outlays. Under the mixed-economy model adopted by leftist governments, states re-nationalized key national industries, arguing that privatization reduced competition, raised prices, increased unemployment, and robbed the state of significant capital and tax resources.

The two models also differed in government spending and tax policy. Neoclassical economics advocates for low government spending, which is justifiable mainly for providing proper public goods or correcting for negative externalities. Taxes should also be kept low to encourage private investment. On the contrary, mixed-economy models require higher levels of government spending and taxation to finance expanded state services and public enterprise.

Welfare and poverty alleviation strategies are the fourth set of indicators that distinguishes the neoclassical model from the mixed-economy one (Esping-Andersen 1991). Neoclassical economic model welfare programs require strict means testing and offer meager short-term benefits, thus pushing individuals back to work at any price. In seeking better poverty alleviation, left governments attempted to de-commodify basic services more, aspiring to universal coverage of citizens. Benefits tended to be more generous, long-term, and available to broader categories of persons in need.

4.3 Analytic Framework

We argue that whether the business and agrarian elites of small economies on the periphery of the world capitalist system oppose, support, or consent to more mixed-economy models favoring development with greater social equity hinges on the balance of power between them and governments seeking to implement such programs. That balance depends on the power resources that business and landowning elites muster in relation to those left-oriented governments' commands. In this chapter, we analyze how the correlation of forces influences a left-oriented government's relative autonomy from business and landowning elites and, in turn, the leverage that economic elites possess to limit the implementation of mixed-economy programs. To pinpoint the factors that explain variation over time of this correlation of forces, we look at the changing distribution of power resources in three interrelated but analytically separate fields – economic, political, and social – and at the international economic factors that tilt the balance in favor of or against capital owners.

We anchor our approach in the "political sociology of political economy" to shed light on the politics of policy choice (Gourevitch 1986). At heart, what is at stake are conflicts over a nation's economic and social development model. The policy requires politics and which policies 'win' depends in the first instance on the relative strength of contending social forces, which, in turn, depends on their economic, political, and social power resources.

Economic power hinges on the effective possession of economic resources. For capital and landowners, it is the capacity to generate investment, stable economic growth, and employment. This is known as the 'structural power' of business in capitalist economies (Lindblom 1977). The degree to which states and the governments that run them are dependent on the private sector for investment, growth, and employment affects their degree of autonomy from capital. International economic factors, such as the fluctuations in the price of commodities and the relative role of capitalists vis-à-vis domestic and international markets, can increase or decrease the economic power that different economic elites wield.

Political power stems from state structures – in the form of channels of access to policymaking – and, by extension, from the political organizations that seek to occupy them. On the one hand, state structures establish decision-making rules and procedures: the more porous they are to business and landowning interests, the more capable economic elites are of influencing policy outputs. This direct influence on policymaking has often been referred to as 'instrumental power' of capital (Miliband 1969; Fairfield 2015). As a result, the more instrumental power elites have, the more difficult it will be for left governments to implement heterodox development models. On the other hand, states are also *arenas* in which contending social forces vie for support through elected class-based intermediary organizations (Collier and Collier 1991; Mann 1993; Gourevitch 1986). Here, we mainly refer to political parties whose electoral success increases the capacity of the social sectors they represent to steer policymaking. The electoral strength of pro-business parties directly impacts the power resources that economic elites muster and, as a result, the capacity of left governments to move away from the policies preferred by economic elites.

In addition to the political power of their party linkages, the social power of class and ethnically based groups depends on the level of development and cohesiveness of their interest organizations (Rueschemeyer et al. 1992). Following Silver (2003), we focus on class associational power and collective power. *Associational power* refers to the degree of organizational density and coordination *within* a class, ethnically, or territorially defined social group. Among business elites, this applies to distinct sectors, such as chambers of industry, commerce, import–export firms, and finance. *Collective power* refers to horizontal linkages *across* class, ethnically, and territorially organized social groups. Among businesses and landowners, this refers to peak associations (confederations) formed by the individual sector-wide business chambers and agricultural activities. The higher the associational and collective power of economic elites, the more cohesive they are and the more social-associational power they wield.

4.4 Methodology

We adopt a methodology that combines process tracing with controlled comparison to show how variation over time in power resources within and across our two cases accounts for shifts in economic elites' support, acquiescence, or opposition to mixed-economy models. While process tracing guarantees attention to processes within each case and illuminates the causal pathways connecting the explanatory factors to our outcome of interest, we select cases that allow us to conduct a controlled comparative analysis to maximize control over alternative explanations (Slater and Ziblatt 2013).

The cases we analyze in this chapter, Bolivia and Ecuador, also offer an excellent paired comparison to evaluate factors that contributed to the relative durability (Bolivia) or fragility (Ecuador) of these socio-economic projects after business and agrarian elites turned against them following a period of concession. Space does not permit, but one could extend the analysis to other cases. Uruguay also offers a case of relative durability, and one factor, the strength of popular sector and left-party connections, is even stronger than in Bolivia (Anría et al. 2022; Anría and Bogliaccini 2022). Argentina and Brazil occupy a middle position with somewhat weaker popular sector-left political party linkages. Therefore, we see more attenuated swings between market and mixed-economy models depending on whether conservative and left-leaning political parties govern (Silva 2017).

We establish the position of business and agrarian elites based on their revealed preferences in public media, archival, and secondary literature accounts. We trace the balance of power between economic elites and left governments over three periods. These are the initial resistance of elites when the left governments assumed office, a period of rapprochement, and renewed business and landowner opposition.

4.5 Economic Elites and Left Parties: The Neoliberal Period

Business support for market reforms depended on the international competitiveness of their sectors and whether assets were fixed (brick and mortar) or liquid (portfolio). Commercial, financial, and extractive industries headed the list, along with the construction sector, which benefitted from expanding finance and credit. Industrial and landowning sectors supported trade and financial market liberalization if competitive with imports or export-oriented. Under market reforms,

Bolivian and Ecuadorian business and landowning elites with these characteristics prospered, often in association with international capital, as the state retreated (Conaghan and Malloy 1995).

The retreat of the state from economic activity expanded the private sector's role as the engine of economic growth, thus augmenting its structural power because economic growth and employment – closely linked to political stability – depended more on it. Thus, most Bolivian and Ecuadorian political parties, including the center-left, supported market-affirming policies, which left opposition to market reform without effective parliamentary representation. Under these conditions, business elites' instrumental power also expanded. Influential business leaders enjoyed direct access to high-ranking officials and technocrats, so did their business chambers, and connections to political party leadership helped advance business policy preferences (Conaghan and Malloy 1995; Crabtree 2020). The most privileged sectors tended to be financial, commercial export–import, and agro-export.

Pro-market social forces benefitted from a favorable balance of power between 1984 and 2005. The Latin American debt crisis of the 1980s, plus a shift in the international sources of financing to private financial markets in the 1970s and 1980s, left Latin American states without the resources to manage more statist economic policies and expansive social policies. In the context of severe economic dislocations and high inflation, major political parties that had represented disadvantaged social sectors collapsed or became electorally unappealing. Indeed, even when left populist parties won the presidency, they wound up supporting market reforms, ultimately weakening their electoral appeal as voters abandoned them.

In Ecuador, between 1984 and 2005, all presidents supported market reforms, even those who had run anti-neoliberal electoral campaigns. Rodrigo Borja (1988–1992) of the Democratic Left party, who opposed them, was forced to sign IMF (International Monetary Fund) stabilization programs. Lucio Gutiérrez (2003–2005), of the new Patriotic Society party, who campaigned on a progressive anti-neoliberal platform, received the backing of the IMF once in office, and needing business support to revive the economy, he pushed economic stabilization and structural adjustment programs (Campello 2015). Likewise, all Bolivian presidents between 1985 and 2006 supported market reforms regardless of the historical ideological positions of their parties (Crabtree 2020). Thus, the formerly left Revolutionary Nationalist Movement initiated market reforms, followed by the Revolutionary Left Movement and the National Democratic Alliance. The three parties not only agreed that market reforms were necessary for economic growth in a changing international political economy, but they also formed shifting alliances for presidential elections to ensure their political dominance.

4.6 Economic Elites and Left Governments: From Opposition to Collaboration

The favorable balance of power for socio-economic and political forces that supported free-market economics began to change in the early 2000s. The volatility of economic growth, deepening income inequality, rising unemployment, the rapid expansion of precarious employment (the 'informal' sector), and the collapse of public services undermined pro-market forces.

By the same token, those developments increased the relative power of anti-neoliberal forces. Their associational and collective power grew as marginalized social sectors organized to resist market economics. These famously included indigenous people's organizations, as well as the 'informal' sectors, in alliance with declining unions. Together, they organized anti-neoliberal mobilization cycles that shook Bolivia and Ecuador's political foundations. Moreover, as socio-economic conditions deteriorated, citizens abandoned established political parties and turned to outsider parties built on the back of anti-neoliberal mobilization (Silva 2009). Those parties differed markedly. Bolivia's Movimiento al Socialismo (MAS) was an organic party of highland indigenous peasants, lowland First Nations indigenous peoples, frontier people, and informal sector urban dwellers alongside 'invited' urban middle-class members. Evo Morales, of indigenous peasant extraction and leader of the coca union federations, headed the party. Ecuador's Alianza País (AP) was a top-down electoral vehicle formed by disaffected center-left political elites to support unorthodox economist Rafael Correa's presidential campaign. Notably, AP had an uneasy relationship with powerful indigenous people's organizations united in the Confederación de Nacionalidades Indígenas del Ecuador (CONAIE).

The balance of political power turned decisively against business elites when these outsider political parties convincingly won presidential elections: Evo Morales and the MAS in 2005 with 53.7 percent of the vote to the conservative PODEMOS party's 28.6 percent and AP's Rafael Correa in the second-round balloting with 56.7 percent to the conservative opposition's 43.3 percent. Despite notable differences, these leaders and their parties shared a similar socio-economic platform. They were committed to reforming neoliberal capitalism. They sought to develop a mixed economy, one with a greater direct role for the state and extension of social citizenship rights to marginalized groups. This entailed nationalization and/or greater regulation and taxation of international and domestic companies in key export sectors, utilities, transportation, and banking; promotion of small and micro-business as well as small agricultural peasant and indigenous holdings; expansive social policy in public health, education, pensions, and infrastructure development; raising minimum wages. To facilitate these changes, Morales and Correa supported constitutional reform to provide the legal basis for the change in the development model. By the early 2000s, the commodity boom provided national treasuries with sufficient resources to ensure a measure of autonomy from business interests and govern on the left. Curiously, Bolivia and Ecuador's post-neoliberal development program did not involve strengthening labor unions, with whom Morales and Correa maintained a rocky relationship.

4.6.1 Initial Opposition

Business elites felt threatened by this socio-economic and political agenda. They believed it would restrict investment opportunities because of regulation and competition by the state and that they would be forced to pay higher taxes to support increased fiscal expenditures. Even if labor unions were not favored, higher wages, particularly minimum wages, would add costs to business. Moreover, the incoming governments would be hostile to business elites and landowners, and they could expect their political influence – their instrumental power – to wane once government officials excluded them from policymaking networks. For these reasons, business and landowning elites strongly opposed incoming left governments, hoping to constrain their plans to govern capital. However, business opposition was more united and violent in Bolivia than in Ecuador.

4.6.1.1 Bolivia

In Bolivia, political opposition primarily came from powerful agribusiness (mainly soya) and natural gas interests in the lowland departments of Santa Cruz, Pando, Beni, and Tarija – the so-called Half Moon. Their economic power was substantial because they were the principal contributors to export-led economic growth at the turn of the century after the decline of tin in the highlands. They rejected Morales' agrarian 'revolution' and the nationalization of the burgeoning gas industry. In alliance with conservative political parties, they maneuvered in the constituent assembly to derail or delay the process and organized intense public protests. Confrontations became increasingly polarized as the lowland departments began to talk about secession in constitutional debates over departmental autonomy (Farthing and Kohl 2014).

The Department of Santa Cruz, and its eponymous capital city, was the epicenter of opposition. Political, social-associational, and economic power converged in the alliance between the departmental government, the civil society organization Comité Cívico Pro Santa Cruz, and the Santa Cruz Federation of Private Entrepreneurs (Federación de Empresarios Privados de Santa Cruz – FEPSC). The FEPSC included regional business associations such as the Eastern Chamber of Agriculture (Cámara Agropecuaria del Oriente, CAO) and the Chamber of Industry and Commerce (Cámara de Industria, Comercio, Servicios y Turismo, CAINCO) (Eaton 2011; Gamarra 2008).

Violent confrontations mounted in 2008, but the lowland opposition suffered two important political reverses in 2008. First, Evo Morales overwhelmingly won a recall vote in August 2008 (61.4–38.6 percent). Second, in September, a confrontation between peasant supporters of the government and opposition forces in Pando, in which local opposition officials were complicit, ended in the deaths of at least a dozen pro-government demonstrators. The MAS government responded by removing and prosecuting the Pando's Prefect (governor) along with several other officials. This decisive action deflated the more violent confrontations and forced the opposition to concentrate more on parliamentary obstruction and negotiation.

Lowland landowner and business opposition and their political allies did not manage to attain its maximal goals of achieving regional autonomy, ousting Evo Morales, and torpedoing the constituent assembly. However, as Wolff (2016) argued, their main purpose was defensive. They ultimately sought to constrain the

MAS government's political project; to a certain extent, they succeeded and struck a compromise. The draft constitution was revised between 2008 and 2009, especially regarding regional control over land tenure. In a key concession to Santa Cruz business concerns, land reform would contain a 'non-retroactivity clause,' exempting existing landholdings from the new 5,000 hectares limit on the size of agrarian properties (Eaton 2011).

4.6.1.2 Ecuador

In Ecuador, opposition to Correa's government was more geographically diffused and thus more fragmented along sectoral and regional lines. Although Guayas province and its capital city, Guayaquil, were a center of opposition, it did not galvanize fierce resistance as Santa Cruz did in the Bolivian case (Eaton 2011). The business sectors that were squarely on the losing end of Correa's economic agenda were the banking and the export sectors (particularly those with windfall profits during the commodity boom) (Ospina Peralta 2015). Landowners who paid higher property taxes and certain importers who paid higher tariffs also saw their interests affected.

Correa targeted business more selectively than Morales, with a particular focus on the underregulated banking sector. He tightened regulations and taxed interbank transactions, thus significantly reducing their profits (from 20 to 12 percent) and raising revenue for government projects (Chiasson-LeBel 2019). To undercut their outsized political influence, Correa also prohibited financial conglomerates from owning media companies through which they manipulated public opinion.

However, some of the policies implemented by Correa affected business elites' influence in general. In particular, the permanent closure of traditional institutional paths expressly established to channel business association influence in policymaking, including their express prohibition in the 2008 constitution, came as a huge blow to the instrumental political power of the country's economic elites (Chiasson-LeBel 2019). Similarly troubling was Correa's plan to strengthen state taxing institutions and to fund expanded state economic and social policy by raising taxes, including on private enterprise. As a result, on a rhetorical level, the main business associations closed ranks in public opposition to these policies in the early years of his government (Chiasson-LeBel 2019). In January 2008, 130 business leaders of 30 national business associations publicly rejected key government policies (Wolff 2016). Exporters were particularly vehement as well because Correa opposed free trade agreements with the US and the EU.[2]

In practice, however, opposition from business and landowning elites was neither as strong nor as radical as in Bolivia. In Ecuador, economic elites could not do much to derail the constituent process that Correa initiated. Apart from being more fragmented, Ecuadorian economic elites had weaker representative associations than Bolivia from the outset, as they were accustomed to guaranteed institutional access to policymaking. They did not need strong, coordinated national federations and confederations, and when these were abolished, their fragmentation precluded vigorous collective action beyond rhetoric. Also, Ecuador had no conditions for the convergence of economic, political, and social-associational power that we saw in Santa Cruz (Eaton 2011).

4.6.2 Strategic Cooperation

We saw that the balance of power turned against business and landowning elites by the mid-2000s. When left governments took office in Bolivia and Ecuador, the commodity boom gave them a measure of autonomy from business' structural power, and business elites also lost much of their privileged access to policymakers. Politically, the business also lost influence as Morales' MAS in Bolivia and Correa's AP in Ecuador gained majorities in the legislature. The period of full-on opposition to their governments ended with the ratification of new constitutions that gave legal standing to the left's socio-economic and political project in September 2008 (Ecuador) and January 2009 (Bolivia). Business and landowning elites thus needed a new approach to dealing with left governments. Meanwhile, Bolivia and Ecuador's left governments were reformist, not revolutionary. They needed a healthy private sector, if nothing else, because the level of hydrocarbon and agro-export revenue was not sufficient to ensure stable, sustained economic growth and employment. They also required a sufficiently cooperative private sector to ensure governability. These circumstances contributed to strategic rapprochement and cooperation.

4.6.2.1 Bolivia

In Bolivia, rapprochement began in 2009–2010 after the new constitution was approved, and it coincided with a split between the lowland political elites and economic elites, with the former wanting to continue scorched-earth opposition and the latter seeking to build bridges (Eaton 2017). The rift between political, social-associational, and economic interests severely debilitated the pro-market coalition, dissipating important power resources (particularly in the political and social-associational fields) and producing an important change in the correlation of forces between government and opposition.

The split became evident as early as September 2009 when CAO and CAINCO extended an olive branch to the MAS government and invited President Morales to inaugurate the Santa Cruz International Fair. The move provoked a strong adverse reaction from the governor, the mayor, and the president of the Comité Pro Santa Cruz, who threatened to resign (Wolff 2019). To avoid raising tensions, Morales thanked but declined the invitation. He did, however, attend the following year's inauguration, when the president of CAINCO talked about "a new phase in the relations between the private sector and the state" (Correo del Sur 2010).

This initial public display of cooperation was followed up in 2011 by meetings with Evo Morales in La Paz, where both sides emphasized their "commitment to support national production and investment in order to generate employment" (América Economía 2011). More high-level meetings followed through 2012, suggesting that lowland private sector leaders no longer thought of Evo Morales' government as an existential threat (Reuters 2012). Meanwhile, the lowland political opposition accused business leaders of abandoning the struggle against Morales and making a pact with the government to safeguard their interests (Wolff 2016; Eaton 2016). Business groups stopped funding the Comité Pro Santa Cruz, thus substantially weakening it (Crabtree and Chaplin 2013, 137; Eaton 2016).

Rapprochement deepened into cooperation in 2013 with a series of high-level, very public meetings between business leaders and the executive. The government agreed to support agro-export expansion, a law to legalize illegal deforestation, and subsidies for energy production for sugar refineries. Morales also promised state investment in infrastructure and legal security (protection from expropriation) for landowners and the private sector more generally (Wolff 2016). These public agreements were backed by policy. For example, the rate of land redistribution declined, landowners enjoyed exemptions from expropriation and from size limits to holdings, restrictions on exports to boost domestic food supply were loosened, and the agro-exporting sector reclaimed its access to the highest policymaking spheres (Wolff 2016). This cooperative relationship continued throughout the second and third term of Morales and was propped up by coordinated initiatives, like the joint creation of the Consejo Económico Productivo in 2017 to foster collaboration in the economic sector (Fides 2017).

4.6.2.2 Ecuador

In Ecuador, rapprochement and cooperation with some economic sectors followed the ratification of the 2008 constitution. Correa's government sought to discipline the private sector so that it contributed positively to national development with a modicum of social equity in full realization that a healthy private sector was a key factor in economic growth and employment. Meanwhile, the private sector understood that it did not have the power to oust Correa or to significantly derail its development program. Correa's administration encouraged the thawing of hostilities in response to the recession-inducing 2008–2009 world financial crisis. He favored some sectors – such as food distribution, real estate, and construction – who then acquiesced to his rule. This process was reinforced by a gradual change in the correlation of forces as a result, on the one hand, of the increase in the private sector's social power and of the political–electoral strategies of powerful banking–export conglomerates, and on the other hand, of the increasing cleavages within the governing coalition.

Given their reduced economic power, their political power at an all-time low, and their lack of mobilization capacity, after Correa's landslide reelection in 2009, Ecuador's economic elites sought to boost their associational and collective power. As national politics became more significant in a country historically marked by regionalism, and given they had lost guaranteed access to policymaking, business elites turned regional and sectorial associations into national ones encompassing many business sectors. This was a bid to "develop more efficient actions to influence public opinion and the state" (Chiasson-LeBel

2019, 161). A key leader in this movement, Richard Martínez, became head of the Committee of Ecuadorian Entrepreneurs (Comité Empresarial Ecuatoriano, CEE), which federates the greatest number of business associations in the country (Chiasson-LeBel 2019, 162) and was eventually appointed Minister of Finance in 2018 under Lenín Moreno. The CEE focuses on trade, labor, taxes, and defense of market principles. This development strengthened the private sector's capacity for collective action.

Meanwhile, to counter the burgeoning left, some banking and export–import conglomerates chose to participate in electoral politics, both for the presidency and for the national legislature and subnational governments. Electing representatives to legislatures offered political power to obstruct and water down Correa policies. This was the case of the banana magnate Alvaro Noboa, from Guayaquil, who credibly ran for president several times, including against Correa in 2006, and headed a party (the PRIAN) with a sizeable presence in the legislature. The party was subsequently dissolved in 2014 due to a precipitous electoral decline. He was followed by Guillermo Lasso, a banking conglomerate magnate, who, on the third try, became president of Ecuador in 2021.

We argued above that the relative autonomy of Correa's government, ironically, depended in part on a healthy, growing but tamed private sector to raise tax revenue for its programmatic goals. The 2008–2009 world financial crisis threatened that balance and served as a catalyst for business–state cooperation, especially with exporters that had initially been hardline opponents of Correa. As we shall see, this was not the case with the banking sector, which remained isolated in its hardline opposition and thus unable to threaten the government.

There are many telling examples of this balancing act. On the one hand, to improve the balance of trade and stimulate domestic production Correa's administration slapped temporary tariff increases on a wide range of imports and regulated food prices for rice, corn, milk, and bread. To raise revenue, the government raised the currency export tax, quintupling it by 2011. On the other hand, to mollify key business sectors, it eliminated tariffs on close to 300 goods, favoring capital goods and equipment for agricultural production. In a cooperative return gesture, "several of the country's largest importers (many with long-standing links to rightwing political parties and the leading chambers of commerce and industry) signed an agreement with the president in 2009 to restrict imports" (Bowen 2014, 108). Correa's government also changed its stance on a free trade agreement with the EU in 2012, which was concluded in 2014, a move that shows that business association representatives had been steadily gaining access to the government. Meanwhile, while they opposed tax increases, economic elites abandoned belligerent rhetoric and recognized that they benefitted from infrastructure development (Wolff 2016, 134). Moreover, in 2013, the government immediately introduced compensatory measures to offset the loss of US trade preference 2013 due to disagreements over drug eradication policies favored by the US, and it reestablished the Ministry of Foreign Trade, which it had abolished earlier. In all instances, business association leaders publicly welcomed these policy initiatives in a spirit of cooperation (Wolff 2016, 134).

4.7 Resurgence of Hardline Opposition to Development with Equity

By 2017–2019, the cooperative spirit of business and landowner elites soured. Several important shifts in the balance of power between capital and social democratic forces influenced this turn. One was economic. The end of the commodity boom around 2012–2014 undercut revenue that supported active state involvement in the economy and society. This decline in revenues reduced the degree of state autonomy from capital, as it increased the dependence of the former on the latter for economic growth and employment. As we shall see, business and landowning elites exploited the strengthening of their structural power to push back on social democratic programs.

The second element in the power shift was political and associational. The decline in resources for social democratic programs, among other factors, caused dissension in the political parties that dominated left governments. Rifts between ruling left parties and the social organizations that linked those parties to the electorate became more common. These developments weakened the left parties' mobilization capacity, both electorally and extra-electorally.

Business and landowning elites exploited these weaknesses. They used their growing structural power to wring policy concessions from left governments or their successors, aided by rapprochement with the IMF, whose loan conditionality requirements favored austerity and market-oriented structural adjustment. The political weakness of ruling left governments incentivized economic elites to unite in opposition to their social democratic agenda and to strengthen their relationship with pro-market conservative parties in the hopes of defeating them electorally. These factors had somewhat different weights in each of our two cases.

4.7.1 Bolivia

In Bolivia, the business elite's turnaround from a cooperative to an oppositional stance to state-led development with equity had more to do with political than economic factors. Compared to Ecuador, the effects of the commodity boom's decline were not as severe because Morale's government's prudent macroeconomic policies maintained fiscal, monetary, and foreign exchange stability and sustained economic growth. Instead, the unraveling of the socio-political coalition that supported his government presented an opportunity for the hardline political right and business elites to renew their alliance in opposition to Morales and his socio-economic project (Brown 2022; Wolff 2020). In November 2019, they forced Morales to resign and established a caretaker government that favored market-driven development.

The resurgence of opposition to Morales' government turned on his persistent efforts to run for reelection in 2019, even though the term limits established by his own constitution forbade it. Morales' reelection bid sparked cycles of mobilization by opposition political forces and middle-class citizens. The polarized conflict revived the languishing conservative political opposition to the MAS government. It re-launched former president Carlos Mesa (2003–2005) as the standard bearer of the center-right. Perhaps more importantly, it revitalized the radical far-right of the lowlands, the same ones that had so implacably opposed Morales when he initially became president. Key Santa Cruz-based party and Civic Committee leaders made common cause with disgruntled informal sector leadership and allied political representatives and took the limelight in violent protests in various cities. Lowland business and agro-exporting elites turned from cooperation with Morales' government to the growing clamor for Morales' removal. The encompassing business confederation, somewhat more cautiously, also joined the opposition. Morales' reelection bid also destabilized the social coalition that supported the MAS, as his cooperative practices and past meddling in the internal leadership of various MAS-affiliated organizations provided a breeding ground for coalition infighting (Brown 2022).

The timing of the business' turn from cooperation to opposition supports the conclusion that the debilitation of Morales' strong social support base and electoral domination was the principal reason for it. Wolff (2022) shows how national business associations were cautious at first, and as Morales weakened, they became more emboldened. When the opposition called for a 'civic strike' in February 2018 commemorating the 2016 referendum, the CEPB (Confederation of Private Entrepreneurs of Bolivia) – the main umbrella business association – demurred and left it up to member associations to participate. Many of the principal associations did not, including three from the lowlands. In December 2018, in response to the Court's ruling on Morales' candidacy for president, the CEPB again refrained from signing on to the political opposition's calls for mobilization. Although the lowland FEPSC followed suit, CAINCO joined in at the behest of the Santa Cruz Civic Committee.

The situation changed after the October 2019 presidential election. Some major business associations continued to emit measured pronouncements about the political unrest engulfing the nation. CEPB and CNI released statements urging opposing sides to moderate polarization while at the same time recommending that the national legislature call a second round of voting. However, once Áñez replaced Morales, the CEPB threw its full support behind her. Meanwhile, CAINCO went a step further, calling for Morales' resignation only after the OAS (Organization of American States)' November 10 recommendation (Wolff 2020, 145). Other business associations, especially from the lowlands, took a more militant stance. The CAO, after labeling Morales' decision not to call a second round of voting undemocratic, unequivocally called for his overthrow in defense of democracy. The Exporters' Association of Santa Cruz took a similar stance, emphasizing the negative consequences of political instability for business (Wolff 2020, 146).

Áñez's interim government staunchly supported market development and, once installed, business and landowning elites, represented by their business associations, declared their allegiance to it. Indeed, they celebrated its arrival. They extolled the reestablishment of democracy and order in line with constitutional norms (Brown 2022, 179). Áñez government's pronounced pro-business and lowland support base led to ministerial appointments that favored pro-market representation (many from Santa Cruz) and afforded business elites easy access to policymaking. These included the Minister of Finance and Economy, the Minister of Environment and Water, and the Minister of Productive Development and Rural Economy. The new government also created a new Productive Development Council in which business associations had ample representation (Página Siete 2020).

Nevertheless, except for COVID-19 pandemic-related measures, the interim government did not significantly change economic policy, although it would have liked to. That may have been because other factors did not tilt the balance of power sufficiently in their favor, as the MAS remained politically strong and could regain part of the associational and collective power it had lost over the years. On the one hand, the decisive factor was that while presidential succession was, to put it kindly, 'irregular,' Bolivia's democratic regime remained, and the MAS, given legislative results in the October 2019 elections, had won a majority in the Congress. Indeed, a *Masista* was president of the Senate. Hence, the MAS remained a political force to be reckoned with. On the other hand, Morales' exit from power freed MAS-affiliated social movements from the debilitating cooptative relations that they entertained with the state. In a renewed context as opposition actors, social movements were able to regroup and reassert their autonomy and capacity for contestatory mobilization against the state. Ultimately, it was the MAS, both in the institutional arena and in the streets, that held Áñez's government's feet to the fire with respect to holding new presidential elections as soon as possible, COVID-19 notwithstanding (Ortiz et al. 2020).

The interim government did implement some economic policy changes that favored agro-exporters, principally from the lowlands. For example, it liberalized agrarian and agro-industrial exports on which there had been quotas, such as bovine, cattle, and chicken meat, corn, sugar, sunflower, and soy oils (Wolff 2020). The interim government also floated the privatization of companies, such as Boliviana de Aviación, and opening lithium mining to foreign companies. However, demonstrations pushing for presidential elections and against privatization kept it from acting. This is probably because, as a presidential candidate, Áñez sought to avoid open confrontation over such a conflictive policy initiative, especially since the MAS was still an electorally powerful party and its presidential candidate led by a significant margin in the polls.

4.7.2 Ecuador

In Ecuador, business elites' reversion to united hardline arose in a specific conjuncture: a poor macroeconomic position due to a decline in international oil prices, and the 2017 presidential election in which Correa's vice president, Lenin Moreno, only narrowly beat Guillermo Lasso and his Creating Opportunities party (CREO). The former weakened state autonomy and increased the structural power of capital. The latter debilitated pro-state development forces politically. Both contributed to tensions between the Correa and Moreno factions of the party that business elites and conservative parties exploited.

Oil prices declined in 2011 from a high of $150 p/b to a low of $47 p/b in 2016[3]; the gross domestic product's (GDP) growth followed the downward trend, from a year-end high of 7.9 percent in 2011 to negative 1.5 percent in 2016 and less than 1 percent growth after that to 2018. Correa was reluctant to cut public spending and flatly rejected the IMF and economic austerity. When Moreno took over the presidency, Ecuador's current account was in deficit (0.7 percent of GDP), and its fiscal deficit expanded to 6 percent of GDP by 2017 (Wolff 2018, 283). The level of public debt turned into a major source of tension between Correa's faction of the ruling AP party and Moreno's. Moreno declared Ecuador in serious economic difficulties due to Correa's fiscal sleight of hand and said that he, Moreno, would have to fix the problem.

The second source of debilitating tension was that Moreno had campaigned as a consensus-builder. Correa was committed to developing state autonomy and took a hardline toward all organized interest groups, including businesses, shutting them out of the policy process. This characteristic contributed to accusations of abrasive, authoritarian behavior that fanned socio-political conflict. Moreno promised a more inclusive, consultative, and deliberative policymaking style in which all organized interest groups – business, labor, and indigenous people's organizations – would participate in solving pressing public issues.

Upon taking office, Moreno made good on these promises. He established National Dialogue Roundtables on the business climate, labor relations, the fiscal deficit, natural resource development, and socioenvironmental conflict, among others. Participants joined at the presidency's invitation, not by right. Most of the Roundtables operated between July and October 2017. The Roundtables revealed Moreno's government's belief in private sector-friendly policies as the key to economic reactivation instead of state intervention to protect domestic markets and state autonomy.

Moreno's preference for private sector-led development caused a rift with Correa's faction of AP. This rift deepened when, in 2018, Moreno organized a constitutional amendment referendum on seven questions that arose from the Roundtable dialogues, many of which were designed to weaken Correa's faction of AP. They all passed handily, and one result was that Jorge Glas, Moreno's vice president and a Correa loyalist, was successfully prosecuted for corruption. Correa was indicted *in absentia*, and the Correa faction of AP created a new political party without, however, being able to mobilize its core constituents against Moreno's pro-market reversal.

In mid-2018, Moreno unambiguously threw his support to orthodox economic stabilization and market-oriented structural reforms by appointing Richard Martínez, former president of the CEE, as Finance Minister and invited an IMF team to Ecuador. Ecuador signed a US$ 8 bn Extended Loan Facility with the IMF in early 2019. The IMF loan package supported two key pillars of the Ecuadorian government's reform agenda. First, it boosted competitiveness and job creation, which involved loosening labor and financial sector regulation. Second, it strengthened fiscal sustainability and dollarization, which entailed public sector wage cuts, terminating fuel subsidies, slashing expenditures on capital investment, goods, and services, and raising taxes (low even by Latin American standards). Economic elites, through their representative associations and supporting political

1 Neoliberal Period		
Power Resources	**Bolivia**	**Ecuador**
Economic	(+) State retreat	(+) State retreat
Political	(+) State penetration	(+) State penetration
Social	(-) Division national and regional	(-) Fragmentation

2 Initial Opposition to Government Seeking Mixed Economy with Social Equity		
Power Resources	**Bolivia**	**Ecuador**
Economic	(+) Heritage of neoliberalism	(+) Heritage of neoliberalism
Political	(-) Right party crisis	(-) Right party crisis
Social	(+) Convergence of interests in Santa Cruz	(-) Fragmentation

3 Acquiescence and Cooperation		
Power Resources	**Bolivia**	**Ecuador**
Economic	(-) Commodity boom	(-) Commodity boom
Political	(-) Right party crisis	(+) "Business" parties
Social	(-) Split in Santa Cruz coalition	(-) Fragmentation

4 Resurgent Opposition		
Power Resources	**Bolivia**	**Ecuador**
Economic	(+) End of commodity boom	(+) End of commodity boom
Political	(+) Revived right parties	(+) Cooptation of Moreno
Social	(+) Renewed Santa Cruz coalition	(+) National business associations

Figure 4.1 Evolution of economic elites' power resources in Bolivia and Ecuador.

Source: Elaboration by authors.

parties, threw their weight in support of the IMF negotiations and most of the conditions of the loan agreement.

The graph below (Figure 4.1) summarizes the evolution of power resources in the hands of economic elites throughout the four periods analyzed. Arrows between tables indicate the direction of the transition from one period to the next – from (1) neoliberalism to (2) the initial opposition against left-wing governments to (3) the period characterized by acquiescence to the new economic model to (4) the last phase of renewed opposition to the mixed-economy model. Plus and minus signs within the tables indicate whether the power resources possessed by economic elites in each of the three fields were high/increasing or low/decreasing in each period.

4.8 Conclusion

In this chapter, we have sought to explain the conditions under which the business and agrarian elites of small economies on the periphery of the world capitalist system might swing their support from neoclassical market economics to more mixed-economy approaches to development with equity. We argued that the variation in the level of opposition of economic elites to a state-led development model is a consequence of shifts in the balance of power between them and governments that seek to implement that model. We showed how that is what happened in the cases of Bolivia and Ecuador under the governments of Evo Morales and Rafael Correa, respectively. As long as the two countries' economic elites could take advantage of state dependence on private capital (i.e., structural power) and enjoyed extensive influence in policymaking (i.e., instrumental power), their opposition to more state participation in the economy was unyielding. Yet, when the boom in commodity prices decreased the reliance of the state on private capital, and the election of left-wing parties to the executive blocked access to policymaking circles, economic elites in Bolivia and Ecuador reluctantly accepted the transition to a more state-led economic model. The end of the commodity boom and the internal division within left-wing governing coalitions gave once again business and agrarian elites the upper hand in the conflict over the developmental model, as they were able to regain control of the executive in both countries.

In Bolivia, the tenure of the right in power was brief, as the de facto government of Áñez was defeated in the elections of October 2020 by MAS candidate and former Minister of Economy Luis Arce. With Arce as president, Bolivia has returned to a mixed-economy model of development with equity, and the relationship with economic elites has been more cooperative. In Ecuador, on the contrary, the political problems inside *Correismo* and its poor presence in the social-associational space prevented it from making an electoral comeback after the return to a neoclassical economic model under Moreno. Members of the business elite Guillermo Lasso and Daniel Noboa (Alvaro's son) won the presidency in 2021 and 2023, respectively. Their victories marked the deepening of the process of re-neoliberalization and the consolidation of the neoclassical economic model with a significant reduction of the role of the state in the economy. The country is now going through a severe economic and social crisis, but whether it will swing back to a macroeconomic model of state-led development remains to be seen.

Notes

1 Throughout the chapter we refer to business and landowning elites as "economic elites," and we distinguish them from political elites, i.e., high-ranking state officials and party cadres.
2 In this they most closely resembled Bolivia's agro-exporting elites (Bowen 2014).
3 See: Macrotrends.2022. *Crude Oil Prices – 70 Year Historical Chart*. www.macrotrends.net/1369/crude-oil-price-history-chart (June 23, 2022).

References

América Economía. 2011. "Bolivia: gobierno y empresarios acuerdan trabajar juntos para enfrentar la crisis." *América Economía*, August 24. www.americaeconomia.com/economia-mercados/finanzas/bolivia-gobierno-y-empresarios-acuerdan-trabajar-juntos-para-enfrentar-la (July 15, 2022).

Anría, Santiago, and Juan Bogliaccini (2022) "Empowering Inclusion? The Two Sides of Party-Society Linkages in Latin America." *Studies in Comparative International Development* 57, 410–432.

Anría, Santiago, Verónica Pérez Betancourt, Rafael Piñero Rodríguez, and Fernando Roesnblatt. 2022. "Agents of Representation: The Organic Connection between Society and Leftist Parties in Bolivia and Uruguay." *Politics and Society* 50 (3), 384–412.

Bowen, James D. 2014. "The Right and Nonparty Forms of Representation and Participation: Bolivia and Ecuador Compared." In *The Resilience of the Latin American Right*, edited by Luna, Juan Pablo, and Cristóbal Rovira Kaltwasser, 94–116. Baltimore, MD: Johns Hopkins University Press.

Brown, John. 2022. *Deepening Democracy in Post-Neoliberal Bolivia and Venezuela: Advances and Setbacks*. New York: Routledge.

Campello, Daniela. 2015. *The Politics of Market Discipline in Latin America: Globalization and Democracy*. New York: Cambridge University Press.

Chiasson-LeBel, Thomas. 2019. "Neoliberalism in Ecuador after Correa." *European Review of Latin American and Caribbean Studies/Revista Europea de Estudios Latinoamericanos y del Caribe* 108, 153–174.

Collier, Ruth Berins, and David Collier. 1991. *Shaping the Political Arena: Critical Junctures, the Labor Movement, and Regime Dynamics in Latin America*. Princeton, NJ: Princeton University Press.

Conaghan, Catherine M., and James M. Malloy. 1994. *Unsettling Statecraft: Democracy and Neoliberalism in the Central Andes*. Pittsburgh, PA: University of Pittsburgh Press.

Correo del Sur. 2010. "Expocruz, todo un símbolo nacional." Correo del Sur, September 19. https://hemeroteca.correodelsur.com/2010/0919/1.php (July 15, 2022).

Crabtree, John. 2020. "Democracy, Elite Power and Civil Society: Bolivia and Peru Compared." *Revista CIDOB d'Afers Internacionals* 126, 139–161.

Crabtree, John, and Anne Chaplin. 2013. *Bolivia: Processes of Change*. London: Zed Books.

Eaton, Kent. 2011. "Conservative Autonomy Movements: Territorial Dimensions of Ideological Conflict in Bolivia and Ecuador." *Comparative Politics* 43 (3), 291–310.

———. 2016. "Challenges of Party Building in the Bolivian East." In *Challenges of Party-Building in Latin America*, edited by Levitsky, Steven, James Loxton, Brandon Van Dyck, and Jorge I. Domínguez, 383–411. New York: Cambridge University Press.

———. 2017. *Territory and Ideology in Latin America: Policy Conflicts between National and Subnational Governments*. Oxford: Oxford University Press.

Esping-Andersen, Gøsta. 1991. *The Three Worlds of the Welfare State*. New York: Cambridge University Press.

Fairfield, Tasha. 2015. *Private Wealth and Public Revenue in Latin America*. New York: Cambridge University Press.

Farthing, Linda C., and Benjamin H. Kohl. 2014. *Evo's Bolivia: Continuity and Change*. Austin, TX: University of Texas Press.

Fides. 2017. "Morales y empresarios privados deciden crear un consejo económico productive." *Agencia de Noticias Fides*. www.noticiasfides.com/economia/morales-y-empresarios-privados-deciden-crear-un-consejo-economico-productivo-378902 (July 15, 2022).

Flores-Macías, Gustavo A. 2012. *After Neoliberalism? The Left and Economic Reforms in Latin America*. Oxford: Oxford University Press.

Gamarra, Eduardo A. 2008. "Morales and Democracy." In *Constructing Democratic Governance in Latin America*, edited by Domínguez, Jorge I., and Michael Shifter, 124–151. Baltimore, MD: Johns Hopkins University Press.

Gourevitch, Peter. 1986. *Politics in Hard Times: Comparative Responses to International Economic Crises*. Ithaca, NY: Cornell University Press.
Lindblom, Charles E. 1977. *Politics and Markets: The World's Political-Economic Systems*. New York: Basic Books.
Mann, Michael. 1993. *The Sources of Social Power: Volume 2, the Rise of Classes and Nation-States, 1760–1914*. Cambridge: Cambridge University Press.
Miliband, Ralph. 1969. *The State and Capitalist Society*. New York: Basic Books.
Ortiz, Pablo, Fernando Molina, Verónica Rocha Fuentes, and Julio Córdova Villazón. 2020. "¿Por qué volvió a ganar el MAS? Lecturas de las elecciones bolivianas." *Nueva Sociedad* (Octubre). https://nuso.org/articulo/Bolivia-Luis-Arce-Evo-Morales/ (July 15, 2022).
Ospina Peralta, Pablo E. 2015. *Grandes empresas, crisis económica y revolución ciudadana: informe de coyuntura, noviembre de 2015*. Quito: Comité Ecuménico de Proyectos (CEP).
Página Siete. 2020. "Gobierno y empresarios privados crean Consejo Nacional de Desarrollo Productivo." *Página Siete*. www.paginasiete.bo/economia/gobierno-y-empresarios-privados-crean-consejo-nacional-de-desarrollo-productivo-EFPS245760 (July 15, 2022).
Reuters. 2012. "Morales suma a empresarios en acuerdo de Gobierno en Bolivia." *Reuters*. January 11. www.reuters.com/article/latinoamerica-bolivia-cumbre-idLTASIE80B00620120112 (July 15, 2022).
Rueschemeyer, Dietrich, Evelyne Huber Stephens, and John D. Stephens. 1992. *Capitalist Development and Democracy*. Cambridge: Polity.
Silva, Eduardo. 2009. *Challenging Neoliberalism in Latin America*. New York: Cambridge University Press.
———. 2017. "Reorganizing Popular Sector Incorporation." *Politics & Society* 45 (1), 91–122.
Silver, Beverly J. 2003. *Forces of Labor: Workers' Movements and Globalization Since 1870*. Cambridge: Cambridge University Press.
Slater, Dan, and Daniel Ziblatt. 2013. "The Enduring Indispensability of the Controlled Comparison." *Comparative Political Studies* 46 (10), 1301–1327.
Wolff, Jonas. 2016. "Business Power and the Politics of Postneoliberalism: Relations Between Governments and Economic Elites in Bolivia and Ecuador." *Latin American Politics and Society* 58 (2), 124–147.
———. 2018. "Ecuador after Correa. The Struggle over the 'Citizens' Revolution.'" *Revista de Ciencia Política* 38 (2), 281–302.
______. 2019. "The Political Economy of Bolivia's Post-neoliberalism." *European Review of Latin American and Caribbean Studies/Revista Europea de Estudios Latinoamericanos y Del Caribe*, 108, 109–129.
———. 2020. "Las élites económicas en la Bolivia contemporánea." In *Nuevo Mapa de Actores en Bolivia: Crisis, polarización e incertidumbre (2019–2020)*, edited by Souverein, Jan, and José Luis Exeni Rodríguez, 139–163. La Paz: Friedrich Ebert Stiftung Bolivia.
______ 2022. *The Local Turn and the Global South in Critical Peacebuilding Studies*. Frankfurt: Peace Research Institute.

5 Entrenching Mexican Corporate Elites in Global Corporate Networks (and Vice-Versa)

Alejandra Salas Porras and
Martí Medina Hernández

5.1 Introduction

Beginning in the 1980s, a process of recomposition of economic and political elites in Mexico has accompanied and intertwined with the transformation of a previously state-centered, nationalist, and protectionist model of development into an increasingly neoliberal and outward-looking approach firmly centered in the market. From a global perspective, this is a striking example of a rapid, albeit peaceful, neoliberal takeover of state power and the corresponding large economy of the Global South. The Mexican turn to a predominantly neoliberal regime—that is, one in which most policy decisions are subordinated to the logic of the market—is particularly relevant not only because it happened so quickly, surprising even the potential opposition, but also because it involved an intense collaboration and interaction among state, corporate, and intellectual elites.[1] Neoliberalism has become the dominant political-economic ideology, embodied in the Washington Consensus, itself consisting of a set of recommendations backed by the international financial institutions, for example, the International Monetary Fund (IMF) and the World Bank (WB). Mexican state elites have followed this policy advice closely, particularly via the opening of the economy to trade and investment, privatization of state companies, elimination of subsidies, and, in general, reducing most forms of state participation in the economy (Salas Porras 2017, 2020).[2]

This process was sparked by the crisis of import substitution industrialization (ISI) strategies, which could no longer sustain growth due to the level of debt they entailed, giving way to alternative policy proposals that empowered neoliberal-leaning agencies and elites. Thereafter, such state elites strengthened their position, while developmentalist and nationalist elites were displaced from the most influential offices in the state apparatus, often provoking tensions and political divisions.[3] Further, large Mexican corporations, who needed to export an increasingly greater proportion of their output due to the contraction of domestic markets, supported this shift in the development model, reinforcing the process even if it meant dismantling industrial chains and narrowing still-shrunken domestic markets. These and other social costs notwithstanding, the movement toward a market-centered economy has rapidly pushed forward as the new state elites gained control of key agencies and the corporate elite opened to global markets.

DOI: 10.4324/9781032636764-6

5.2 Crisis of the Import Substitution Industrialization Model

Throughout three decades (1950s–1970s), Mexican political elites enhanced state autonomy concerning both foreign and domestic capitals. They developed policy capacities and significantly enriched policy spaces, allowing the planning and pursuit of short- and long-term policy objectives, as well as convincing business elites about the opportunities industrialization projects entailed. To increase national investment, a set of incentives was offered, including fiscal, financial, and other subsidies that substantially reduced risk, made investments profitable, provided stability, and increased trust. The economy was diversified, the internal market was enhanced, and growth rates increased rapidly. Greater planning capacity and autonomy enabled the state to undertake an ambitious process of *Mexicanization*, which limited the percentage of FDI allowed in key economic sectors, inducing joint ventures between foreign and Mexican business elites. Additionally, a drive to diversify into more advanced and promising sectors led state elites to undertake massive public investment projects in areas, such as steel and metal tools, petrochemicals, and telecommunications, among others (Salas Porras 2017). They carried out large infrastructure projects (for example, dams, underground transport, highways, and airports), encouraging the formation of highly sophisticated infrastructure construction private firms. Despite these and other achievements, the ISI model in Mexico did not increase business productivity or lead to higher standards of competitiveness in exchange for protection and subsidies, nor did it curb rent-seeking behavior, collusion of monopolistic interests, or corruption practices of different sorts (Salas Porras 2017).

Yet, notwithstanding the shortcomings in how the ISI model was implemented, the economy grew at an average rate of 6.8%–6.7% during the 1960s and 1970s, respectively (The World Bank 2021), rapidly industrializing and diversifying several economic sectors, constituting what is referred to as 'the Mexican miracle.' While the primary sector[4] decreased participation in GNP from 13.1% to 6.3% in the period from 1965 to 1980, manufacturing increased participation from 18.6% to almost 22% in 1988 (The World Bank 2021). However, the model depended on the imports of capital goods, which demanded increasingly higher amounts of hard currency, as economist Jaime Ross (1993) thoroughly documents. Until the 1960s, these funds were provided mostly by revenues from agricultural and mining exports, and from the 1970s onward, oil exports became more and more important. However, oil production required huge investments, deepening the level of debt and making the model increasingly vulnerable. When oil prices fell and interest rates increased simultaneously in the 1980s, the model became both unsustainable and politically indefensible. To renegotiate foreign debt, Mexico was required by the IMF to adopt structural adjustment programs to contain the public deficit and public expenses in general. The economy virtually came to a halt with an average growth rate of 1.93% throughout the 1980s and a negative growth in per capita terms according to the World Bank (2021) and only 2.63% between 1995 and 2007, with productivity[5] increasing only 14% throughout this period (OECD 2021). Such complications created a favorable situation for a group of technocrats to radically transform the model of development (Salas Porras 2017) and for the corporate elite to profit from both the neoliberal reforms and the globalizing trends these reforms unleashed. Consequently, the Mexican corporate elite has become involved in a dynamic and multifarious integration with global elites and circuits of accumulation that transform the corporate network in several ways and enhance the structural power that the most important family groups already possess.

5.3 Structure of the Chapter, Sources, and Methodology

The purpose of this chapter is twofold: first, to discover the main strategies followed by the most salient members of the corporate elite to integrate into global circuits of accumulation. It is argued in the first four sections that the main strategies include (i) the expansion of trade and investments to an increasingly greater number of countries, a process that intensified since the 1990s; (ii) cross-border interlocks among corporate elites produced by Mexican directors positioned on the boards of foreign-controlled transnational corporations (TNCs)[6] or foreign directors positioned on the boards of Mexican controlled corporations; (iii) property connections with global asset managers and other institutional investors who hold securities in Mexican listed companies; and (iv) a greater expansion into foreign security markets to raise capital. All these strategies feature feedback into one another, imbricating national and transnational corporate interests and opening new opportunities for accumulation. The second purpose is to examine how this multilevel integration affects crucial characteristics of the Mexican corporate network (MCN). It is argued in the last section that although some global corporate practices affect the composition of the boards and the network as a whole, the network remains increasingly centered around family interests as the most important way to protect the national corporate elite from foreign penetration.

Several sources were used to investigate the main strategies followed by the Mexican corporate elite in integrating into global circuits of accumulation: for the expansion of trade and investment into global markets, we selected the corporations that were listed on the Mexican Stock Exchange (MSE) and that were identified as global—having assets in two or more countries—by the business magazine *Expansion* (Revista Expansión 2020). Then, we collected data regarding the percentage of foreign sales, the regions where they have expanded, the number of subsidiaries in those regions, and the year of expansion. Unless otherwise specified, most of the information was found in the Annual Meeting Reports.

The second integration strategy, cross-border interlocks, required identifying three different mechanisms: (i) Mexican directors in foreign-controlled corporations listed on the MSE, (ii) Mexican directors in TNC headquartered abroad, and (iii) foreign directors in Mexican-controlled corporations listed on the MSE. Information for the first mechanism came from foreign corporations listed in 2020 on the MSE, considering only Mexican directors having at least three positions on company boards. Mexican directors positioned on the board of foreign corporations trading debt securities on the MSE were also included in this case, in particular, Deutsche Bank, Scotiabank, and HSBC.

To discover the second strategy of integration (ii), we surveyed biographies of multiple directors in our dataset, in the Annual Meeting Reports and in the main Mexican business sources of information. At least 28 Mexican directors are affected by this type of cross-border interlock, including those holding only one position on foreign boards. Although this procedure may have underestimated the number of Mexican directors, the authors believe it illustrates this relatively new practice among the Mexican corporate elite.

The presence of foreign directors in Mexican-controlled corporations was investigated using the information provided by the boards of Mexican corporations with minority foreign investment and double-checking the nationality of directors with foreign names.

To check property connections with global asset managers who hold securities in Mexican listed companies, we used the information provided by the financial investment advisor Market Screener (MarketScreener Website n.d.). To examine their expansion through their participation in foreign security markets, we obtained the information through the MSE's web page.

To examine the impact of the mentioned processes on the MCN, we constructed a database consisting of the corporations listed on the MSE and their board of directors in 1980, 1990, 2000, 2010, and 2020. The database was processed with the help of different software: 'tidyverse' (1.3.0), 'graph' (1.2.4.2), and 'visNetwork' from the R-Programming Language (Almende et al. 2009; Csardi and Nepusz 2006; R Core Team 2019; Wickham et al. 2019).

5.4 Expanding into Global Markets

The expansion of trade and investment in foreign countries was the first strategy employed by the Mexican corporate elite to become global. This outward expansion has accelerated since the 1990s (Garrido 1999; Salas Porras 1998): as can be seen in Table 5.1, out of a total of 140 corporations listed on the MSE in 2020, at least 52 have become global corporations (according to the Mexican business journal *Expansion*), that is, corporations with assets in 2 or more countries. Table 5.1 shows that out of these 52 public companies, 1 became transnational in the 1970s, 3 in the 1980s, 17 in the 1990s, 18 from 2000 to 2010, and 7 from 2011 to 2020 (6 with no information available). Expanding into global markets is, therefore, an ongoing process.

This process is the upshot of cyclical processes of accumulation, entailing concentration and centralization of capital at a national level first (Peres 1998; de los Rios 2007; Salas Porras 2002), and is the most common path followed by corporate elites not only in Latin America (Chudnovsky et al. 1999) but throughout the world (Carroll 2009; Murray 2012). Despite this expansion into foreign markets, most of these global corporations continue to hold controlling positions in Mexico and have diversified into the most attractive sectors, such as the energy sector, which has been increasingly opened to private investment after reforms introduced in 2013 and earlier. Thus, in the past two decades, Slim, Bailleres, Servitje, and other members of the Mexican corporate elite have invested in this sector, demonstrating that the national market remains a crucial source for accumulation (Regalado 2021)

Since the 1990s, once large Mexican corporations controlled large chunks of the national market in their specific spheres of activity, cross-border mergers and acquisitions became the most important mechanism whereby these corporations continued the process of concentration and centralization of capital, seizing the opportunities provided by the liberalization of the Mexican economy, with particular regards to trade and investment agreements with industrialized countries (Garrido 1998, 1999). In this way, they gained controlling positions in the regional or global markets where they operate and, as a consequence, by 2020, they substantially increased the proportion of sales outside Mexico, up to 79% of Cemex total sales, 76% of Grupo Cuervo's, 68% of Vitro's, 71% of America Movil's, and 71% of Bimbo's (see Table 5.1).[7]

Table 5.1 shows that some Mexican corporations have a truly global reach, while others have a more regional focus, although in both cases, they usually achieve controlling positions in consumer or intermediate goods. Out of the 52 TNCs listed on the MSE, at least 10 have become truly global, having affiliates in 2 or more continents, the most outstanding being America Movil (with assets in 18 countries in Latin America and 8 in Europe), but Cemex, Alfa, Bimbo, and GRUMA have also notably expanded to many countries throughout the world. Those with a more regional focus include Grupo Mexico, ARCA, Kuo, Elektra, Bachoco, and FEMSA. In most cases, they expanded primarily through mergers and acquisitions, except for GRUMA, which multiplied subsidiaries, creating plants from scratch.

From 1989 to 2005, Mexican corporations invested almost $US33.8 billion in cross-border acquisitions, nearly 23.6 billion from 2000 to 2005 (de los Rios 2007), although each Mexican TNC followed a different path. Cross-border mergers and acquisitions changed corporate practices, particularly relationships with the financial institutions facilitating these transactions. JP Morgan, Goldman Sachs, and other financial corporations were particularly active in identifying opportunities, negotiating the terms of buyouts, and engineering prospectus to finance acquisitions. In this way, Mexican corporate elites expanded their business abroad, and, in the process, they became entangled not only with financial but policy networks as well. Thus, to undertake mergers and acquisitions in other countries, they relied on national profits in addition to a combination of new stock and bonds offered through international security markets, greatly accelerating capital mobilization and furthering the concentration and centralization of capital.

After the liberalization of the economy in the 1980s, internationalization became one of the main strategies the Mexican corporate elite followed in order to defend their national base of accumulation while also providing new opportunities abroad to continue the process of capital accumulation in global markets. Crucially, this means national and global circuits of accumulation became tightly intertwined, depending increasingly on one another and maximizing profit-making opportunities. Therefore, entry into foreign markets can be considered a strategy to accumulate further and defend positions at home. By way of such expansion, elites have participated in restructuring the global economy, including a redistribution of

Table 5.1 Mexican Global Corporations Listed on the MSE

Corporation	*Sector*	*US$ sales (millions) in 2020*	*% Foreign sales*	*Regionsc (# subsidiaries)*	*Expansion*
AMERICA MOVIL[a]	TELECOMMUNICATIONS	$53,412	71.3%	LA (19), US (1), EU (3)	1990s
FEMSA	HOLDING	$26,867	35%	LA (14)	1990s
ALFA	HOLDING	$17,908	69.7%	LA (13), EU (18), NA (9), AS (2)	1990s
ALPEK	PETROCHEMICALS	$6346	61.2%	LA (6), NA (2), EU (1)	1990s
NEMAK	AUTOPARTS	$4102	>48%	LA (2), EU (18), NA (6), AS (5)	1990s
BIMBO	FOOD	$15,479	71%	LA (1), EU (2), NA (2)	1980s
CEMEX	CONSTRUCTION	$13,409	79%	LA (8), EU (9), US (3), AS (3), AF (1), ME (2)	1990s
G MÉXICO	HOLDING	$10,907	68.7%	LA (4), US (7), EU (1)	1990s
COCA-COLA FEMSA	BEVERAGE AND DRINKS	$10,311	>44%	LA (9)	1990s
ARCA	BEVERAGE AND DRINKS	$8751	59.1%	LA (11), US (9)	2000s
ORBIA ADV. CORP.	PETROCHEMICALS	$7135	80.6%	LA (14), EU (29), NA (9), AS (2)	2000s
CHEDRAUI	SELFSERVICE STORES	$6863	43.6%	US (2)	2010s

ELEKTRA	HOLDING	$6310	14.4%	LA (8)	1990s
CARSO[a]	HOLDING	$5434	25.6%	LA (7), EU (1), US (2)	1990s
GRUMA	FOOD	$4103	75.8%	US (11), LA (9), EU (9), AS (3)	1970s
AEROMEXICO	AIRLINES	$3646	58.2%	EU (1)	–
BACHOCO	FOOD	$3269	39.2%	US (1), EU (1)	2010s
ALSEA	RESTAURANTS	$3083	50.5%	LA (14), EU (2)	2000s
G SANBORNS	DEPARTMENT STORES	$2825	1%	LA (2)	2000s
VITRO	GLASS PRODUCTS	$2226	68.4%	LA (1), NA (3)	1980s
INDUSTRIAS CH	STEEL PRODUCTS	$2003	41%	US (4), EU (2), LA (3)	2000s
G SIMEC		$1812	45.3%	US (5), EU (2), LA (2)	2000s
BIO PAPPEL	PAPER	$1375	23.6%	US (8), LA (3)	1990s
QUALITAS	INSURANCE PRODUCTS	$1919	10%	US (1), LA (3)	2000s
GIGANTE	HOLDING	$1720	19.5%	LA (5)	1990s
G CUERVO	ALCOHOLIC DRINKS	$1575	75.6%	NA (2), EU (2)	2000s
ELEMENTIA	CONSTRUCTION	$1374	NA	US (2), LA (4)	2000s
VOLARIS	AIRLINES	$1843	26.6%	LA (4)	2000s
GENTERA	FINANCIAL SERVICES	$1276	30%	LA (2)	2010s
HERDEZ	FOOD	$1189	8.3%	US (7), LA (1)	2000s
G FAMSA	DEPARTMENT STORES	$1089	23.2%	US (2)	2000s
RASSINI	AUTOPARTS	$1087	>11%	US (2), LA (1), UE (1), AS (1), ME (1)	1980s

(Continued)

Table 5.1 (Continued)

Corporation	*Sector*	*US$ sales (millions) in 2020*	*% Foreign sales*	*Regionsc (# subsidiaries)*	*Expansion*
LAMOSA	CONSTRUCTION	$951	<22.7%	LA (3)	–
G INDUSTRIAL SALTILLO	HOLDING, AUTOPARTS	$908	68.4%	US (1), EU (1), AS (2)	2010s
CEMENTOS DE CHIHUAHUA	CONSTRUCTION	$954	73.1%	US (9)	2000s
IDEAL[a]	CONSTRUCTION	$913	NA	LA (>1)	–
GRUPO DESC[b]	INDUSTRIAL AND IMMOBILIARY	$2360	54.4%	US (3), EU (3), AS (3)	2010s
ASUR	AIRPORT SERVICES	$892	38.6%	LA (2)	2000s
TV AZTECA	MEDIA	$679	4.9%	US (2), EU (1), LA (5)	2000s
CIE	ENTERTAINMENT	$621	3.6%	LA (5), US (1)	1990s
GENOMMA LAB	PHARMACEUTICAL	$676	56.7%	LA (16), US (1), EU (1)	2000s
INTERCERAMIC	CONSTRUCTION SUPPLIES AND FIXTURES	$554	26%	US (5), LA (1), AS (2)	1990s
G ACCEL	LOGISTIC AND TRANSPOR	$483	86.3%	US (1)	–
ROTOPLAS	CONSTRUCTION SUPPLIES AND FIXTURES	$429	42.7%	LA (4)	–
G POCHTECA	PETROCHEMICALS	$336	>29.2%	LA (>1)	2000s
VISTA OIL & GAS	OIL AND GAS	$425	99%	LA (5)	–
FINANCIERA INDEPENDENCIA	FINANCIAL SERVICES	$308	26.4%	US (1), LA (1)	2000s

PROMOTORA AMBIENTAL	PROFESSIONAL SERVICES	$266	15.6%	LA (3)	1990s
G MINSA	FOOD	$257	NA	EU (1), AS (1)	1990s
G VASCONIA	CONSUMER GOODS	$163	NA	EU (1)	1990s
H. CITY EXPRESS	HOTELS AND TURISM	$167	6.8%	LA (2)	2010s
COMP. MINERA AUTLAN	MINING	$429	46.5%	EU (1)	2019

Sources: Own elaboration with information from the business magazine Expansión (Revista Expansión 2020), the MSE (Grupo BMV n.d.), the financial investment advisor MarketScreener website (MarketScreener Website n.d.), corporate annual reports and websites.

Notes

[a] Controlled by Carlos Slim.

[b] Before Kuo.

[c] Subsidiaries outside Mexico, according to annual meeting reports (some of them just reported the most significative), included those with more than 50% ownership. Subsidiaries are counted by country and different legal personalities. For example, AMX Argentina and AMX Paraguay are treated as two. Meanwhile, Coca-Cola Femsa in Centroamerica is treated as one because it has no legal divisions. Russia and Turkey are treated as European countries.

US=United States, LA=Latin America, EU=Europe, AS=Asia, NA=North America (Canada and US), AF=Africa, ME=Middle East.

markets across sectoral and regional levels. At the same time, it unleashed cross-border interlocking, particularly with institutional investors who helped finance the expansion.

5.4.1 Cross-Border Interlocking

The transnational expansion of large Mexican corporations has been driven by interlocking with corporate interests from different countries, as Mexican boards include directors from foreign companies holding stock or as members of the Mexican corporate elite positioned on the boards of TNCs located inside or outside the country.

Thus, cross-border interlocking includes those generated by (i) Mexican directors positioned on the boards of foreign-controlled corporations listed on the MSE, (ii) Mexican directors positioned on the boards of TNCs and financial institutions headquartered abroad, and (iii) foreign directors positioned on the boards of Mexican-controlled corporations with minority foreign investment.

Very few foreign-controlled industrial corporations operating in Mexico integrate members of the national corporate elite into their boards, supporting the idea that they operate as enclaves. In contrast, foreign-controlled banks often invite Mexican directors to their boards, particularly the Spanish banks BBVA and Santander (BSMX), which, out of 33 and 11 directors on their boards, respectively, have integrated 5 and 4 Mexican links in 2020. These banks have two or more positions in the network and are among those with the highest degree of interlockings, particularly when compared to the number of directors integrated by other foreign banks (HSBC, Scotia Bank, and Deutsche Bank). This shows a clear interest in connecting with the most central members of the MCN, profiting in this way from their social capital. This is a very common practice among Spanish corporations, not only in banking but also in the energy sector (Salas Porras 2017).

Cross-border interlocking between national and global corporate elites is increasingly generated outside the country by Mexican directors positioned on the boards of TNCs and financial institutions headquartered outside the country. A thorough examination of the most important sources for Mexican big business[8] shows that at least 37 members of the Mexican corporate elite are positioned on the boards of corporations headquartered in the Global North, particularly those of financial corporations—among others, Blackrock, Citigroup, Goldman Sacks, Deutsche, Barclays, and BBVA—connecting these corporations with powerful members of the Mexican corporate elite, including Slim, Bailleres, Diez Morodo, and Chico Pardo, two of whom are included on the Forbes' list of billionaires (see Table 5.2). This trend reveals that the inter-penetration of Mexican and global elites has become a two-way process that has intensified over the last two decades and can be interpreted as part and parcel of the process of globalization examined in the previous section, particularly the interaction with the financial institutions brokering mergers and acquisitions.

Additionally, some Mexican-controlled corporations listed on the MSE have foreign investment in joint ventures or strategic alliances that affect connections

Table 5.2 Mexican Directors on Boards of TNCs Headquartered Abroad

Mexican director	*Board of Mexican corporation*	*Board of TNC*	*Origin*[b]	*Sector*
Aboumrad Gonzalez, Alejandro	IDEAL, MFRISCO	CEMENTOS PORTLAND VALDERRIVAS SA	SP	Construction Services
Bailleres Gonzalez, Alberto[a]	DINE, FEMSA, FRES, GNP, GPH, GPROFUT, KUO, PEÑOLES, TLEVISA	JP MORGAN INTERNATIONAL COUNCIL	US	Financial
Berrondo Avalos, Eduardo	CMR, CREAL, GFMULTI	HEMISPHERE MEDIA GROUP	US	Media
Canal Hernando, Jose Manuel	DINE, GENTERA, KUO, RLH	BANK OF AMERICA	US	Financial
Chedraui Eguia, Jose Antonio	BANORTE, CHDRAUI, TLEVISA	BODEGA LATINA CORP.	US	Groceries stores
Chico Pardo, Fernando Gerardo	ASUR, GISSA, PMCPAC, POSADAS	CARRIX	US	Transportation & Logistics
		SSA MARINE INC	US	Transportation & Logistics
Cura, German	TS	FREYR	US	Battery cells for energy storage
De Angoitia Noriega, Alfonso	CABLE, FEMSA, GFNORTE, TLEVISA	LIBERTY LATIN AMERICA LTD	US	Media
		UNIVISION	US	Media
Del Valle Perochena, Antonio	ELEMENT, MEXCHEM	BYLINE BANCORP	US	Financial
Del Valle Perochena, Juan Pablo	ELEMENT, ORBIA	JOHNSON CONTROLS INTERNATIONAL PLC	US	Battery cells for energy storage
Elias Ayub, Alfredo	AGUA, GFNORTE	AVANGRID	US	Energy
Esteve Recolons, Jorge C	AEROMEX	ECOM ATLANTIC INC	US	Agricultural Producers
Fernandez Carbajal, Francisco Javier	ALFA, CEMEX, FEMSA	VISA	US	Financial
		MELLMO INC	US	Technology
Fernandez Carbajal, Jose Antonio	FEMSA, KOF, PEÑOLES	HEINEKEN	NL	Alcoholic Drinks
Garza Egloff, Francisco Rogelio	AXTEL, GISSA, R	LINDLEY	PE	Non Alcoholic Beverage

(*Continued*)

Table 5.2 (Continued)

Mexican director	*Board of Mexican corporation*	*Board of TNC*	*Origin*[b]	*Sector*
Garza Sada, Armando	ALFA, ALPEK, AXTEL, CEMEX, FEMSA, LAMOSA, LIVEPOL, NEMAK	MELLMO INC	US	Technology
Gonzalez Laporte, Claudio X	ALFA, GCARSO, GISSA, GMEXICO, KIMBER	GENERAL ELECTRIC	US	Electrical Equipment
Gutierrez Hernandez, Arturo	AC	KKR & CO INC	US	Financial
Gutierrez Munoz, Jorge Ricardo	ICA, LAB	ARCOS DORADOS HOLDING INC	US	Restaurants
Kalach Mizrahi, Rafael Moises	AMX, G CARSO	COLTEJER	COL	Textile
Kuri Kaufmann, Gerardo	ELEMENT, MFRISCO, SITES	CEMENTOS PORTLAND VALDERRIVAS SA	SP	Construction Services
	ELEMENT, MFRISCO, SITES	REALIA BUSINESS SA	SP	Real Estate Properties
Larson, Michael J	FEMSA	ECOLAB INC	US	Water treatment
		WESTERN ASSET PREMIER BOND FUND	US	Financial
		REPUBLIC SERVICES INC	US	Waste disposal company
Milan Haddad, Divo	ELEMENT, ORBIA	QUONIA SOCIMI	SP	Real Estate Properties
Ortiz Martinez, Guillermo	ASUR, ORBIA, VITRO	BETTERWARE DE MEXICO	US	Multilevel marketing
Phillips Margain, Guadalupe	ICA, OMA	LOS PORTALES	PE	Real Estate Properties
Rivero Larrea, Jose Antonio	ALPEK, AUTLAN}	GFM RESOURCES LIMITED	CA	Mining Exploration
Robles Miaja, Rafael	AEROMEX, ASUR, LALA, TRAXION	US COMMERCIAL CORP SA DE CV	US	Consumer Elec & Applc Stores
Rocca, Gianfelice Mario	TS	TERNIUM	US	Steel Industry

Table 5.2 (Continued)

Mexican director	*Board of Mexican corporation*	*Board of TNC*	*Origin*[b]	*Sector*
Rodriguez Torres, Juan	ELEMENT, GSANBOR, MFRISCO, SITES	REALIA BUSINESS SA	SP	Real Estate Properties
		CEMENTOS PORTLAND VALDERRIVAS SA	SP	Construction Services
		REALIA BUSINESS	SP	Real Estate Properties
Salazar Lomelin, Carlos Vicente	GAV, ALSEA, BBVA	BBVA	SP	Financial
Salem Slim, Alfonso	ELEMENT, GIGANTE	NATURGY ENERGY	SP	Gas and Electricity
Santos Reyna, Jorge Humberto	AC, R	LINDLEY	PE	Non Alcoholic Beverage
Senior Hernandez, Enrique Francisco Jose	KOF, TLEVISA	UNIVISION	US	Media
		CINEMARK HOLDINGS INC	US	Entertainment Facilities
Serra Puche, Jaime	AGUA, ALPEK, TS, VITRO	BBVA	SP	Financial
Slim Domit, Marco Antonio[a]	AMOVIL, GCARSO, GFINBUR, IDEAL	BLACKROCK	US	Financial
Tellez Kuenzler, Luis Manuel Enrique	CULTIBA, GAP	CHUBB LIMITED	SW	Insurance company
Zambrano Benitez, Enrique De Jesus	ALPEK	DILA CAPITAL ACQUISITION CORP.	US	Financial

Sources: Bloomberg (Bloomberg n.d.) and MarketScreener (MarketScreener Website n.d.).

Notes

[a] Present in Forbes list of billionaires.

[b] NL=Netherlands, GE=Germany, CA=Canada, SP=Spain, PE=Peru, COL=Colombia, SW=Switzerland.

between the Mexican elite and broader transnational networks, particularly with the US corporate network. Cross-border interlocks produced by foreign directors positioned on Mexican-controlled corporations tie 13 Mexican-listed corporations with 15 American corporations, overlapping the networks of these 2 countries (3 directors from Delta, for example, are Aeromexico board members, and 2 from Ford are on the Nemak board). Further, four Spanish, four Italian, and one German director are also positioned on the boards of Mexican-listed corporations, although they may represent interests of a different origin.

In short, cross-border interlocks intertwine Mexican and global elites in several ways and at different levels, creating spaces where they build and expand common economic interests and social understandings and where corporate practices are disseminated. However, most cross-border interlocks produced by Mexican corporate elites connect them with North American and European corporate elites, and, as Cárdenas (2015) shows, there are hardly any cross-border corporate networks connecting them with other Latin American corporate elites. This is more striking when considering that several of the most important Mexican TNCs expanded first toward other countries in Latin America (for example, America Móvil, Bimbo, FEMSA, and GMEXICO).

5.4.2 Interlocking with Institutional Investors

As institutional investors become an important source of capital, the weight of transnational finance capital in the MCN grows.[9] Although they have been present since the beginning of the 20th century and earlier yet (Hawley and Williams 2000), their presence expanded significantly in the 1990s as a wave of institutional investors (mutual, pension, and insurance funds) provided the financial resources needed for their international expansion. When credits became increasingly scarce as a source of funding, Mexican corporations organized roadshows to present investment opportunities to institutional investors seeking more attractive returns but not necessarily interested in influencing decision-making.

Making primary and secondary stock offerings in this way became a very common practice throughout the 1990s. Several Mexican groups (for example, FEMSA, Vitro, and CEMEX) used this mechanism to finance cross-border acquisitions. Although initial institutional investors were generally short-term investors, not interested in exerting corporate control, their leverage was occasionally felt when they were unsatisfied with corporate strategies, opting for an exit course of action. This was seen in 1994 when, when complaining that Cemex was expanding far too fast and had not previously disclosed its investment plans, investors sold a considerable number of shares, thereby dumping the price (Salas Porras 1998).

A second wave of institutional investments flowing into large, Mexican-listed corporations has been undertaken by asset managers who 'seek to replicate existing stock indices,' in contrast to the first wave of institutional investors aiming to outperform stock market returns (Fichtner et al. 2017, 299). New asset managers found in the Mexican network include Black Rock and Vanguard (Murray and Peetz 2012), having made inroads into MCN during the last decade with relatively small ownership shares (see Table 5.3), particularly when compared with the shares held by financial firms in other Latin American countries (Cárdenas et al. 2020).

Black Rock holds additional stock in Mexican corporations via different affiliates—among others, BlackRock Advisors (UK), BlackRock Asset Management Deutschland AG, BlackRock Asset Management North Asia, BlackRock Fund Advisors, BlackRock Investment Management (UK), and

Table 5.3 Presence of Global Asset Managers (2020)[a]

Asset manager	*Origin*	*Presence in no. of Mexican Corp.*	*Average % equities (min/max)*
Dimensional Fund Advisors	US	59	1.59 (0.0015, 26)
The Vanguard Group, Inc.	US	53	1.67 (0.48, 3.2)
BlackRock	US	43	2.17 (0, 43.7)
Norges Bank Investment Management	NOR	43	2.28 (0.073, 16)
Invesco Advisers, Inc.	US	15	2.51 (0.039, 8.57)
Fidelity Management & Research Co. LLC	US	13	2.13 (0.0085, 5.13)
The Caisse de dépôt et placement du Québec	CA	13	6.81 (0.14, 60)
APG Asset Management NV	DU	10	2.76 (0.15, 12.7)
Capital Research & Management	US	10	1.79 (0.48, 4.9)
Allianz Global Investors US LLC	US	9	0.34 (0.002, 1.94)
SSgA Funds Management, Inc.	US	7	0.12 (0.0005, 0.37)
William Blair Investment Management LLC	US	7	0.92 (0.042, 3.25)
JPMorgan	US	6	2.3 (1.49, 3.26)
Charles Schwab Investment Management, Inc.	US	5	0.23 (0.036, 0.36)
Goldman Sachs Asset	US	5	1.02 (0.019, 1.61)
Handelsbanken Fonder AB	SW	5	12.19 (1.76, 50)
Massachusetts Financial Services Co.	US	5	2.01 (0.21, 6.3)
Thornburg Investment Management, Inc.	US	5	2.15 (0.01, 7.47)

Source: Own elaboration with data from financial investment advisor MarketScreener (MarketScreener Website n.d.).

Note

[a] Asset managers having the largest blocks of shares (present in five or more Mexican corporations) in 2020 (18 out of 182 foreign asset managers with presence in at least one corporation in MCN).

BlackRock Mexico—articulating in this way a complex web of investments that amounts to almost 43% of GICSA, 5.1% of KOF, and 4.6% of GAP (Grupo Aeroportuario del Pacífico).

However, as can be seen in Table 5.5, most of the 18 asset managers concentrating the largest blocks of shares in Mexican listed corporations in 2020 hold relatively small percentages of total stock, as is the case in most countries (Carroll 2012). Fourteen are based in the US, and out of these, the most important are BlackRock, Dimensional Fund Advisors, and the Vanguard Group, with investments in 43, 59, and 53 publicly listed Mexican corporations, respectively.

In this second wave, asset managers with stock in Mexican corporations have exerted influence on corporate decisions in two ways: by coordinating proxy voting or interacting directly with management or members of the boards. Voice corporate strategies whereby asset managers coordinate proxy voting (that is, a mechanism by which voting power is delegated to a representative) have become an instrument to centralize and aggregate power against or in favor of management during annual general meetings. In addition to proxy coordination, large asset managers discuss strategies directly with members of the boards, with whom they sometimes have lasting relationships, allowing them to build consensus around common interests and preferences (for example, Carlos Slim, as has been previously seen, has even become a member of the board of Blackrock; Fichtner et al. 2017).

In short, since the 1990s, institutional investors have facilitated the internationalization of large Mexican corporations, intertwining national and transnational circuits of accumulation. During the first wave, mutual, pension, and insurance funds accepted greater risks as long as high returns were guaranteed and occasionally used exit power to influence corporate decision-making. In the second wave, institutional investors have tended to have greater sway in defining strategic decisions, promoting harmonization with corporate practices in the Global North.

5.4.3 Expanding onto Global Stock Exchanges

Some of the largest corporations listed on the MSE are also listed on other stock exchanges, which have become an increasingly important source of funding as international bank credits have become increasingly scarce. Thus, global bonds and notes traded in international markets increased from 28.6% of the long-term capital market in 2002 to 56.1% in 2019, while loans decreased from roughly 37% to 19% in the same period. The New York Stock Exchange (NYSE) is the most important for Mexican corporations, both in terms of new offerings and the volume of trading.

Mexican corporations listed in the NYSE, NASDAQ, Madrid, and London Stock Exchanges must comply with a series of regulations that require producing regular information regarding their performance and all corporate decisions that may impact stock prices. Auditing, disclosure, and accountancy practices must meet global standards stemming from global regulatory bodies, such as the International Accounting Standards Committee and the International Organization of Securities Commission. These standards serve as centrifugal forces, compelling the corporate governance of Mexican corporations to follow the guidelines and practices of a global technocracy, acting as independent professional directors[10] or members of auditing, accounting, and law firms.

5.4.4 Continuity and Change in the Mexican Corporate Network (MCN) and Practices

According to a longitudinal analysis dating back to the 1980s (Salas Porras 2006, 2012), family clusters have remained central in the structure of the MCN and in the Mexican system of capital mobilization, whether they include a bank or not in the cluster. The firms belonging to each of these family clusters are tightly intertwined through both ownership interests as well as interlocking between the members of the boards. There is strong continuity among the main families constituting the network throughout the period examined. Although they move and articulate among themselves differently, most have remained central in the network since the 1980s (for example, Slim's family), and in some cases even before (Bailleres). Until the 2000s (see Figures 5.1–5.5), there was a high degree of overlapping across family clusters, but since they have tended to withdraw to singular family spheres of influence, intensifying interlocking between members of the family and coupling the network structure more tightly with the ownership structure, in this way avoiding foreign penetration into the national corporate community.

Thus, Slim's family cluster is integrated through seven large and diversified holdings, including IDEAL (construction and infrastructure), SANBORNS (commerce), CARSO (industry), FRISCO (mining), INBURSA (finance), TELMEX, and AMERICA MOVIL (telecommunications). Intercorporate holdings and pyramiding among all these affiliates facilitate the mobilization of capital according to expected rates of profit and expansion plans. The boards of these holdings and the numerous affiliates, each controlling two or more members of the family in common, increase the density and intensity of connections within the cluster (the wider the line in the figures, the more intense the connection between two corporations, that is, the greater the number of directors in common) (see Figures 5.3–5.5).

In the 1980s (Figure 5.1), this cluster was closely connected with two business groups, Bimbo and GMexico. In the 1990s (Figure 5.2), this family, whose main

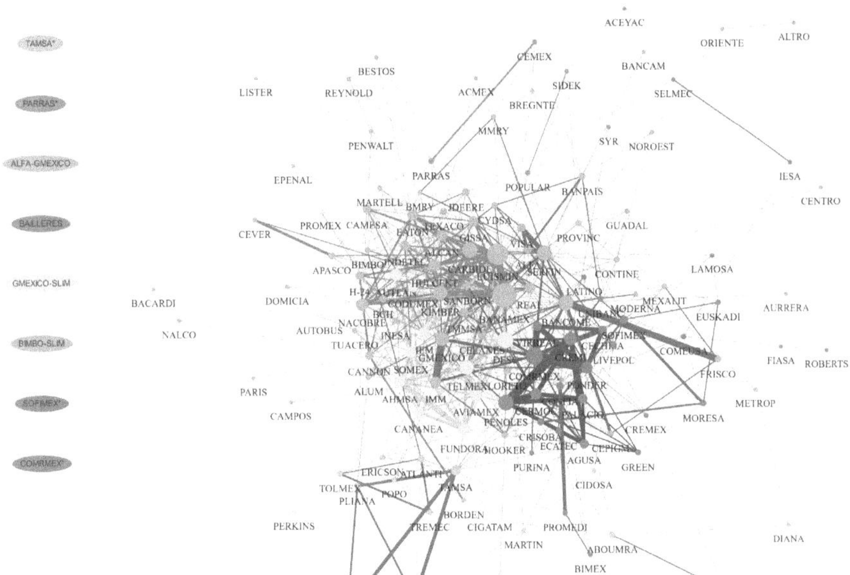

Figure 5.1 Mexican corporate network in 1981.

Source: Own elaboration.

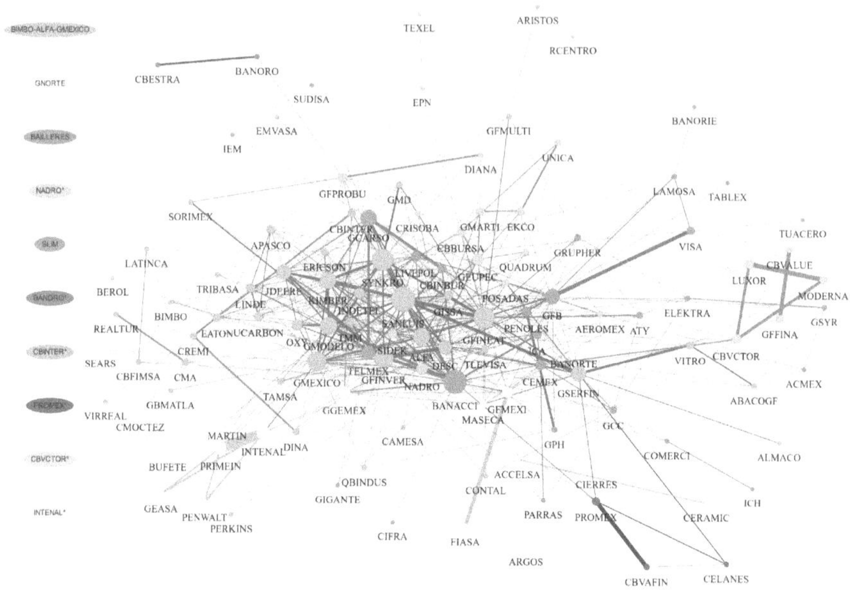

Figure 5.2 Mexican corporate network in 1990.

Source: Own elaboration.

stockholder, Carlos Slim, ranked fifth on the 2021 Forbes list with assets worth 63 billion dollars, moved to the center of the network, consolidating a cluster that remains tightly interlocked through family interests, as can be appreciated in Figures 5.1–5.5. However, since then, as connections within the cluster have intensified, those outside the family cluster have become more limited, and from the 2000s onward (see Figures 5.3–5.5), most of the firms in Slim's cluster were controlled by the family.

Bailleres, who, according to Forbes, is the fourth richest Mexican executive with a fortune amounting to $9.2 billion in 2020, has controlled large stakes in financial (GNP), mining (Peñoles), and commerce activities (GPH) since at least the 1950s. The corporations he controls have remained tightly interlocked, and while featuring some connections with other family clusters (for example, GMEXICO and KUO), this cluster has fewer cross-family links than other family groups.

As can be seen in the graphs below, in 1981 and 1990 (Figures 5.1 and 5.2), the core of the network intertwined the most important family clusters and interests, showing a clear-cut pattern of centralization. From 2000 onward (Figure 5.3), connections among clusters became increasingly scarce. By 2010 (Figure 5.4), most clusters (see, for example, Slim's, Bailleres', and Alfa-Femsa) moved toward the margins of the network, expanding the distance among themselves, disarticulating the core, and decentralizing the network structure. By 2020, the position

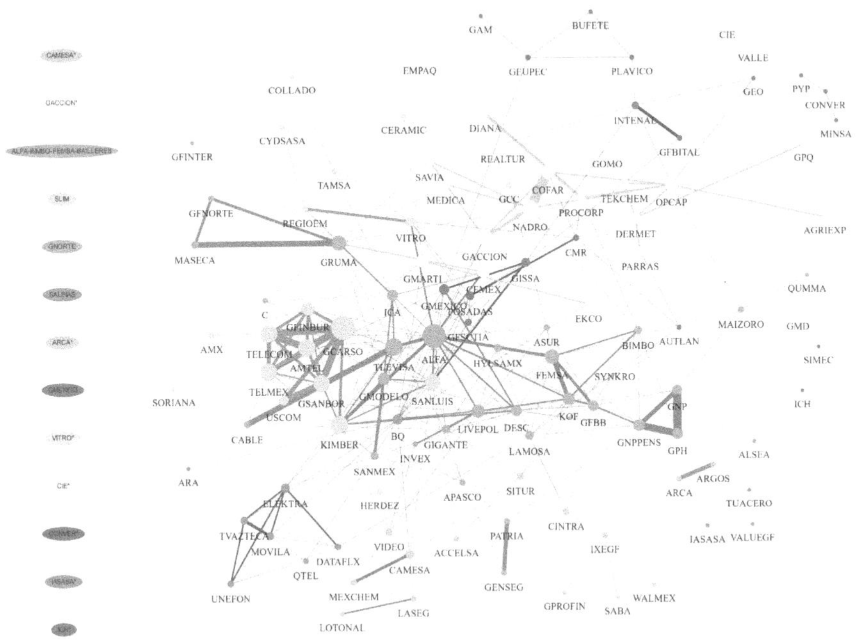

Figure 5.3 Mexican corporate network in 2000.

Source: Own elaboration.

of Salinas-Pliego (the third richest man in Mexico, according to Forbes) had become marginal since its main companies (ELEKTRA and TV AZTECA) had no connections in the network.

Retreat toward family spheres of influence can be regarded as a defensive strategy to avoid hostile takeovers and other aggressive corporate strategies that are very common in the context of globalization, with similar reactions vis-à-vis Europeanization found by Dudouet et al. (2012) in Holland and Italy.

Despite several national crises, including the debt crisis of 1982, the currency crisis of 1987, and the financial crisis of 1995 (Griffith-Jones 1997), as well as the ensuing accommodations, bankruptcies, displacements, and takeovers by foreign capital (for example, the breweries Modelo and Cuauhtémoc and the spirit corporations Bacardí and Cuervo), and rising groups and families (Cinepolis belonging to Ramírez Magaña's family, though this group is not listed on the MSE), cohesiveness has remained very high throughout this period. However, density (that is, the number of connections with respect to all possible connections) tended to decrease, falling from 7.9% in 1981 to 4.24% in 2020, as the number of directors and interlocks per firm and the number of interlocks per director decreased throughout the period (see Table 5.4). This is a trend common in Western countries, as Heemskerk (2007) and Schifeling and Mizruchi (2014) have pointed

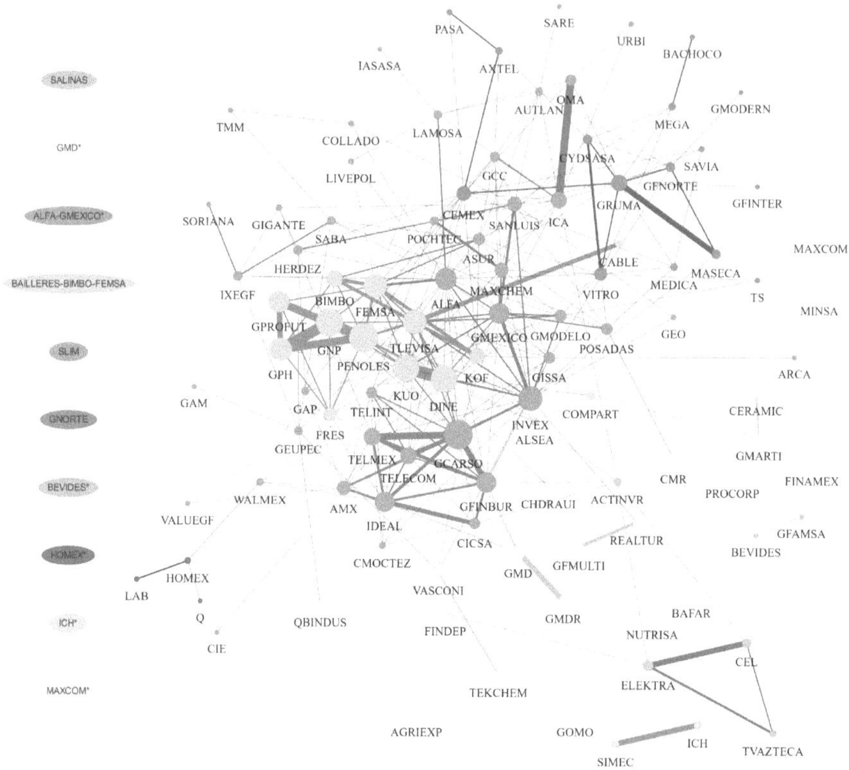

Figure 5.4 Mexican corporate network in 2010.

Source: Own elaboration.

out. Nonetheless, keeping high degrees of cohesiveness remains important and is particularly striking when compared to thinner networks in other Latin American countries, as Cardenas (2016) thoroughly documents.

The concentration of interlocks demonstrates the concentration of social capital (Table 5.5). Considering only directors in listed corporations participating in the stock market in 2020, a total of 41 big linking actors (with more than three positions in the network) concentrated almost 12.55% of all interlocks in the network. Directors having only independent positions in the network (480/1381) generated 7442 interlocks in 2020, that is, 33% of all interlocks, mobilizing knowledge and social capital throughout the network and making the network more consistent with the professional and technocratic criteria of global corporations.

The changing characteristics of the network and the composition of the boards of Mexican corporations run parallel, facilitate, and respond to increasingly intense interaction with corporate elites in the Global North. In contrast, the Mexican

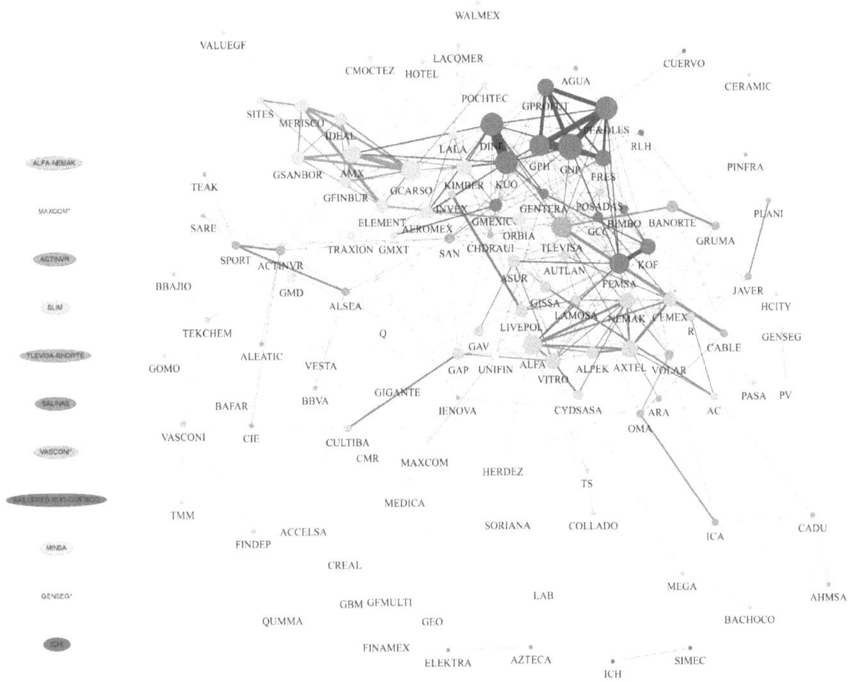

Figure 5.5 Mexican corporate network in 2020.

Source: Own elaboration.

corporate elite pursue a combination of intersecting paths whereby they integrate into a global corporate community.

5.5 Discussion

The strategies followed by the Mexican corporate elite to become transnational are interdependent and increasingly intertwined, reinforcing one another and opening new opportunities for capital accumulation. This elite expanded foreign direct investments mainly through cross-border mergers and acquisitions engineered and funded to a great degree by global financial institutions. Out of the 140 corporations listed on the MSE in 2020, at least 100 have become entangled in cross-border activities of different sorts, engaging in 1 or more of the strategies examined to become transnational. In the case of cross-border interlocks, out of the 1929 Mexican directors in the MCN in 2020 (including both capital and debt markets), at least 54 have made cross-border interlocks. Still, only 20 of the 61 big linking actors (producing 4 or more interlocks) point to a high concentration of cross-border connections in the 'inner core' of the Mexican corporate elite, that

Table 5.4 Accumulation of Positions

Year	*Density (%)*	*No. of firms*	*No. of seats*	*No. of directors*	*No. of multiple directors (%)*	*Directors holding two seats (%a)*	*Directors holding three to five seats (%a)*	*Directors holding six to ten seats (%a)*	*Directors holding more than ten seats*
1981	7.9	138	1738	1218	252 (20.7)	134 (53.2)	98 (38.9)	16 (6.4)	4
1990	7.6	128	1776	1282	284 (22.2)	117 (41.2)	93 (32.8)	13 (4.6)	1
2000	3.2	154	1457	1162	168 (14.5)	105 (63.5)	53 (31.6)	10 (6)	0
2010	4.2	131	1482	1162	185 (16)	114 (61.6)	63 (34)	8 (4.3)	0
2020	4.2	140	1732	1381	200 (14.5)	122 (61)	70 (35)	8 (4)	0

Source: Own elaboration with data from MSE (Grupo BMV n.d.).

Note

[a] Percentage of multiple directors.

Table 5.5 Interlocks

Year	*Seats per firm*	*Directors per firm*	*Multiple directors per firm*	*Interlocks of firms*	*Interlocks per firm*	*Interlocks of directors*	*Interlocks per director*
1981	12.59	8.8	1.8	2380	17.2	26,444	21.7
1990	13.87	10.0	2.2	1910	14.9	32,046	25.0
2000	9.46	7.5	1.1	1098	7.1	15,490	13.3
2010	11.31	8.9	1.4	1148	8.8	17,470	15.0
2020	12.37	9.9	1.4	1246	8.9	22,204	16.1

Source: Own elaboration with data from MSE (Grupo BMV n.d.).

is, in the group of very large businessmen who have the organizational capacity to accumulate capital not only in different sectors but in different institutional settings too. This group has become highly intertwined in global corporate networks, concentrating the capacity to reorganize the geographic and sectoral distribution of markets.

With this process of transnationalization, some corporate governance practices have changed considerably, intensifying centrifugal trends to adapt to the US guidelines in several ways: corporate independent directors, who until recently were mainly shareholders from other corporations, have an increasingly professional profile (for example, fiscal lawyers, accountants, professional auditors) and are more observant of the standards set by international organizations, while asset managers and institutional investors have become, in this way, more outward-oriented. In short, corporate practices increasingly resemble those of global corporations, changing the profile of directorships, boards, and corporate governance. All these practices make large Mexican corporations more responsive to the guidelines and performance criteria that emphasize short-term financial results at the expense of long-term planning and investment. The harmonization of corporate governance and practices is a crucial component of the globalization of the Mexican corporate elite.

Notes

1 Following Scott (2008), in this chapter, elites are defined as all those actors—individual or collective—who control resources of different sorts—economic, political, or ideological—and use them to influence through different mechanisms—more or less coercive or persuasive—the course of economic and political events, processes, and policy decisions. Thus, although elites are recruited from social classes, not until they become involved in wielding their power can they be considered elites. As Scott contends, elites controlling resources from different spheres (the state, parties, corporations, and knowledge production institutions, among the most important) increasingly interlock, interact, and aggregate power to make their voices heard. Consequently, although it becomes increasingly difficult to draw clear-cut frontiers, according to their main field of influence, elites can be differentiated into state, corporate, and intellectual elites.

2 Neoliberalism has been defined as a 'thought collective' (Mirowski and Plehwe 2009), that is, 'a multi-centric movement anchored in a network of think tanks and pro-market institutions that connect political, economic and scientific elites' (Undurraga 2016, 15), and whose main purpose was to remove the obstacles that collectivism and state-centered economies implied for a free market society. It emerged in the 1930s as a reaction to collective trends (Keynesianism, Fabianism, neo-corporatism, communism, and fascism), which they believed jeopardized personal freedoms (Eagleton-Pierce 2018). However, it was, from the very beginning, a very heterogeneous and contradictory movement that gradually spread throughout the world before it achieved consensus in the 1980s around a set of economic and social policies that were nevertheless implemented at different pace across regions and countries (Crouch 2011; van Apeldoorn and Overbeek 2012). The superiority of a society centered on the market, competition, and the individual is the main idea underlying all the policies that reached consensus in the 1980s around the neoliberal project, which, according to Springer (2016, 2) '[...]fosters an individual ethic that allows selfishness to reap its own rewards,' validating in this way the commodification and appropriation of collective and state property and naturalizing the conviction that—as Thatcher contended—there is nothing else to society than the sum of individual interests, preferences, and desires.

3 In 1988, for example, a fraction split from PRI due to differences and disaffections with the new neoliberal policy orientation.

4 Including agriculture, forestry, and fishing.

5 Measured as GDP per hour worked.

6 Transnational corporations are defined as corporations integrated across two or more countries, holding assets in more than one country.

7 According to Chudnovsky et al. (1999), the internationalization of firms advanced first in those Latin American countries that introduced the first neoliberal reforms.

8 MSE web database (Grupo BMV. n.d.), annual reports, biographies in financial magazines, and financial investment advisor MarketScreener (MarketScreener Website n.d.).

9 Davis and Steil (2004, 12) define these investors '[...] as specialized financial institutions that manage savings collectively on behalf of small investors toward a specific objective in terms of acceptable risk, return maximization, and maturity of claims.' However, what is considered acceptable changes depending particularly on how the trade-off between these terms is perceived.

10 Independent directors are those not having an executive position or investment in the firm.

References

Almende, B. V., Benoit Thieurmel, and Titouan Robert. 2016. visNetwork: Network Visualization using 'vis.js' Library. R package version 1.0.0. https://cran.r-project.org/web/packages/visNetwork/visNetwork.pdf

Bloomberg. n.d. "Bloomberg." Bloomberg.Com. www.bloomberg.com/europe.

Cárdenas, Julián. 2015. "Are Latin America's corporate elites transnationally interconnected? A network analysis of interlocking directorates." *Global Networks* 15 (4), 424–445.

———. 2016. "Enredando a las elites empresariales en América Latina: Análisis de redes de interlocking directorates y propiedad en México, Chile, Perú y Brasil." *America Latina Hoy* 73, 15–44.

Cárdenas, Julián, Francisco Robles-Rivera, and Diego Martınez-Vallejo. 2020. "Los dueños de América Latina: Análisis de las redes entre los propietarios transnacionales de las grandes empresas." *Revista CIDOB d'Afers Internacionals* 126, 17–40.

Carroll, William K. 2009. "Transnationalists and national networkers in the global corporate elite." *Global Networks* 9 (3), 289–314.

———. 2012. "Capital relations and directorate interlocking: The global network in 2007." In *Financial elites and transnational bussiness. Who rules the world?*, edited by Murray, Georgina and John Scott, 54–75. Cheltenham: Edward Elgar.

Chudnovsky, Daniel, Bernando Kosacoff, and Andrés López. 1999. *Las Multinacionales Latinoamericanas: Sus Estrategias en un Mundo Globalizado*. Buenos Aires: FCE.

Crouch, Colin. 2011. *The strange non-death of neoliberalism*. Cambridge: Polity.

Csardi, Gabor, and Tamas Nepusz. 2006. The igraph software. *Complex Systems* 1695, 1–9.

Davis, E. Philip, and Benn Steil. 2004. *Institutional investors*. Cambridge: MIT Press.

de los Rios, Cortés. 2007. "Mergers and acquisitions in Mexico, 1986–2005." *Economía UNAM* 4 (12), 60–92. www.scielo.org.mx/scielo.php?script=sci_arttext&pid=S1665-952X2007000300004 (December 20, 2020).

Dudouet, François-Xavier, Eric Grémont, and Antione Vion. 2012. "Transnational business networks in the eurozone: A focus on four major stock exchange indices." In *Financial elites and transnational bussiness. Who rules the world?*, edited by Murray, Georgina and John Scott, 124–145. Cheltenham: Edward Elgar.

Eagleton-Pierce, Matthew. 2018. "Neoliberalism," In *Palgrave handbook on contemporary international political economy*, edited by Shaw, Timothy, Laura Mahrenbach, Craig Murphy, Renu Modi, and Xu Yi-Chong. Houndmills: Palgrave.

Fichtner, Jan, Eelke M. Heemskerk, and Javier García Bernardo. 2017. "Hidden power of the big three? Passive index funds, re-concentration of corporate ownership, and new financial risk." *Business and Politics* 19 (2), 298–326.

Garrido, Celso. 1998. "El liderazgo de las grandes empresas industriales mexicanas." In *Grandes Empresas y Grupos Industriales Latinoamericanos*, edited by Wilson Peres, 397–472. México City: Siglo XXI-CEPAL.

———. 1999. "The Mexican case." In *Las Multinacionales Latinoamericanas: Sus Estrategias en un Mundo Globalizado*, edited by Chudnovsky, Daniel, Bernando Kosacoff, and Andrés López, 165–258. Buenos Aires: FCE.

Griffith-Jones, Stephany. 1997. "Causes and lessons of the Mexican Peso crisis." *WIDER working papers (1986–2000)* 1997/132. Helsinki: UNU-WIDER.

Grupo BMV. n.d. "Información de Emisora." *Grupo BMV*. www.bmv.com.mx/es/emisoras/informacion-de-emisoras (July 11, 2021).

Hawley, James P., and Andrew T. Williams. 2000. *The rise of fiduciary capitalism: How institutional investors can make corporate America more democratic*. Philadelphia: University of Pennsylvania Press.

Heemskerk, Eelke M. 2007. *Decline of the corporate community: Network dynamics of the Dutch business elite*. Amsterdam: Amsterdam University Press.

MarketScreener Website. n.d. *MarketScreener*. www.marketscreener.com/ (April 1, 2021).

Mirowski, Philip, and Dieter Plehwe, eds. 2009. *The road from Mont Pèlerin. The making of the neoliberal thought collective*. Cambridge: Harvard University Press.

Murray, Georgina. 2012. "Australia's ruling class: A local elite, a trinational capitalist class or bits of both." In *Financial elites and transnational bussiness. Who rules the world?*, edited by Murray, Georgina and John Scott, 193–219. Cheltenham: Edward Elgar.

Murray, Georgina, and David Peetz. 2012. "The financialization of global corporate ownership." In *Financial elites and transnational bussiness. Who rules the world?*, edited by Murray, Georgina and John Scott, 26–53. Cheltenham: Edward Elgar.

OECD. 2021. *GDP per hour worked (indicator)*. https://doi.org/10.1787/1439e590-en (August 5, 2021).

Peres, Wilson, ed. 1998. *Grandes Empresas y Grupos Industriales Latinoamericanos*. México City: Siglo XXI-CEPAL.

R CORE TEAM. 2019. R Development Core Team. R: A Language and Environment for Statistical Computing. http://dx.doi.org/www.R-project.org

Regalado Jacobo, Hugo José. 2021. "¿A quien benefició la privatización en Mexico? Conformación de elites, beneficios y diversificación." *Presentation at the Conference "Explorando las élites y la riqueza en América Latina" in Guadalajara, México*, December 10, 2021.

Revista Expansión. 2020. Estas son las 500 empresas más importantes de México 2020. *Expansión*. https://expansion.mx/empresas/2020/07/15/estas-son-las-500-empresas-mas-importantes-de-mexico-2020 (August 5, 2021).

Ros, Jaime. 1993. "Mexico's trade industrialization experience since 1960: A reconsideration of past policies and assessment of current reforms." *Kellogg Institute working paper 186* (January 1993). http://kellogg.nd.edu/publications/workingpapers/WPS/186.pdf (August 5, 2021).

Salas Porras, Alejandra. 1998. "The strategies pursued by Mexican firms in their efforts to become global players." *Cepal Review* 65, 133–153.

———. 2002. "Avenidas de desarrollo de los grandes grupos empresariales mexicanos." *Revista Mexicana de Sociología* LXIV (1), 141–185.

———. 2006. "Fuerzas centrífugas y centrípetas en la red corporativa mexicana (1981–2001)." *Revista Mexicana de Sociología* 68 (2), 331–375.

———. 2012. "The transnational class in Mexico: New and old mechanisms structuring corporate networks (1981–2010)." In *Financial elites and transnational bussiness. Who rules the world?*, edited by Murray, Georgina and John Scott, 146–176. Cheltenham: Edward Elgar.

———. 2017. *La economía política neoliberal en México ¿Quién la diseñó y cómo lo hizo?* Madrid: Akal.

———. 2020. "Transnational state elites and the neoliberal Project in Mexico" *New Global Studies* 15 (1), 23–46.

Schifeling, Todd, and Mark S. Mizruchi. 2014. "The decline of the American Corporate Network, 1960–2010." In *The power of corporate networks*, edited by David, Thomas, and Gerarda Westerhuis, 31–47. New York: Routledge.

Scott, John. 2008. "Modes of power and the reconceptualization of elites." *Sociological Review* 56 (1), 25–43.

Springer, Simon. 2016. *The Discourse of Neoliberalism. An Anatomy of a Powerful Idea.* New York: Rowman & Littlefield International.

Undurraga, Tomás. 2016. "Business, politics and ideology: Neoliberalism and capitalist class formation in Argentina and Chile (1990–2014)." *Revista de Ciencia Política* 54 (2), 177–210.

van Apeldoorn, Bastiaan, and Henk Overbeek. 2012. "Introduction: The life course of the neoliberal project and the global crisis." In *Neoliberalism in crisis*, edited by Overbeek, Henk, and Bastiaan van Apeldoorn, 1–22. London: Palgrave Macmillan.

Wickham, Hadley, Mara Averick, Jennifer Bryan, Winston Chang, Lucy McGowan, Romain François, Garrett Grolemund et al. 2019. Welcome to the tidyverse. *Journal of Open Source Software* 4 (43), 1686. https://doi.org/10.21105/ joss.01686

The World Bank. 2021. *Crecimiento del PIB (% anual) [Data file]*. https://datos.bancomundial.org/indicator/NY.GDP.MKTP.KD.ZG?locations=MX (August 5, 2021).

Part II

Elites and the State in Latin America

6 Chile and the Contemporary Power of Capital

Peripheral Predatory Rentier Capitalism and the Political Practices of Business Elites

Fernando Ignacio Leiva

6.1 Why Chile Matters?

Despite displaying some of the worst wealth and income distribution indicators in the world, Chile had been constantly touted over the past decades as an economic and political success story. This long-standing fable, exulting it as a model of governability and economic accomplishment that other Latin American countries should emulate, was finally punctured by the October 18, 2019, popular uprising that shook the country to its very foundations.[1] Before the October 2019 *estallido* (and on the basis of highly selective indicators),[2] praise gushed enthusiastically for Chile's economic performance and statecraft[3] even though the country's richest decile consistently appropriated close to 36% of national income, by far the largest portion among OECD countries (OECD 2021). A quarter century of center-left governments failed to stem this trend. Quite the contrary, thanks to policies that further commodified social reproduction, center-left administrations contributed to socio-economic disparities and popular discontent by actively strengthening capital's hegemony over all aspects of social life (Leiva 2021). The 2022 World Inequality Report indicates how income and wealth remain highly concentrated to a much higher degree than the world average: In 2021, Chile's top 10% received 58.9% of income (as opposed to 52.4% for the world) and controlled 80.4 % of the wealth, a much higher proportion than the 76% owned by the planet's richest decile (see Table 6.1). Focusing on wealth and not just income, the World Inequality Database shows that for 2022, the top 1% received 80.6% of the country's wealth, while the bottom 50% of the population was in debt and actively dispossessed receiving a negative 0.6% of the country's wealth (–0.6%).[4]

How can we explain such record levels of income and wealth inequality? Are these mainly a product of the business elite's influence over the policymaking realm? How are they connected to the contemporary structure and functioning of Chilean capitalism?

The failure of "progressive neoliberal" policies to meaningfully reduce inequality's lacerating effects plonks before us a perplexing set of issues: Why have Chile's corporate elites remained able to continually appropriate both figuratively and literally the "lion's share" of the country's wealth and income? (López, Figueroa, Gutiérrez 2013). Or stated more plainly, "Why [do] the rich tend to stay rich, no matter what

DOI: 10.4324/9781032636764-8

Table 6.1 Chile: 2021 Indicators of Wealth and Income Inequality

World Inequality Report 2022	Share of Income (%)		Share of Wealth (%)	
	World	*Chile*	*World*	*Chile*
Top 1%	19.3	26.5	38	49.6
Top 10%	52.4	58.9	76	80.4
Middle 40%	39.5	30.9	22	20.6
Bottom 50%	8.5	10.2	2	-0.6

Source: Compiled by author based on data provided by World Inequality Report, 2022.

the rest of society wishes?" (Palma 2020, 93). Attempts to answer these questions highlight the importance of theoretical frameworks capable of slashing through self-serving right-wing and center-left rhetoric that for years successfully foisted the now-dethroned myth of Chile as an exemplar. These questions also underscore the importance of analytical tools adept at deciphering how capitalist accumulation, social development, and modes of political mediation entwine, reproduce, and normalize extraordinarily high levels of inequality observed in much of the world today. At times of protracted sluggishness of the world economy, planet-wide climate disasters, global geopolitical reordering, and devastating consequences from the Covid-19 pandemic (Bull and Rivera 2020), holistic frameworks capable of discerning how "the evolution of the economy and the political go together and mutually condition one another" become indispensable and urgent (Amable and Palombarini 2021, 9). This chapter explores the interconnected aspects behind this complex array of issues by tackling two specific and delimited questions.

First, does the "elite capture of the state"-thesis (ECS hereafter), which has gained growing popularity among academics and in public discourse (OXFAM 2017; Crabtree and Durand 2017), offer us a sufficiently capacious analytical framework for unraveling the nature of those forces, logics, and practices that today enable inequality to persist and grow in Chile and Latin America? In other words, can the ECS thesis convincingly explain why the rich always seem to stay rich, "no matter what, no matter the cost" (Palma 2020)?

Second, given Chile's "pole position" in trailblazing the path toward global neoliberal modernity, it behooves us to also ask about the modalities through which in recent decades Chile's corporate elites exercise their power over society. What allows them to unfailingly appropriate extraordinarily high levels of surplus and profits? Or, put slightly differently, what kind of political practices have Chile's dominant classes used to create conditions for reproducing and intensifying wealth and income inequality over time? Does ECS fully account for such practices, revealing their underlying foundations and characteristics?

These questions gain greater saliency at this historical juncture, a "liminal time" in which, despite popular social mobilizations forcing Chile's economic and political elites to grudgingly task a Constituent Convention with writing a new charter to replace Pinochet's 1980 Constitution, efforts to bring about such political change were thwarted. Additionally, the December 2021 election of Gabriel Boric further highlights the importance of having a suitable diagnosis of the roots of inequality. Only thus can we assess whether this new, younger, left-leaning coalition arising from the 2011 student mobilizations will be more effective in tackling the political, economic, and cultural means through which inequality manages to persist and whether it will do a better job in this regard than the previous Concertación (1990–2010) and Nueva Mayoría (2013–2017) administrations.

As Chilean society stumbles onto a still open-ended historical cycle, debates about the relationship between the roots of inequality and capitalist accumulation, about the state's role and the desired scope for democratic public policymaking, draw renewed interest not just from pundits and academics; these issues are also part of quotidian discussions in households, communities, and workplaces. How is persistent inequality connected to the contemporary structure and functioning of Chilean capitalism? Why is Chile a "global winner" when assessed using a much less known Socio-economic Dysfunction Index,[5] a measure of economic malaise, financialization, tax evasion, ecological damage, exclusion, alienation, and militarism, ranking at the very top right behind Nigeria and Russia?

6.2 The Elite Capture of the State Thesis and Its Limitations

Initially welcomed for "bringing politics back" into conversations about inequality, the ECS thesis perceptively referenced elite influence over policymaking precisely at a time when Latin American public opinion was peeling back the veil of Odebrecht's extensive corrupting influence over presidents and many of the region's governments.[6] Initially, elite capture of the state was defined as

> the exercise of abusive influence by an elite, for its own interests and priorities and in detriment to the common interest, over the cycle of public policies and state entities, with potential effects on inequality and the correct exercise of democracy.
>
> (OXFAM 2017, 12)

In such a context, ECS authors highlighted how the elite capture of the state offered a convincing explanation for the region's deepening level of inequality as it involved among other aspects (1) a "blocking of public initiatives with redistributive impact" and (2) a "maintenance or strengthening of a narrative or line of discourse that justifies privileges" (OXFAM 2017, 13).

With the benefit of hindsight and relying on a strategic relational approach influenced by a critical cultural political economic perspective (Sum and Jessop 2013; Leiva and Chiasson-LeBel 2018; Leiva 2021), we can now ascertain *four substantial shortcomings* in the ECS thesis. Indeed, despite its contributions, ECS misses key pieces of the puzzle and fosters the erroneous notion that freeing the state and fiscal policy from elite capture is a sufficient condition for combatting inequality in the region. Certainly, greater democratic control over public policy is necessary, but as I sketch below, and as the Chilean case suggests, a horizon of much broader amplitude is required if we are to successfully tackle the roots of inequality.

The first and most glaring flaw of ECS is its under-theorization of the linkages between the nature of Latin American capitalism and mechanisms of class formations and class processes that produce and reproduce inequality over time. Contemporary forms of production, appropriation, and distribution of the social surplus among the population are heavily influenced by legacies of what previous theorists labeled peripheral and dependent capitalism (Bambirra 1972; Marini 1974; Prebisch 1984; Katz 2018). Later, as Latin American, and Caribbean societies transited through neoliberal restructuring and globalization, these traits morphed into what I denote *peripheral rentier capitalism*, a concept that, as I sketch in the next section, extends Brett Christophers (2020) analysis to our hemisphere. Even if Latin American and Caribbean societies were to gain greater ability to tax the proverbial 1% and shape fiscal policy to serve the "common good," the systemic impacts of economies based mostly on the export of raw materials with low levels of processing still structurally condition societal options and well-being. To tackle inequality, we need to wrestle with and transform the form that rentier capitalism assumes in Latin America, where, as I show using Chile as an example, it takes a highly predatory and violent form. ECS is unprepared to enlighten a path forward for confronting such a challenge.

Second, ECS deploys a rather limited theory of the state. Indeed, it enacts a markedly liberal conception that undertheorizes the state by envisioning it as an autonomous agent that arbitrates conflicts among stakeholders instead of a structure or social relation built upon past and ongoing class conflicts (Leiva and Chiasson-LeBel 2018). It conceives the state as a defender of the common good temporarily diverted from its natural role on account of undue influence gained by elites. More critical conceptions of the state, including materialist ones influenced by different and evolving strands of the Marxist tradition (Poulantzas 1973; Das 1996; Jessop 2016), envision the state as both a crystallization and arena of conflict among classes and social forces, constituting a key site where class domination is produced, reproduced, and contested.

Third, by over-emphasizing how the elite capture of the state hijacks the possibility of enacting public policies to serve the common good, ECS diverts much-needed attention from a critical assessment of the role of the center-left and left political coalitions in government. Both in Europe (UK, France, Spain, Greece) and Latin America (Chile, Brazil), center-left governments have played a crucial role in buttressing and intensifying neoliberal reform agendas by providing the intellectual and political conditions for what some have called "progressive neoliberalism" (Fraser 2019). Focusing on the politics of recognition rather than redistribution or transformation, such efforts, despite momentary and socially important gains, ultimately failed to stem systemic income and wealth disparities. Even when Latin America's more "hard-core" or "carnivorous" left has been in government, as in Bolivia, Ecuador, and Venezuela, significant obstacles arising from the contemporary nature of global capitalism, the exhaustion of the commodity super-cycle, and a prevalence of personalist or vertical top-down political cultures posed multi-dimensional obstacles for addressing inequality (Gaudichaud et al. 2022). The experience of Latin America's first "Pink Tide" starkly reminds us that addressing inequality is more complex than just overcoming the "elite capture of the state," or that it can be solved merely by expanding short-term consumption opportunities for the most disenfranchised sectors of the population.

The fourth and final limitation arises when ECS is tasked with accounting for the current political practices of business elites. As I argue below, ECS upholds what has become a rather antiquated and stationary conception of politics, focused exclusively on "state-centric" forms of political mediation. As the Chilean case shows, if we are to understand contemporary forms of capitalist power and how political practices by Latin America's ruling classes and economic elites produce and intensify rising inequality, we need a viewfinder with a broader and sharper scope. Only then, can we understand how and why capitalist elites are enacting new forms of politics that extends *well beyond the state and formal political systems* and is producing new forms of capital-state-civil society articulations to manage the status quo (Leiva 2023).

In this sense, ECS provides inadequate explanations for how the region's corporate elites manage conflicts, attempt to produce legitimacy, engage in new forms of governance, and consciously seek to produce subjectivities; all essential tasks to keep Latin America's highly predatory form of rentier capitalism alive and thriving. In a nutshell, despite ECS's contributions to public debates, we still need a more holistic analytical framework capable of unraveling how the economy and the political mutually condition each other under present historical conditions.

In what follows, I direct our attention to two of the above limitations to roughly sketch out an alternative framework better endowed for exploring connections between capitalist accumulation, social development, and emergent forms of political mediation that constitute the region's actually existing capitalism.

6.3 Rentier Capitalism in the Global North and Global South

Over the last decade, a gamut of authors has stressed the importance of analyzing the qualitatively new material foundations upon which the valorization of capital unfolds. For them, it is the materiality of such transformations, not the elite capture of the state, that constitutes the key analytical entry point for understanding the root causes of spiking inequality. Working from disparate heterodox theoretical traditions and mostly focusing on Europe and the United States, these authors [i.e., Lapavitsas (2013); Piketty (2014, 2020); Durand (2017); Zubboff (2019); Lazonick and Shin (2020); Christophers (2020)] underscore how contemporary inequality is rooted not so much on who controls policymaking, but rather on historically significant mutations in the very nature of contemporary capitalism and their consequences. Given the scope of this chapter, a thorough discussion of these works is out of the question. I can only sketch here how their lines of inquiry depart from the analytical emphasis at the heart of the ECS thesis.

Whether alluding to how $r > g$, that is, how returns on capital (r) historically grow faster than the growth of income (g) in the economy (Piketty), the rise to predominance of fictitious capital (Durand), the emergence of surveillance capitalism (Zubboff), or new forms of value extraction linked to evolving corporate structures (Lazonick and Shin), each of these authors underlines the importance of examining transformations in the political economy foundations of capitalism itself. They persuasively argue that macro-structural mutations at the core of capitalist societies create systemic conditions for inequality to thrive. These authors echo what Marx stressed more than a century and half ago about capitalism and the accumulation of capital: As production becomes more social in character and global in scale, the appropriation of the social surplus becomes more and more concentrated in the hands of a small minority through both old (fictitious capital) and qualitatively new mechanisms (digital platforms).

Among these works Brett Christophers' seminal 2020 book *Rentier Capitalism, Who Owns the Economy and Who Pays for It?* warrants special attention. Based on a close study of the United Kingdom, Christophers offers a useful typology for envisaging the multi-pronged reach of contemporary rentier capitalism (see Table 6.2). He demonstrates how it is no longer just the exploitation of labor (surplus value extracted from living labor) that today sustains capitalist profits. Rent, that is, income based on monopoly control of valuable assets, increasingly has

Table 6.2 Forms of Contemporary Rentierism in the UK

Asset	*Primary Means of Gaining Asset Control*	*Principal Income Stream*
Financial	• Creation of credit money by private banks • Acquisition of financial assets in primary and secondary markets	• Interest • Dividends • Capital goods
Natural resource reserves	• Leasing agreements with mineral rights owners	• Product sales
Intellectual property	• Registration of rights (e.g. patents, trademarks with state intellectual property offices)	• Product sales • Royalties
Digital platforms	• Organic creation	• Commissions • Advertising fees
Service contracts	• Bidding process (various)	• Service fees
Infrastructure	• Privatization of state-owned enterprises • Licensing by government • Organic creation	• Service fees • Licensing fees
Land	• Acquisition in markets • Privatization of public sector landholding	• Ground rent

Source: Table P-1, Brett Christophers (2020) Rentier Capitalism (Verso).

become fundamental to the point where "a full-fledged comeback and proliferation of forms of rent" characterizes the current transformation of capitalism.[7] Combining heterodox with orthodox notions to better account for this new reality, Christophers defines rent as, "income derived from the ownership, possession or control of scarce assets under conditions of limited competition" (Christophers 2020: xxiv). Hence, monopoly control over rent-bearing assets linked to financial, natural resources, land, intellectual property, service contracts, infrastructure, and digital platforms, alongside the exploitation of living labor, that is "having rather than doing," constitutes the defining structure, dynamics, and contradictions of 21st-century capitalist economies and societies.

6.4 Rentier Capitalism in the Global South

If we are to extend this framework to the Global South, to Latin America and specifically Chile, we need to investigate and reconceptualize how rentier capitalism's "darker side" manifests itself (and originates) in the "periphery." Whether on account of "unequal and combined development," "accumulation by dispossession" (Harvey 2005), the "coloniality of power" (Quijano 2000), the extractive operations of capital (Gago and Mezzara 2017), or imperialism's much debated contemporary nature,[8] Chile's neoliberal capitalism has matured morphing into a highly dependent and violent form of predatory rentierism (see Table 6.3).

"Peripheral rentier capitalism" thus describes the politico-economic nature of contemporary Chile and increasingly other societies in Latin America. Peripheral rentier capitalism captures the underlying structure and dynamics resulting from an amalgamation of three trends. First, lasting legacies of colonialism, imperialism, and dependency condition these countries' role in the international division of labor as suppliers of raw materials with scant or very low levels of processing.[9] As a result, extractivism, understood as the removal of large amounts of natural resources with minimal processing destined for export (Acosta 2013; Gudynas 2021), has become prevalent again in the 21st century. Second, the consolidation of a mature neoliberal system of domination originally birthed through state terror and unrestrained market forces accentuates the monopoly power of capitalist elites, freeing them from constraints imposed by previous social contracts, such as having to assume their share of costs for the production and reproduction of society. Later, as a new neoliberal common sense organized social life based on individualism, debt, and precarity, monopoly control over public assets and the commons managed to survive and even thrive despite multiple crises and contradictions. Third, financialization and digitalization of capital accumulation and social existence collude to intensify processes of deterritorialization/reterritorialization and de-temporalization/re-temporalization that end up undermining previously known repertoires that had underpinned social solidarities and forms of collective action.

Peripheral rentier capitalism stems from multi-faceted processes such as these, which permanently exacerbate its predatory and hierarchical characteristics. On the one hand, capitalist elites knit together new and evolving forms of exploitation and appropriation to take advantage of these aforementioned dynamics, exponentially

Table 6.3 Chile's Predatory and Dependent Rentier Capitalism

	Global North	*Chile*
Asset	Primary means of gaining asset control (UK)	Primary Means of Gaining Asset Control
Financial	• Creation of credit money by private banks • Acquisition of financial assets in primary and secondary markets	• Appropriation of forced savings of workers through the private social security (AFP system) • Forgiveness of private banks' subordinated debt • Financial Extraction ("ghost" intermediation commissions)
Natural resource reserves	• Leasing agreements with mineral rights owners	• Pillaging of the state and society • Predatory privatization of water and ecosystems • Royalty scams in copper and lithium • Appropriation of the commons
Intellectual property	• Registration of rights (e.g. patents, trademarks with state intellectual property offices	• Stricter standards than WTO standards agreed in bilateral US-Chile Free Trade Agreements • Royalties
Digital platforms	• Organic creation	• Commissions • Advertising fees
Service contracts	• Bidding process (various)	• Service fees
Infrastructure	• Privatization of state-owned enterprises (SOEs) • Licensing by government • Organic creation	• Privatization and transnationalization of SOEs • Predatory licensing fees • Speculative operations on permits
Land	• Acquisition in markets • Privatization of public sector landholding	• Violent restitution of landlords' property rights • Encirclement and strangulation of small property owners • On-going military and police operations against Mapuche communities • Territorial planning transformations giving MNC more power in the processes (Leiva 2019)

Source: Compiled by author. "Chile Column" from various sources. "Global North" column from Christophers (2020). Table P-1.

scaling up their class power. On the other hand, the exploited and oppressed find difficulties in making the passage from resistance and episodic explosions of discontent to effective strategies for overthrowing such a system and replacing it with an alternative social order.

The rise to prominence of a new type of "hybrid rentier-capitalists"[10] endowed with the capability of deftly combining the exploitation of labor with the appropriation of rent is what lies behind the growing gap in wealth and power that separates them from the majority of the population. In sum, in Chile and much of the Global South, inequality is materially and discursively anchored on the exploitation of the labor force, the expansion of predatory rentierism, and the expanding pillage of the commons.

6.5 Chile's Peripheral and Predatory Rentier Capitalism

Four vignettes presented below underscore how the origins, structure, and functioning of Chile's rentier capitalism are characterized by its peripheral, predatory, and violent character. Achieving monopoly control and maintaining it hinges on using all necessary means—coercion, competition, corruption, dispossession, and destruction of human and non-human lives—to ensure that rent continues flowing. The four snippets below highlight how the "peripheral," "predatory," and "violent" qualifiers conform to the core of its success and denote a political-economic assessment, not a moral condemnation. At the same time, these qualifiers also underscore how Christophers' framework needs to be thoroughly reworked to account for rentier capitalism's evolution in the periphery. In Chile and the Global South, extra-economic as well as economic compulsions shape and continue to shape the contours of rentier capitalism and its "social structures of accumulation" (Wolfson and Kotz 2010). Not only must we account for different economic activities through which rentier capitalist appropriate rent and exercise control over income-bearing assets, but we must also expand our historico-analytical perspective to include non-economic interventions that allow them to colonize an expanding realm of socio-ecological systems. One author working in the Marxist ecofeminist tradition sagely states that "in addition to the appropriation of surplus value produced by wage-labor, capitalism relies on the ongoing and violent expropriation of women, indigenous peoples, nonhuman animals, and the biosphere" (Oksala, 2018, 222 cited by Schild 2019).

By considering how contemporary forms of value appropriation interact with corporate political practices, we can map more precisely the material and semiotic terrain upon which contemporary hybrid capitalist-rentier elites construct and expand their domination. Additionally, such a more granular topography helps us make sense of the multiple struggles against inequality unfolding in the streets of Chile, Colombia, Puerto Rico, Ecuador, and elsewhere. Upgrading our understanding of how the economic and political co-constitute contemporary forms of class domination can evidence the extent to which the "elite capture of the state" is but a sliver of a much more complex process.

6.5.1 First Vignette: The Great Pillage Made Possible by Blood and Terror

After the September 11, 1973, coup, thanks to the military and the Chicago Boys, Chile's capitalist class set out to overturn the Popular Unity's policies, especially its Area of Social Property. Between 1978 and 1990, assets estimated with a value of US$ 2.5 billion dollars, or 6.4% of GDP, were transferred to the private sector (Monckeberg 2001). Research later carried out by a Congressional committee estimated the present value of such transfers to be closer to US$ 6 billion (Cámara de Diputados 2004). However, the actual value of assets appropriated by Chile's corporate capitalist conglomerates and their allies thanks to the military regime was much bigger. Previously cited figures accounted for only 30 of the largest enterprises from a total of 725 public firms privatized at bargain rates. Many of these firms were taken over by Pinochet's inner circle, including his then son-in-law, Ponce Lerou, who seized control of SOQUIMICH (now SQM) for which he paid something like US$ 262 million below its real value. In addition to transferring state and socialized corporations to large capitalists, the military also rolled back more than a decade of land reform. Thus, close to 15,000 properties formerly under public ownership were transferred to new owners, 11,000 of these going directly to private hands. We are talking about nearly 8 million hectares (almost 20 million acres) formerly under public ownership. Of these about 20% remained under peasant control, but the rest went to private owners.[11]

Hence, state terror laid the late 20th-century foundations for Chile's rentier capitalism and neoliberalism. State violence made monopoly control over assets in mining, finance, infrastructure, and both agricultural and urban land possible. The concomitant set of tax, commercial, investment, financial, and property rights policies that enabled local and foreign rentiers to thrive and expand were all rooted in economic restructuring made possible through brutal repression of civil, political, and democratic rights. State terror and violence were thus the first political technologies deployed to establish the foundations of contemporary neoliberal Chilean capitalism.

6.5.2 Second Vignette: An Ongoing Gift to Mining Transnationals

Chile is the top exporter of copper in the world, producing about 31% of global output in a sector dominated by private transnational corporations. Since the 1973 military coup, thanks to neoliberal foreign investment, mining, and water laws enacted by Pinochet's civilian-military dictatorship, nationalized copper mines were left defenseless to encirclement by private transnational corporations. Since 1990, all civilian governments have kept the norms governing mining operations unchanged. Extremely lax rules governing mining rent have allowed mining transnationals to freely earn hundreds of billions of dollars. One study published by ECLAC estimates that private multinationals have appropriated gratuitous rent totaling US$ 114 billion in 2005–2014, representing an annual average flow equivalent to 5.1% of the country's GDP over these years (Sturla et a. 2018). The study points out that

> the resources thus gifted averaged US$ 11.4 billion per year between 2005 and 2014. It has been estimated that free education in the country, understood as full State funding at all levels of education, requires additional financing equivalent to almost US$ 5 billion per year. It is also estimated that the recently enacted tax reform will raise US$ 6 billion per year at most. In other words, the wealth transferred annually to these large transnational companies in 2005–2014, could have financed free complete education, and the remaining US$ 6.4 billion could have been used to definitively upgrade the healthcare and pensions systems.
>
> (Sturla et al. 2018: 114)

Extraordinary rents from Chile's copper riches are just one example of how monopoly control over natural resources extracted for export generates huge income streams for globally connected rentier capitalists. Another study calculates that 87% of Chile's exports comprised copper, lumber and cellulose, fish, lithium, and agro-commodities are based on monopoly control over the natural commons and extensive depredation of ecosystems.[12] Yet, it would be a mistake to consider that this appropriation of resources happens only in "traditional" economic sectors far from Chile's urban center. The income stream and profitability of technologically intensive activities by global digital platforms also depend on the ongoing appropriation of the commons, in this case, water. When Google announced the installation of a Data Center in Santiago's Cerrillos district, involving an estimated US$ 200 million investment, it was discovered that such a facility would require an estimated 169 liters of water per second to cool its servers.[13] In a country experiencing a 13-year drought, with a capital city of almost 7 million people atop an aquifer already declared endangered, this project was approved without an environmental impact study, showing us how predatory rentier capitalism operates by using water for profit, not for sustaining life.

6.5.3 Third Vignette: Zombie Enterprises and the Zombie King

During the 1990s, some of the country's most important rentier-capitalist conglomerates, such as Luksic, Piñera, Penta, Solari, Ponce Lerou, and others, expanded their profit-making by discovering how to take advantage of "zombie enterprises." Billionaire Sebastián Piñera became the "Zombie King" for pioneering this unique strategy to avoid paying taxes on profit (Guzmán and Rojas 2017). Taking advantage of Zombie enterprises was perfectly legal, and under the advisement of their tax lawyers and specialized tax accountants, profitable holding companies managing these conglomerates found they could dodge paying taxes on profits by merging profitable operations with "dead" or shell enterprises that, existing only on paper, still carried huge accounting losses. Research by CIPER showed that at least 47 corporations tied to these conglomerates used this strategy to avoid paying close to Ch$ 1 billion in taxes. Between 1997 and 2001, Sebastián Piñera—for example the poster boy of Chilean rentier capitalists—managed to save Ch$ 2,800 million (approx. US$ 5 million) in taxes.[14] In 2002, the Luksic conglomerate also resorted to zombie enterprises to wipe Ch$ 39,682 million in profits (approx. US$ 58 million) and Ch$ 28,551 million (approx. US$ 30 million) from its books.[15]

6.5.4 Fourth Vignette: Financial Tribute and the Great Con by AFPs

Perhaps the starkest incarnation of the predatory nature of Chile's rentier capitalism is the privatized social security system created under Pinochet, the hated Asociaciones de Fondos Previsionales (AFPs), which operates literally as a life-draining, society-wide, financial extraction system. Seven private pension management companies, or AFPs, extract society's surplus, appropriate it, and control its allocation. In 2020, these seven AFPs controlled US$ 201 billion, a sum representing 81.7 % of Chile's GDP. Eleven and a half million workers with individual accounts managed by the AFP system are obligated by law to deposit 10% of their monthly wages in these privately managed funds.[16] In turn, each of the AFPs is controlled by large transnational rentier capitalists corporations.[17] The largest AFP in terms of size of managed funds is Habitat with US$ 56.5 billion, an amount roughly equivalent to 23% of Chile's GDP, and controlled by Prudential (USA) and the Cámara Chilena de la Construcción. The second largest, Provida, manages funds totaling US$ 49.4 billion (or 20% of GDP) and is controlled by Metlife (USA). The third in size, Capital, managing US$ 38.8 billion in funds (equivalent to 15.8 % of the GDP) is controlled by Colombia's Sura group; Cuprum's US$ 35.7 billion or 14.5 % of GDP is controlled by Principal (USA).

By investing in workers' forced savings and paying out miserable pensions, the AFPs reap huge profits. During the first quarter of 2021 alone, AFPs made US$ 145.6 million in profits or approximately US$ 1.6 million per day. The "beauty" behind the system's design is to be found in the attempt to link materially, discursively, and existentially, the fate of millions of Chile's underpaid and super-exploited workers with the AFP's ability to further expand their power. Such leverage allows predatory rentier conglomerates to wield extraordinary levels of economic and political power based on "owning" not "doing." All of it linked to the huge sums they control and the power of deciding where to allocate them to maximize private profits and monopoly control.

During 2021, 12 banks belonging to the largest domestic (Luksic, Solari, Hurtado, Matte) and foreign (Morgan, Santander) conglomerates received investments of US$ 23.9 billion from the AFPs, an amount equivalent to 8.8% of the country's GDP.[18] Chile's economic conglomerates thus become a destination for workers' savings, enabling these *grupos económicos*, all of them hybrid capitalist rentiers, to further expand their own monopoly power. The Ponce Lerou conglomerate, for example, through investments from AFPs in four of its companies (SQM, Nitratos, Oro Blanco, and Norte Grande), received 2020 US$ 1.333 billion (0.5% of GDP).[19] Surplus extracted from living labor is transformed into a means for expanding the capacity to appropriate rents by Chile's transnationalized rentier capitalists and their global allies.

Yet, for the overwhelming majority of male and female workers, the results of Chile's privatized social security system have been truly catastrophic: In 2020, for example, out of the 102,000 individuals who retired under the AFP system, only

Table 6.4 Financial Assets of Chile's Super Rich: High and Ultra High Net Worth Individuals

Tranches of Net Worth Value of Financial Assets Controlled (US $ millions)	*Number of Individuals*	*Financial Assets (US$ millions)*	*Per Capita Value of Financial Assets (US$ million)*	*Percentage of Private Wealth*
High Net Worth Individuals				
$1 to $5 million: lower HNW	18,152	27,839	1.5	
$5 to $100 million	5,690	70,761	12.4	
>$100 million: Ultra HNW	140	88,740	633.9	18
SubTotal Super rich	23,982	187,340		33

Source: "Los súper ricos en Chile: Cúantos son, cúal es su patrimonio y dónde invierten su dinero," *El Mercurio,* November 6, 2019.

50% of them were able to fund a monthly pension of US$ 100.13 (Ch$ 75,000), and even half of those who had managed to save during 30–35 years of working life through this system for their retirement managed to self-finance a monthly income of Ch$ 287,0000, equivalent to US$ 383.31, or approximately only 85% of the legal minimum wage (Ch$ 337,000).[20] (see Table 6.4).

The four vignettes above are just the tip of the iceberg. They suggest the need to explore how complex processes of class domination and class power perpetuate Chile's predatory, transnationalized, financialized, and digitalized rentier capitalism, and in turn, how these dynamics deepen inequality.

6.6 An Expanded Framework to Account for the Contemporary Politics of Capital

So then how does paying attention to the nature and dynamics of predatory rentier capitalism alter our understanding of corporate elites' political practices? Or stated differently, how does the rise to predominance of hybrid rentier-capitalists compel us to rethink in a more holistic manner how the economic and political realms connect and interact? And why is such reconceptualization indispensable for unearthing the root causes of deepening inequality today? The following three interconnected postulates encapsulate a rudimentary answer to such questions:

1 Rentier capitalism makes control of the political realm—the state and civil society—more necessary than at any other previous historical moment.
2 Rentier capitalism makes it both materially and semiotically easier for rentier capitalists to exercise political control and domination over society to an extent never experienced before.

3 Latin America's peripheral predatory rentier capitalism continually expands the frontiers of the 'political' beyond traditional state institutions and conventional forms governance to encompass ever more sprawling realms of sociality and social life.

Let us briefly examine these axioms to highlight how rentier capitalists in Chile (and increasingly Latin America) wield political resources comprising mechanisms and processes vastly greater than those initially cataloged by the ECS thesis. Given space limitation, I provide only a sketch of how dependent predatory rentier capitalism secretes novel and highly contradictory forms of articulation between profit-making, *the* disciplining of populations, and political domination. This dense constellation of power relations lies at the origins and lifeblood of contemporary inequality.

Political Control as an Imperative: Under rentier capitalism, the source of revenue is anchored not so much on "doing"—i.e. exploiting living labor in the *production* of commodities, but rather on "owning," that is on *exercising monopoly control* over an expanding collection of income-yielding assets. As a result, what becomes vital is not just "politics" but political domination *tout court.* To create conditions for the valorization of capital, rentier–capitalist conglomerates must engage in political practices unfolding not only at firm-level labor processes but must also establish social and ideological control over the different circuits of valorization. Such control is crucial for ensuring the continuity of processes of dispossession and for constantly retracing the boundaries between the commodified and non-commodified realms of social and natural life.

New Capillaries for the Flow of Capitalist Power: The cultural logic of peripheral predatory rentier capitalism creates conditions "from above" as well as "from below" that make it materially and semiotically easier for rentier capitalists to exercise their domination. Predatory rentier capitalism has concentrated enormous material and communicative resources in the hands of a minuscule minority of rentier capitalists—140 individuals classified by Boston Consulting Group as the "ultra-high net worth individuals" who in Chile possess 18% of the country's private financial wealth constitute the ultra-privileged core of that 1% who owns 49.5% of the country's wealth, while the bottom 50%, as we saw in Table 6.1, literally owns nothing and lives in perpetual debt. This minuscule nucleus of rentier capitalists and their retinue of sub-contracted politicians, think tanks, pundits, media, and epistemic communities under their command—not the institutions of a receding liberal democracy—are really those who today manage the valorization of capital, concoct the ideas, forge the rules, and produce the subjectivities that anchor their power. Daily existences shaped by precarity, individualism, debt-based consumption, and alienation digitally pounded across times dedicated to work, social reproduction, and leisure create emotional infrastructures and subjectivities highly vulnerable to the class power of rentier capitalists.

The three postulates listed above suggest that to fully map the range of political resources wielded by the contemporary rentier capitalist class, we need to examine *the whole gamut of articulated market, state, and civil society resources forged, mobilized, and brandished by Chile's ruling class over the past five decades of neoliberalism*. Though the "elite capture" of the state thesis alerts us to some of the mechanisms that continually hollow out liberal democracy (i.e. revolving doors, corporatist agenda setting, interlocking directorates, legal and illegal campaign contributions, and tax havens), we need a much more systemic view.

6.7 For an Expanded Notion of the Political Realm

By compiling a directory of eleven capture mechanisms, the ECS thesis draws attention to the more grotesque, yet effective modalities corporate elites deploy to ensure that fiscal and tax policies favor their class interests (see Table 6.5). Yet, as previously indicated, the ECS narrative is limited by its neglect of the rentier,

Table 6.5 Political Resources of Capital: Elite Capture or Technologies of Class Domination?

	Capture Mechanisms by Elites ECS (OXFAM 2017)	*Technologies of Domination*
Focus of analysis	• State-focused, understood as an institution • Traditional political system • Elite control over fiscal and tax policies	• Interconnectedness of accumulation, hegemony, and subjectivity • Systemic perspective • Contestation and conflict as analytical entry points
Mechanisms	1. Communications and media campaigns 2. "Revolving door" 3. Extraordinary regulatory procedures 4. Exploitation of weaknesses in the political and electoral system 5. Advocacy and lobbying 6. Technical smokescreen 7. Exploitation of regulation and regulatory frameworks 8. Prosecution in constitutional courts 9. Bribes and influence peddling 10. Marches and protests 11. Opacity in tax havens	1. State terror and targeted assassination of land and human rights defenders. 2. Cooptation of social movements 3. Cruel pedagogies of the market 4. Debt 5. Territorial dialogues and early community participation as forms of hegemonic participatory politics 6. Corporate-Private-NGO corporations for territorial management 7. "Privatization" of traditional state responsibilities (production of social cohesion, territorial management).
Solution	• Restore majoritarian control over state institutions	• Construct a counter-hegemonic bloc. • Radical democratization of economic, political, and cultural structures

Source: Compiled by author. Column 2 on the basis of Table 2, OXFAM (2017), page 15. Column 3 based on Leiva (2018).

dependent, and predatory nature of Latin American capitalism and by its privileging of a state-centric approach. Such a perspective fails to account for the full range of political resources through which today's rentier capitalists forge and reforge their domination to ensure their continued exploitation of labor and appropriation of value.

In contrast to ECS' focus on traditional political institutions, the systemic approach advocated here envisions the political realm as dialectically linked to broader processes of class domination that continually interconnect capitalist accumulation with efforts to refurbish bourgeois hegemony and the production of subjectivities (Leiva 2010, 2023; Leiva & Chiasson-LeBel 2018). Such a perspective investigates the logic, strategies, and tactics of political action of different social actors from a relational perspective: as incessantly being molded by contestation and conflict. It focuses on broader dynamics of class domination, not just on disputes over fiscal and tax policy formulation, by paying close attention to (1) the hegemonic project brandished by the more dynamic capitalist factions—the hybrid rentier-capitalists—leading the power bloc; (2) the types of class consciousness emerging from concrete historical moments; and (3) the array of political technologies crafted and operationalized to address challenges posed by different historical junctures in contested territories (Leiva 2023). As Table 6.5 portrays, these two explanatory frameworks not only have different entry points but also lead to distinct strategies of action to effectively combat inequality.

6.8 Conclusion: Going beyond the Elite Capture of the State Thesis

The longevity of Chile's neoliberal system of domination offers us a trove of materials for exploring how the interlinked political, economic, and cultural dimensions of capitalist class power and domination have evolved over the past decades.[21] These entwined pillars and capillaries of class power—economic, political, and cultural—abetted by the right-wing as well as center-left administrations, both committed to ensuring governability of the status quo, produce and reproduce Chile's dependent and predatory rentier capitalism. Here we find the root of the ruling class's capacity to appropriate inordinately high levels of income and wealth, deepening inequality in the process.

By shifting our entry point beyond from just the limited design of public policy perspective to more complex processes of class formation and class domination, we can visualize a broader range of phenomena than those delimited by the ECS thesis. Beyond a state-apparatus-centric perspective, an analysis of contemporary political practices of corporate elites must account for those collateral agents that play a key role in shoring up the political domination of capital. These include (1) firm-based strategies that seek to create both loyal customers (customer loyalty campaigns, customer clubs) as well as manage employees civic involvement through company orchestrated volunteer and philanthropic campaigns; (2) business associations (Consejo Minero, SOFOFA, Confederación de la Producción y el Comercio; American-Chilean Business Chamber, etc.; (3) think tanks (Instituto Libertad y Desarrollo, Corporación de Estudios Públicos [CEP], Fundación

Futuro, Espacio Público, CIEPLAN, Fundación Siglo 21, etc.); (4) political parties (UDI, RN, Partido Republicano, Partido Por la Democracia, Partido Demócrata Cristiano, Partido Socialista); (5) consulting firms specializing in corporate image, branding, and crisis management (Tironi Asociados, Azerta, Imaginacción, Extend Comunicaciones, Casa de la Paz, etc.); (6) corporate foundations and corporate philanthropic initiatives (Fundación A. Luksic, Fundación Futuro, Techo Chile, etc); (7) epistemic communities that play a crucial role in formulating and disseminating hegemonic concepts (Centro de Políticas Públicas, Universidad Católica; World Bank, IDB, UNDP, COES, an connected research networks on various topics); and finally, (8) alliances and networks at the transnational, national, and local scales too numerous to itemize that produce, circulate, and embed imaginaries and discourses that across different conjunctures and landscapes reproduce the power of peripheral predatory rentier capitalists. In sum, we need to investigate vast flora and fauna, a densely entwined cognitive and communicative ecosystem ignored by the ECS thesis, that scaffolds those mechanisms of class domination that today produce and deepen inequality.

The Chilean case merits close attention for it is emblematic of how, under mature neoliberal capitalism, corporate practices expand the boundaries of the political. In the 50 years since bloody 1973 overthrow of Salvador Allende, different facets of Chile's neoliberal system of domination illustrate how a ruling class wields its power and political influence depending on a shifting balance of class forces and the robustness of their hegemony. Contrary to the limited scope afforded by the "elite capture of the state" perspective, the Chilean case illuminates the broad range of extra-state political practices that, operating on multiple realms, scales, and temporalities, constitute, preserve, and reproduce class power.

Unraveling the roots of inequality requires thus a thorough understanding of how capitalist exploitation, appropriation, and political domination are currently produced and renewed in the face of rising societal discontent, mounting popular resistance, and deepening crises. This becomes even more imperative in our current historical conjuncture characterized, first, by a capitalism that has "metastasized" into rentier capitalism, and second by a global neoliberalism incapable of dealing with the multi-dimensional crises afflicting it. In such context, the elite capture of the state framework (ECS) proves to be too restrictive to fully account for how capitalist elites today maintain their power, manufacture consent, and strive to restore their hegemony as it deteriorates.[22] ECS does not provide a sufficiently comprehensive scope or sharp enough tools to explore the linkages between inequality and those relations of appropriation and exploitation inherent to Latin America's rentier capitalism.

Additionally, Chile illustrates why ECS lacks competence for scrutinizing how one of the region's most dynamic capitalist power blocs expands the very frontiers of the "political." Indeed, ferociously powerful and hybridized rentier-capitalists like the Luksic, Matte, Angelini, Paulmann, Solari, and Ponce Lerou economic conglomerates,[23] along with their foreign multinational corporate allies, are enacting a new capitalist class consciousness: an understanding that as rentier capitalists they must attend not only to the valorization of capital increasingly reliant on the extraction of value and dispossession of communities but also must directly participate in the production of ideas, rules, and subjectivities. Historically, Chile's capitalist class has demonstrated a remarkable class consciousness and ability to learn and recover from momentary setbacks by defining new strategic lines of action that ensure their continued domination over society. Today, Chile's capitalist class strives to reconfigure its relationship with the state and society by endorsing a "new citizenship of capital" that politically intervenes in all realms of the country's social, cultural, and spiritual life. Some business leaders linked to lumber and cellulose, transport, and power generation actively endorse the use of the military, counter-insurgency operations, increased police repression, and the creation of paramilitary groups to crush demands by the Mapuche people and nation as well as other communities in movement. Others continue seeking the incorporation of political parties, intellectuals, private consulting firms, think tanks, NGOs, university departments, philanthropic entities, and international development agencies behind efforts to devise, launch, and operationalize refurbished political technologies better capable of molding the behavior of the subaltern.

Chile is the one place in the Americas where elite "capture" of the state was carried out literally by "fire and blood" in the military coup of 1973, and such "capture" was later baked into the 1980 Constitutional order that has prevailed despite the 2019 popular uprising or *estallido social*. Such "capture" was deeply imprinted onto the political culture and praxis of right-wing, center-left, and left politicians and parties that conform to the institutional political system. The ECS thesis fails to explain how elected officials, intellectuals, "think tanks," and transversal epistemic communities across the political spectrum, including the center-left, willingly and loyally serviced the interests of transnational capital.[24]

In these "liminal times," we must boldly imagine and forge innovative paths capable of profoundly transforming power relations in society if we are to succeed in addressing the causes of inequality. As argued here, a logical first step should be to inquire how, under peripheral predatory rentier capitalism, class power and class domination are enacted.

Notes

1 International elites were finally forced to reckon with their bloated rhetoric on Chile and with the lingering effects of October 2019 popular uprising as vividly illustrated by the article, "Chile, Once Considered Latin America's Finland, is in Trouble," *The Economist*, October 31, 2021.

2 See for example "La engañosa manera de medir la desigualdad de ingresos." La Tercera, July 29, 2013. www.latercera.com/voces/la-enganosa-manera-de-medir-la-desigualdad-de-ingresos/ (February 22, 2024). Chile's official poverty rate is 10.8% of the population. A more realistic and comprehensive calculation carried out by Fundación Sol puts the real rate at 39.8 percent of the population. See Fundación Sol, (2021) "La pobreza del modelo chileno. La insuficiencia de los ingresos del trabajo y pensiones." www.fundacionsol.cl/blog/estudios-2/post/la-pobreza-del-modelo-chileno-2021-6791 (February 22, 2024).

3 Check out how Chile is ranked by the World Bank's Government Effectiveness Index.

4 See World Inequality Database for Chile at https://wid.world/country/chile/. (February 22, 2024).
5 See Jorge Buzaglo, and Leo Buzaglo, "Socio-Economic Dysfunction Index – a failure index," Real-World Economics Review Blog, April 13, 2022. https://rwer.wordpress.com/2022/04/13/socio-economic-dysfunction-index-a-failure-index/ (February 2022, 2024).
6 ODEBRECHT

> Using a complex network of shell companies, off-book transactions and off-shore bank accounts, and a dedicated bribery division, Odebrecht paid more than $780 million in bribes to government officials, their representatives and political parties in countries across Latin America and the Caribbean. This conduct helped it win contracts and other benefits totaling $3.34 billion, according to the U.S. Department of Justice, which has described the scheme as "massive and unparalleled." (www.icij.org/investigations/bribery-division/bribery-division-what-is-odebrecht-who-is-involved/
>
> (February 22, 2024))

7 Vercellone (2008) cited in the epigraph in Christophers (2020) book.
8 See for example "You live on the other side of imperialism", https://mronline.org/2021/08/04/prashad-to-harvey- A full version of the debate is available on YouTube www.youtube.com/watch?v=CcX2O47NZucyou-live-on-the-other-side-of-imperialism/
9 Central America and Mexico are incorporated into the international division of labor via other means, namely export processing zones that are capital intensive (in Mexico) and labor intensive in Central America, non-traditional agricultural exports, services, tourism, and fundamentally through the export of labor.
10 Manuel Riesco coined the very useful concept of "hybrid rentier-capitalists" for the case of Chile (Riesco 2010).
11 "El saqueo de la dictadura militar al patrimonio estatal: Los orígenes del actual sistema económico neoliberal," www.elciudadano.com/portada/el-saqueo-de-la-dictadura-militar-al-patrimonio-estatal-los-origenes-del-actual-sistema-economico-neoliberal/09/12/ (February 22, 2024).
12 "Chile. ¿A costa de qué?: Estudio señala que 87% de las exportaciones son producto de extracciones de bienes comunes naturales," *Resúmen Latinoamericano*, March 21, 2022. resumenlatinoamericano.org/2022/03/21/chile-a-costa-de-que-estudio-senala-que-87-de-las-exportaciones-de-chile-son-producto-de-extracciones-de-bienes-comunes-naturales/ (February 22, 2024).
13 Las zonas oscuras de la evaluación ambiental que autorizó "a ciegas" el megaproyecto de Google en Cerrillos. Investigación CIPER 25, May 2020. www.ciperchile.cl/2020/05/25/las-zonas-oscuras-de-la-evaluacion-ambiental-que-autorizo-a-ciegas-el-megaproyecto-de-google-en-cerrillos/ (February 22, 2024).
14 "Así operaban las empresas zombis de Piñera," https://pousta.com/empresas-zombis-pinera/
15 "Cómo empresas de Luksic y Juan Cúneo usaron zombis para no pagar impuestos," CIPER, www.ciperchile.cl/2017/08/16/como-empresas-de-luksic-y-juan-cuneo-usaron-zombis-para-no-pagar-impuestos/ (February 22, 2024). US equivalent calculated by author by using the June 30 exchange rate for each respective year.
16 Superintendencia de Pensiones, "Estadísticas de Pensiones, Afiliados/as AFP," www.spensiones.cl/apps/loadEstadisticas/genEstadAfiliadosCotizantes.php?id=inf_estadistica/aficot/mensual/2022/04/01C.html&p=M&menu=sci&menuN1=afil&menuN2=afp&orden=10&ext=.html (February 22, 2024).

17 Marcos Kremmerman, "¿Quiénes son las empresas dueñas de las AFP y cuánto dinero administran?" www.youtube.com/watch?v=7GPOfQHOjac (February 22, 2024).
18 Fundación Sol, Fundación SOL en base a Superintendencia depensiones al 29 de octubre de 2021.
19 Data compiled by Fundacion Sol was converted by author to US dollars equivalents using Ch$ 723.59 - US$1.
20 See Fundación Sol (2021). "Pensiones sin Seguridad Social ¿Cómo se calcula el monto de las pensiones en Chile?" www.fundacionsol.cl/blog/estudios-2/post/pensiones-sin-seguridad-social-como-se-calcula-el-monto-de-las-pensiones-en-chile-2021-6784#o_wblog_post_main (February 22, 2024).
21 Jose Gabriel Palma (2019b) offers an eye-opening account of this inability.
22 A great example of these efforts is the World Economic Forum's The Great Reset initiative, www.weforum.org/great-reset (February 22, 2024).
23 For more details about these conglomerates, see my paper "Hacia un enfoque sistémico, relacional y de economía política cultural crítica para investigar el accionar de las elites empresariales y el poder contemporáneo del capital."
24 During the last month of the Piñera administration, Daniel Matamala published the opinion piece "¿Dónde está el piloto?" *La Tercera,* October 3, 2021. He commented on how the

> government insists on confessing its impotence, electoral candidates become incapable of leading even their own supporters, legislators fall prey to panic, the ranks of the technocracy are ignored, and the power centers exercising effective control *(los poderes fácticos*) have become irrelevant. Not even the large economic conglomerates, despite preserving untouched all their sources of power, remain able to dicate public policies as they had done during the [pre-October 2019] *Ancien Regime.*
>
> My translation.
>
> The original reads: Dónde está el piloto> El gobierno se empeña en confesar su impotencia, los candidatos no lideran ni a sus partidarios, los parlamentarios se dejan llevar por el pánico, la tecnocracia es ignorada, los viejos poderes fácticos son irrelevantes. Tampoco los grandes grupos económicos, pese a mantener intactas las fuentes de su poder, son ya capaces de dictar políticas públicas como lo hacían durante el Antiguo Régimen.

References

Acosta, Alberto. 2013. "Extractivism and neoextractivism: two sides of the same curse," In *Beyond Development. Alternative Visions from Latin America*, edited by Lang, Miriam, and Dunia Mokrani, 61–86. Quito: Transnational Institute.
Amable, Bruno, and Stefano Palombarini. 2021. *The Last Neoliberal: Macron and the Origins of France's Political Crisis.* New York: Verso.
Bambirra, Vania. 1972. *El capitalismo dependiente latinoamericano.* Santiago de Chile: Prensa Latinoamericana.
Bull, Benedicte, and Francisco Rivera. 2020. "COVID-19, elites and the future political economy of inequality reduction in Latin America" *ECLAC Review* 132, 77–91.
Cámara de Diputados. 2004. *Informe de la Comisión Privatizaciones.* Santiago de Chile: Cámara de Diputados.
Christophers, Brett. 2020.. *Rentier Capitalism. Who Owns the Economy and Who Pays for It?* London; New York: Verso Books.

and Timothy D. Clark, 23–56. Cham: Springer International Publishing.

Crabtree, John, and Francisco Durand. 2017. *Peru: Elite Power and Political Capture*. London: Zed Books

Das, Raju. 1996. "State Theories: A Critical Analysis." *Science & Society* 60 (1), 27–57.

Durand, Cédric. 2017. *Fictitious Capital. How Finance is Appropriating Our Future*. London; New York: Verso Books.

Fraser, Nancy. 2019. *The Old is Dying and the New Cannot Be Born*. London; New York: Verso.

Gago, Verónica, and Sandro Mezzadra. 2017. "A Critique of the Extractive Operations of Capital: Toward an Expanded Concept of Extractivism." *Rethinking Marxism* (29) 4, 574–591.

Gaudichaud, Franck, Jeffery Webber, and Massimo Modonesi. 2022. *The Impasse of the Latin American Left*. Durkham, NC: Duke University Press.

Gudynas, Eduardo. 2021. *Extractivisms. Politics, Economy and Ecology*. Halifax: Fernwood Publishing.

Guzmán, Juan Andrés, and Jorge Rojas. 2017. *Empresarios zombis. La mayor elusión tributaria de la elite chilena*. Santiago de Chile: Catalonia.

Harvey, David. 2005. *A Brief History of Neoliberalism*. Oxford: Oxford University Press.

Jessop, Bob. 2016. *The State: Past, Present, and Future*. Cambridge: Polity Press.

Katz, Claudio. 2018. *La teoría de la dependencia, cincuenta años después*. Buenos Aires: Batalla de Ideas.

Lapavitsas, Costas. 2013. *Profiting Without Producing. How Finance Exploits Us All*. London; New York: Verso.

Lazonick, William, and Jan-Sup Shin. 2020. *Predatory Value Extraction: How the Looting of the Business Corporation became the U.S. Norm and How Sustainable Prosperity Can Be Restored*. London; New York: Oxford University Press.

Leiva, Fernando I. 2010. "Acumulación, cohesión social y subjetividad en el capitalismo latinoamericano contemporáneo. El aporte de la economía política cultural crítica." Congreso de la Asociacion Centro-Americana de Sociología (ACAS), August 4, 2010, San José.

———. 2018. El 'dialogo territorial' y la 'participación temprana' como dispositivos de despojo. Las nuevas estrategias de las empresas extractivistas.

———. 2019. "Economic Elites and New Strategies for Extractivism in Chile." *European Review of Latin American and Caribbean Studies* 108: 131–152.

———. 2021. *The Left Hand of Capital: Neoliberalism and the Left in Chile*. New York: SUNY Press.

———. 2023. "Beyond Corporate Social Responsibility: New Territorial Management Strategies for Defeating Community-Based Resistance to Extractivism," In *From Extractivisms to Sustainability. Lessons from Latin America*, edited by Henry Veltmeyer, and Arturo Esquerra-Cañete, 181–201. New York; London. Routledge.

Leiva, Fernando I, and Thomas Chiasson-LeBel. 2018. *Sharpening Our Tools, Linking Our Endeavors: Research on Recent Transformations of Latin America's Capitalist Class, Corporate Strategies and the Role of Economic Elites*.

López Vega, Ramón., Eugenio Figueroa Benavides, and Pablo C. Gutiérrez .2013. La 'parte del león': Nuevas estimaciones de la participación de los súper ricos en el ingreso de Chile. *University of Chile Working Papers* 379, 1–32.

Lordon, Frederic. 2014. *Willing Slaves of Capital. Spinoza and Marx on Desire*. New York; London: Verso.

Marini, Ruy Mauro. 1974. *Subdesarrollo y revolución*. México City: Siglo XXI Editores.

Monckeberg, Maria Olivia. 2001. *El saqueo de los grupos económicos al Estado de Chile.* Santiago de Chile: Ediciones B.
OECD. 2021. "Income distribution," *OECD Social and Welfare Statistics* (database), https://doi.org/10.1787/data-00654-en (February 22, 2024).
Oksala, Johanna. 2018. "Feminism, Capitalism, and Ecology." *Hypatia* 33 (2), 216–234.
OXFAM. 2017. *Captured Democracy: How Elites Capture Fiscal Policy, and its Impact on Inequality in Latin America and the Caribbean 1990–2017.* Oxfam.
———. 2020."Why the rich always stay rich (no matter what, no matter the cost)." *ECLAC Review* 132, 93–132.
Picketty, Thomas. 2014. *Capital in the Twenty-First Century.* Cambridge: Harvard University Press.
———. 2020. *Capital and Ideology.* Cambridge; London: Harvard University Press.
Poulantzas, Nicos. 1973. *Political Power and Social Classes.* London: New Left Books.
Prebisch, Raúl. 1984. *Capitalismo periférico: Crisis y transformación.* México City: Fondo de Cultura Económica.
Quijano, Anibal. 2000. "Coloniality of Power and Eurocentrism in Latin America." *International Sociology* 15 (2), 215–232.
Riesco, Manuel. 2010. "¿Capitalistas o rentistas?" September 9, 2010. www.economia.manuelriesco.cl (February 22, 2024).
Schild, Verónica. 2019. "Feminisms, the Environment and Capitalism: On the Necessary Ecological Dimension of a Critical Latin American Feminism." *Journal of International Women's Studies* 20 (6), 23–43.
Sturla, Gino, Ramón López, Eugenio Figueroa, and Simón Accorsi. 2018. "La riqueza regalada a la gran minería del cobre en Chile: nuevas estimaciones, 2005–2014". *Cepal Review* 24, 107–129.
Sum, Ngai Ling, and Bob Jessop. 2013. *Towards a Cultural Political Econom*y. Cheltenham; Northampton: Edward Elgar Publishing
Tironi Eugenio, and José Ossandón, eds. 2013. *Adaptación: La empresa chilena después de Friedman.* Santiago de Chile: Ediciones Universidad Diego Portales.
Vercellone, Carlo. 2008. *The New Articulation of Wages, Rent and Profit in Cognitive Capitalism. The Art of Rent.* London: Queen Mary University School of Business and Management.
Wolfson, Martin H., and David M. Kotz 2010. "A Reconceptualization of Social Structure of Accumulation Theory," In *Contemporary Capitalism and Its Crises: Social Structure of Accumulation Theory for the 21st Century*, edited by McDonough, Terrence, Michael Reich, and David M. Kotz, 72–90. Cambridge: Cambridge University Press.
Zubboff, Shoshana. 2019. *The Age of Surveillance Capitalism. The Fight for a Human Future at the New Frontier of Power.* New York: Public Affairs.

7 Business and State Relations in Uncertain Times

Alliance Recalibration in Nicaragua

Rose J. Spalding

This chapter begins with the observation that economic elites develop not simply in response to economic openings but also in relation to their political interactions with the state. Policies that favor the interests of business elites, such as a shift toward privatization and increased tax exonerations, or that promote the expansion of specific sectors, such as trade agreements and deregulation, do not emerge automatically as a byproduct of market competition or technological change. They develop in response to relational dynamics that unfold in complex intra-elite negotiations. Despite the critical role of business and state relations in shaping the flow of resources and opportunities, this dynamic has been under-researched and analyzed. Along with the other contributions to this collection, my chapter sheds new light on these relations.

The Nicaraguan case demonstrates how political change intersects with and shapes elite formation and recomposition. As Nicaragua underwent revolution and warfare, democratization and de-democratization, economic sanctions and reinsertion, business–state relations shifted in tandem, reflecting the construction of new barriers and opportunities. This study provides insights into the dynamics of elite strategic recalibration under conditions of political uncertainty.

Following a decade of revolutionary change in the 1980s, the Nicaraguan business elite reconfigured in response to post-revolutionary market reform in the 1990s that produced new trade and investment flows and altered the domestic institutional architecture. Although some traditional economic elites were hard-pressed to make the requisite transitions in terms of technology and production processes, others flourished under expanding economic conditions and, along with former revolutionaries-cum-entrepreneurs, emerged as part of the post-revolutionary elite. The 2007 return to the presidency of *Frente Sandinista de Liberación Nacional* (FSLN) leader and former revolutionary Daniel Ortega raised questions about the emerging interface between economic and political elites in the context of once-again shifting international alliances and post-neoliberal policy adjustments. Increased repression and instability in 2018 propelled business–state relations into another cycle of adjustments. The intersection between the state and business elites was renegotiated and reconfigured in each phase.

DOI: 10.4324/9781032636764-9

To analyze this interplay, this chapter is organized into seven sections. The first section reviews theoretical claims about state and business relations in Latin America. The second examines the relationship between the Nicaraguan business sector and the state during the revolutionary 1980s. The third traces the reconstitution of the elite during the neoliberal transition that followed. The fourth section focuses on the formal organization of the business sector and documents the post-revolutionary development of Nicaraguan business chambers and associations. It gives particular attention to the period beginning in 2006 when the prospect of Daniel Ortega's return to the presidency led to a "defensive encompassing organization" (Schneider 2004, 36) and the strengthening of business sector coordination. The fifth section analyzes the new forms of state–business collaboration that developed in the 2007–2018 period, following Ortega's return to power. The sixth section examines the breakdown of relations following de-democratization and rising repression in 2018–2023. The final section returns to the question of mutual dependence that shapes state and economic elite interactions, analyzing shifting alliance strategies and the continuing areas of tension.

This analysis draws on long-term observation of business–state relations in Nicaragua, beginning during the period of the Sandinista Revolution (1979–1990) and concluding in the aftermath of the turbulent 2018 protest cycle. During the 1980s and 1990s, I conducted over 100 interviews with Nicaraguan business elites, a subset of whom became recurring sources of information in the following decades (Spalding 1994). Their experiences and insights figure sharply on the page in the analysis that follows. This chapter builds on that foundation and adds 34 interviews I conducted with Nicaraguan business leaders between 2006 and 2018. It also draws on archived papers and publications of the Consejo Superior de la Empresa Privada (COSEP), Nicaragua's business peak association.

7.1 Business–State Relations: Theoretical Considerations

As this volume demonstrates, the relationship between economic and political elites has become a topic of intense study and debate among academic analysts (Durand and Silva 1998; Schneider 2012; Bull and Aguilar-Støen 2015; Fairfield 2015; North and Clark 2018; Ondetti 2021). Researchers deploy diverse models to capture these dynamics, ranging from pluralist frameworks, which interpret the business sector as one of many groups that combine and compete to establish temporary sway over state actions, to orthodox Marxist frameworks, that highlight the hegemonic role of capital and the reactive role of the state, an "executive committee" relegated to managing the common affairs of the bourgeoisie. Others emphasize the "relative autonomy" of the state, as state managers act to protect their own power or corporatist vision of national development, particularly during times of stress (Block 2020 [1977]). In that framework, state actors operate with relative independence, detached from the preferences of other social and economic actors, even in putatively democratic regimes (Nordlinger 1982). Still others employ a hybrid model, underscoring the persistent structural power of business elites but diagnosing a fluid relationship wherein state–business relations respond to shifting institutional and agentic dynamics (Martin and Swank 2012; Cárdenas 2016; Wolff 2016). In this more dynamic framing, business and state actors are understood as deeply interconnected and engaged in a process of mutual co-construction.

The present study is situated in this latter camp. It calls attention to ongoing negotiations between economic and political elites and identifies the mechanisms they employ and the circumstances under which they deploy them. In this model, elite interests may converge around a cohesive set of goals in particular policy arenas, but business and state leaders may also diverge, leading to tensions and conflicts that disrupt and reconfigure processes of engagement.

Business elites have a wide repertoire of strategies they can adopt—instrumental and structural, individual and collective, formal and informal, associational and electoral—as they pursue their goals (Schneider 2013; Fairfield 2015).[1] In addition to the obvious sources of instrumental power, such as campaign contributions and media ownership, business elites have indirect levers that increase their influence. The need that political leaders have for private sector investment and growth in order to achieve state consolidation and stability gives the business sector enduring structural power, which political elites ignore at their peril. At the same time, business elites' ability to exercise this influence depends on the extent to which they attenuate the differences among themselves through negotiation, persuasion, intimidation, or exclusion of weaker segments. One mechanism for promoting business sector coherence is the formal business sector association.

Although historically state-dependent and fragmented in many countries, Latin America's business sector often gained organizational capacity during the late-20th-century market transitions (Durand and Silva 1998). Complex multi-sectoral peak associations worked to unify the business voice and amplify its impact on both domestic policy and international agreements. In Mexico and Chile, strong business associations were found to play a strategic role in crafting specific provisions in NAFTA and in the Mercosur trade agreement (Teichman 2001; Schneider 2004, 221–30). Business representatives, who were more expert in their industries than government officials, actively collaborated in these negotiations to secure their preferences, advancing recommendations on tariff schedules and timetables. In her study of Chilean free trade negotiations, Bull (2008) found that business elites used control over not just capital but also knowledge to influence the shape of the trade text. The professional staff of business associations, some of whom rotated between private sector and government roles, blurred the distinction between public and private and helped to synchronize business and government positions.

Market reform deals both winning and losing hands to business elites, however, commonly leading to fragmentation and organizational reconfiguration. Hierarchies among business groups with differential access to policymakers can lead to policy reforms that favor some interests over others. Detailed case studies of privatization in Latin America and Europe, for example, challenge conventional arguments about privatization policy's purely ideological or technocratic base, even in neoliberal showcases like Pinochet's Chile or Thatcher's Britain. Close academic analysis frequently identifies ways in which a handful of conglomerates gained privileged access to policy arenas and shaped particular reforms to their benefit (Schamis 2002; Manzetti 2009). Hellman (1998) notes the problem of "state capture" in post-communist systems, in which insiders aligned with emerging economic interests to stall economic reforms at an equilibrium point that fell short of full transition, a strategy that allowed them to extract rents and non-competitive benefits, to the detriment of other business sectors and the broader society. Aaron Schneider (2012, 34–40) uses the tools of "fiscal sociology" to demonstrate how the structure of business alliances affects state-building processes via tax regimes in Central America. The particular coalitional formation between state–elites and economic elites may direct economic policy to different benchmarks.

This chapter homes in on the processes that shaped the shifting business–state relations as they unfolded across four decades of transitions in Nicaragua. Rather than focus on the specific interactions at one critical juncture, it addresses the processes involved in elite relational shifts and reversals over time. It asks: What are the circumstances under which business elites and state actors collaborate in the co-construction of social and economic policy? Under what circumstances do elite strategic negotiations falter and open conflicts erupt? To answer these questions, this chapter pays close attention to the impact of uncertainty and perceptions of threats on the strategic calculations of business leaders. At issue are a series of theoretical concerns, including the ability of state managers to ensure stability and order, the ability of state actors to reliably expand economic opportunities that reward business interests, and the ability of business elites to coordinate a collective response and exercise cohesive sectoral leverage in a politically volatile context. These themes became recurring elements in the cycles of conflict and alliance that are traced in the following sections.

7.2 Nicaraguan Elites, in War and Revolution

Historically, the economic activities of Nicaraguan elites were centered on the agro-export production of coffee, cotton, and cattle (Bulmer-Thomas 1987). The sector developed in close proximity to the Somoza dynasty (1936–1979), as agro-export production expanded and Central American Common Market-supported industrialization was launched. Three main business groups were constructed in the 1960s and 1970s, each aligned with a different banking interest (Strachen 1976). Using both rewards and pressures, Somoza allies extended their presence into the business community as competitors and partners.

This relationship generated tensions, especially under Anastasio Somoza Debayle (1967–1972 and 1974–1979), as corruption levels escalated and political violence increased. As the threat of disorder rose in the early 1970s, the business community began to organize around this discontent. A business peak association, COSEP, was formed in February 1972, bringing together business leaders across a dozen sectoral networks and chambers (see Appendix). This business coalition provided organizational space in which to coordinate deepening elite opposition to the regime. In the wake of massive corruption involving the misappropriation of relief aid following the 1972 Managua earthquake, business leaders called for administrative and political changes to improve accountability and transparency (Spalding 1994; COSEP 2012b).

In a noteworthy development, prominent producers came to support the FSLN-led uprising against the dynasty, actively cultivating diplomatic support for the insurgency and providing financial resources and protection to the rebels. Following the 1978 assassination of one of their own, *La Prensa* editor Pedro Joaquín Chamorro, a growing number of business leaders endorsed recurring general strikes, contributing to an escalation of the conflict and Somoza's ultimate departure from power the following year.

Although business representatives were initially incorporated into the revolutionary government, and some disaffected youths from elite families joined the revolutionaries in the political takeover, the relationship between much of the business elite and the Sandinista regime quickly soured. Under FSLN leader Daniel Ortega, the Sandinista Revolution created a mixed economy that prioritized state-centered accumulation. The new government seized the assets of the Somoza family and its allies, thus acquiring extensive agricultural holdings and a large network of industrial and commercial firms. Private banking collapsed during the insurrection and was replaced by state-owned banks. The government quickly assumed monopoly control over the export of major commodities, eliminated private trading firms, and imposed increasingly complex regulations on trade and domestic transactions. As the 1980s wore on, other expropriations followed, targeting some top business leaders.[2] By the end of this era, about 30% of GDP was controlled by the state sector, and the private sector faced extensive regulation (Spalding 1987; Conroy 1990; Martínez Cuenca 1990; Solà Montserrat 2007). Traditional elites lost economic and social power; a subset moved into self-exile, generally to the United States.

Conflict over the regime's self-styled "socialism" and alliance with Cuba fueled the "contra" war, which the Reagan administration (1980–1988) sponsored and financed in an effort to overthrow the Sandinista government. With the economy contracting, hyperinflation raging, and the war imposing large human and material costs, Nicaraguan voters chose a change of course in the 1990 presidential election. The George H. W. Bush administration (1988–1992) funded Violeta Chamorro's campaign against Sandinista leader Daniel Ortega and greeted her victory with a promise of additional assistance.

Chamorro's election was followed by a 16-year period in which leaders from the business community took the political helm, adopting a direct governance model employed by business elites-cum-presidents elsewhere in the region (Nercesian 2020). Arnoldo Alemán (1997–2002), former head of Nicaraguan coffee growers and mayor of Managua, succeeded Chamorro, followed by Enrique Bolaños (2002–2007), an agro-industrialist who rose to fame as COSEP president in the embattled years of the revolution. During the post-revolutionary period, Nicaraguan economic elites experienced both the dislocation of market transition and new opportunities, leading to further reconfiguration.

7.3 Nicaraguan Elites, Post-Revolutionary Market Reform

As elsewhere in Central America, market reform in the 1990s opened important opportunities in the financial sector (Segovia 2005; Colburn and Sánchez 2000, 71–74), and the private banking sector quickly reemerged. Eleven private banks set up shop between 1991 and 1994, including five that proved durable. Credomatic/BAC and LAFISE Bancentro marked the return of Nicaraguan banking entrepreneurs who had networked with financial operations abroad, particularly in Miami. Transnationalized through self-imposed exile, these returning Nicaraguan bankers were the first in Central America to expand into the regional market, offering credit card services, currency exchange, and offshore banking (Segovia 2005, 47; Mayorga 2007).

Between 1994 and 2002, three multi-year structural adjustment loans were signed with the IMF. Public sector employment (including the armed forces) dropped from 290,000 to 80,000 between 1990 and 2000 (Government of Nicaragua 2000, 15). Once the economy stabilized, the government moved to privatize the remaining state banks, telecommunications, and electricity, and further liberalized trade under the second structural adjustment plan launched in 1999 (IMF 1999; Solà Montserrat 2007, 130–47).

Market transition produced some quick benefits and encouraged a durable period of business–state collaboration through the 1990s and early 2000s. Inflation dropped from a catastrophic 13,490% in 1990 to 12% in 1996 (Solà Montserrat 2007, 117), and economic growth resumed in 1994, after almost a decade of contraction, in part due to rapidly expanding export processing zones. Non-traditional agricultural exports became another source of growth, strongly encouraged by USAID. Rapid privatization and new regulations lacked transparency and allowed rent-seeking behavior, and well-placed investors soon moved to extract regulatory and tax concessions (Mayorga 2007; Medal 2012). Prominent Nicaraguan business leaders reorganized themselves into "diversified business groups," defined as "a collection of firms operating in different sectors, subject to centralized ownership and financial control by a single family or family network" (Bull 2013, 268).

The Pellas Group, under the leadership of Carlos Pellas Chamorro since 1985, grew to include 21 affiliated companies in 2012. Beginning with Nicaragua Sugar Estates Limited, the family business founded in 1890, the Pellas Group came to encompass an array of financial, commercial, energy, and tourism operations, including several companies located elsewhere in Central America.[3] The LaFise Group, established in Miami in 1985 with the participation of Nicaraguan exiles, focused on financial services, including foreign debt rescheduling and currency conversion in Central America. With Nicaraguan banker Roberto Zamora Llanes as president, LaFise financial services transnationalized, opening operations in 11 countries (Nicaragua, Honduras, Costa Rica, Panama, Guatemala, El Salvador, Dominican Republic, Venezuela, Colombia, Mexico, and the United States).

Nicaragua's relatively low crime rate, compared to El Salvador, Honduras, and Guatemala, and low production costs, compared to Costa Rica, attracted investor attention, as did deregulation and a strengthening record of investment protection. Several Nicaraguan business groups partnered with transnational corporations, including La Perfecta (with Parmalat in 1999), Tip Top (with Cargill in 2000), and Café Soluble (with Nestle in 2006) (Rocha 2011). Nicaragua also attracted investments from economic groups elsewhere in Central America, including the Salvadoran Grupo Taca, which made airline acquisitions throughout the region, and the Salvadoran Grupo Poma, with investments in major malls, including Managua's Metrocentro (Segovia 2005, 154–65).

As the banking sector, non-traditional exports (including *maquila* production), agro-industry, and new waves of commerce expanded, Nicaraguan elites gained organizational capacity. Entrepreneurs in this renovated elite embraced and promoted deepening market reform. Looking to serve as domestic partners to incoming foreign investors and as exporters to more legally secure markets in the North, these sectors provided active support for regional integration and free trade agreements with the United States (CAFTA), Canada, and the European Union (Spalding 2014).

The relationship between the business sector and the FSLN was generally adversarial in the post-revolutionary period, particularly in the COSEP wing, but these links were multifaceted and complex. In the 1980s, some producers, characterized by the Sandinista government as "patriotic," acquired land or made new investments that positioned them well for the subsequent neoliberal transition (Spalding 1994). Others included elite family members who had taken positions in the Sandinista government; with the 1990 electoral ouster of the FSLN, they now resumed their place in family businesses, searching for opportunity. Some segments of the post-revolutionary elite were former Sandinista officials who had acquired assets in the "piñata," the transition-era appropriation of state property following the FSLN's 1990 defeat. To the extent that these emerging elites identified with the FSLN, the *embourgeoisement* of the party leadership began to reshape the economic orientation of the FSLN itself.

7.4 Business Sector Reorganization

As new economic sectors emerged in the 1990s, business chambers reorganized around growth industries. Chambers were established in the banking, free trade zone, mining, and tourism sectors and allowed sectoral leaders to better coordinate around shared interests (see Appendix for a list of COSEP organizational affiliates across time). The Association of Nicaraguan Producers and Exporters (APEN) was created in 1991, with USAID covering its initial operating expenses. The American Chamber of Commerce (AMCHAM)-Nicaragua, which had been founded in 1975 but ceased to function once the Reagan administration halted trade with Nicaragua during the Sandinista Revolution, now reopened and quickly added members.

As Nicaragua's 2006 election wheeled into view, with the right-wing coalition split and Ortega now in the lead, Nicaragua's business elites eyed the future with uncertainty. COSEP's highly politicized leaders of the 1980s and 1990s spiraled off into political parties and electoral campaigns and were replaced by new business association leaders. Incoming leaders were a generation younger than their predecessors and intersected differently with the era's conflicts. According to then-rising COSEP leader José Adán Aguerri, the new generation moved to "substitute our new vision for that of our parents" (Aguerri 2006). Redefining their organizational strategy, they prided themselves on their pragmatism and focused on lobbying instead of confrontation. Priorities now emphasized expanding investment opportunities, targeted policy pressure, and improving membership services.

Facing the imminent return to power of the FSLN, Nicaragua's business leaders took two steps to strengthen their organization and insert it more fully into the policy planning process. First, they formally connected the country's top business groups to COSEP's organizational apparatus by creating an advisory board composed of the country's preeminent business figures. Second, they expanded the organization's breadth by securing the affiliation of previously independent businesses and chambers. COSEP affiliates also opened their doors to business owners who had been officials in the Sandinista government or their close family members as the push for pragmatic coordination superseded old ideological battles.

7.4.1 COSEP's Advisory Board (Junta de Consejeros)

Traditionally, the country's largest business groups had little need for formal chamber organizations. Their high profile as investors, technological leaders, and employers allowed them to negotiate directly with the Nicaraguan government and gain personal access to representatives of friendly countries and international financial institutions. Although these elites often had an indirect connection to the formal business chambers, they generally associated through managers of their enterprises or occasional donations to support particular initiatives. The absence of comprehensive elite links diminished COSEP's ability to speak on behalf of business as a whole or to coordinate a common business position.

Following long conversation about the need to thicken connections in uncertain times, COSEP announced the creation of a *Junta de Consejeros* in August 2006, naming 11 major business leaders to its newly created advisory board (Aguerri 2012). Those named included movers and shakers in the country's main financial establishments and the heads of major export and business consortia.[4] Members were selected through a laborious process in which both COSEP's *junta directiva* (composed of presidents and two other members of each affiliated chamber) and prospective *consejeros* themselves had mutual veto power over the nominees (COSEP 2007b, 24).

The restructuring improved COSEP's bargaining position by reinforcing its stature as the sector's formal voice. At the same time, this step made COSEP more dependent on the contributions and input of the dominant business groups, papering over differences that emerged between these more transnationalized elites and those more focused on the domestic market.

7.4.2 COSEP's Expanding Organizational Breadth

COSEP's second step involved broadening its base by recruiting new chambers and members. Ortega's 1990 electoral loss and the following economic transition encouraged the resuscitation of old business chambers that had disappeared during the revolution. As Appendix indicates, three chambers that had been active in the 1970s but dissolved or fractured during the Sandinista Revolution reemerged in the post-revolutionary period and rejoined COSEP. In addition, several new chambers were developed in the 1990s in response to economic openings. Three of these associations now joined COSEP, raising the organization's chamber tally to 11 by 2007. Over the next 15 years, COSEP's associational network expanded to 26 affiliates, with five new chambers joining in 2008 alone (COSEP 2008).[5] Resuscitated and redefined in the second Ortega period, COSEP now drew almost all of the country's major business organizations into its orbit.

Organizational reconfiguration and expansion partly responded to the dual perception of threat and opportunity. In a process that Ben Ross Schneider (2004, 36) labeled "defensive encompassing organization," business sector unity can emerge in response to a perceived potential threat. The impending return of Sandinista leader Daniel Ortega to the presidency raised an alert with the business community, given the historical clash between the FSLN and economic elites. At the same time, the new Ortega regime called for creating a "grand alliance," including partnership with the business sector in the design of a new national development strategy. The residual threat posed by the return to power of a historical adversary, combined with the opportunity to engage in structured collaboration, encouraged a new consolidation cycle between the Nicaraguan state and business leaders.

7.5 The Return of Ortega: The "Dialogue and Consensus Model"

Daniel Ortega was re-elected in 2006 under terms negotiated in the Alemán-Ortega "governability" pact in 2000.[6] The Ortega camp had worked hard to project a post-partisan image during the campaign, forsaking its traditional red and black colors in favor of bright pink, and proclaiming its commitment to reconciliation with former adversaries. Along with his courtship of the Catholic Church and ex-contra leadership, Ortega sought to build stronger connections with the business community. He named a business leader as his vice presidential running mate, selecting Jaime Morales Carazo, a former banker whose expropriated home had become Ortega's residence and office following Somoza's ouster. This odd alliance signaled that the self-declared "second phase of the Sandinista revolution" would differ from the first.

In its post-revolutionary incarnation, the Ortega regime was well-motivated to improve its relationship with the business sector. Not only did it depend on business investment for jobs and growth, it also needed business approval to secure international finance and attenuate U.S. government animosity, which continued to flicker. For their part, business leaders were also motivated to promote improved relations. Heavily dependent on exonerations and the light regulatory regime that facilitated growth during the market transition and on international loans and market access that required official cooperation, they needed to gain access to state actors who would be attentive to business concerns.

Four days after Ortega's November 5th electoral victory, COSEP President Erwin Kruger, along with *Junta de Consejeros* members and the leaders of several affiliated chambers, met with Ortega and his business sector intermediary, Vice President Morales Carazo, to initiate a dialogue (COSEP 2007e, 79). This interaction launched a series of meetings through which the business sector was formally incorporated into a consultative process with the government. Over the following months, the COSEP group designed a "development axes" process, in which COSEP *consejeros* and chamber leaders met regularly with the Ortega's lead adviser for economic affairs, *Comandante* Bayardo Arce. Together they developed a discussion framework organized around 13 key themes. Business leaders sorted themselves into working groups based on their expertise and areas of interest and began work on a development agenda.

Seven of the 11 high-powered COSEP *consejeros* joined these working groups (COSEP 2007c, 22). These business leaders included the presidents of the country's three largest bank groups, Carlos Pellas (BAC), Ramiro Ortiz (BANPRO), and Roberto Zamora (LaFise-BANCENTRO), who all joined the working group on finance, along with COSEP President Erwin Kruger. Pellas, whose family's traditional holdings in the sugar industry had been expanded into ethanol production and who was developing a luxury tourism project in the Tola area, also joined the sugarcane and tourism working groups. BANPRO's Ramiro Ortiz and COSEP Vice President José Adán Aguerri joined the energy subsector as did four others who represented companies with investments in this field. Other chamber leaders, including former Sandinista officials or their family members, took seats in the working groups on food chains and tourism.

Although Ortega continued to criticize U.S. "imperialism" and aligned closely with Venezuelan President Hugo Chávez, the government's relationship with Nicaraguan business elites and foreign investors proved generally cooperative. COSEP leaders and *consejeros* began meeting periodically with Ortega in formal sessions that were hosted by the Harvard-affiliated Central American Business Administration Institute, INCAE, located on the outskirts of Managua. Policy discussions led to new forms of collaboration, including creating a Follow-Up Commission (*Comisión de Seguimiento*), requested by COSEP and established by Ortega in March 2009. This commission, formally composed of three representatives each from COSEP and the government, established a process of monthly meetings in which proposals were made and views were exchanged.

In 2008, COSEP introduced a modernized outreach strategy designed to influence the legislative agenda. It hired a lobbyist and designated selected COSEP leaders to cultivate relationships with each party bench. According to its internal analysis, COSEP successfully collaborated on 124 laws that were approved by the legislature during the 2008–2017 period (COSEP 2016a, 9; COSEP 2016b, 34; COSEP 2018, 18). In 2010, over 60% of all approved laws, and all but one of the economic laws, were found to involve the active collaboration and endorsement of COSEP delegates (COSEP 2011, 44).

The growing number of government-sponsored institutions and councils on which COSEP secured formal representation facilitated this outreach effort. By 2011, COSEP had official status on oversight boards for 11 public–private institutions, ten councils, four ministries and government agencies, and the presidential commissions on investment and trade facilitation, all in addition to the *Comisión de Seguimiento* which guaranteed a monthly exchange with high-ranking FSLN officials (COSEP 2012a, 2–3). In 2013, COSEP (2013, 32) reported securing official representation in 39 public–private boards, with another ten slots proposed or underway.

These formal positions gave the business sector a seat at the table for board meetings of the central bank and the newly created state development bank, *Banco Produzcamos*, as well as an array of institutes governing social security, technical education, tourism, and competitiveness. Under the new Minimum Wage Law #625, which was finalized in June 2007, COSEP representatives were incorporated into the tripartite commission that negotiated bi-annual wage increases for workers in eight economic sectors (Tuckler 2008, 24–25).

The business sector's willingness to accept real wage increases in the 2009–2012 period was viewed by the government as a sign of cooperation, as was business acceptance of the 2009 Fiscal Equity Law, which modestly increased tax revenues as the government worked to stave off fiscal crisis during the global recession. When the government was pressured by the IMF to address tax loopholes and subsidies, it returned to tax reform in 2012, and business leaders were given a privileged position in the negotiation process. The *Ley de Concertación Tributaria* was elaborated in a closed-door process in consultation with business and labor representatives and then approved quickly by the FSLN-controlled legislature in November 2012 (COSEP 2012c).

The new protocol for collaboration, officially labeled the "Dialogue and Consensus Model," was widely accepted in the business community. The business sector made certain concessions to the government, leaving political affairs largely to the political class, and, in return, received opportunities to make their case about desired legislation, urgent priorities, and the requirements of a supportive business climate. The Ortega government's ability to ensure labor peace, promote macroeconomic stability, foster economic growth, increase foreign investment, and expand export markets trumped the recurring problems of institutional weakness and limited transparency. The unanimous re-election of COSEP President José Adán Aguerri for 11 straight terms (2007–2020) demonstrated broad-based business support for this collaboration.

Contrary to fears of renewed strife or economic contraction, the Nicaraguan economy experienced increased growth under the Ortega administration, with the GDP growth rate surpassing both the Latin American and Central American average (ECLAC 2020, 160). International financial flows assisted this growth. One of Ortega's first actions after his 2007 inauguration was to join the Venezuela-sponsored Bolivarian Alliance (ALBA). Between 2008 and 2018, Venezuelan loans, donations, and investments in Nicaragua totaled US$4.9 billion (BCN 2019, 15), reaching around 7% of GDP before peaking in 2012 (IMF 2012, 13). Venezuelan aid funded a host of public initiatives, including an urban transportation subsidy, livestock and microcredit transfers, housing construction and improvements, and a monthly wage boost for low-salary government workers (BCN 2013, 11). Directly or indirectly, these transfers provided an economic stimulus to several sectors, including big business.

In addition to aid from Venezuela, the Ortega government secured loan commitments from the Inter-American Development Bank (IDB) and the Central American Bank for Economic Integration (BCIE). External donations and long-term development loans helped the country to weather the 2009 recession and pursue multiple social and economic development objectives with only modest increases in taxes. Although Venezuelan aid was controversial with both domestic and international critics due to concerns about transparency and the potential volatility of funds that depended on political ties (IMF 2012, 11–13), both the Venezuelan and conventional multilateral bank funding proved a stimulant to the Nicaraguan economy, helping to smooth government–business relations and encourage business cooperation.

Business leaders proved useful allies to the regime. In June 2012, high-profile Nicaraguan business leaders joined a delegation traveling to Washington, DC to lobby against a threatened U.S.-aid cutoff to the Ortega government.[7] Faced with the prospect of a U.S. veto of substantial development loans negotiated with the IDB and World Bank, the Nicaraguan business leaders formed a united front with the Ortega government to make the case that the waiver of sanctions (signed routinely by U.S. presidents since the 1990s) should continue. The willingness of these economic leaders to take action that buffered the Ortega regime reflected the balance of state–business relations at that juncture. Unlike their predecessors in the 1980s, Nicaraguan business elites in this period worked to avoid destabilization of the Ortega government, even as they registered a call for institutional strengthening (COSEP 2021).

Regime critics labeled the business sector's approach "corporatist" and accused it of promoting elite interests while ignoring the state's anti-democratic turn (Chamorro 2017). Aguerri, however, claimed that the new "COSEP Model" was designed to break with a long history of political confrontation that had undermined national development. Describing his support for the new approach, Aguerri (2017) explained: "The model begins with the understanding that our delay (*atraso*) in relation to the region and the world is because for decades we've been prisoners of confrontation and political intolerance…It's worth asking," he continued, rhetorically, "Have the confrontations of the past left us with the country that we want?" "What's distinctive about the recent years," he concluded, "is that we've been constructing our own model, born of the realities that we've been called to confront by the problems of today, not those of yesterday." The substance of this model, he summed up, is "dialogue and consensus."

7.6 Political Crisis and Business–State Rupture

Orchestrated performances and economic growth belied simmering political tensions associated with Ortega's tightening grip on power. By 2016, Ortega was sworn in for his third consecutive term. Having used the courts to eliminate term limits, named his wife, Rosario Murillo, as vice president, and secured FSLN control over the legislature, courts, electoral authorities, and most local governments, Ortega had achieved unfettered political control (Sánchez and Osorio Mercado

2020). When conflict over a proposed social security reform prompted a protest on April 18, 2018, and repression triggered a rapidly growing protest cycle, the regime responded with persistent and open violence. Claiming that demonstrators were attempting a "coup," the regime unleashed a crackdown that left at least 109 dead and 1400 injured in the first six weeks alone (GIEI 2018).

Accused of complicity based on the Dialogue and Consensus Model, COSEP leaders now joined the swelling political opposition in denouncing the repression. Aguerri resigned his official positions on government boards and joined the Alianza Cívica, which became the public face of the opposition. When asked by journalists if the dialogue model had been a mistake, Aguerri (2018) replied,

> If I had known that the result of this process was going to be what happened after April 18th, my response is 'obviously.' I would not at any point have taken this route if we had known this was going to be the final outcome.

Highlighting a line he declared the business sector would not cross, he concluded: "It's not the same negotiating under autocratic conditions as negotiating in a situation of assassinations, repression, [and] destruction." Aguerri, along with the presidents of all of COSEP's chambers and the AMCHAM leadership, signed a letter calling for Ortega's resignation. Even top business figures stepped away from the alliance. In a rare interview in May 2018, Carlos Pellas (2018) described the dialogue model as "worn out" and, expressing outrage at the violence, called for an "orderly transition" via early elections.

Explaining how a business–state alliance that persisted for over a decade now ruptured brings us back to our opening questions. What are the circumstances under which business–state collaboration tends to advance? What are the circumstances under which it breaks down? Nicaraguan business leaders, forged by the bitter experience of conflict and severe economic loss during the revolutionary 1980s, were primed to seek less acrimonious relations as the former revolutionaries returned to power. And those titular revolutionaries, having overseen a severe economic collapse at least partly of their making and having suffered three straight demoralizing electoral losses, were also primed to seek new forms of collaboration with former adversaries. Recognizing what was at stake, business and state leaders reorganized and constructed a new form of collaboration that hinted at an alliance. As the Ortega regime consolidated power, based on some combination of approval, acquiescence, and disengagement, the opening of economic opportunities, accompanied by the appearance of stability and order, fostered a new era of business collaboration.

But mounting evidence of public frustration put elite assumptions about stability into question. As with the Somoza era defection of prominent business elites, the veneer of cooperation wore thin as the alliance hit disruptive barriers. Operating as an alliance of convenience, the linkages that had supported business collaboration with the regime proved less attractive "in a situation of assassinations, repression, [and] destruction." Business elites revisited their calculations as order and stability were no longer ensured.

In the months and years that followed, repeated efforts by Catholic Church leaders to negotiate a resolution failed, and the Ortega regime became increasingly autocratic, banning protests, criminalizing opponents, and closing down a broad swath of civil society. COSEP leaders refused to renew the business–state dialogue until the institutional crisis was addressed, but their stance had little effect. Long associated with the dialogue model, Aguerri was replaced when his term as COSEP president ended in 2020, and Michael Healy, president of the agricultural chamber and forceful critic of the regime, stepped into the breach. The economy entered a three-year decline in the wake of the crisis and deteriorated further when COVID-19 hit.

As the 2021 presidential election approached, the regime doubled down on the repression. Additional opponents were arrested, starting with seven prominent figures vying to lead the electoral opposition. Newly approved laws required the leaders of foundations and NGOs who received foreign funds to register as "foreign agents." Bank accounts of FUNIDES-associated business leaders (including two *consejeros*) were frozen, and security forces arrested an array of opponents, generally under Ley 1055, the Act to Defend the Rights of the People to Independence, Sovereignty and Self-Determination, approved by a rubber stamp legislature in December 2020. Between June and October 2021, three COSEP leaders—José Adán Aguerri, Michael Healy, and COSEP Vice President Alvaro Vargas—were detained and imprisoned. In 2022, they, along with opposition political, student, and peasant leaders, were convicted and given lengthy prison sentences (between 9 and 13 years). They were released in February 2023 as part of a mass expulsion of 222 political prisoners, having lost their Nicaraguan citizenship, properties, bank accounts, and business assets (Report of the Group of Human Rights Experts on Nicaragua 2024).

Nicaragua's business climate was further damaged as the U.S. and allied governments imposed sanctions on a host of Nicaraguan individuals and entities, including Rosario Murillo and several of her children with Ortega, along with a long list of elected and appointed government officials at both the national and local levels (Taft-Morales 2022). Under the Nicaragua Human Rights and Anticorruption Act (NICA Act) of 2018, the U.S. Congress prohibited U.S. support for new multilateral loans to Nicaragua. U.S. sanctions prohibited travel and transit, froze assets, and banned U.S. companies and residents from doing business with targeted individuals and entities. The growing number of sanctions on Nicaraguan leaders and the threat that Nicaragua could lose access to U.S. investment and market opportunities under CAFTA-DR created another round of mounting uncertainties for business elites.

The widely discredited November 2021 re-election and January 2022 inauguration of Ortega for a fourth straight five-year term signaled that the regime would not be easy to dislodge. As time passed without a strategy for formal government engagement, some business leaders began to speak openly about a renewal of dialogue. Signs of re-accommodation emerged as the criminal prosecutions of Ortega's political adversaries advanced, with dialogue now defended as a strategy to get charges against imprisoned business leaders dismissed or reduced

(Redacción Central 2022). Under the acting leadership of César Zamora, president of the Nicaraguan Chamber of Energy (CEN), COSEP moved toward normalization of business–state relations in 2022, with its Consejo Directivo unanimously approving a resolution in favor of a return to dialogue as "the only instrument that would allow Nicaraguans the find the path to the reunification of the family" (COSEP 2022). These moves ultimately failed to protect the organization from regime crackdown, and COSEP lost its legal status in 2023, as did 17 of its affiliated members, some of which date their legal founding back to the 1950s and 1960s (Ministerio de Gobernación 2023).

7.7 Summary and Conclusions

Seeking to interpret shifts in business–state relations under conditions of post-neoliberalism in Bolivia and Ecuador in the 2000s, Jonas Wolff (2016) tracked a move toward increased reliance on dialogue and negotiation during the administrations of Evo Morales and Rafael Correa. This development came about as business leaders lost what Tasha Fairfield (2015) called "instrumental" or political power while retaining or increasing what she called "structural" power, or control over investment and growth. Business leaders' loss of political power following the election of left-leaning administrations required them to become more accommodating to state preferences, while their continued power over investment and job growth required the governments to be attentive to business needs. The result, Wolff argued, was "a process of rapprochement that has led to a fairly stable pattern of negotiation and dialogue" (p. 126).

Wolff offers an engaging, if streamlined, analysis of this temporary recalibration, and some of these processes were at play in Nicaragua after Ortega returned to the presidency in 2007. However, the longer-term analysis of business–state relations in Nicaragua demonstrates that varied processes affect the interactions of economic and political elites and that their engagement patterns are also diverse.

As this chapter illustrates, business–state relations are not predetermined by fixed structural conditions that deliver predictable performances and unwavering results. Instead of conceptualizing these bonds in terms of static connections dictated by business dominance over the state or state control over the business arena, they are better understood in more dynamic terms characterized by strategic calculations and shifting balances. As business elites recalibrate their assessments of opportunities and threats, different business groups and associations may adjust their stance regarding preferred levels of cooperation with political elites. The outcome may be a close alliance characterized by a high degree of collaboration. It may also be conflictual and adversarial, characterized by disruption, noncompliance, and defection.

This review of business–state interactions in the Nicaraguan case demonstrates how the relationship has cycled through various modalities over time. Cooperation between business leaders and the Somoza dynasty ruptured as regime corruption and misrule in the 1970s triggered rising instability, ultimately leading major business figures to collaborate with a revolutionary movement in the push for political change. That alliance unraveled in the following years and gave way to overt conflict with the Sandinista government during the revolutionary 1980s. Ortega's electoral defeat in 1990 permitted the political ascent of the business class in the 1990s and early 2000s, in which the line between business and state managers blurred. Business leaders and pro-business technocrats populated key ministries and official positions and, with support from the U.S. government and international financial institutions, presided over a market transition process that stimulated new investments and sectoral growth.

The electoral defeat of this post-revolutionary coalition and Ortega's return to power in 2007 brought new challenges and invoked unexpected forms of collaboration. The hardships associated with confrontation and crisis during the previous Sandinista era, combined with signals of the FSLN's internal evolution, encouraged the pursuit of a mediated dialogue with pro-business actors in the FSLN camp. Responding to the uncertainties associated with regime change, economic elites engaged in strategic negotiations to improve business leverage and secure reliable access to resources. The resulting 2007–2017 Dialogue and Consensus Model introduced a new era of cooperation and concession.

The resulting alliance promoted sustained economic growth, even as the Ortega regime steadily consolidated political control. Ultimately, however, the destabilizing consequences of permanent rule and the exclusion of opposition voices undermined the façade of regime legitimacy and brought into question Ortega's ability to preserve order without escalating violence. International condemnation and mounting sanctions further undercut elite accommodation. Under these conditions, the business–state alliance unraveled.

Mapping these processes of cooperation and conflict allows us to identify circumstances under which business–state relations tend to shift. Three conditions stand out as particularly relevant. The first concerns the ability of state leaders to ensure order and stability. The second concerns the extent to which state managers develop policies that serve to advance business opportunities. The third relates to the level of direct access to state decision-makers that business representatives are able to secure. Together, these conditions shed light on the processes that tip business–state relations in different directions.

As we have seen in this chapter, a regime's inability to ensure order and preserve stability serves as a recurring catalyst for business defection, as does the perception that the regime could become a direct threat to property rights and capital accumulation. State use of heavy-handed repression to maintain control and the alienation of traditional partners such that international trade and investment are seriously affected tend to exacerbate uncertainties and pause business support.

In contrast, the perception that state managers can manage conflict successfully by deescalating protest mobilizations, for example, or by gaining public acceptance in credible electoral contests encourages business elites to seek pathways to accommodation. The regime's ability to create economic opportunity by securing new lines of aid and trade, as with the Ortega regime's cooperation agreement with Venezuela, while maintaining loans and aid flows with established international partners and conventional multilateral lenders, tends to elicit business elite approval.

The ability of business elites to reconfigure and expand internal alliances in preparation for a strategy shift may also encourage concessions from state managers and facilitate cooperation. By hiking up the prospects of shared gains and raising the costs associated with political conflict, business elites can improve their leverage in negotiations with the regime. Whereas organizational weakness and internal fissures in the business community may weaken the sector's bid for recognition and results, associational expansion and cohesion can help business elites secure privileged access to state leaders and the economic decisions they approve. On the other hand, that same organizational cohesion may elicit harsh treatment by the regime in the event of elite defection.

In the Nicaraguan case, economic growth, increased foreign investment, macroeconomic stability, and labor quiescence initially provided concrete evidence of the viability of collaboration, from a business point of view. The government's willingness to repeatedly accommodate business preferences in taxation and incentives further demonstrated the utility of cooperation. As the regime broadened its political base, winning additional (if increasingly controversial) terms in 2011 and 2016, the business sector settled into a routinized (if not institutionalized) dialogue with officials that delivered mounting gains.

Top government officials listened to what business elites wanted in regularly scheduled sessions and attended to their priority concerns about energy supplies, infrastructure, property guarantees, and political access. The Ortega government continued to provide a spaghetti bowl full of exemptions, loopholes, and special benefits, as had its predecessors, assisting investors in the export processing zones, agricultural, forestry, mining, tourism, and renewable energy projects. Lengthy tax holidays, tariff exemptions, and export bonuses were maintained and increased, and officials did not pursue tax evasion aggressively (Medal 2012, 16). COSEP's privileged position as the portal in these negotiations helped to strengthen the organization, further encouraging business collaboration.

This top-heavy alliance proved unstable, however, and, after a decade in power, the Ortega regime began to lose traction. Ultimately, growing unease over the regime's dynastic features and the withering of political checkpoints, combined with clashes with students and Catholic Church leaders, fueled a political crisis. As episodic bouts of low-level repression gave way to paramilitary mobilization and politicized deployment of security forces, regime support eroded. U.S. sanctions allowed Ortega to play the imperialism card, a traditionally effective strategy in a country long-battered by U.S. hegemonic pretensions. But the ferocity of the crackdown, ban on protests, brusque clearing out of independent civil society organizations, and long prison sentences for opposition figures made it difficult to sustain the pretense of broad public approval. Under these circumstances, the Dialogue and Consensus Model came to an end.

This study highlights the recurring pattern of relational switchbacks that affect the shape of business–state relations. Although the magnitude and frequency of these shifts may be more pronounced in Nicaragua than elsewhere, given the country's recent history of political volatility, such shifts are not uncommon in other parts of Latin America. The significance of these ruptures and recalibrations call attention to the need to open the processes of consultation and collaboration to a broader array of civic actors. They also call for continued theorizing and research about the political dynamics shaping intra-elite relations. The results of the Nicaraguan case highlight the protean features of business–state relations under conditions of sustained political uncertainty, as variability and fluidity persist as defining characteristics.

Acknowledgments

The author thanks Eric Hershberg and other participants in the Central American Elites research group for valuable comments on an earlier version of this chapter, which was published as "Los empresarios y el Estado posrevolucionario: El reordenamiento de las élites y la nueva estrategia de colaboración en Nicaragua." *Anuario de Estudios Centroamericanos,* 43 (2017), 149–188. DOI 10.15517/AECA.V43Io.31556. She also thanks Nikki Hughes for research assistance and DePaul University's College of Liberal Arts and Social Sciences for research support.

Notes

1 Following Higley and Gunther (1992, 8), elites are defined here as the "principal decision makers in the largest or most resource-rich political, governmental, economic, military, professional, communications, and cultural organizations and movements in a society." Business elites are those who, often operating through formal and informal business groups that oversee complex multi-sectoral holdings, play a leading role in shaping the contours and operations of their national economy. See discussion of business groups in Schneider (2013) and Bull and Aguilar-Støen (2015). In my framework, business elites also include the top leadership of national business associations who serve as the spokespeople and negotiators for business collective interests in both national and international venues.

2 The land holdings of COSEP President Enrique Bolaños were expropriated in 1985, and the Pellas family temporarily lost the San Antonio sugar mill, its flagship investment. These properties were returned in the 1990s.

3 Pellas Group activities in Nicaragua included auto sales, rental and repair, industrial production, telecommunications, insurance, health services, television, wireless communication, warehouse and shipping, sports facilities and upscale real estate and luxury tourism development ventures, with partnered investments in Costa Rica and Panama.

4 The members of COSEP's original *junta de consejeros* were José Antonio Baltodano Cabrera, Alberto Chamorro Chamorro, Ernesto Fernández Holmann, Miguel Gómez César, Ignacio González Holmann, César Augusto Lacayo Lacayo, Rene Morales Carazo, Ramiro Ortiz Mayorga, Carlos Pellas Chamorro, Roberto Zamora Llanes, and Miguel Zavala Navarro. This list included the presidents of leading private banks (Ramiro Ortiz Mayorga, Roberto Zamora Llanes, Carlos Pellas Chamorro, and Ernesto Fernández Holmann), along with leaders of major commercial and export operations from the

Grupos CALSA (César Augusto Lacayo Lacayo) and Mercon (José Antonio Baltodano Cabrera). Two other business leaders, Juan Bautista Sacasa (president of BDF) and Jaime Rosales (Compañia Cervecera de Nicaragua), were added in 2012, and a third, Jaime Montealegre (real estate, offshore investments), in 2013 (COSEP 2007b, 10–11; COSEP 2016a, 5; Aguerri 2012).

5 New chambers represented businesses in the export processing zones; agrochemical distributors; coffee, tobacco, and African palm exporters; housing and real estate developers; mining and forestry businesses; and business services in the private health sector, telecommunications, energy, advertising, and microfinance.

6 Electoral rules allowed a winner to emerge in first round of voting if they secured a minimum of 35% of the vote and the second ranked candidate trailed by more than 5 percentage points. Ortega returned to the presidency in January 2007 with only 38% of the votes.

7 Allegations of fraud in the 2008 municipal elections and deterioration in the quality of the presidential election process in 2011 fueled opposition claims against Ortega in Nicaragua and in Washington. Cuban–American Republican leaders in the U.S. Congress and the outgoing U.S. ambassador to Nicaragua, Robert Callahan, called for the Obama administration to apply sanctions against the Nicaraguan government. Thwarted at the time, this move succeeded following the sociopolitical crisis of 2018.

References

Aguerri, José A. 2006. President of CACONIC and Vice-President of COSEP. Author interview. June 29.

———. 2012. President of COSEP. Author interview. December 13.

———. 2017. El corporativismo y los tres diálogos (2). *Nicaragua empresaria en linea.* https://cosep.org.ni/abril-4-del-2017/ (June 17, 2022).

———. 2018. [Interview] with Carlos Salinas Maldonado, "Los empresarios nos equivocamos con Daniel Ortega." *El País.* https://elpais.com/internacional/2018/06/04/america/1528141024_018748.html (June 17, 2022).

AP. 2021, November 8. "Nicaragua's Ortega decries foes who question his re-election." *AP News.* https://apnews.com/article/elections-boycotts-united-states-election-2020-central-america-f6814f4bce601643c6c0bf31496cb695 (June 17, 2022).

BCN. 2013. *Informe de cooperación oficial externa 2012.* Managua: BCN.

———. 2019. *Informe de cooperación oficial externa 2018.* Managua: BCN.

Block, Fred. 2020 [1977]. "The Ruling Class Does Not Rule (with 2020 epilogue)." *Jacobin.* April 24. https://jacobin.com/2020/04/ruling-class-capitalist-state-reform-theory (June 17, 2022).

Block, Fred, and Marian Negoita. 2016. "Beyond Embedded Autonomy: Conceptualizing the Work of Developmental States." In *The Asian Developmental State*, edited by Yin-wah Chu, 57–72. New York: Palgrave Macmillan.

Bull, Benedicte. 2008. "Policy Networks and Business Participation in Free Trade Negotiations in Chile." *Journal of Latin American Studies* 40(2), 195–224.

———. 2013. "Diversified Business Groups and the Transnationalisation of the Salvadorean Economy." *Journal of Latin American Studies* 45(2), 265–295.

Bull, Benedicte, and Mariel Aguilar-Støen, eds. 2015. *Environmental Politics in Latin America: Elite Dynamics, the Left Tide and Sustainable Development.* New York: Routledge.

Bulmer-Thomas, Victor. 1987. *The Political Economy of Central America since 1920.* Cambridge: Cambridge University Press.

Cárdenas, Julián. 2016. "Why Do Corporate Elites Form Cohesive Networks in Some Countries, and Do Not In Others? Cross-national Analysis of Corporate Elite Networks in Latin America." *International Sociology* 31(3), 341–363.

Chamorro, Carlos F. 2017, May 8. "¿"Modelo COSEP," o el régimen de Ortega?" *Confidencial*. www.confidencial.com.ni/opinion/modelo-cosep-regimen-ortega/ (June 17, 2022).

Colburn, Forrest D., and Fernando F. Sánchez. 2000. *Empresarios Centroamericanos y Apertura Económica*. San José: Editorial Universitaria Centroamericana.

Conroy, Michael E. 1990. "The Political Economy of the 1990 Nicaraguan Elections." *International Journal of Political Economy* 20(3), 5–33.

COSEP. 2007a. Firma del convenio COSUMIPYME. *Memoria 2005–2007*. Managua: COSEP, 30.

———. 2007b. Junta de Consejeros. *Memoria 2005–2007*. Managua: COSEP, 10–11, 24.

———. 2007c. Los ejes de desarrollo, una estrategia de crecimiento y equidad social. *Memoria 2005–2007*. Managua: COSEP, 20–22.

———. 2007d. *Memoria 2005–2007*. Managua: COSEP.

———. 2007e. Visitas y eventos. *Memoria 2005–2007*. Managua: COSEP, 76–82.

———. 2008. Sector privado se fortalece con cinco nuevas cámaras al COSEP. *Revista COSEP*, 3 (May/June), 12.

———. 2011. *Revista COSEP: Nicaragua Empresaria* 15 (March).

———. 2012a. *Gestión Anual 2011*. Managua: COSEP.

———. 2012b. *Revista COSEP: Nicaragua Empresaria*, Edición Especial: 40 años, fortaleciendo al empresario hacemos grande a Nicaragua, 23 (September).

———. 2012c. "Proceso de concertación tributaria, un hecho inédito para nuestro país." *Revista COSEP: Nicaragua Empresaria* 25 (November/December), 46–49.

———. 2013. "Representación institucional." *Revista COSEP: Nicaragua Empresaria* 26 (February/March), 32.

———. 2016a. "Incidencia legislativa." *Revista COSEP: Nicaragua Empresaria* 44 (January/February), 9–10.

———. 2016b. "Informe de la Trigésima Segunda Legislatura, enero a diciembre 2016." *Revista COSEP: Nicaragua Empresaria* 49 (November/December), 34–44.

———. 2018. "Trabajando por la institucionalidad económica." *Revista COSEP: Nicaragua Empresaria,* 56 (January/February), 18.

———. 2021. *COSEP 2007–2019: Institucionalidad Democrática*. https://cosep.org.ni/download/institucionalidad-democratica-2007-2019/ (June 17, 2022).

———. 2022, January 27. Comunicado. (Tweet) https://twitter.com/COSEPNicaragua/status/1486815127525539844?ref_src=twsrc%5Etfw (June 17, 2022).

Durand, Francisco, and Eduardo Silva, eds. 1998. *Organized Business, Economic Change, and Democracy in Latin America*. Miami: North-South Center Press, University of Miami.

Economic Commission on Latin America and the Caribbean (ECLAC). 2020. *Economic Survey of Latin America and the Caribbean*. Santiago: ECLAC.

Fairfield, Tasha. 2015. *Private Wealth and Public Revenue in Latin America: Business Power and Tax Politics*. Cambridge: Cambridge University Press.

GIEI (Grupo Interdisciplinario de Expertos Independientes). 2018. *Nicaragua: Informe sobre los hechos de violencia ocurridos entre el 18 de abril y el 30 de mayo de 2018*. December 21. https://gieinicaragua.org/giei-content/uploads/2019/02/GIEI_INFORME_DIGITAL_07_02_2019_VF.pdf (June 17, 2022).

Government of Nicaragua. 2000. *A Strengthened Growth and Poverty Reduction Strategy.* Managua: República de Nicaragua. https://publications.iadb.org/publications/english/document/Nicaragua-A-Strengthened-Growth-and-Poverty-Reduction-Strategy.pdf (June 17, 2022).

Hellman, Joel S. 1998. "Winners Take All: The Politics of Partial Reform in Postcommunist Transitions." *World Politics* 50(2), 203–234.

Higley, John, and Richard Gunther, eds. 1992. *Elites and Democratic Consolidation in Latin America and Southern Europe.* Cambridge: Cambridge University Press.

IMF. 1999. *Nicaragua: Enhanced Structural Adjustment Facility, Economic Policy Framework Paper for 1999–2001* (August 23). www.imf.org/external/np/pfp/1999/nicarag/ (June 17, 2022).

———. 2012. Nicaragua: Ex Post Assessment of Longer-Term Program Engagement. *IMF Country Report No.12/258*. September. www.imf.org/en/Publications/CR/Issues/2016/12/31/Nicaragua-Ex-Post-Assessment-of-Longer-Term-Program-Engagement-26236 (June 17, 2022).

Manzetti, Luigi 2009. *Neoliberalism, Accountability, and Reform Failures in Emerging Markets: Eastern Europe, Russia, Argentina, and Chile in Comparative Perspective.* University Park, PA: Pennsylvania State University Press.

Martin, Cathie J., and Duane Swank. 2012. *The Political Construction of Business Interests: Coordination, Growth, and Equality.* Cambridge: Cambridge University Press.

Martínez Cuenca, Alejandro 1990. *Nicaragua: Una Década de Retos.* Managua: Nueva Nicaragua.

Mayorga, Francisco J. 2007. *Megacapitales de Nicaragua.* Managua: Ediciones Albertus.

Medal, José L. 2012. *Hacia un presupuesto público para promover el desarrollo de Nicaragua.* FUNIDES Serie de Estudios Especiales, 12. March.

Ministerio de Gobernación. 2023. "Acuerdo Ministerial No. 27-2023-OSFL." *La Gaceta.* March 6, http://digesto.asamblea.gob.ni/consultas/util/pdf.php?type=rdd&rdd=%2F2oPobuaqUQ%3D. (April 11, 2024).

Nercesian, Inés. 2020. *Presidentes empresarios y Estados capturados.* Buenos Aires: Teseo.

Nordlinger, Eric A. 1982. *On the Autonomy of the Democratic State.* Cambridge, MA: Harvard University Press.

North, Liisa L., and Timothy D. Clark, eds. 2018. *Dominant Elites in Latin America.* Cham: Springer International Publishing.

Ondetti, Gabriel. 2021. *Property Threats and the Politics of Anti-Statism.* Cambridge: Cambridge University Press.

Pellas, Carlos. 2018, May 30. [Interview] with Eduardo Enríquez. Carlos Pellas: Solución a crisis de Nicaragua pasa "por adelanto del elecciones." *La Prensa*.www.laprensani.com/2018/05/30/politica/2427376-carlos-pellas-solucion-a-crisis-de-nicaragua-pasa-por-adelanto-de-elecciones (June 17, 2022).

Redacción Central. 2022, January 27. "Empresarios liderados por César Zamora cocinan un posible diálogo con Ortega." *Nicaragua Investiga.* https://nicaraguainvestiga.com/politica/73649-empresarios-liderados-cesar-zamora-cocinan-posible-dialogo-ortega/ (June 17, 2022).

Report of the Group of Human Rights Experts on Nicaragua. 2024. Human Rights Council, 55th Session (26 February-3 April 2024), www.ohchr.org/en/hr-bodies/hrc/regular-sessions/session55/list-reports (April 11, 2024).

Rocha, José. L. 2011. "Remittances in Central America: Whose Money Is It Anyway?" *Journal of World-System Research* 17(2), 463–481.

Sánchez, Mario, and Hloreley Osorio Mercado. 2020. "Abril 2018, Nicaragua: El desafío de la democracia frente al autoritarismo." In *Nicaragua 2018: La insurrección cívica de abril*, edited by Manuel Ortega Hegg, Irene Agudelo Builes, Jessica Martínez Cruz, Mario Sánchez, Hloreley Osorio Mercado, Jessica Pérez Reynosa, Sergio Ramírez, Hellen Castillo Rodríguez, Juan P. Gómez and Oscar Navarrete, 73–116. Managua: UCA Publicaciones.

Schamis, Hector E. 2002. *Re-Forming the State: The Politics of Privatization in Latin America and Europe.* Ann Arbor: University of Michigan Press.

Schneider, Aaron. 2012. *State-Building and Tax Regimes in Central America.* Cambridge: Cambridge University Press.

Schneider, Ben Ross. 2004. *Business Politics and the State in Twentieth-Century Latin America.* Cambridge: Cambridge University Press.

———. 2013. *Hierarchical Capitalism in Latin America: Business, Labor, and the Challenges of Equitable Development.* Cambridge: Cambridge University Press.

Segovia, Alexander. 2005. *Integración Real y Grupos de Poder Económico en América Central.* San José, Costa Rica: Fundación Friedrich Ebert.

Solà Montserrat, Roser. 2007. *Un Siglo y Medio de Economía Nicaragüense: Las Raíces del Presente.* Managua: Universidad Centroamericana, Instituto de Historia de Nicaragua y Centroamérica.

Spalding, Rose J, ed. 1987. *Political Economy of Revolutionary Nicaragua.* Boston: Unwin and Hyman.

———. 1994. *Capitalists and Revolution in Nicaragua: Opposition and Accommodation 1979–1993.* Chapel Hill, NC: University of North Carolina Press.

———. 1998. "Revolution and the Hyperpoliticized Business Peak Association: Nicaragua and el Consejo Superior de la Empresa Privada." In *Organized Business, Economic Change, Democracy in Latin America*, edited by Francisco Duran and Eduardo Silva, 147–179. Miami: North-South Center Press.

———. 2014. *Contesting Trade in Central America: Market Reform and Resistance.* Austin: University of Texas Press.

Strachen, Harry W. 1976. *Family and Other Business Groups in Economic Development: The Case of Nicaragua.* New York: Praeger.

Taft-Morales, Maureen. 2022, June 3. "Nicaragua in Brief: Political Developments and U.S. Policy." *Congressional Research Service.* https://sgp.fas.org/crs/row/R46860.pdf (June 14, 2022).

Teichman, Judith A. 2001. *The Politics of Freeing Markets in Latin America: Chile, Argentina, and Mexico.* Chapel Hill, NC: University of North Carolina.

Tuckler, Donald M. 2008. "Salario mínimo: un nuevo marco legal rige su establecimiento." *Revista COSEP* 1 (January/February), 24–25.

Wolff, Jonas. 2016. "Business Power and the Politics of Postneoliberalism: Relations Between Governments and Economic Elites in Bolivia and Ecuador." *Latin American Politics and Society*, 58(2), 124–147.

Appendix

Table A7.1 Consejo Superior de la Empresa Privada (COSEP)[a] Chamber Affiliates

	1975	*1979*	*1990*	*2007*	*2012*	*2022*
Cámara de Comercio de Nicaragua (CACONIC) (later Cámara de Comercio y Servicios de Nicaragua (CCSN)[a]	X	X	X	X	X	X
Cámara de Industrias de Nicaragua (CADIN)[a]	X	X	X	X	X	X
Cámara Nicaragüense de la Construcción (CNC)[a]	X	X	X	X	X	X
Instituto Nicaragüense de Desarrollo (INDE)	X	X	X	X	X	X
Asociación de Productores de Arroz de Nicaragua	X	Joined UPANIC				
Sociedad Cooperativa Anónima de Algodoneros	X	Joined UPANIC				
Sociedad Cooperativa Anónima de Cafeteros	X	Joined UPANIC				
Asociación de Ganaderos de Nicaragua	X	Joined UPANIC				
Unión de Productores Agropecuarios de Nicaragua (UPANIC)[a]		X	X	X	X	X
Confederación de Asociaciones Profesionales de Nicaragua (CONAPRO)		X	Fractured	X	X	X
Asociación de Instituciones Bancarias de Nicaragua	X	Dissolved				
Asociación de Criadores de Ganado Brahman de Nicaragua	X	Dissolved				
Asociación de Distribuidores de Vehículos Automotores (ANDIVA)[a]	X	Dissolved		X	X	X
Cámara Nicaragüense de la Industria Pesquera (later Cámara de Pesca de Nicaragua-CAPENIC)[a]	X	Dissolved		X	X	X
Asociación de Productores y Exportadores de Nicaragua (APEN)[a]				X	X	X
Asociación Nacional de Avicultores y Productores de Alimentos (ANAPA)[a]				X	X	X
Cámara Nacional de Turismo (CANATUR)[a]				X	X	X
Asociación Nicaragüense de Formuladores y Distribuidores de Agroquímicos (ANIFODA)[a]					X	X

(*Continued*)

Table A7.1 (Continued)

	1975	*1979*	*1990*	*2007*	*2012*	*2022*
Asociación Nicaragüense de la Industria Textil y de Confección (ANITEC)[a]					X	X
Cámara de Urbanizadores de Nicaragua (CADUR)[a]					X	X
Cámara Minera de Nicaragua (CAMINIC)[a]					X	X
Cámara Nicaragüense de la Salud (CANSALUD)					X	
Federación Cámara Nicaragüense de Zonas Francas (FCNZFP)					X	X
Asociación de Exportadores de Café Nicaragua (EXCAN)[a]					X	X
Asociación de Bancos Privados de Nicaragua (ASOBANP)[b]					X	
Cámara Nicaragüense de Internet y Telecomunicaciones (CANITEL)						X
Asociación Nicaragüense de Instituciones de Microfinanzas (ASOMIF)[a]						X
Asociación Nicaragüense de Distribuidores de Productos Farmacéuticos (ANDIPROFA)[a]						X
Asociación Nacional de Reforestadores (CONFOR)						X
Cámara de Energía de Nicaragua (CEN)[a]						X
Cámara Nicaragüense de Tabacaleros (CNT)						X
Asociación de Puestos de Bolsa de Nicaragua (ASOBOLSA)						X
Organización Nicaragüense de Agencias de Publicidad (ONAP)						X
Cámara de Productores de Palma Africana (CAPROPALMA)[a]						X

Sources: Spalding (1994, fn 42, 248); Spalding (1998, appendix, 181); COSEP (2007d, 7); COSEP (2008, 12); www.cosep.org.ni, accessed October 1, 2012; Aguerri (2012); and https://cosep.org.ni/que-es-cosep/, accessed February 25, 2022.

[a] Lost legal status in March 2023.

[b] Under special regimen.

8 From Plutocracy to Modernity in Bolivia

Economic Elites Adapting to the State Transformation under the MAS Government

Thomas Chiasson-LeBel

8.1 Introduction[1]

Over the last decade, the concept of state capture has regularly been used in and about Latin America to critique the growing influence of economic elites on state decision-making processes (Cañete Alonso 2018; Castellani 2018; Durand 2016, 2019a, 2019b,; Nercesian 2020). To what extent is this influence new, and is the concept of state, capture the best way of "capturing" the dynamic at play? More than a pun, the latter question touches on a theoretical discussion regarding the nature of the state. I will address this debate by discussing the relationships between the state and economic elites[2] in Bolivia following the election of Evo Morales to the presidency in 2005. The Bolivian situation is especially relevant since Evo Morales and his party, the MAS-IPSP, were clearly not the representatives of traditional economic elites. They are of peasant and Indigenous origin, with strong historical linkages to social movements, and yet they are being accused of having merely reproduced internal colonialism by relying on extractivism (Tapia Mealla, 2022). In such a context, is state capture the primary method by which economic elites reproduce their power over politics?

Mainstream institutionalist theories of the state (Dahl 1971; Dryzek and Dunleavy 2009, Chapter 2) start from the premise that the modern democratic state is an autonomous apparatus. Changing coalitions of agents alternatively take control over this apparatus as an instrument to implement policies by balancing their program with the interests of other constituents. In such a view, economic elites are only one group among others whose interests are counterbalanced by the plurality of expressed interests. Plurality explains state autonomy: it is not that economic elites do not have an essential influence on the state, but that they are not alone. The state is not "their own"; therefore, the best analytical point of departure is state autonomy.

The concept of state capture that is sometimes presented as a theory of its own (Durand 2019b, 15) fits well within this instrumental conception: an economic elite seizes more than its fair share of influence, provoking a risky imbalance. Although I agree that economic elites have too much power, I would like to challenge this perspective because of its instrumental connotation of the state. I will do so from two angles. First, from a Marxist-inspired theoretical perspective, in a capitalist society state managers' dependency on successful economic

DOI: 10.4324/9781032636764-10

dynamics for the reproduction of the state itself (taxes) and their own reproduction within it (easier re-election for incumbents when the economy is growing) grants economic elites a very specific place among the agents that influence the state. These agents require particular attention because they are within a structure that creates a perpetual form of state capture, and this interpretation nourishes various theories that stress how state autonomy is only *relative*. Second, from an empirical point of view, a look at Bolivia's history and, more specifically, its state–economic elites interactions highlights the belief among economic elites that the state must be theirs and represent their interests because their economic interest is the general interest. Therefore, turning the state into an instrument that serves other needs, even conquering a relative state autonomy, is itself an object of struggle.

Evo Morales and his government achieved a greater autonomy via a process that some qualify as elite circulation (Espinoza 2015). But then, the economic elites' means of influencing society and the state were used to fence off state interventions and defend their space of action. The economic elites did so through investment decisions, or what Tasha Fairfield (2015) qualifies as "structural power."[3] Structural power is clearly acknowledged by economic elites, who are also conscious that the anticipation of their decisions by state managers can have an effect. In this particular case, the economic elites also acted within the space of civil society, or what Fairfield groups under the concept of "instrumental power." I am therefore arguing against several conceptions of the state: while the instrumental view tends to downplay the structural limitations, I also disagree with structuralist perspectives that undermine the importance of class power within and without the state. In other words, I suggest, with Bob Jessop (2002, 2007) and Simon Clarke (1991), that the state, its autonomy, and the boundaries of its actions are themselves an object of class struggle. This does not mean that the state has no possibility to act upon and within society, but that this very capacity is always relational; that is, it is dependent upon how other social forces are organized and act, accepting or curtailing such capacities.

To support this argument, I will first present a short theoretical discussion inspired by Marxist debates on the nature of the state. I then introduce a brief outline of the recent literature on the history of elite-state interaction in Bolivia since the early twentieth century. This is followed by a discussion of several interviews with leaders of the main business associations in Bolivia about their conception of the state and their relationship with the MAS government. In 2018, I mapped out the most important business associations (chamber of commerce, association of industrial producers, and regional and national federations grouping them) and interviewed numerous spokespersons of these associations along with other businesspeople and academics. They serve as the empirical base for the discussion, and my interpretation of these interviews is followed by a conclusion that ties all the pieces together.

8.2 Marxist Debates on the Nature of the State and on State Capture

This short theoretical prolegomenon does not seek to summarize the history of state theory to this day. It rather aims to contrast various perspectives on the nature of the state and confront them with the experiences of post-neoliberal governments, and in doing so introduce the most appropriate one from which to understand the situation of Bolivia, which has experienced several transitions. In return, this reflection contributes to informing our understanding of the state in general. I start with "state capture" because it has recently circulated in and about Latin America. Francisco Durand (2019a) defines state capture as "forms of excessive (legal) and undue (illegal) influence on public policies that favors private interests" (p. 1).[4] This approach raises an interesting and necessary critique of the power imbalances that allow specific sectors to dominate the realms of civil and political societies and sway the state to their advantage. With respect to elite studies, the concept of state capture follows the lines drawn by Wright Mills (2000), for whom the convergence of corporate, military, and political elites around common views renders democracy meaningless. Nevertheless, the concept of state capture offers an instrumentalist view of the state: as a neutral instrument, the state is sometimes illegitimately seized and used for specific interests. This conception is problematic not so much when it points to the undue influence exerted by economic elites, but because it connotes that this is an exception. The wave of post-neoliberal governments in South America, which by late 2000 governed two-thirds of Latin America (Levitsky and Roberts 2011, 1), has clearly shown instead the limitations encountered by forces who criticize economic elites when they attempt to use the state for other ends than those defined by the economic elites (Chiasson-LeBel and Larrabure 2019). With the current wide consensus regarding the limited achievements of the first wave of post-neoliberal governments, instrumentalist perspectives should tell us why, if the state is a tool, it always pushes in the same general direction.

The concept of state capture nevertheless offers a more subtle understanding than the reductionist Marxist view summarized by the abuse of Marx's quotation from the *Manifesto* in which the "executive of the modern state is but a committee for managing the common affairs of the whole bourgeoisie" (Marx and Engels 1893, 10). The reductionist view assumes that the actual people who control the state are aware of their role as representatives of the bourgeoisie and constantly create an artificial discourse that veils their real goals. That is the kind of conclusion one finds in Raul Zibechi and Decio Machado's *Cambiar el mundo desde arriba* (2017), which suggests that post-neoliberal governments were essentially emerging elites that developed social policies to conceal the unspeakable truth: they forged alliances with traditional elites to modernize capitalism (p. 128). The main issue with this interpretation is fundamentally empirical: over a decade of interviewing members of economic elites in Bolivia, Ecuador, and Venezuela, I found only a small handful of businesspeople expressing some degree of satisfaction with the left wing in power, and those who did were the most reliant on state protection and support for their business. The idea of a conspiracy based on a secret alliance between post-neoliberal governments and traditional elites involves too many people to be convincing. Moreover, were said alliances real, traditional economic elites would not have been so enthusiastic about getting rid of the "left" in power.

There is, nevertheless, a more subtle explanation for the limited achievements of post-neoliberal governments, and it is a structuralist one. Instead of relying on a specific set of omniscient Machiavellian agents, the structuralist explanation fuses capitalist social relations with the state, making the latter a dependent variable of the capitalist structuring of society. From this perspective, the state is merely a gear within capitalist society, and changing the government can only modify the pace of the dynamic but not its direction. This model was eloquently developed by John Holloway (2010), who suggests that the fundamental functions accomplished by the state, that of reproducing the social divisions and identity cleavages that maintain capitalism, cannot be transformed by occupying state power. The issues with the structuralist perspective relate to the limited degree of agency it includes, and the absence of autonomy the state is left with in the context. It can hardly explain the variations Latin American states have experienced in the last few decades. It is tempting to conclude that such variations result from domestic structural differences; but then, what accounts for structural variations, if not the history of local struggles? Though the global economic structure definitely influences the state and its policies, the translation of global economic crises into variegated forms of impacts and reactions by Latin American states means that there is more to it than simply a mechanical transmission of the structure.

Marxist state theories have thus developed the concept of relative autonomy to overcome the impasses of both instrumentalist and deterministic structuralist theories of the state. According to this view, the state is not a neutral instrument, nor merely a tool controlled by the bourgeoisie, nor even entirely determined by the structure. Rather, the state is formally autonomous and therefore has specific capacities, but its autonomy is limited or "relative." The ensuing debate focuses on what curtails this autonomy. Fred Block (1977), inspired by structuralism, argues that those who manage the state are autonomous, but they need a good level of economic activity because it guarantees some support from the population and also finances the state through taxes. Therefore, in capitalist societies, state managers will develop the consciousness of what is good for capital in general and will dispute this vision with all classes in society, including short-sighted capitalists. This structuralist-class perspective reduces the class agency to a minimum, since it is derived from the structure. Indeed, Block titled one of his articles "The Ruling Class Does Not Rule" essentially to show that the reproduction of capitalism happens even without requiring the agency of the capitalist class. In other words, and to use Fairfield's (2015) distinction between structural power (derived from investment decisions and their anticipation by state managers) and instrumental power (the conscious and concrete exercise of political pressures), there is no need for capitalists to make use of instrumental power, which Block qualifies as a subsidiary, because state managers will reproduce capitalism in order to reproduce the state and maintain themselves within it. The structural dynamic of the sum of investment decisions will be sufficient to push state managers to maintain the general capitalist orientation of society. The relative autonomy comes from workers who pressure the state to maintain the economy sufficiently embedded and to ensure just enough happiness to prevent a revolution. It is the balance between the consciousness of state managers, the pressure of the working class, and the structural dynamic of capitalism that provides the general path of reproduction for a capitalist state. Here, economic elites do not need to partake in politics, and there is no need for instrumental power, because their investment is already sufficient as a political message.

The main issue with this explanation is its exclusion, or reduction as *a subsidiary* factor, of the agency of capitalist classes and its actual ruling out of the starting points that we identified: what if there is a somewhat organized and conscious capitalist class that captures the state? What if the combination of structural and instrumental powers curtails the capacity of state managers to establish a tax system that would consolidate the state apparatus? That is the kind of scenario Tasha Fairfield (2015) identifies, especially for Chile and Bolivia: the power of economic elites has historically curtailed the autonomy of the state to the point of questioning its existence. In order to integrate the concerns outlined above, I suggest a class-relational perspective: it is the balance of forces in society that determines what the state is and what it can do, as well as its boundaries and specificities:

> *the state's structural powers or capacities, their structural and strategic biases, and their realizations do not depend solely on the nature of the state as a juridico-political apparatus [...] They also depend on diverse capacities-liabilities and forces that lie beyond it.*
>
> (Jessop 2007, 6)

From this perspective, it is the struggles between agents that determine what the state is and what it can do, i.e., its autonomy. The structural power derived from the capitalists' position within the productive structure is obviously tremendous. Other agents, including state managers and workers, contribute to it when they organize their actions for the well-being of capitalism as a whole or that of a specific industry – when, for instance, employees ask the state to protect their employment in a certain industry. Nevertheless, the instrumental power of agents is also tremendously important, and not just "subsidiary"; it defines the evolution and transformation of the main trends at the local level. However, no single class determines the results; a relational perspective suggests that the balance of their respective power accounts for the results, including the construction of institutions to resolve their disputes.

From this perspective, the state is itself the product of class struggles, just like its autonomy. What I suggest is that we cannot start from the liberal premise of a neutral or autonomous state. Autonomy is itself the object of a class struggle, relative to it, and the structural force of capitalism is insufficient to explain the degree of autonomy. Understanding this degree requires an active investigation into class organizations, their strategies, and their capacities, which are tied to the economic activity that economic elites control. To make sense, this relative autonomy must be studied from a relational perspective in which the struggles of some sectors are placed in the context of the actions of other sectors of society.

8.3 Historical Background on the Bolivian and Cruceña Economic Elites

Lorgio Orellana Aillón (2016) documents the historical elite-state relationship in Bolivia. Combining interviews with high-positioned state actors who were removed from office upon the election of Evo Morales with a critical interpretation of Bolivian literature and political theorists, Orellana Aillón eloquently narrates the sequence of construction, displacement, and resurgence of a *power elite* (Wright Mills, 2000): a racial- and economic-based "caste," self-styled as the "decent people" (*gente decente*), that dominated economic and political power for most of the twentieth century, with the exception of the 1952 revolution. Initially composed of families of land and mine owners – who strongly identify with their European descent to differentiate themselves from the Indigenous majority – they combined their wealth with their privileged access to higher education to forge an oligarchy still identifiable today by their family names. Until very recently, this oligarchy not only controlled the leading businesses in the country but also staffed many of the higher state positions. Xenophiles who admire whatever comes from Europe or North America, they built up a sense of entitlement to control the state that persisted even through the 1952 revolution.

Where Felipe Burbano de Lara's seminal work (2014, 69) maintains that the 1952 revolution ended the oligarchic state, Orellana Aillón (2016, Chapter 2) shows the continuities. He convincingly argues that even though the revolution did displace this oligarchy from state power, the middle-class intellectuals who led the transformation failed to produce the cultural change that would have delegitimized oligarchic rule.[5] This cultural feature, along with the reconstitution of the army with US support[6] and the economic difficulties that the revolution encountered in the late 1950s, incentivized a turn toward international institutions for assistance, and a pro-business space that the heirs of the oligarchy could occupy upon their return to the country after the counter-revolutionary coup of 1964 was reinstated.

Orellana Aillón identifies a regional shift in the composition of the elites after the counter-revolution that he nevertheless understates to underline the continuity. The oligarchy that controlled the state was initially based in the Andes (Cochabamba, La Paz) and directed by medium silver and tin mine owners who had diversified their activity through trade and finance. Its economic profile started to change with both the revolution and Hugo Banzer Suárez's dictatorship (1971–1978). Despite their significant differences, both the revolution and the Banzer regime promoted the development of an agro-export sector in Bolivia's Eastern lowlands. The economic elites from Santa Cruz, geographically remote from the center of state power established in La Paz at the turn of the twentieth century, had already developed a strong regional identity. Their province was at the margins of the silver and tin booms of the late nineteenth and early twentieth centuries and experienced an economic surge during the same period thanks to a completely different activity: forest extraction of rubber tree sap (Espinoza 2015, 262–267). With inefficient communication channels to the main axis of accumulation in the Andes, the lowland elites developed a strong regional identity with links to international markets through alternative routes crossing Paraguay and Brazil. Although the region's economy was relatively weak in the first half of the twentieth century, it developed a set of regional organizations that defended the local interests (committees, Orientalist party) against the dominance of La Paz (Burbano de Lara 2014, 55–60). In the 1930s, this regional identity was strong enough to win a greater share of the oil rent for the region (11% of raw production) than had ever been the case with other minerals (Burbano de Lara 2014, 67–69). Lowland regional elites were showing their capacity to limit the central state autonomy to preserve more power locally.

The region experienced its most important economic surge during the second half of the twentieth century. In addition to hydrocarbons, several factors contributed to the economic surge of the region: support for the colonization of the Eastern lowlands in response to the Chaco War (1932–1935), the capacity of local elites to concentrate plots of lands distributed by the 1952 revolution to weakly organized peasants, and state support for the modernization of agriculture. The region's share in the country's GDP grew from 2.6% in 1952 to 9.1% in 1964, 16.3% in 1971, and 19.2% in 1977 (Burbano de Lara 2014, 97). While some members of the regional elites were recent European migrants attracted by the availability of large land estates, others were descendants of long-established Spanish families, and the economic boom also attracted investors from other parts of the country (Prado Salmón et al. 2007, 171–175). The Banzer dictatorship crowned this surging economic elite by linking it to the state's power. Proudly from Santa Cruz himself (Burbano de Lara, 2014, 96), Banzer found support in the agribusiness elites of his home region and helped them in return by subsidizing cotton production and other agro-export products, thus reinforcing the economic capacity of large landowners (Hylton and Thomson 2007, 87–88). He managed to integrate this emerging elite with the older oligarchy from the highlands within his government: almost half of his first cabinet was composed of people from Santa Cruz (Burbano de Lara, 2014, 93), while he named to key state offices several foreign-trained sons of returning members of the previous oligarchy who had been exiled by the 1952 revolution (Orellana Aillón 2016, Chapter II.2.3).

Even though Banzer was successful in uniting the economic elites of the Eastern lowlands and the Altiplano behind his dictatorship, regionalist feelings remained strong in Santa Cruz, sustained by a set of local institutions feeding the regional identity. Not only were the chambers of commerce, industry, and agriculture of the Eastern lowlands specifically strong and united through their own regional organizational infrastructure, but they had also supported the Pro Santa Cruz Civic Committee (CCPSC) since 1950. Built on over half a century of regionalist demands, from federalism to decentralization of power and a fairer economic integration, the committee developed a strong regionalist discourse defending the imaginary of *cruceñidad*: a specific ethnocultural identity based on the happy mixing of races, which had given birth, in its most radical interpretation, to the idea of a specific national identity: the *Camba* nation (Argirakis 2011). This identity, like most, makes sense when contrasted with an alterity, in this case, the *Colla* nation, described as the mostly Indigenous people who live in the mountain range. According to Argirakis (2011), Santa Cruz's regional identity has historically been successful in subsuming other conflicts, notably the class tension that accompanied the fast economic growth of the region. This success justified the economic elites' conduction of the region by turning their economic achievements into a tenet of the regional identity.

With the democratic transition in the 1980s and the continued growth of the lowland economy, presidents tended to include an important share of representatives from Santa Cruz in their governments. Carlos Mesa Gisbert, the vice president who became president after the resignation of Gonzalo Sánchez de Lozada in 2003, asserts, after listing all the ministers from Santa Cruz since 1982, that "[…] it is an indisputable fact that cruceña elites controlled the Bolivian economy from the central state during the whole democratic period until [his] arrival to government in 2003" (Mesa Gisbert 2018, 213). Although this supports Orellana Aillon's depiction of the unity of the country's economic elite, Santa Cruz's regional identity remained sufficiently strong that, despite its influence on the central state, economic elites from the region still convey this narrative of distance from political power. A current member of these elites would ask in this sense:

> *How many presidents were cruceños in the history of Bolivia? Three, two were assassinated and Banzer who was a dictator. After that, when have we ourselves been part of government? When?*
>
> (Bo-CA2)[7]

Among the interviewees, one of the most adamant advocates of regional identity in the business field similarly said:

> *Compared to the other departments, Santa Cruz has a unique character, and it's not only cultural, because we are culturally very distinct, but it's also in terms of its social and business structures. In Santa Cruz, we value institutions because we've always been far from the political power and from state's perks. Santa Cruz is self-made and developed by itself with its own institutions in the almost total absence of the state. Civic, professional and business institutions, were created and they all agree to generate the conditions and promote Santa Cruz's development. There is a Cruceña institutional logic that is different from the paceña institutional logic, which is much more related to public authority. Cruceña business institutions stand by themselves.*
>
> (BO-CF1)

This situation is at the core of our concern. Since the 1970s, the economic elites of Santa Cruz grew into Bolivia's dominant capitalist faction and became increasingly involved in state power, but simultaneously sustained a regional identity discourse that allowed them to have their cake and eat it too: they had an important influence on state policies and could mobilize the regional identity as a discursive shield when things were not happening as they desired.

8.4 The Election of Morales and Santa Cruz Elites' Reaction

During the two decades preceding Evo Morales' victory, the strong influence of the lowland fraction of the elites over the state is instructive about the relationship of society and state. Only very strong popular movements (Webber 2009), such as the Water War and the two Gas Wars (Webber 2009), would force the government to backtrack on the elites' neoliberal program. Even when the central government promoted a neoliberal program that corresponded to the one embraced by Santa Cruz's economic elites, they were simultaneously buttressing the regional identity discourse as a response to the popular movements in the Altiplano that opposed it. When the highlands social movement issued the 2003 October Agenda demanding a referendum to support the nationalization of hydrocarbons and a constituent assembly (Burbano de Lara 2014, 317), elites in Santa Cruz promoted their own agenda through the Pro Santa Cruz Civic Committee (CCPSC). The CCPSC's first memorandum threatened to separate the region from the country if the autonomy of the departments and the cultural specificity of Santa Cruz were not recognized. Its leader, Rúben Costas, was flanked by the leader of one of the most powerful business associations in the region, the Chamber of Agriculture of the Orient (CAO), when he made this position public in 2003, before large crowds that demonstrated the CCPSC's strong mobilization capacity (Burbano de Lara, 2014, 322). Two weeks later, the CCPSC's strength was also displayed when some of its supporters engaged in street fights against peasant-Indigenous protesters who demanded Sánchez de Lozada's resignation. The economic elites defended the regional identity against the highlands social movements opposing neoliberalism. Simultaneously the umbrella organization for business interests from the region, the *Federación de empresarios privados de Santa Cruz* (FEPSC), withdrew from the confederation encompassing business interest associations throughout the country, the Confederation of Private Entrepreneurs of Bolivia (CEPB). Although a representative of one of the business associations from Santa Cruz downplayed the importance of this rupture (Interview BO-FE1), it demonstrates that the strength of the regional identity movement at the time should not be underestimated. It is a sign that Santa Cruz economic elites were displeased with their peers from the highlands for being too soft in front of anti-neoliberal protests.

The election of Evo Morales and a majority of MAS members in the National Assembly in 2005 represented the end of this win-win situation for Santa Cruz: they still had a strong regional identity to back them up, but they had lost their privileged access to state power. Jeffery Webber (2011) argues that the MAS was then shifting from an Indigenous-revolutionary agenda to a white-mestizo reformist attitude (2011), but it was still far from being the kind of voice the economic elites wanted to hear, and the tension kept growing: while the MAS summoned the assembly to inscribe its post-neoliberal and pluri-cultural aspirations in the constitution, Santa Cruz economic elites were promoting regional autonomy through a referendum to capitalize their identity achievements into useful political leverage over both local and national institutions.

This confrontation led to a *catastrophic stalemate* (García Linera 2008): a social and institutional confrontation between two groups leading to a crisis of the state without any group succeeding in making their solution the hegemonic one. The MAS supporters could not have the constitution adopted without support from some members of the opposing elites, even though the economic project of the elites of Santa Cruz had been widely rejected in the previous years, and they mostly offered a regionally centered political project. Tensions were causing intense regional protests and fueling racial hatred against Indigenous people that went so far as to cause the death of several Indigenous people in a "massacre" driven by racial, ethnic, social, and cultural motives (Comisión para el esclarecimiento de los hechos de Pando 2008).

The solution to the stalemate was not simple. The MAS conceded more powers to the regions in the new constitution project, but this concession did not seem enough. More importantly for the purpose of this article, a targeted repression spread an intense fear among the most right-wing members of the economic elites. Individuals suspected of planning the assassination of the president were killed in 2009 during a police "counterterrorist" intervention known as the *Caso Rozsa*, while others were jailed under accusations of having funded the terrorist cells (Prado Araúz 2018; Valverde Bravo 2012). Given the family ties between the accused funders of the plot and those specific representatives of the right-wing economic elites who most supported the identity discourse, these events threw a chill on the economic elites' overt support of identity discourse and the Pro Santa Cruz Civic Committee (CCPSC). Some even went into exile by fear of repression (Bo-CC1). Such intervention placed a wedge between the most right-wing faction of the economic elites, who were very attached to the regional identity discourse, and the ones who prioritized their business interests. As the leadership of several business associations changed, the government's attitude also changed, and a more fluid relationship between the MAS government and the Cruceña elites was slowly established. The following section analyzes this shift with a thorough interpretation of interviews with representatives of the economic elites that were conducted in late 2018.

8.5 Adaptation: Modernization from the Elites' Point of View

The following section offers an interpretation of a series of 19 interviews conducted with spokespersons of business associations and other entrepreneurial think tanks in Bolivia in late 2018.[8] The excerpts quoted here are drawn from interviews with members of the elites from Santa Cruz, since they were at the core of the change in class attitude that transformed the catastrophic stalemate into a peaceful coexistence, at least until the coup of October 2019. In analyzing the interviews, I identified four themes around which concerns of the elites congealed despite their variations with respect to their relationship to the state and the regional identity.

8.5.1 The Primacy of Cruceñidad: The Regional Identity

To understand the evolution of the relationship between the state and the *Cruceña* economic elites, one must appreciate the strength of the regionalist feeling that cuts across business sectors. Prior to the class unity with economic elites from other regions, and despite tensions between businesses – such as that surrounding prices between primary producers and the industries they supply – their unity as a regional class facing the central state is clearly expressed. For instance, one former leader of an agricultural chamber and one of the most acceptant of maintaining good relationships with the MAS government said:

> *We've always been hand in hand, always when there is a demand that one of us needs or that we see convenient to implement for the whole country [...] we work together, we present ideas together, we make the efforts as a group in the relationship with the government so that norms, decrees and laws are adopted [...] even if obviously, sometimes our interests are opposed.*
>
> (Bo-CA2)

What is striking about this quotation is that the interviewee was clearly talking about the other business associations from the region, not elsewhere in the country. The unity and integration at the regional level reinforce the elites' consciousness of their structural power and help them build apparatuses of instrumental power. For instance, in 1986, during a period of hyperinflation, they founded the Bolivian Institute of Foreign Trade (IBCE), a think tank supported by the main regional business associations, but with sufficient autonomy to appear as a credible voice representing business interests in general, although its board of directors is entirely controlled by business associations from Santa Cruz.

The change in the relationship with the state governed by the MAS pushed this alliance to focus on entrepreneurial-business identity rather than the more regionalist-ethnic trend that, nevertheless, remains very strong in the region:

> *The predominant discourse is that we are regionalist, but the reality is that Santa Cruz is the department that without a doubt receives the most diverse Bolivian migration. There are Bolivians of higher classes who have migrated from various departments to produce here because the money is here.*
>
> (Bo-CA2)

This quotation highlights the business mindset as a marker of identity for the region that is gaining importance.

8.5.2 Consciousness of Structural Power

Economic elites in Santa Cruz share a great awareness of their structural power, that is, the power they derive from their position in the capitalist structure as those who make investment decisions. They conceive of the regional economy as the driving force of the whole country, and this regional drive comes from the private initiative rather than from state policies, public investments, or hydrocarbon reserves. Therefore, they consider it a question of time before the government agrees to the rightfulness of their positions:

> *The [Santa Cruz Department] raises more taxes, it is the department that brings the most to the GDP, that generates 26% of jobs in the country, so the government says: "We cannot always be [opposing them]."*
>
> (Bo-CA1)

In many instances, their discourse underlines their awareness that the tensions with the government affected private investment and forced the government to adjust:

> *It is true that at the beginning, there was no investment because of fear. Why? Because there was this discourse that [the MAS government] would take everything away, we would be stolen and stripped of our lands.*
>
> (Bo-CA2)

According to the interviewees, the government could survive this lack of private investment because of the oil bonanza, and by piling up international reserves to resist markets' ups and downs. However, this way of dealing with structural forces is not eternal, and once it was confronted with the economic reality of changing hydrocarbon prices, the government had to adapt its politics to support the economic elites' demands. The protracted economic crisis would explain why transgenic crops and biofuel production, which the economic elites had long demanded but which were initially rejected by the MAS government, were eventually accepted. This acceptance should not, though, be seen as a true alliance:

> *The government is tight income-wise. It has to be creative, it's as simple as that, because the extractive era is already…[…] That's why it opened-up to biofuels, because there were no options… So the discourse ends when the economy squeezes you.*
>
> (Bo-CA1)

> *In other words, there is not a firm conviction that the government is in favour of the business sector, it is only a necessity because the economy requires that it be so, and you know that there is nothing blunter than reality.*
>
> (Bo-CF1)

8.5.3 The Narrative Regarding the Change in Attitude

Structural power plays an important role in explaining the rapprochement between economic elites and the state, but it is not sufficient. A change in attitude from both sides was necessary, and the discourse explaining this change differed from one business spokesperson to another. The interviews sought to understand whether the elites thought that it was the state that had changed, the economic elites, or a bit of both. Most would say it was a bit of both, but the emphasis varied greatly. Those who were most opposed to the government and most attached to the Cruceña identity said the government forced economic elites to behave differently:

> *There was obviously a transition, a change of conduct, of attitude on both sides. Business leaders were harassed, intimidated by the political power. The political power took the decision to destroy the business leadership, the civic leadership [referring to the CCPSC], and they did it. You certainly know about how he did it, especially with the terrorism case [Rozsa case] […]. Thereafter came a change in the leadership, mostly on the business side: business leaders were renewed around 2010.*
>
> (Bo-CF1)

Nevertheless, some business leaders proudly asserted that an important change was made by economic elites themselves, even naming the leaders who conducted the shift:

> *Together with a group of people who work for business associations, we drove and managed this change of attitude.*
>
> (Bo-FE1)[9]

> *I obviously think that it is a job we did by ourselves, but the government took part in it. It was a courtship that lasted for a long time, an infatuation that took a long time to become concrete because there was initially a total lack of trust. There were tensions because we did not think that talks were sincere, but with time, we worked on it and noticed results.*
>
> (Bo-CA2)

These contrasting accounts show how the change came from a complex conjuncture involving actors from all sides. Structural pressure likely influenced the government, but the latter was also instrumental in severing some of the ties between the economic elites and the institutions supporting the regional identity discourse in Santa Cruz. Some resisted this evolution, which was nevertheless seized by other business leaders who permitted the flourishing of the more modern approach to the economic elites' political role, whereby their instrumental power prioritized the well-being of capital over other political interests.

8.5.4 The Changing Relationship to the Regional Identity Narrative

Though business elites are still very much attached to the regional identity, the new business leadership collapses this cultural difference into a sectoral difference: the dominance of certain economic sectors within Santa Cruz, such as large agriculture, forestry, or hydrocarbons, explains the tensions with other regions (Bo-CA1 and Bo-FE1). The weakening of the historically strong ties between the CCPSC, which promotes regional identity, and the business elites contributed to the acceptance of a modern relationship in which a formally autonomous state will nevertheless cave in to structural economic necessities when proper use of instrumental power by a united capitalist class equates the general interest with their own. One leader of a chamber that publicly supported the CCPSC explained this phenomenon as follows:

> *There were obviously troubles with some people, like the Civic Committee that was opposed to Evo Morales coming [to the regional fair], but these are things you need to accept because the President is the President. He was elected by Bolivians, and he sadly is the President even if he is not from your party.*
>
> (Bo-CA2)

This tension between business spokespersons and regional identity apparatus shows the progressive non-linear evolution of the elites–state relationship. Those who accepted the modernization of the relationship trust their structural power and understand that alliances with business elites from the highlands will make them all stronger. Those who feel the most deprived of state representation maintain a more confrontational attitude, and while they see the importance of instrumental power, they still tend to reject alliances with economic elites from La Paz.

However, even those who accept the autonomy of the state still lament the lack of direct representation of people from Santa Cruz in the MAS government and particularly of the Cruceña economic elite:

> *What does La Paz produce? Nothing! The headquarters of the state are there, and those people make presidents and ministers, but we don't even have a minister in this government. Santa Cruz does not have one. In the next elections, we will be the home of 50% of the voters. Do you think it is right that there be no leader from Santa Cruz? Fifty percent of the voters of the country? Can you imagine? It can't be! Why? Why are they not giving us space?*
>
> (Bo-CA2)

8.5.5 The Resulting Relationship to Instrumental Power

As discussed above, the Bolivian state has historically been captured by economic elites. In spite of what contemporary *Cruceña* elites argue, there were channels to relay the economic elites' demands directly to the executive. That could explain why apparatuses of instrumental power had less salient roles than direct representation. Instrumental power technologies acted mostly as safety valves or as places to mobilize the economic elites behind a unified program, and one that could place other political concerns, such as *Cruceña* identity, ahead of business ones. The paradox of the recovery of state autonomy seems to be that, once facing the structural powers of economic elites, the MAS' main response was actually to cede instrumental power by opening channels of negotiations where economic elites could directly access the political society. Offering open dialogue about economic issues between the highest state officials and chambers' spokespersons was the way for the MAS government to curtail their actions in the space of civil society and limit their ties with regional identity organizations. Having some avenues to dialogue with state officials would diminish their need for aggressive public interventions, as some of the interviewees have noted:

> *We, as the federation of entrepreneurs, we made the decision not to communicate messages to the state through the media. It is a decision that has been made. If I have a problem with you, I am going to talk to you and I will tell you: "I disagree with the colour of your shirt." But I will not summon a press conference to publicly say that your shirt is the ugliest in the world. This is trust building because you do not maintain a double discourse.*
>
> (Bo-FE1)

> *This has always been my politics: never in my term as a leader, never in my years as a president of the XXX [in the agricultural sector] has there been a strike [by agricultural entrepreneurs], and normally, under previous management, there have been blockades, marches, but I always tried instead to sit down at the table, 50 times, 100 times if necessary, but in the end, having a position and a dialogue where the person, the government, independently of how hard it is, understands that he's causing harm [...]. With time, I have demonstrated through facts, and through the laws that we developed, and there were 36 under my rule if you count laws, decrees, resolutions and norms, that benefitted my sector and the whole country. So I think that it has been demonstrated that it works and obviously, until now, I maintain a very cordial relationship with the government, and with the governorship controlled by the opposition.*
>
> (Bo-CA2)

The confidence in their structural power meant that they could choose the best instrumental means at their disposal. They were aware of the range of their strategies: as long as the dialogue works, they have no reason to risk damaging it by intervening in the media or going on strike. The use of the media is nevertheless possible if the former strategy does not yield the expected results. However, the double play on regional identity and economic factors needed to be shifted to a more modern approach to the relationship in which economic interests could prevail.

This relationship appears to have contributed to containing the development of other tools of instrumental power much in use in other countries, such as the extensive use of corporate social responsibility (Chiasson-LeBel 2019a, 2019b) or territorial planning (Leiva Letelier 2019, 2022), that are, admittedly, little developed in Bolivia. Instead, through this strategy, some business leaders have acquired privileged contact with the president, even opening doors for direct representation within the state:

> *This earned me different considerations from the president [Morales], who sees me with a different face, no as an enemy, not as somebody who uses the institution to do politics. More so: he offered me twice to be part of his government, but I am not a politician, I don't like politics [...]. Moreover, I have a meeting tomorrow with the president for a tax-related question regarding slaughterhouses. I don't have any position anymore, I am not an elected official of the association anymore, I am a nobody, but the president called me because he believes in mi.*
>
> (Bo-CA2)

8.6 Interpretation and Conclusions

From this brief interpretation, one can notice a few important things to support the theoretical position we presented regarding the state. More than a mere structural determination, a relational-class perspective is important to understand how things have evolved during the MAS government prior to the 2019 coup. First, it undermines the structuralist perspective because the agency of the capitalist class was initially strongly marked by the identity struggle in Santa Cruz. The regional identity position was so important in defining the class identity of elites in the region that it blocked possible dialogues for several years. This regional identity was also successful at aligning popular classes who tended to be less belligerent than their peers from the Altiplano and were more likely to partake in the *cruceñidad.*

The class position of economic elites initially hindered the economy through its structural consequences, and it superseded their own economic interests for several years. After the government/state push to break the instrumental power tied to regional identity, changes in attitude from both the government and the economic elites themselves resulted in greater opportunities for a dialogue, which also meant a greater correspondence between the economic interests of the capitalists and their actual priorities. The importance of the relational-class agency is also exemplified by the elites changing their attitudes for the dialogue to be possible and for this dialogue to result in a policy change. While the economic elites were right in asserting the importance of their structural power, had they decided to double down on the regional identity discourse they could have perpetuated a catastrophic stalemate.

Moreover, the rapprochement happening several years prior to the policy change by the MAS, when it accepted biofuel production, is a good signal of the importance of the class agency in actually reproducing the structure. This long confidence-building process created the possibility for the government to trust that an adjustment of its policies would really produce the expected structural effects, such as private investment, job creation, and economic growth, and eventually compensate for the political cost of abandoning its party line. By contrast, such confidence was never established in Venezuela, where the leader of the main business federation headed a coup attempt in 2002, and the government's trust in private investment was never restored.

This analysis also reveals the limitations of the concept of state capture. State capture supposes that the state is primarily neutral but becomes biased when economic elites seize an undue influence on political processes. First, the autonomy of the state should not be assumed but studied as an empirical question. In the case discussed here, the autonomy, defined as a state not essentially controlled by the economic elite, had to be won via intense protests that Webber (2011) qualifies as a revolutionary period. Second, the revelations of the economic elites tend to show a more complex relationship: even without capture, it appears that the state autonomy can be curtailed when economic elites either block its political process, as in Bolivia during the catastrophic stalemate, or combine their structural and instrumental powers. Therefore, although the concept of state capture alerts us to the potential danger ensuing from economic elites' capacity to align state institutions toward private ends, it does not account for the complexity of the potential pressures economic elites can exert on the state in a capitalist society, where a combination of structural and instrumental power is sufficient to produce such private goals even without capture. Third, the revelation that a former chamber leader from Santa Cruz was invited to become part of the Morales' government shows that elites are not necessarily the main active agents of a capture: their astute play within a modernized relationship pushes governments to integrate economic elites as a way to deal with their structural and instrumental power.

The interviews also demonstrate the complexity of the construction of state autonomy. Economic elites do not expect the state to be neutral: the state must serve their interests because they are equated with economic growth, and growth is the general interest. Elites have tools to publicly defend this chain of equivalence in the public discourse, notably through think tanks and other means of instrumental power. Therefore, the contradiction of building state autonomy in a capitalist society with strong regional elites in a dependent economy such as that of Bolivia is that when state autonomy is used for purposes other than those desired by the elites, the consequences can be harsh on the economic structure since it quickly erodes business confidence, or may nourish a separatist movement.

Nevertheless, the achievements of the MAS controlling the state and placing a wedge between the far-right identity discourse and the more liberal economic elites in Santa Cruz should not be minimized. This could, in the long run, help to undermine the structural support for an identity discourse in the region that fuels racist hatred, but it comes at the cost of leaving more room to certain elites' interests within the state.

Finally, the findings of this article corroborate my earlier work on Ecuador and Venezuela (Chiasson-LeBel 2016), in which the issue with the first wave of the pink tide in South America is related to the over-confidence left-leaning governments had in the instrumental autonomy of the state. Keeping the economic elites unchecked has been revealed to be a concern in all cases. Seeing how the next wave deals with economic elites should serve as inspiration for future research.

Notes

1 Special thanks to Guillermo P. Delgado for comments on an earlier version.
2 In this chapter I use the word elite according to the sociological tradition, to mean the people who are dominant in their sphere of activity. Therefore, economic elites, mostly used in the plural form, are the ones who dominate the economy. In a capitalist society, economic elites consist mainly of capitalists, those who own the means of production, but also include spokespeople of business associations who publicly voice their interests. The term capitalists also refer to the capitalist class, the organized expression of economic elites conscious of their common interest. Said class is often divided into fractions; thus, there can be capitalist classes, and the division is not necessarily strictly according to economic activity (agriculture, industry, commerce, etc.). There can be regional and racial divisions within the capitalist class between these fractions.
3 Tasha Fairfield identifies Block (1977) and Lindblom (1977) as the creators of the concept.
4 All translations of interviews and texts originally written in Spanish are mine.
5 Like the belief in a specific ruling entitlement for those possessing a foreign higher education diploma, this explains why, even in the early 2000s, presidents would lie about their academic success to legitimize their rule.
6 I owe this argument to Guillermo P. Delgado.
7 The alphanumeric codes following quotations refer to interviews and are meant to preserve the confidentiality of the participants. See the list of participant organizations and interviewees in Annex for details.

8 The interviews were conducted as part of a SSHRC-funded post-doctoral research project that compared economic elites' reactions to the left in power in Ecuador and Bolivia. Semi-structured interviews lasted about 60 minutes and were based around a series of questions about their interpretation of the political conjuncture of the last 15 years and their relationship to the current state and government. Transcribed interviews were entered into a computer-assisted qualitative data analysis software, then codified and recodified to identify shared meanings. Results regarding Ecuador were published elsewhere (Chiasson-LeBel 2019a, 2019b, 2020).
9 To preserve the confidentiality of the participants and other people, it seemed inappropriate to reproduce here the list of names the interviewee offered.

References

Argirakis, Helena. 2011. "El Comité Cívico Pro Santa Cruz como aparato ideológico de la élite cruceña." *Revista Mojón* 21 1 (1). http://mojon21.blogspot.com/2011/04/el-comite-civico-pro-santa-cruz-como.html (March 20, 2023).

Block, Fred. 1977. "The ruling class does not rule: Notes on the Marxist theory of the state." *Socialist Revolution* 33, 6–28.

Burbano de Lara, Felipe. 2014. *La revuelta de las periferias: Movimientos regionales y autonomías políticas en Bolivia y Ecuador*. Quito: Flacso.

Cañete Alonso, Rosa. 2018. *El gobierno de unos pocos. Democracias capturadas: Mecanismos de captura de la política fiscal por parte de las élites y su impacto en la desigualdad en América Latina y el Caribe (1990–2017)*. Lima: Oxfam; Clacso. https://d1tn3vj7xz9fdh.cloudfront.net/s3fs-public/file_attachments/democracias_capturadas_full_es.pdf (March 20, 2023).

Castellani, Ana. 2018. Lobbies y puertas giratorias: Los riesgos de la captura de la decisión pública. *Nueva sociedad* 276, 48–61.

Chiasson-LeBel, Thomas. 2016. "Neo-Extractivism in Venezuela and Ecuador: A weapon of class conflict." *The Extractive Industries and Society* 3 (4), 888–901.

———. 2019a. Conglomérats nationaux et espace public: Stratégies de politisation de l'activité économique sous un gouvernement de gauche en Équateur. In Julián Durazo Herrman, *Les espaces publics, la démocratie et les gauches en Amérique latine* (pp. 21–47). Québec: Presse de l'Université Laval.

———. 2019b. "Neoliberalism in Ecuador after Correa: A surprise turn or according to economic elites' plan?" *European Review of Latin American and Caribbean Studies*, 108, 153–174.

———. 2020. Tres periodos de relaciones entre las élites y el Estado: Una comparación entre los casos de Venezuela y Ecuador. In Liisa North, Blance Rubio, Alberto Acosta, and Carlos Pástor, *Concentración económica y poder político en América Latina* (pp. 93–136). Buenos Aires, México. Quito: CLACSO. Friedrich-Ebert-Stiftung. FES Transformación. Universidad Andina Simón Bolívar.

Chiasson-LeBel, Thomas, and Manuel Larrabure. 2019. "Latin America's changing balance of class forces: An introduction." *European Review of Latin American and Caribbean Studies* 108, 87–107.

Clarke, Simon, Ed. 1991. *The state debate*. London: Palgrave Macmillan.

Comisión para el esclarecimiento de los hechos de Pando. 2008. *Informe de la comisión de UNASUR sobre los sucesos de Pando. Hacia una alba de justicia para Bolivia*. Informe de UNASUR sobre Pando. Quito: UNASUR.

Dahl, Robert A. 1971. *Polyarchy: Participation and opposition*. New Haven: Yale University Press.

Dryzek, John, and Patrick Dunleavy. 2009. *Theories of the democratic state*. London: Palgrave Macmillan.

Durand, Francisco. 2016. *Cuando el poder extractivo captura el Estado. Lobbies, puertas giratorias y paquetazo ambiental en Perú*. Lima: Oxfam.

———. 2019a. "La captura corporativa del Estado en América Latina." *trAndeS Working Paper Series*. Berlin: Lateinamerika-Institut (LAI); Freie Universität.

———. 2019b. *La captura del Estado en América Latina: Reflexiones teóricas*. Lima: Fondo Editorial; Pontificia Universidad Católica del Perú.

Espinoza, Fran. 2015. *Bolivia: La circulación de sus élites (2006–2014)*. Santa Cruz: El País.

Fairfield, Tasha. 2015. *Private wealth and public revenue: Business power and tax politics in Latin America*. Cambridge: Cambridge University Press.

García Linera, Álvaro. 2008. "Empate catastrófico y punto de bifurcación." *Crítica y emancipación: Revista latinoamericana de Ciencias Sociales* 1 (1), 25–33.

Holloway, John. 2010. *Change the world without taking power: The meaning of revolution today*. London: Pluto Press.

Hylton, Forrest, and Sinclair Thomson. 2007. *Revolutionary horizons: Past and present in Bolivian politics*. London; New York: Verso.

Jessop, Bob. 2002. *The future of the capitalist state*. Cambridge: Polity Press.

———. 2007. *State power: A strategic-relational approach*. Cambridge: Polity Press.

Leiva Letelier, Fernando I. 2019. "Economic elites and new strategies for expanding extractivism in Chile." *European Review of Latin American and Caribbean Studies* 108, 131–152.

———. 2022. *Left hand of capital: Neoliberalism and the left in Chile*. New York: SUNY Press.

Levitsky, Steven, and Kenneth M. Roberts, Eds. 2011. *The resurgence of the Latin American left*. Baltimore: Johns Hopkins University Press.

Lindblom, Charles E. 1977. *Politics and Markets: The World's Political Economic Systems*. New York: Basic Books.

Marx, Karl, and Friedrich Engels. 1893. *Le manifeste du parti communiste*. http://classiques.uqac.ca/classiques/Engels_Marx/manifeste_communiste/manifeste_communiste.html (March 20, 2023).

Mesa Gisbert, Carlos. D. 2018. *Presidencia sitiada: Memorias de mi gobierno*. La Paz: Fundación Comunidad; Plural Editores.

Nercesian, Ines. 2020. *Presidentes empresarios y Estados capturados*. Buenos Aires: Teseo.

Orellana Aillón, Lorgio. 2016. *Resurgimiento y caída de la gente decente: Un sendero en la formación de una clase-etnia dominante en Bolivia (1940–2003)*. La Paz: Muela del Diablo.

Prado Araúz, Gary. 2018. *El indebido proceso: Análisis jurídicio y político de investigación preliminar del 'caso terrorismo'*. Santa Cruz, Bolivia: GP Producciones.

Prado Salmón, Fernando, Susana Seleme Antelo, and Claudia Peña Claros. 2007. *Poder y elites en Santa Cruz: Tres visiones sobre un mismo tema*. Santa Cruz: CEDURE.

Tapia Mealla, Luis. 2022. *The production of local knowledge: History and politics in the work of René Zavaleta Mercado*, edited by Freeland, Anne, and Sinclair Thomson, (p. 465). London: Seagull Books.

Valverde Bravo, Carlos. F. 2012. *¡Maten a Rozsa!: El rompecabezas de una conspiración*. Santa Cruz: El País.

Webber, Jeffery R. 2009. *Red October: Left-Indigenous struggle in Bolivia, 2000–2005.* Toronto: University of Toronto. http://ezproxy.library.yorku.ca/login?url=http://search.proquest.com/docview/816335013?accountid=15182 (March 21, 2023).

———. 2011. *From rebellion to reform in Bolivia: Class struggle, Indigenous liberation and the politics of Evo Morales.* New York: Haymarket Books.

Wright Mills, C. 2000. *The power elite.* Oxford: Oxford University Press.

Zibechi, Raúl, and Decio Machado. 2017. *Cambiar el mundo desde arriba: Los límites del progresismo.* Bogotá: Huaponi Ediciones.

Annex

Table A8.1 List of Participant Organizations and Interviewees

Name of the organization	*Type*	*Region*	*Interviewees*
Confederación de Empresarios Privados de Bolívia (CEPB)	Confederation of business associations – whole country		1
Cámara Nacional de Industrias (CNI)	Confederation of business associations – whole country		1
Cámara Nacional de Exportadores de Bolivia (CANEB)	Confederation of business associations – whole country		1
Cámara de Hidrocarburos y Energía de Bolívia (CBHE)	Business association – whole country		1
Cámara Forestal de Bolívia	Business association – whole country		1
Cámara Nacional de Comercio (CNC)	Business association – whole country		1
Federación de Empresarios Privados de La Paz	Confederation of business associations – regional	La Paz	1
Cámara Agropecuaria del Oriente (CAO)	Business association – regional	Santa Cruz and Eastern lowlands	3
Cámara de Industria, Comercio, Servicios y Turismo de Santa Cruz (CAINCO)	Business association – regional	Santa Cruz	1
Federación de Empresarios Privados de Santa Cruz (FEPSC)	Confederation of business associations – regional	Santa Cruz and Eastern lowlands	2
Instituto Boliviano de Comerico Exterior (IBCE)	Business think tank – regional/national	Santa Cruz and Eastern lowlands	1
Cámara de Exportadores de Santa Cruz	Business association – regional	Santa Cruz	1
Comité Civico Pro Santa Cruz (CCPSC)	Regional identity organization	Santa Cruz	1
Leaders of conglomerates form Eastern lowlands	Businessmen		3
Other informants (Academics, Journalists, Researchers)			5

Part III

Elites, Wealth, and Power

9 Earning but Not Leading

Argentina's Economic Elites and the Exercise of Power in Global Capitalism

Mariana Heredia

9.1 Economic Power and Distributive Struggles in Argentina

In March 2008, the Argentine government announced the so-called Resolution 125, which modified the tax rates (of the export retention tax) for the main agricultural products of the country. Given the rise in international prices, the government aimed to moderate the impact on the domestic market and to give the Treasury a share of the extraordinary profits. No one expected that the reactions to this measure would be so intense. Not only did the leading representatives of producers reject the resolution, but there were also protests from agricultural businessmen, who started mobilizing in different parts of the country. Instead of backing down, President Cristina Fernández de Kirchner pressed forward, accusing the producers of organizing "pickets of abundance" (Presidential Speech, March 25, 2008). The conflict dragged on for weeks, and the opposition to the measure brought together what began to be referred to as the countryside (el campo) and urban sectors dissatisfied with the government's policies and backed by the mainstream media. Far from dividing the opposition, the government stoked the polarization by summoning its supporters within unions, social movements, human rights organizations, Peronism, and the left in a renewed struggle against corporate powers. After public protests escalated, the President sent the bill to Parliament, where, after a tie, the Vice-President rejected the measure. It was the end of Resolution 125 and the deepening of a conflict that would not cease in the years to come.[1] While the Kirchnerist movement aligned itself more and more with Peronist symbology and intensified its economic positions blamed as "populist," the denunciation of the "oligarchy" could once again be heard in official speeches.

The Latin American governments of the beginning of the 21st century, described as being center left, did not bring anything new regarding the tensions with capital and business. In the words of Pablo Stefanoni (2016, 99):

> It seems as if, due to the political-intellectual shortcomings of the new left, the socialism of the 21st century did not confront the capitalism of the 21st century, but rather that of the 20th century and sometimes that of the 19th century.

DOI: 10.4324/9781032636764-12

Indeed, comparing these governments to the neoliberalism of the period before, several analysts emphasize their common quest for the region's autonomy, greater social justice, and more endogenous growth (Chodor 2015). There were different degrees to this wager. Venezuela took on its most radical form, while Chile, Brazil, and Uruguay were more moderate (Levitsky and Roberts 2011). In any case, it is often stated that after the financial crisis of 2008 and the recomposition of right-wing forces, the rhetoric and policies adopted brought social confrontation back to life (Ellner 2019). However, little is said about how these governments defined and fought against as economic powers.

Argentina did not have to wait until the 21st century to mobilize its lower and working classes, challenge its ruling classes, and experiment with egalitarian-inspired public policies. Within Latin America, this country stands out for its tumultuous socio-political history due to a succession of weak civilian and military governments throughout the 20th century and its unique level of militancy both when it comes to the activism within its society and the democratic governments that confront the representatives of the business community. In contrast to other countries that are notable for the reproduction capacity of the elites and the subjugation of the lower classes, Argentina stands out for its porous access to the highest positions[2] and for the importance of Peronism, a political movement with loyal voters and the capacity to win competitive elections, with union power to challenge employers and uphold labor legislation (Torre 1983; Etchemendy and Collier 2008) and a symbolic influence that exalts egalitarianism and rejects social hierarchies (O'Donnell 1984).

The results are clear for those with an optimistic view of social conflict. Comparative data illustrating Argentina's situation highlight that it is one of the continent's most integrated and egalitarian nations. According to the Gini index by income, which measures inequality levels, in 2019, Argentina had lower inequality than Brazil, Mexico, and Chile.[3] It is also undisputable that its human development indexes were high, above the average figures for the region among the wealthiest Latin American countries, and close to the Organisation for Economic Co-operation and Development (OECD) average.[4] These social conditions were ultimately linked to labor protection and welfare institutions, among the region's most extensive.[5]

However, the lack of definition of the economic power confronted and the optimistic social indicators could hide a more complex situation. If Argentina has one story to tell in this last cycle of capitalism, it reveals the potential and limits of traditional distributive struggle. Do capital and the means of restraining its prerogatives take on the same form in the 21st century as in the mid-20th century? The case of Argentina allows us to document the extent to which social mobilization and confrontational government policies have been and continue to be an excellent strategy to undermine the privileges of the elites and achieve a more egalitarian society.

While systematizing and combining quantitative and qualitative evidence, this chapter analyzes events since the 1970s to test the implications of socio-political confrontation in a globalized world. On the one hand, using a variety of background and statistical information, the study presents the continuities and ruptures in the composition of economic power in Argentina, demonstrating that it's most concentrated sectors are inseparable from international and institutional dynamics and that they have experienced peculiar instability in recent decades. On the other hand, comparative statistical information shows that erratic macroeconomic management reduced the reproductive capacity of companies and business owners and resulted in moderate economic growth and negative societal consequences. Finally, based on research on sectoral representatives and interviews on their ways of relating with the State,[6] this chapter reveals the dislocation between the structural and instrumental power of the elites in Argentina. This includes the intense militancy of business owners and the persistent, fundamental division between them.

The region's center-left governments and those led by Néstor and Cristina Kirchner in Argentina did not confront all the economic power, nor did they succeed in awakening the business elites to a more significant commitment to the fate of their societies. While large companies, especially those that export raw materials, remain competitive on the global markets but lack strong political influence, domestically oriented companies are more cohesive and organized and have strong partisan ties. That said, whereas fragmentation made it difficult to establish sustainable socioeconomic policies over time, persistent macroeconomic instability led the significant economic actors of the country to the same adaptive behavior: low investment and capital flight. The data we will present here reveals something that is not usually observed through the indicators that are typically used to evaluate relative social equalization: Argentina also stands out among its peers for its moderate growth, the deterioration of its social equity over time, and for the relative emancipation of its occasional winners from the rest of society.

9.2 Whose Power? What Power? A Historical and Conceptual Revision

Two separate bodies of literature have analyzed the effect of capital accumulation on contemporary social inequalities. On the one hand, Thomas Piketty (2013) helped revitalize studies that stressed the need to center the production and circulation of wealth. On the other hand, as part of a long tradition, analyses of the relationship between states and business owners paid particular attention to capital's forms of collective action (Evans 1995; Schneider 2004) and its efforts to influence public policies.

The remarkable contribution of Tasha Fairfield (2010) is located at the intersection of these analyses and takes an interest in Argentina. Concerned with tax policies in the region and their potential to reduce social inequalities, the author distinguishes between two forms of power of capital. On the one hand, she refers to structural power as the ability to intervene in the economic sphere through decentralized decisions in search of greater profits. Although these are individual actions, they have far-reaching consequences: they can determine levels of investment, growth, and job creation. According to the author, the main structural power of capital is "the threat of disinvestment" (Fairfield 2010, 40). On the other hand, Fairfield introduces instrumental power, referring to the collective action of capitalists when coordinating and organizing to influence the political sphere.

These strategies include the formation of business associations, the financing of electoral campaigns, the links between businesspeople and officials, etc.

Fairfield (2010) alludes to another important dimension that she presents in less detail: the specific content of the deployed actions. This dimension could be anchored in the contribution of Isaac Ariail Reed (2020). Dominant groups who intervene on behalf of capital can enjoy two contrasting capacities: they can be "rectors" of order through the acquired and inertial power to hold on to certain privileges, or they can be "authors," seeking to have a disruptive and instituting influence on the course of events.

Both structural and instrumental powers resist this type of categorization. On the one hand, structural power can reproduce over time when specific production, circulation, and wealth distribution practices are sustained. It can also have a disruptive character when, in moments of crisis or radical innovation, it significantly disrupts the normal functioning of the economic structure or dynamics. On the other hand, instrumental power can be content with collaborative relationships and enduring influence vis-à-vis the authorities and public opinion that allows the status quo to be reproduced, or it can acquire an instituting character when the representatives of economic power seek to influence the adoption of specific policies that benefit them.

Fairfield concludes that these forms of power do not necessarily converge. However, in analyzing Argentina, she establishes that the country's relative social equality and the recent ability of its authorities to advance more progressive tax policies can be explained by the mobilization of civil society and, thus, the relative weakness of the elites.

Recognizing the significant contribution of this analysis, this chapter questions its hypothesis and examines the transformations of economic power in Argentina. To this end, it stresses that the composition and powers of capital mutate throughout history and that the most recent cycle of capitalism – with its commercial and financial globalization processes – has led to the relative emancipation of socioeconomic elites from the fate of their countries of origin. Latin America mainly depends on exogenous dynamics over which it has no control. It cannot be considered a sum of nations or a region with geographically circumscribed capitals but rather as one of the many arenas where capital has been able to take root or take flight more quickly in recent decades than in the past. If, in the words of Susan Strange (1986), financialization contributed to likening capitalism to a "casino," speculative effervescence is even more significant in countries with unstable macroeconomic institutions.

In Latin America, contrary to what critical theorists postulated in the mid-19th century, the relationship between economic elites and the masses cannot be reduced to a zero-sum game in which activism necessarily forces business owners to give in and negotiate. In the region's long history, the primary source of wealth has been the intensive exploitation of nature more so than the hiring and mobilization of large workforces. Since the 1970s, the flight to liquidity and financialization has increased the separation between wealth accumulation and reinvestment. Escape mechanisms have been consolidated, encouraging the search for quick profits and discouraging long-term investment. Therefore, the distributive struggle cannot only be analyzed in a closed and synchronic manner but requires a more open and diachronic perspective that lets us perceive how much of the wealth generated in times of prosperity allows for growth and social progress.

9.3 Who's Who? Capital in Recent Argentina

Who is part of the capital in contemporary Argentina? How much have socio-economic elites changed over time? To address these two questions, this chapter will use a broad definition that includes those economic agents of the private sector who make significant decisions regarding the flows and uses of financial and material assets. Thus, those persons who impact the growth, employment, and dynamics of the country's economy at any given time. Without a doubt, large companies' owners, shareholders, and managers constitute essential members of economic power, but they do not necessarily exhaust it. The funds available for direct deposits or real investments have always sat latent until changes in domestic regulations allowed or encouraged their actual use.

In many countries, stock exchanges are the best place for companies and shareholders to meet. They are used as sources of information for analyzing the economic power of each country and its evolution over time. However, unlike in Anglo-Saxon countries, Mexico and Brazil, the Argentine stock exchange occupies a marginal role. It does not offer a good vantage point for analyzing private-sector businesses. This is because of three features of the Argentinian stock exchange:

1 As we shall see, most large companies operating in the country are subsidiaries of multinationals listed elsewhere.
2 The nationally created companies that opened their capital preferred to do so abroad with higher traded volumes.
3 Local economic groups with diversified businesses avoid submitting to the formalization and transparency requirements for stock exchange listing.

The Buenos Aires Stock Exchange's big business has been and continues to be public sector securities (Heredia 2008). There is no indisputable source with which one can build a detailed portrait of the capital of Argentina. As with other countries, the solution has been to use a combination of available data sets. One is the National Survey of Large Companies conducted by the National Institute of Statistics (INDEC's *ENGE – Encuesta Nacional a Grandes Empresas*). Another is the rankings in local business magazines that list the private companies with the highest level of sales in the local market. A third one is *Forbes* magazine's podium of millionaires. This information, however, is not without bias. The first data set reproduces an anachronistic criterion of ownership. It does not specify whether they are part of the same economic group, which is crucial to observe concentration levels, market power, and capacity of influence. The second is based on the participants' self-reporting and excludes agricultural and livestock farms and financial companies. Specific statistics on banks and large companies and detailed sectoral surveys are often used to make up for these shortcomings. The last data set celebrates a minority of prominent magnates without carefully considering their position in the domestic economy.[7] The literature on this topic usually highlights three criteria to describe economic power in Argentina:

1 The sector of activity (which refers to the good or service produced and the relationship with nature, labor, and the international market).
2 The origin of capital (local or foreign character of shareholders and owners)
3 The size of enterprises (which refers to the levels of concentration or competitiveness of their markets).[8]

There is no undisputed source of information, and all of them have been elaborated separately. Nevertheless, it becomes clear that Argentina is not unique among the rest of the large Latin American nations. It features a high level of concentration in the largest companies. According to Ben Schneider (2009), the Argentinian economy can be described as a "hierarchical market economy" in which multinationals and diversified economic groups with standards similar to those of the industrialized countries coexist with small or medium-sized enterprises (SMEs), which employ low-skilled workers in less developed ways of production. Significant productivity disparities are also observed by at the Economic Commission for Latin America and the Caribbean (ECLAC) (also known by its Spanish acronym CEPAL: Comisión Económica para América Latina y el Caribe, see ECLAC 2013).

Among those at the very top, the importance of foreign capital is evident. Although land ownership (the great source of the country's wealth) remained in the hands of Argentines for a decade, most large companies have been in the hands of foreign capital. During the post-war period, the State and, to a lesser extent, the national bourgeoisie managed to take over a significant proportion of strategic sectors, including manufacturing (Rougier and Raccanello 2021). However, even then, 60% of the top 50 companies were externally owned (Castellani and Heredia 2020, 472). A similar dependence is observed in financing. A local capital market never developed in Argentina, even more than in other emerging economies. Productive investments were propitiated by the State while, during periods of financial openness, the country was subject to cycles of massive inflows and retractions of foreign direct investments (Bortz 2018).

Since the end of the 19th century, the primary sector has remained necessary since the 1970s, with the increasing involvement of foreign actors. Argentina's highest profit margins have never been obtained in the sector that employs the most salaried workforce but from those activities that exploit nature most intensively. One way to observe this is to examine how generated wealth is distributed between business owners and the workers engaged in production. Using long-term estimates (from 1950 to 2007), Kidyba and Vega (2015)[9] establish that primary activities (agriculture, livestock, forestry, fishing, and mining) show higher levels of productivity and allow business owners to retain a more significant portion of the generated wealth. In 1950 and even in 1970, business owners held on to 67%

of the profits generated by these activities, reaching 81% by 2007. In turn, by being independent of the domestic market demand, these activities also tended to be more stable and immune to the ups and downs of the national economy. Besides, Argentine exports have been composed of a limited basket of commodities. In 2018, agricultural (23%), agro-industrial (37%), and, to a lesser extent, fuel and energy (7%) accounted for 67% of Argentine exports.[10]

The continued relevance of commodities does not mean that individual winners remain the same. Since the 1970s, the agricultural export sector has undergone profound changes. Although the heirs of traditionally powerful families are still around, the new agribusiness model is characterized less by the accumulation of large tracts of land than by the integration of financial, technical, and managerial resources that allow to increase the scale and reduce risks (Gras and Cáceres 2017). The heterogeneity of actors involved in production (Gras and Hernández 2016) contrasts with the concentration of suppliers and exporters. Carlos Freytes and Juan O'Farrell (2017) argue that these downstream, most international, sections of the chain are those with the highest degree of concentration. While inputs are provided by some global players such as Monsanto, Syngenta, Bayer, or Dow, less than ten companies commercialize the grains exported by Argentina (*Idem*, 185). The concentration is even more significant in the mining and oil sector, where the required investments ensure that foreign companies are the main protagonists. According to INDEC data (2019), 39 of the 44 large companies that worked in mines and quarries and 61 of the 80 that produced fuels, chemicals, and plastics relied on foreign direct investment. According to Schorr and García Zanotti (2022), 70% of Argentine exports in 2019 were concentrated in 200 companies and more than half in the first 50.

However, the importance of primary exports for the Argentine economy today should not make us overlook the wealth other sectors in Argentina generate. While primary activities accounted for only 10% of Argentina's Gross Domestic Product (GDP) in 2018, industrial activities accounted for 23%, and the heterogeneous service sector for the remaining 67%.[11] These sectors also consist of large companies, many of which are multinationals. According to INDEC, 177 of the 270 large industrial companies in the country could be characterized as foreign (INDEC 2019). Nevertheless, the breakdown by individual companies is misleading. This is due to parts of the national bourgeoisie that prospered under state protection after the Second World War expanding to other sectors. With a tentacular logic, these companies such as Acindar (steel), Bridas (oil), Celulosa Argentina (paper/cellulose), Pérez Companc (oil), and Techint (construction) combined their original activity with ventures into finance or services (Azpiazu, Basualdo, and Khavisse 2004 [1986], 41). The issue is that the State has played and continues to play a fundamental role in strengthening these national groups. Castellani (2009) analyzed that the State helped Sade and Techint with public works, supported Bridas and Pérez Companc with oil contracts, and promoted Acindar and Celulosa with industrial policies. According to Gaggero and Schorr (2017, 60), by the beginning of the 21st century, almost 80% of the overall turnover of national private companies came from companies belonging to six conglomerates. They were then joined by others whose prosperity was once again fostered by the public sector. Thus, the authorities' decisions regarding infrastructure, the media, gambling, or promotional schemes generated possibilities to amass large new fortunes.

In this sense, scholars must carefully analyze capital ownership, as subtle differences have to be acknowledged. While at the beginning of the 21st century, in line with the new forms of global governance, most of the multinationals operating in the country have been publicly traded corporations with professionally managed activities, the national business groups continue to be organized under the mostly centralized control of the founding owner. There is a certain opposition between these two worlds of international corporate powers on the one side and the local business community – the national economic groups- on the other. Furthermore, at certain economic junctures, these differences are of great importance. If commercial and financial borders are closed, businesspeople from concentrated sectors tend to control their markets and most of the economy. The domestic capital market is so tiny that they are the ones who can influence the exchange rate, impact new investment projects, and mobilize their networks while creating preferential conditions. However, when the economy opens up and external capital becomes available, this international attention can be both a threat and a reward for national business owners and their managers.

9.4 "Lose-Lose": Argentina's Decline in a Globalized World

After the Second World War, as in other large nations of the continent, Argentina's rulers pursued import substitution to diversify the country's productive structure and encourage full employment. Various policies were implemented to shift surpluses from the countryside to the city and target consumption. The State's fiscal crisis, the inflationary spiral, radicalization, and political violence closed this cycle and created the conditions for significant reforms.

It is difficult to pinpoint a clear trend in Argentina's economic orientation since then. Most authors distinguish three major stages. The first, which began with the dictatorship in 1976, created the conditions for an extraordinary process of financial valorization through the liberalization of the capital account and the deregulation of the banking and financial system. These measures led to a cycle of speculation and debt with regressive economic and social consequences. These changes were accompanied by large transfers of public resources to concentrated local capital through various mechanisms (differential prices in public procurement, tax exemptions, and preferential financing, among others: Castellani 2009; Schvarzer 1981). This organization continued with nuances until 1988 when the fiscal and external crises made it impossible to simultaneously sustain the interest payment on the national debt and the subsidies to capital.

The second stage began precisely after the hyperinflationary crisis of 1989 with a change in the orientation of the State. During this period, structural reforms were implemented in line with the ideals of the so-called Washington Consensus: trade and financial liberalization, market deregulation, and privatization of public enterprises. From 1991 onward, inflation was halted thanks to the "convertibility plan," which fixed the exchange rate by law and restrained the issuing of money to the evolution of reserves. As in other countries, the reforms led to a profound recomposition of capital, integrating it into the world and weakening the less competitive groups. Compared to other countries in the region, this recomposition has not been successfully established. 2001, the exchange rate became unsustainable, which led to a new crisis.

In the aftermath of this neoliberal adjustment period, the administrations of Eduardo Duhalde, Néstor Kirchner, and Cristina Kirchner revived the role of the State. Due to increased demand and rising world market prices for commodities exported by Argentina, the governments sustained the domestic market expansion, the protection of local production, and the progressive redistribution of income until 2015. However, since 2007, several macroeconomic indicators have shown signs of deterioration of this favorable condition (Kulfas 2016). Once again, Argentina entered a cycle of inflation and stagnation. The liberalization measures implemented by the government elected in 2015 did not manage to reverse these problems but aggravated them by fueling sizeable public debt.

These newest events also had consequences on Argentina's economic elites. To examine the impact of the political instability on the country's companies and financial leaders, the author and Ana Castellani have analyzed the medium-term evolution of the country's top 50 companies. Based on the abovementioned rankings, we found that.

> only 13 of the companies that occupied positions in the top 50 in 1976 were still in the ranking in 2015. This reveals a stability rate of only 26%. However, only 4 of these 13 had also climbed within the ranking. Of the 13 companies that successfully reproduced themselves over time, only three were nationally owned, eight were subsidiaries of foreign companies, and two were partnerships between national and foreign capital. In addition, three of them changed owners and names.
>
> (Castellani and Heredia 2020, 473)

In contrast to the 1990s, the recomposition of the business community experienced a period of stability and consolidation during the Kirchnerist decade (2004–2015). Afterward, the government of Mauricio Macri (2015–2019) once again disrupted companies' configuration by introducing liberalization policies. Cassini, García Zanotti, and Schorr (2020, 212–213), in their analysis of the evolution of sectoral prices and their impact on the profitability of companies, reveal a significant downturn. Considering the wealth of the rich Argentines, *Forbes* magazine comes to a similar conclusion. In its own words, the Argentine ranking "[...] powerfully reflects the greatest process of wealth destruction in its history. It shows the impact of long years of stagflation, devaluation, and massive job losses accelerated recently by the COVID-19 pandemic and the bad business climate."[12] According to the magazine, in 2020, wealthy Argentinians accumulated almost 20% less wealth than in 2019, which showed a 17% reduction compared to 2018. The analyses of Piketty's research group draw the same conclusions (de Rosa, Flores, and Morgan 2020).

Suppose specific policies (many of which target economic liberalization and were adopted between 1989 and 2015) and the country's zigzagging economic orientation caused essential changes among Argentine business owners and their profit margins. Did this lead to a more egalitarian redistribution of wealth?

Instead of settling for a synchronic analysis of socioeconomic indicators, it is worth looking at their evolution over time. Such an approach reveals that Argentina's situation is less remarkable and promising. The limits of the country's economic growth are well-known. In the last five decades, Argentina has experienced a relative stagnation of the economy compared to regional averages.[13] But social conditions have also evolved negatively. On the one hand, the evolution of income inequality reveals that while other countries in the region managed to reduce the gap between the highest and lowest income deciles, in Argentina, the gains were elusive, and the aggregate trends were regressive. Although the average Gini coefficient between 1974 and 2019 (0.450) shows that the country is one of the least unequal in the region, inequality has been increasing, with a positive difference of 0.079 between the mid-1970s and the present. On the other hand, although Argentina featured more extensive labor protections and vigorous attempts to encourage the labor force's formalization, labor informality levels remained high. According to Beltranou and Casanova (2013, 38), 44% of working Argentines were informally employed. This combined effect probably explains why, if we look ECLAC data, urban poverty data from 2018 to 2019, Argentina was above the regional average, with almost one-third of the population in poverty, a percentage just below that of Mexico (31%) and higher than that of Brazil (less than 20%) and Chile (around 15%).[14]

In short, if the analysis of this last cycle of capitalism reveals anything, it is that beyond the crises and rebounds, not only have Argentine companies and business owners found it difficult to reproduce their advantages but also, at the same time, the levels of growth, social inclusion, and social welfare have been deteriorating. Unlike what happened in other regions where the strengthening of the economic power of large companies and fortunes was accompanied by poverty reduction, as in China (a win–win logic), or those where this enrichment came at the cost of higher levels of inequality and poverty, as in the United States (in a win–lose game),[15] in Argentina, everyone seems to have lost.

9.5 Loud-Mouthed and Brawny: Dislocated Powers, Convergent Learnings

At this point, one could conclude that capital in Argentina remained structurally and instrumentally passive in the face of adversity. However, this is not true. Those who highlight the militancy of Argentine society are usually only referring to the mobilization and organizing power of the lower classes. However, businesses of different sectors and sizes have developed numerous entities representing them. The first business associations were created in the late 19th and early 20th centuries to organize and promote various economic activities in the country. When labor conflicts increased, these and other associations channeled the growing concerns of employers (Rapalo 2012). The first Peronist government (1946–1955) even helped relaunch business associations in two ways.

1. It encouraged the sectoral associations to become the unions' counterparts in the collective bargaining agreements established by law in 1953. The workers' demands, spurred on by the delays resulting from price inflation, ensured these entities would remain in operation.
2. As the Peronist government increased the state's influence in orienting business activities, businesses helped and harmed by state action had to negotiate with the government. As Novaro (2019, 94–95) shows, business associations multiplied and diversified as time passed: between 16 and 25 new entities were created per decade between 1950 and 2000.

This fragmented activism only resulted temporarily in unification. The hundred-year-old entities linked to the most significant sectors of the economy (the Argentine Industrial Union, the Argentine Rural Society, and the Argentine Chamber of Commerce, among others) continued to have more significant influence and presence in the press and came informally together only incidentally. In 1959, several of these entities formed the *Acción Coordinadora de Instituciones Empresarias Libres* (ACIEL – Coordinating Action of Free Enterprise Institutions) to oppose the continuation of the trade union model created by Peronism and the rehabilitation of the *Confederación General Económica* (General Economic Confederation) which had accompanied that administration. A similar group was built in the mid-1970s to denounce the Peronist government's irregularities and encourage the 1976 coup d'état. Large businesses came together again in the 1980s with the Captains of Industry and in the 1990s with the group of eight (the eight leading centennial business corporations).[16] Although there are more elitist entities, such as the Argentine Businessmen's Association (AEA) or the Institute for the Entrepreneurial Development of Argentina, none of them managed to claim exclusive representation of the economic power in the country, not even the most concentrated.

To what extent does this concern for the organization and buttressing of instrumental power evidence the strength or weakness of economic power in Argentina? For Tasha Fairfield, as for other authors, this "associativism" could be considered an additional task faced by capital in Argentina due to the weakness of the elites. However, framing the issue in aggregate terms would be a mistake. Economic power cannot be singularized in Argentina, nor can the structural and instrumental capacities of different actors in the national economy align coherently.

Few would doubt the structural power of the agricultural sector. As mentioned above, since the end of the 19th century, its production has been crucial for obtaining foreign currency, collecting taxes, and providing goods such as cereals and meat, which are fundamental to the food basket of domestic households. However, as Fairfield (2010) demonstrates, the instrumental power of the "*campo*" (countryside) is comparatively weak. Rural elites have threatened not to liquidate crops and tried evading controls. They repeatedly mobilized (as in 1988 and 2008) against the national government. However, given the nature of their activity (land exploitation), they are rooted in the territory. Thus, despite their demands, nothing prevented that; as Hora (2002) and Freytes and O'Farrell (2017) demonstrated, agricultural exports were among the most taxed activities during much of the 20th century and so far in the 21st century. Their producers had little access to the high spheres of political power in democratic governments. Their instrumental capacity is weak.

The opposite has occurred in the industrial sector, whose instrumental power has been greater than its structural power. As we have seen, the position of a significant portion of the manufacturing business sector in Argentina rested mainly on the protection of public authority. The need for frequent collective bargaining in an inflationary society and the need to obtain strategic advantages for different branches led these business leaders to engage in political action very actively. This does not mean that a straightforward project or common and lasting interests prevailed among them. As Schvarzer (1991) and Dossi (2019) show, if anything characterized the industrial sector in Argentina, it was the plurality of organizations and the permanent fracture of its central entity (the Argentine Industrial Union).

The structural and instrumental power mismatch is clearly observable within the industrial sector. The *Unión Industrial Argentina* (UIA – Argentine Industrial Union) represents large companies, and the *Confederación Argentina de la Mediana Empresa* (CAME – Argentine Confederation of Medium-Sized Enterprises) encompasses small and medium-sized companies. Since smaller companies are more numerous, and their survival depends on their representatives and governmental decisions, at the beginning of the 21st century, CAME's resources and activities were greater than those of its counterpart. The testimony of an advisor of both entities is telling. She said that while the UIA has a small budget (from annual conferences and members' contributions), the CAME benefits from a workers' training fund deducted from salaries for training purposes. The UIA employs about 15 people, but the CAME has recourse to more than 70. The former occupies only one building floor, but the latter three. Even the behavior of the leaders of both associations is different. When the conversation with the advisor occurred, the UIA was headed by a millionaire who avoided ostentation and went to work in jeans and with an average car. The director of CAME, however, was a producer from a province, moved around in a convertible car, required his employees to dress in elegant sports clothes, and organized meetings that looked like weddings (Advisor in an interview with the author, January 2020).

As they generated more employment than the primary sector, the industrialists also had the support of the unions and the sympathy of a large part of the Peronist leaders. When the author interviewed one of the leaders of the *Unión Obrera Metalúrgica* (UOM – Metalworkers Union), one could get the impression that Argentine business owners could rely on trade unionists. Even more so, the unionists defended the sector's interests even more vehemently than the company owners. In the words of the prominent leader of the UOM, who at that time was close to those in the nation's presidential offices, "When they have a problem with the government, the business owners call me. And with a couple of phone calls, I solve it for them" (interview of February 2021).

A restless work of representation mediates structural and instrumental power, making it possible to move from individual to collective action and interact with the authorities. In the case of Argentina, it is evident that the most competitive and profitable sectors are different from those with the most active and influential business organizations. Only at the beginning of the 21st century did businessmen coalesce in a center-right party with electoral effectiveness (*Propuesta Republicana*, the PRO), who's economic management in the national government (2015–2019) proved nonetheless frustrating. Furthermore, small and medium urban entrepreneurs hold a close relationship with trade unions and the Peronist party, which promised stable government and extended growth cycles. Thus, when analyzing economic power, it becomes clear that the brawniest are not always the loudest, and the loudest are not necessarily the brawniest, or rather, that the two forms of power (structural and instrumental) do not necessarily coincide. The back-and-forth of macroeconomic policies in Argentina is an expression of tied forces where sometimes the brawniest and sometimes the loudest prevail, depending on the will and vigor of the State.

However, the fact that for decades, elites depended on political decisions to change couleur means that they learned an important lesson: when the elites are influential, they can win, but it is difficult for any of them to achieve lasting imposition and leadership. As Novaro (2019, 55) points out, in the face of political agitation, Argentine business owners developed a relationship with the State that was "increasingly politicized and deinstitutionalized." As the research I conducted with business owners from different sectors of activity reveals, the socioeconomic elites who operate in Argentina need to constantly be vigilant of the political dynamics. Those with the capabilities will focus on networking, negotiating decisions or specific advantages, and accessing privileged information, while those lacking these capabilities move forward with caution and prefer to avoid the risks of lasting commitments. Those who might be able to invest are even warier: due to the high interest rates Argentina is reaching, investors require high, short-term returns. Thus, different types of elites have little faith in capturing "the" State, also recognizing the necessary compromises that this would entail. Instead, at most, they aspire to survive and guide specific state decisions for their practical benefit and risk containment.

In an attempt to mediate between the perspectives that highlight either the impotence or the omnipotence of the economic elites in Argentina, José Nun argued that these elites do not have a shared and defined identity. However, he pointed out that those who managed to consolidate themselves in different businesses developed "that short-term orientation of a speculative nature, guided by quick profit rather than by productive investment" (Nun 1987, 112–113). In moments of economic busts, when the first alarms begin to sound, the emerging capital flight, prolonged stagnation, and the generalized non-fulfillment of tax and labor responsibilities are the flip side of a State that fails to create a stable order in which it can engage and discipline the elites.

It is, therefore, not surprising that two other characteristics differentiate Argentina from other Latin American countries. On the one hand, in 2019, investment levels were slightly below the average for the region but exhibited the most significant contraction from the 1970s to the present. Indeed, when looking at gross fixed capital formation as a percentage of GDP – the measure usually used to measure investment – in the 1970s, Argentina's values were higher than those of its Latin American peers and close to France's or the United States. However, 50 years later, they are lower than those of its peers.[17] On the other hand, if evasion and tax avoidance are worrying features of globalized economies in general, they do not affect all countries equally. While specialists estimate that approximately 10% of the world's gross product is in tax havens, the proportion reaches 40% or 50% of the GDP in countries such as Argentina or Greece (Alstadsæter, Johannesen, and Zucman, cited by Alvaredo et al. 2018, 264). Asset outsourcing – legal or illegal – remains one of the most salient features of the Argentine upper classes (Gaggero, Rúa, and Gaggero 2015).

9.6 Conclusion

Capital and its managers behave strategically in any capitalist society to accumulate profits. The unique thing in Latin America today is that there is both financial liquidity and subordinate insertion in international markets, where local currencies and capital markets recurrently face new opportunities and threats. Neither globalization nor the policies adopted by the center-left governments have changed the concentration of most of the continent's major businesses, which confers market power to the leading companies. Thus, these companies can impose on other members of their value chain or consumers.

In this context, Argentina's socioeconomic elites stand out for acting in a framework of significant institutional instability. This, however, does not mean that the same group of people constantly win and never lose. What makes this country's economic "game" unique is that its rounds are shorter, and the results are more provisional. It is true that, in some cases, business profits have gone hand in hand with growth, job creation, and expansion of goods and services produced. In those periods, such as the first five years of the 21st century, it seems as if there was no concentration of economic power when, in reality, capital is profiting. In periods of crisis and desperate decisions, as with the nationalization of debts, some profits are privatized, and the losses are socialized. Some win and some lose according to their economic activity and capacity to escape or face business risks.

In this context, critical social science sometimes falls into a dangerous simplification: the belief that punishing the local rich would mean taming capital. In the last cycle of capitalism, capital managed to free itself from a large part of the conflicts that facilitated a more egalitarian distribution: it has a more global operating board, it has significantly increased the margins of exploitation thanks to new technologies, and it counts on finance as a strategy of valuation without contact (or, at least without direct contact) with the population. It is, therefore, necessary to recognize that the distribution of wealth does not operate in the same way as in the second post-war period when economies evolved with full employment, closed borders, and relatively efficient state institutions. In this more uncertain and porous scenario, the problem for both center-right and center-left administrations has remained the same in Argentina since the mid-1970s (Heredia 2015b): this challenge is how to splice short- and long-term objectives and how to achieve stability and a sustainable compromise between State and Capital. Sometimes, conflict is the prelude to a better future, but it can also become a dilemma where everyone, especially the poorest, is harmed in the long run.

Notes

1 The events have been extensively studied and are reconstructed here based on the work of Pucciarelli (2017).
2 See, among others: Germani (1963), de Imaz (1964), Jorrat (2008), and Heredia (2022).
3 Prepared by the author with data from the World Bank https://databank.bancomundial.org/reports.aspx?source=2&type=metadata&series=NY.GDP.PCAP.KD.ZG# (June 22, 2022).
4 Prepared by the author with UN data: http://hdr.undp.org/en/data (June 22, 2022).
5 This is suggested by many international comparative studies, including those that evaluated the importance of these institutions in confronting the COVID-19 crisis. See Uni Global Union (2021), ILO-ECLAC (2020).
6 Including interviews with agriculture, banking, the stock exchange, and industry representatives: Heredia (2003, 2008, 2015a, 2022).
7 A presentation of all available sources can be found at: https//sigloxxieditores.com.ar/el-99-contra-el-1-de-mariana-heredia (December 22, 2022). They have been critically examined in Balza and Heredia (2021).
8 The most comprehensive and up-to-date work on this topic is the compilation by Schorr (2021), from which this chapter draws in part.
9 In their analysis of the functional distribution of income, the authors differentiate nine sets of activities and indicate the proportion retained by capital (what they call "gross operating surplus") and by labor (or "remuneration of wage labor"; Kidyba and Vega 2015).
10 Prepared by the author according to exports by significant items. Years 1980–2019, Exports, INDEC. www.indec.gob.ar/indec/web/Nivel4-Tema-3-2-40.
11 Prepared by the author with Gross Value Added data for the same period: www.indec.gob.ar/indec/web/Nivel4-Tema-3-9-47 (June 22, 2022).
12 This is stated in the July 2020 edition, www.forbesargentina.com/rankings/ranking-forbes-2020-quienes-son-cuanto-tienen-50-argentinos-mas-ricos-n3469 (December 22, 2022).
13 Latin American countries have more abrupt growth rates than the central countries, with more moderate expansion and contraction cycles. But even compared to the Latin American and Caribbean averages, the Argentine economy has more uneven trends, with steep slopes and rebounds. In aggregate terms, the average GDP per capita growth between 1970 and 2019 was 0.80, compared to 1.47 for the region. Prepared by the author with data from the World Bank: https://databank.bancomundial.org/reports.aspx?source=2&type=metadata&series=NY.GDP.PCAP.KD.ZG# (June 22, 2022).
14 Prepared by the author with ECLAC's data from household surveys of the different countries. https://cepalstat-prod.cepal.org/cepalstat/tabulador/ConsultaIntegrada.asp?idIndicador=3328&idioma=e (June 22, 2022).
15 For a closer look at these global trends, Milanovic (2016) can be consulted.

16 The studies from which these conclusions are drawn include Acuña (1988), Cúneo (1984), and Osteguy (1990), among others.

17 Prepared by the author with World Bank data, available at https://databank.worldbank.org/reports.aspx?source=2&series=NE.GDI.FTOT.ZS&country=# (June 22, 2022).

References

Acuña, Carlos. 1988. "Empresarios y Política (Parte I). La Relación de las Organizaciones Capitalistas con Partidos y Regímenes Políticos en América Latina: Los Casos Argentino y Brasileño." *Boletin Techint* 255, 17–45.

Alvaredo, Facundo, Lucas Chancel, Thomas Piketty, Emmanuel Saez, and Gabriel Zucman. 2018. *World Inequality Report*. World Inequality Database, WID.

Azpiazu, Daniel, Eduardo Basualdo, and Miguel Khavisse. 2004 [1986]. *El nuevo poder económico en la Argentina de los años 1980*. Buenos Aires: Siglo XXI.

Balza, Sonia, and Mariana Heredia. 2021. "La ansiedad de una relación sin compromiso." *Anfibia*. www.revistaanfibia.com/la-ansiedad-de-una-relacion-sin-compromiso/ (December 22, 2022).

Beltranou, Fabio, and Luis Casanova 2013. *La informalidad laboral en Argentina. Segmentos críticos y políticas para la formalización*. Buenos Aires: OIT.

Bortz, Pablo. 2018. "Flujos de capital y endeudamiento externo: algunas reflexiones para América Latina." In *Estudios sobre financierización en América Latina*, edited by Abeles, Martin., Esteban Pérez Caldentey, and Sebastián Valdecantos, 295–321. Buenos Aires: CEPAL.

Cassini, Lorenzo, Gustavo García Zanotti, and Martín Schorr. 2020. "Más negocio financiero, menos producción: la experiencia neoliberal del gobierno de Cambiemos." In *El poder económico en la Argentina desde fines del siglo XIX a la actualidad*, edited by Schorr, Martín, 199–236. Buenos Aires: Siglo XXI.

Castellani, Ana. 2009. *Estado, empresas y empresarios. La construcción de ámbitos privilegiados de acumulación entre 1966 y 1989*. Buenos Aires: Prometeo.

Castellani, Ana, and Mariana Heredia. 2020. "La reproducción fallida de las elites. Inestabilidad transformaciones de las elites empresariales argentinas entre 1976 y 2015." *Revista Española de Sociología (RES)* 29 (3), 467–486.

Chodor, Tom. 2015. *Neoliberal Hegemony and the Pink Tide in Latin America*. London: Palgrave Macmillan.

Cúneo, Dardo. 1984. *Comportamiento y crisis de la clase empresaria*. Buenos Aires: CEAL.

de Imaz, Jose Luis. 1964. *Los que mandan*. Buenos Aires: Eudeba.

De Rosa, Mauricio., Ignacio Flores, and Marc Morgan. 2020. "Inequality in Latin America Revisited: Insights from Distributional National Accounts," *World Inequality Lab – Technical Note No. 2020/02*. World Inequality Database, WID.

Dossi, Marina. 2019. *Los industriales en su laberinto. Las estrategias políticas de la Unión Industrial Argentina durante el auge y la crisis neoliberal (1989–2003)*. Buenos Aires: Editorial Autores de Argentina.

ECLAC. 2013. *Como mejorar la competitividad de las PyMES en la Unión Europea y América latina y el Caribe*. Santiago de Chile: CEPAL/AL-INVEST.

Ellner, Steve. 2019. "Pink-Tide Governments: Pragmatic and Populist Responses to Challenges from the Right." *Latin American Perspectives* 46 (1), 4–22.

Etchemendy, Sebastán, and Ruth Collier 2008. "Golpeados pero de pie. Resurgimiento sindical y neocorporativismo segmentado en la Argentina (2003–2007)." *Revista POSTData* 13, 145–192.
Evans, Peter. 1995. *Embedded Autonomy: States and Industrial Transformation*. Princeton: Princeton University Press.
Fairfield, Tasha. 2010. "Business Power and Tax Reform: Taxing Income and Profits in Chile and Argentina." *Latin American Politics and Society* 52 (2), 37–71.
Freytes, Carlos, and Juan O'Farrell. 2017. "Conflictos distributivos en la agricultura de exportación en la argentina reciente (2003–2015)." *Desarrollo Económico* 57 (221), 181–196.
Gaggero, Alejandro, and Martín Schorr. 2017. "Las grandes empresas nacionales de la Argentina bajo los gobiernos del kirchnerismo." *H-industri@* 11 (21), 54–75.
Gaggero, Jorge, Magdalena Rúa, and Alejandro Gaggero. 2015. "Los activos offshore de los argentinos." *Revista de Derecho Público* 3 (10), 125–158.
Germani, Gino. 1963. "La movilidad social en la Argentina." In *Movilidad social en la sociedad industrial*, edited by Lipset, Seymour and Reinhard Bendix, Apendix, 260–314. Buenos Aires: Eudeba.
Gras, Carla, and Daniel Cáceres 2017. "El acaparamiento de tierras como proceso dinámico. Las estrategias de los actores en contextos de estancamiento económico." *Población y Sociedad* 24 (2), 163–194.
Gras, Carla, and Valeria Hernández. 2016. *Radiografía del nuevo campo argentino*. Buenos Aires: Siglo XXI.
Heredia, Mariana. 2003. "Reformas estructurales y renovación de las elites económicas. Estudio de los portavoces de la tierra y del capital." *Revista Mexicana de Sociología* 65 (1), 77–115.
———. 2008. "La Bolsa de Comercio de Buenos Aires." *Conference Papers of the Center for Migration and Development*. Princeton University.
———. 2015a. "Globalización y clases altas en el auge del vino argentino." *Revista Trabajo y Sociedad* 24. www.unse.edu.ar/trabajoysociedad/24%20Heredia%20Mariana%20clases%20altas%20en%20vino.pdf (June 22, 2022).
———. 2015b. *Cuando los economistas alcanzaron el poder (O como se construyó la confianza en los expertos)*. Buenos Aires: Siglo XXI.
———. 2022. *¿El 99% contra el 1%? Por qué la obsesión por los ricos no sirve para combatir la desigualdad*. Buenos Aires: Siglo XXI.
Hora, Roy. 2002. *Los terratenientes de la pampa argentina, 1860–1945*. Buenos Aires: Siglo XXI.
ILO-ECLAC. 2020. "Coyuntura Laboral en América Latina y el Caribe. El trabajo en tiempos de pandemia: desafíos frente a la enfermedad por coronavirus (COVID-19)." *Boletín No.* 22. www.cepal.org/es/publicaciones/45557-coyuntura-laboral-america-latina-caribe-trabajo-tiempos-pandemia-desafios-frente (December 22, 2022).
INDEC. 2019. *Encuesta nacional a grandes empresas 2017*. Buenos Aires: INDEC.
Jorrat, Jorge Raúl. 2008. "Exploraciones sobre movilidad de clases en Argentina, 2003–2004." *Documento de trabajo* 52. Buenos Aires: IIGG-UBA.
Kidyba, Susana, and Daniel Vega. 2015. "Distribución funcional del ingreso en la Argentina, 1950–2007." In *Serie Estudios y Perspectivas*. Buenos Aires: CEPAL.
Kulfas, Matías. 2016. *Los Tres Kirchnerismos*. Buenos Aires: Siglo XXI.
Levitsky, Steven, and Kenneth Roberts, eds. 2011. *The Resurgence of the Latin American Left*. Baltimore: Johns Hopkins University.
Milanovic, Branko. 2016. *Global Inequality*. Cambridge; London: Harvard University Press.

Novaro, Marcos. 2019. *Dinero y poder. Las difíciles relaciones entre empresarios y políticos en la Argentina*. Buenos Aires: Edhasa.

Nun, José. 1987. "Vaivenes de un régimen social de acumulación en decadencia." In *Ensayos sobre la transición democrática en Argentina*, edited by Nun, José, and Juan Carlos Portantiero, 83–116. Buenos Aires: Puntosur.

O'Donnell, Guillermo. 1984. " '¿Y a mí, qué me importa?'. Notas sobre sociabilidad y política en Argentina y Brasil." *Working Paper 9*, Kellogg Institute. Buenos Aires: CEDES.

Osteguy, Pierre. 1990. *Los capitanes de la industria. Grandes emnpresarios, política y economía en la Argentina de los años 80*. Buenos Aires: Editorial Legasa.

Piketty, Thomas. 2013. *Le capital au XXI siècle*. Paris: Seuil.

Pucciarelli, Alfredo R. 2017. "El conflicto por 'la 125' y la configuración de dos proyectos prehegemónicos." In *Los años del kirchnerismo*, edited by Pucciarelli, Alfredo R., and Ana Castellani, 351–377. Buenos Aires: Siglo XXI.

Rapalo, María Ester. 2012. *Patrones y obreros. La ofensiva de la clase propietaria 1918–1930*. Buenos Aires: Siglo XXI.

Reed, Issac A. 2020. *Power in Modernity*. Chicago: Chicago University Press.

Rougier, Marcelo, and Mario Raccanello 2021. "Estado y poder económico en la industrialización sustitutiva de importaciones." In *El viejo y el nuevo poder económico en la Argentina: del siglo XIX a nuestros días*, edited by Schorr, Martín, 51–92. Buenos Aires: Siglo XXI.

Schneider, Ben Ross. 2004. *Business Politics and the State in Twentieth-Century Latin America*. Cambridge: Cambridge University Press.

———. 2009. "Hierarchical Market Economies and Varieties of Capitalism in Latin America." *Journal of Latin American Studies* 41, 553–575.

Schorr, Martín, ed. 2021. *El viejo y el nuevo poder económico en la Argentina. Del siglo XIX a nuestros días*. Buenos Aires: Siglo XXI.

Schorr, Martín, and Gustavo García Zanotti 2022. "Dinámica comercial externa de la cúpula empresarial argentina el gobierno de Cambiemos (2015–2019)." *Apuntes del CENES* 41 (73), 91–117.

Schvarzer, Jorge. 1981. *Expansión económica del estado subsidiario, 1976–1981*. Buenos Aires: Centro de Investigaciones Sociales sobre el Estado y la Administración.

———. 1991. *Empresarios del pasado. La Unión Industrial Argentina*. Buenos Aires: CISEA-Imago Mundi.

Stefanoni, Pablo. 2016. "¿Alba o crepúsculo? Geografías y tensiones del 'socialismo del siglo XXI'" In *¿Por qué retrocede la izquierda?*, edited by Leiras, Marcelo, Andrés Malamud, and Pablo Stefanoni, 81–117. Buenos Aires: Capital Intelectual.

Strange, Susan. 1986. *Casino Capitalism*. Manchester: Manchester University Press.

Torre, Juan Carlos. 1983. *Los sindicatos en el gobierno 1973–1976*. Buenos Aires: Centro Editor de América Latina.

Uni Global Union. 2021. "*Covid-19: una enfermedad profesional ¿dónde están más protegidos los trabajadores de primera línea?*." www.uniglobalunion.org (December 22, 2022).

10 Discursive Power in Central America

Economic Elites and Disputes over Public Policies during the COVID-19 Pandemic

Francisco Robles-Rivera, Gustavo Fuchs and Ximena Alvarenga Fournier

10.1 Introduction

Faced with one of the most significant socioeconomic crises in the region's history (CEPAL 2020) and armed with weak tax and economic institutions to tackle it (ICEFI 2015; Pérez Sáinz et al. 2011; Sánchez-Ancochea et al. 2015), economic elites' influence in the first months of the COVID-19 pandemic could have catalyzed or put the brakes on redistributive and progressive public policy reform in Central America. Considering recent history, Central American economic elites have opposed redistributive and democratic policies, even during the context of crisis (Rettberg 2016; Schneider 2012). However, literature has identified a "discursive turn" in the renovation and modernization of elites after the peace accords that have increased the significance of institutions and the use of deliberative dialogue in solving social problems (Bull and Aguilar-Støen 2019).

This chapter discusses economic elites' opportunities and limitations for influencing public policy from the perspective of *discursive power*. It considers a first scenario of strong *discursive power* in which economic elites craft and distribute ideas and information, legitimizing them as privileged spokespersons and guaranteeing access to decision-making (Guatemala, Honduras, and Costa Rica). A second scenario of weak *discursive power* is given in cases in which economic elites' capacity to produce ideas is undermined due to political disputes with the government (El Salvador, Nicaragua).

Recent debates over elites' influence in politics have highlighted different types of elite power. On the one hand, instrumental power is characterized by the elites' capacities to operate politically, and on the other hand, structural power is defined by the economic weight the elites have in countries' development (Bernhagen 2008; Fairfield 2015). Another form of power, less discussed in the literature, is elites' *discursive power* (Freedman 2014; Fuchs 2007; Mills 2000). This power consists of elites' capacities and resources for creating, sending, and reproducing information and messages via the media, business associations, public relations campaigns, documents, social media, and experts that shape the norms, identities, and public debate that inform politicians, politics, and the political process as such (Fuchs 2007). In this vein, in recent decades and throughout the world – particularly in Latin America – economic elites have taken advantage of (1) the economic

DOI: 10.4324/9781032636764-13

struggles of media enterprises and (2) cheap information technologies. Both factors enabled elites to buy or set up new media outlets (Robles-Rivera 2020).

In the case of Central America, the media has helped elites maintain a certain degree of political stability and economic growth by reproducing power structures and discourses in a media market that is highly concentrated and dominated by a few business groups (Rockwell and Janus 2003). This structure has been mounted in close cooperation with other members from economic and political spheres through different types of family and business relations and party affiliations. These networks have also allowed economic elites' discourses to hold hegemony over other social groups' discourses and ideas (Robles-Rivera and Voorend 2012; Rockwell and Janus 2003; Wolf 2009).

In this chapter, we examine the discourses of economic elites during the first six months[1] of the COVID-19 pandemic in Costa Rica, El Salvador, Guatemala, Honduras, and Nicaragua. These countries share economic, social, and political characteristics and, despite their differences regarding State-building, are cases that show spaces and conditions for improving redistributive policies (Martinez and Sánchez Ancochea 2022). Moreover, these are cases in which the strength of economic elites is proportional to the weakness of democratic institutions (Bull 2014). This study limits its analysis to economic- and tax-related public statements made by leading business associations of the countries selected. This includes the Coordinating Committee of Agricultural, Commercial, Industrial, and Financial Associations (CACIF) in Guatemala, the National Association of Private Enterprise (ANEP) in El Salvador, the Honduran National Business Council (COHEP) in Honduras, the Council for Private Enterprise (COSEP) in Nicaragua, and the Costa Rican Union of Chambers and Associations of the Private Business Sector (UCCAEP) of Costa Rica.

The study of the leading business associations in each country is justified for various reasons. In the first place, these associations bring together significant companies and corporate individuals alike. More specifically, they gather representatives from the central business associations of each country who are also, by their nature, spokespersons of the dominant economic actors. In the second place, their relevance has accorded them particular political weight as they enjoy privileged access to decision-makers and are regularly consulted by politicians. In the third place, literature has indicated the importance these associations have had in defining public policy in the cases of Honduras, Guatemala, and El Salvador (Bull 2014; Schneider 2012; Wolf 2009). In the fourth place, given the restricted access to the economic elite in particular, the public nature of the associations' statements allows for a certain degree of insight, not without limitations, into the discursive narratives of the elite in general. In the fifth place, the associations enable elites to establish consensuses and socially legitimize the private interests of their peers. Finally, we opted to work with the associations for systematization and analysis given the recurrent, public, and institutional nature of their communications and statements in social media. However, these discursive narratives do not reflect reality comprehensively, given that they are changing and subject to dispute (Bull and Aguilar-Støen 2019). However, their prevalence and the absence of other contending forces in the public sphere make it easier for them to create scenarios for policies to be supported or rejected following their private interests (Bull and Aguilar-Støen 2019).

A comparative analysis of these cases allows us to think about the discursive power of elites on two different levels. In this way, in Costa Rica, Guatemala, and Honduras, faced with the uncertainty of the pandemic and a lack of information, the elite were able to shape the terms of the debate around economic and tax policies, securing access to politicians and creating an identity – a particular "us" (strong discursive power). In Nicaragua and El Salvador, the crisis and individual disputes with the government prevented elites from articulating proposals and/or ideas (weak discursive power). Thus, strong discursive power allows elites to shape the debate and narratives and increase their capacity to exercise influence on an economic and tax agenda that serves their interests. By contrast, weak discursive power reduces elites' political power in formulating and defining public policy.

Next, we offer a conceptual approach focusing on discursive power and its associated capacities to discuss the two proposed models. The chapter will present the study's methodology and the findings in each country, contributing to a comparison of discursive power in the countries studied.

10.2 Discursive Power: Shaping Policies, Norms, and Ideas

Economic elites' discursive power refers to their capacity to influence policy and political processes by shaping ideas and norms (Fuchs 2007; Fuchs and Kalfagianni 2009). It is a power expressed in language (symbols, images, labels) and can be exercised through multiple channels such as advertising, media, and education (Fuchs and Kalfagianni 2009). Generally, this power can occur in framing policy issues, framing actors, and altering social and political norms (Fuchs 2007).

Frames are formed by selecting salient aspects of perceived reality to promote a particular problem definition, diagnose causes, make moral judgments, and propose solutions (Entman 1993). Gamson and Modigliani (1989, 3) describe a frame as a "central organizing idea […] suggesting what is at issue". By establishing causal relations to define problems, frames also ascribe responsibility and, in turn, presuppose proposed solutions (Iyengar 1991). In society, different actors promote their frames of incidents with agendas in sight and seek to position them in public opinion (Entman 2003). In this dispute, elites' frames tend to dominate since elites with disproportionate resources and different relations to the media and institutions promote them. Studies on framing often ignore the dimension or power in the promotion of frames (Carragee and Roefs 2004), so discursive power thus allows for identifying the processes and resources through which elites promote their frames to influence public policy.

We are working from the assumption that discursive power precedes elites' political action. Discursive power allows economic elites to generate identities and common interests by organizing discourses and narratives that give them meaning as a social class. Their economic resources provide them with the means to create and manage ideas and discursive narratives through think tanks, the hiring of consulting teams and lawyers, public relations campaigns, and the purchase of space and time in media publications to promote and reproduce their messages (Davis 2007; Freedman 2014; Robles-Rivera 2020). These include discursive narratives that operate outward (in society) and inward, generating cohesion among elites.

In times of crisis, like the pandemic, and in the face of a growing situation of uncertainty, economic elites' information and expertise on the economy and public policy allow them to extend their economic influence on political spheres (Vogel 1987). It is a question of providing decision-makers – but also the public in general – with documents, analyses, and expert knowledge to change perspectives on a specific topic, extend the possible benefits of a given policy, present new evidence, and, if necessary, block information that could work against their interests (Bernhagen 2008). Furthermore, it works based on the implicit acknowledgment that the country's general welfare is closely linked to the welfare of businesses (Bell 2012; Bernhagen 2008; Marsh et al. 2015). This does not necessarily entail the exclusion of other actors. However, elites have more network ties to international financial bodies, media, and think tanks, making it easier for their discourse to be more readily legitimized by decision-makers.

In the case of Central America, the hegemony of elites' discursive power has been supported by their privileged access to management schools, think tanks, private universities, lawyers, and private consultants, as well as outside influence from international organizations in the construction and formation of ideas (Pérez-Sáinz 2017). In addition, Central American economic elites have formed networks that allow them to influence public policy, given their access to the State through the collective mobilization of resources and the planning of coordinated political actions (Cárdenas and Robles-Rivera 2021). In the face of these prominent interconnections, Central American civil societies are weak and fragmented, with limited capacities for producing ideas and accessing the media to spread their ideas (Bull 2014; Sandoval García 2008; Wolf 2009).

10.3 Two Scenarios of Discursive Power to Influence Public Policies

In this chapter, we categorize discursive power that allows us to access elites' choices and limitations for influencing public policy. Two different scenarios are described in detail, which inform the case studies. One scenario addresses a case in which elites have strong discursive power, defined by extensive capacities for producing and distributing ideas and information that legitimizes them as spokespersons and guarantees their privileged access to decision-making, as well as greater reproduction of their discourses in mass media (Guatemala, Honduras, and Costa Rica). The other scenario is characterized by elites that hold weak discursive power and limited possibilities to produce and distribute ideas resulting from clashes and the erosion of relations with governments (the cases of El Salvador and Nicaragua) (see Table 10.1).

In the case of Guatemala and Honduras, given the governments' uncertainty and lack of information, elites in the form of the CACIF (Guatemala) and the

Table 10.1 Two Scenarios of Economic Elites' Political Influence in Central America

Scenarios	*Country*	*Discursive power*	*Access to policymakers and public opinion*	*Capacities to influence public policy*
Scenario 1	Guatemala Honduras Costa Rica	Major capacities to produce and reproduce discourses and policies through business associations.	Privileged access to policymakers. Elites' discourses are amplified in mass media.	More significant influence over public policies.
Scenario 2	El Salvador Nicaragua	Limited capacities to produce technical expertise and public discourses.	Open confrontation with political elites.	Weaker influence over public policies.

Source: Prepared by the authors.

COHEP (Honduras) produced public policy proposals and documents that centered around discourses on saving the economy, and with it, the country. Through the interconnection of these discourses, elites sought to create a "common us", where attending the crisis depended, in turn, on elites' good work and philanthropic initiatives. This widespread dissemination of their corporate charitable campaigns also allowed them to increase their social capital. In Costa Rica's case, the pandemic coincided with a proposal that promoted a series of pending structural reforms and the creation of a direct channel to the president of the Republic. Economic elites' proximity to mass media helped, in turn, to make their proposals widespread. In all three cases, having an "action plan" enabled elites to communicate directly with the governments. Faced with uncertainty, governments recognized and accepted the limits and scope for constructing public policy broadly defined by elites.

In contrast, the crisis and the disputes with the Bukele and the Ortega governments in El Salvador and Nicaragua prevented these elites from successfully articulating short- and medium-term proposals. Lacking the capacity to communicate proposals and produce information and being in open confrontation with the governments, the discursive power of the elites was weakened. Far from providing more significant inputs on responding to the crisis, their discourses were limited to informing people on hygienic measures and launching complaints against the governments.

Regarding how and to what end discursive power was used, it is evident, at least in the cases of Guatemala, Honduras, and Costa Rica, that it was used to move economic and regressive tax policies forward as well as to promote the pending structural adjustment policies of a neoliberal agenda. Although the discourses of the Nicaraguan elite were not successful, their discourses also included the policies of flexible working hours and reducing, or even eliminating, taxes.

Considering the crises caused by the pandemic, what is discussed here indicates that the discursive turn of strengthening the State and social dialogue has boundaries founded by elites. It is worth noting – as made evident in the El Salvador and Nicaragua cases – that even when economic elites maintain control over critical economic resources, their discursive power can be limited. This is the case if (1) elites lack access to critical information and (2) elites are not included in drafting public policy proposals that provide them with legitimacy and channels to decision-makers as well as public opinion. The following sections will provide the methodology and empirical material of the study.

10.4 Methodology

This chapter is grounded in a comparative approach analyzing countries with similar social, economic, and political characteristics, strong elites, weak institutions, and ample space for redistributive progress. We based our work on a comparative discourse analysis of economic elites' public statements. To this end, we created a new database that tracked the public statements of business associations and their presidents, principally from the social networks of *Facebook* (N=230) and *Twitter* (N=446). The latter took precedence as the primary source of information because it is one of the most used platforms in the selected countries, in addition to *WhatsApp* (Latinobarómetro 2018). The public statements analyzed in these social networks include documents, announcements, press releases, reports, proposals, and recovery plans. By triangulating information, other public statements were scoured from business associations' web pages to complement what was found on the social networks indicated.

One limitation of these sources is that they do not allow us to capture points and events that are by nature non-public, such as consensuses or private meetings held by economic and political elites. Likewise, the nature of the social networks studied means that elites' public discourses are mainly communicative. This focus also excludes other meetings with non-formal associations of businessmen or other think tanks. However, we consider that, given the restricted access to economic elites, this focus allows us to elucidate comparatively the discussions, characteristics, types of relations, and power that elites in general construct.

The study has been carried out in three phases. First, all the statements were transcribed to upload them as text files in the NVivo12 software. These were then structured by case. Following an inductive approach, the statements were reviewed first, and afterward, a variables guide was elaborated (see Table 10.2) to manually code each of the documents. Textual evidence was retrieved for each node from all the documents and by specific country. These dimensions and variables were used as a coding guide (see Table 10.3) for the textual records of statements.

Based on the dispute over positioning frames that arise among different social actors, this study focuses on elites' discursive narratives. The context of the COVID-19 pandemic revealed a more apparent interest in influencing public policy, entailing far more direct questioning of the government by elites. Levels of discursive tension expressed by economic elites in relation to governments'

Table 10.2 Variable Guides and their Descriptions According to the Objective

Objective	*Dimension*	*Variable*	*Description*
Analyze demands and discursive tensions expressed by elites in their communications during the first six months of the pandemic.	Prescriptive and propositional language (deontological markers)	Level of tension (0, 1, 2, or 3)	Type of prescriptive verb used regarding what governments "should do"
	Proportionality of what should be done	Government	Allusion to the specific measure the government should adhere to principally regarding fiscal and economic matters
		Everyone	Allusion to an "us" in terms of the individual and collective responsibilities that society should accept
		Associations should	Allusion to what businesses should do in the context of the pandemic, from what health guidelines to follow to their relationship with collaborators
		Associations do	Account of the actions taken by the associations and/or private sector in the context of the pandemic
	The subject of the demand	Economic Tax	Type and details of the demand according to the topic

Source: Prepared by the authors.

actions are informed by Van Dijk's (1989) typology of discursive styles that is based on a Weberian understanding of power, where power is understood as "the probability that one actor within a social relationship will be in a position to carry out his own will despite resistance" (Weber 1978: 53). This power is reflected in discursive acts characterized by discursive styles, encompassing (1) "direct, pragmatic function (elocutionary force), such as commands, threats, laws, regulations, instructions, and more indirectly through recommendations or advice"; (2) persuasive discourses, like publicity and propaganda, that aim to influence the recipient's future actions; (3) the description of future events, which seeks to dictate future desired and undesired actions; and (4) the influential narrative, which aims to present future scenarios as desired or undesired in order to indicate that actions to be taken (Van Dijk 1989: 27) (see Table 10.2). This typology allows us to combine the principal theorists of framing studies and the concept of discursive power.

To operationalize Table 10.3, we created discursive markers that would identify prescriptive and propositional elements in the texts published by business elites. Working from the premise that the central point of discursive tensions in the context studied is based on an understanding of what "should be" (in this case, what

Table 10.3 Discursive Typology

Type of discursive style	*Indicators*
Direct, pragmatic function	Orders, threats, laws, regulations, instructions, recommendations, advice.
Persuasive	Repetition and argumentation are connected to market oversight mechanisms.
Descriptive with projections into the future	Argumentation and description of future courses of action, warnings, predictions, plans, and possible scenarios.
Influential narrative	A desired or undesired future is presented dramatically, with emotional appeals or other original stylistic forms.

Source: Prepared by the authors based on Van Dijk (1989).

Table 10.4 Levels of Tension and Related Verbs[2]

Level of tension	*Prescriptive verbs*
3	"Exige", "demanda", "denuncia", "urge", "rechaza" (Require, demand, denounce, urge to do, reject)
2	"Insta", "reitera", "insiste", "espera", "advierte", "señala", "alerta" (Call on, reiterate, insist, hope, advise, point out, warn)
1	"Solicita", "sugiere", "pide", "propone", "llama", "recomienda" (Request, suggest, ask for, propose, call for, recommend)
0	"Anuncia", "informa", "comunica", "puntualiza", "manifiesta" (Announce, inform, communicate, specify, express)

Source: Prepared by the authors.

should be the response to the COVID-19 pandemic), value statements were identified based on a pragmatic analysis of the language, identifying deontic modal markers. From this, a scale of tension was devised based on verbal constructions, categorized in accordance to the prescriptive grammar employed (the more prescriptive the text, the higher the tension level), which enabled us to identify and quantify business elites' effort to persuade governments to act in a certain way. As shown in Table 10.4, tension levels were categorized in ascending order from 0 to 3.

10.5 Context: Central America, Economic Elites, Discourses, and Discursive Tensions during the First Months of the Pandemic

In the context of the first six months of the COVID-19 pandemic, economic elites' demands and narratives around what should be done and how to do it varied over time and among the countries studied. Most statements arose as responses to specific measures and actions by individual governments. They enable us to illustrate two central aspects: on the one hand, the economic elites' discursive tensions and demands regarding what governments should do, and, on the other hand, the policies, narratives, and frames proposed by business associations. During the first, second, and third two-month periods of the pandemic, the countries studied underwent changes in the severity of measures and restrictions put into place. As such, data from the Oxford COVID-19 Government Response Tracker (OxCGRT) database's stringency index reports shifts during the first six months of the COVID-19 pandemic regarding the closing of localities and schools as well as travel bans on a value scale from 0 to 100, with 100 being the strictest.

Figure 10.1 shows that the number of restrictive measures increased in the first months of the pandemic in all cases studied, reaching around 100, except Nicaragua, which maintained levels under 25 during all the analyzed months. By September 2020, both Guatemala and El Salvador began to relax measures after having remained under restrictions continuously for five months. In the cases of Honduras and Costa Rica, the stringency levels of the policies dropped starting in August and continued to do so in the following days.

The public statements made by all the business associations studied in the first month of the pandemic, during March 2020, showed acceptance of these measures to contain the spread of COVID-19. In the Costa Rican case, even though the first statements expressed concern about the pandemic, the president of UCCAEP called for caution in pursuing the measures to avoid severe economic repercussions. In addition, like in the case of El Salvador, ANEP initially appealed to build public–private alliances to contain the virus's spread and make collective decisions. In the case of Costa Rica, this request came to fruition, while in El Salvador, a similar

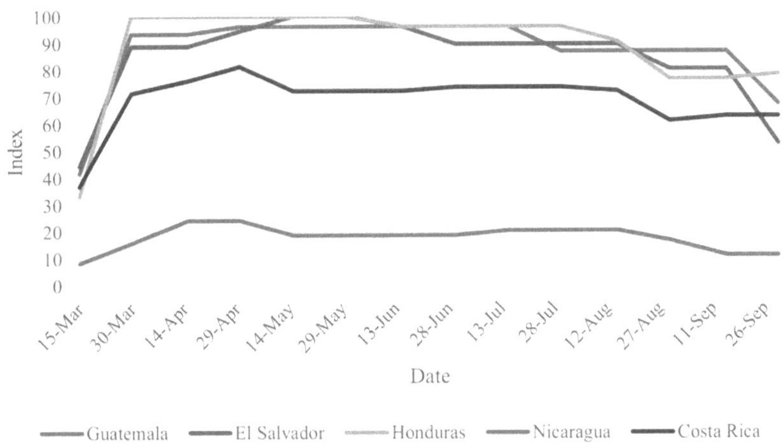

Figure 10.1 Index of bans and closure policies, 2020 (stringency index).

Source: Prepared by the authors based on the Oxford COVID-19 Response Tracker.

petition remained unrealized. On the contrary, in the months analyzed, various points of contention between ANEP and the Salvadorian government can be identified, as shown in the sequence presented in Figure 10.2. Coordination between the private and public sectors was apparent in Honduras starting in April when "Multisector Roundtables" were organized for decision-making.

In Nicaragua, COSEP repeatedly touched on the need for the government to take restrictive measures to contain the spread of the virus in the first trimester. This was in the face of Nicaraguan authorities' inaction and the low level of stringency of their strategies for containing the virus, as shown in Figure 10.1. In the months following this situation, COSEP focused on presenting its proposals and petitions to the business sector and the community at large to exercise collective responsibility around the containment and prevention of COVID-19.

In line with those mentioned above, the public statements of all the business associations studied in the first month of the pandemic, March 2020, expressed an acceptance of restrictive measures implemented to contain the spread of COVID-19. However, as shown in Figure 10.2 the discourses for or against State measures varied over time. At different moments, the business associations discursively communicated their positions on specific issues; sometimes, they even focused on issuing government recommendations.

In general, as Figure 10.2 shows, businesses' statements communicated their positions on specific topics on various occasions; they focused on issuing government recommendations at certain points. In the following sections, the demands and discursive tensions of the business elite from March to September 2020 are explored in detail in each country. As we argue above, this allows us to speak about two types of discursive power: strong and weak.

10.5.1 Guatemala: The Most Influential Association

In Guatemala, the CACIF has been a dominant political actor. Its active political participation has remained intact despite institutional changes in the past (ICEFI 2015; Schneider 2012). This organization has successfully articulated the economic interests of its members and gathered, above all, expertise, knowledge, and information. Against this backdrop, on March 31, 2020, CACIF made public to Alejandro Giammattei's government its plan of short-, medium-, and long-term economic measures based on a system of rigid austerity (issuing bonds to pay for immediate expenses,[3] approving a Paperwork Reduction Act,[4] approving the preferential interest law – Law 4818) and the elimination, reduction, or exemption from different taxes on businesses (social solidarity, revenue, tourism, VAT).

In public discussion of the proposals presented by the association, there was a constant in its reasoning: the reduction/elimination of business taxes and the procurement of temporary resources via domestic borrowing would avoid economic collapse. In a second document from May 2021, CACIF emphasized reviving foreign trade by prioritizing seeking and financing funding from the U.S. through the *United States International Development Finance Corporation* and other

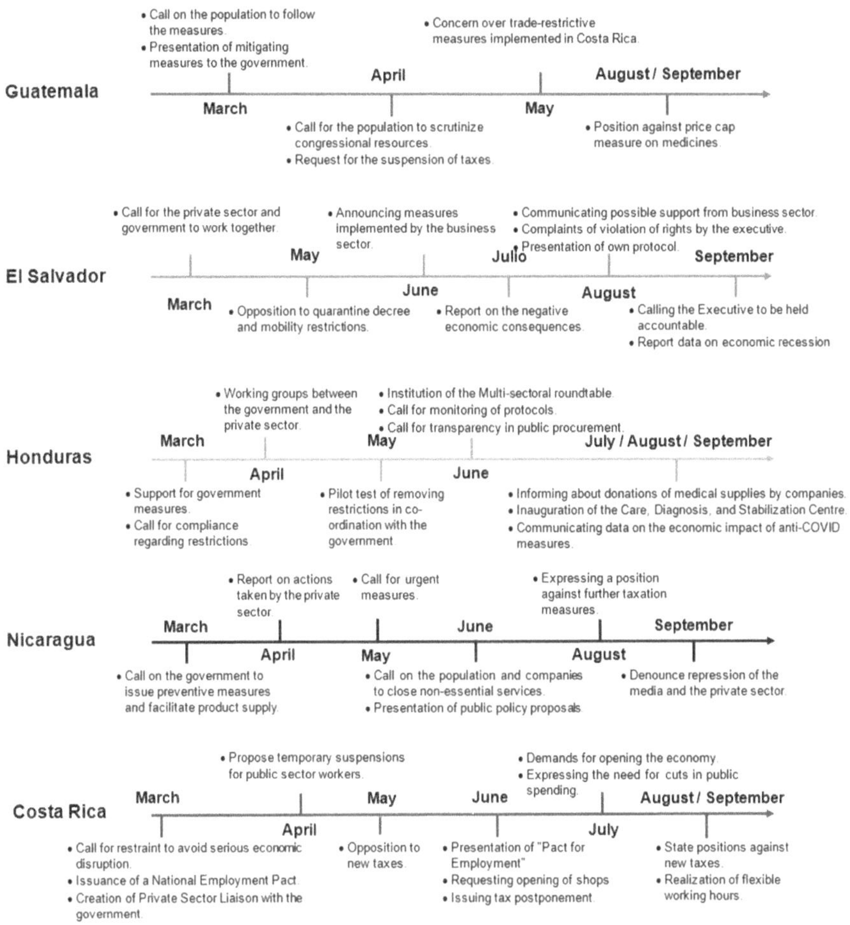

Figure 10.2 Sequence of objectives identified in business statements by country.

Source: Prepared by the authors.

international organizations, a private–public economic recovery commission, and a recovery plan based on remittances and domestic tourism. These proposals underscore the difficulty of implementing institutional changes that assist the State in seeking resources through fiscal reform, for example.

The discourses of Guatemalan elites also emphasized what the government and society should do (see Figure 10.3). In this manner, in publications, which were often accompanied by the hashtag #EnEstoEstamosTodos (#We'reAllInThisTogether), the need to take a constructive attitude of solidarity in the country was reiterated, with the slogan: "It depends on all of us!". On the other hand, when elites spoke about their peers, they referred to their corporate philanthropy work, especially

Figure 10.3 Hierarchic proportionality map of "What Should Be Done" in Guatemala.

Source: Prepared by the authors.

donations made in the form of food, medical equipment, and money to address the emergency under the hashtag #TrabajamosPorTi (#WeWorkForYou).

In this case, elites did not come into conflict with the government. In the face of the urgency of addressing the economic crises spawned by the pandemic, CACIF has fulfilled the role of a privileged private sector partner with the government. At the same time, it offered public policy solutions and intervened directly in crisis management. In terms of online declarations, Guatemalan elites made the fewest statements during the period studied (see Figure 10.4). Additionally, discursive tensions arising from this declaration remained at the lowest levels (1 and 2), and only on three occasions did elites' demands reach their highest point (level 3). It is interesting to note in the Guatemalan case that these discursive tensions did not occur with Giammattei's government but rather with other government bodies such as, for example, the Congress (April 29, 2020), the Superintendence of Tax Administration (SAT), against whom CACIF submitted an application for amparo (enforcement of legal protection) (April 15, 2020) for not deferring tax collection, and local governments (August 11, 2020). The above-mentioned appears to bear on the close relationship and dialogue between elites and the government.

In Guatemala, CACIF exerts strong discursive power, given its high capacity to craft and use public discourse and its channels for the government to translate discourses into public policies. In the trajectory of their discursive narratives, they avoid assigning a more significant role or resources to the State (through taxes, for

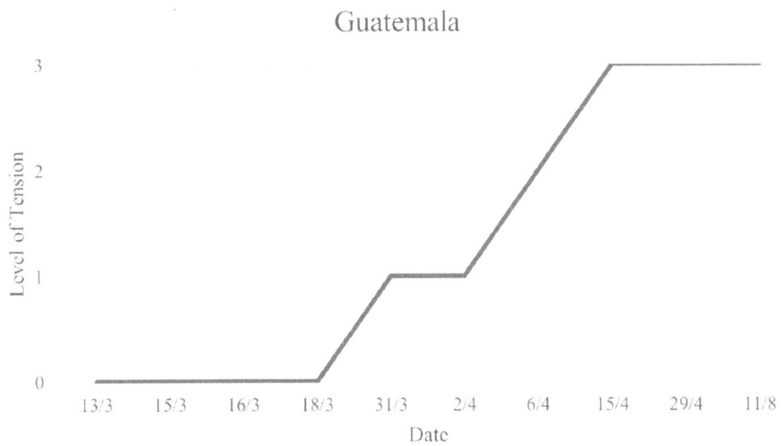

Figure 10.4 Discursive tensions in the case of Guatemala.

Source: Prepared by the authors.

example), they critically depend on outside resources or debt to avoid economic collapse, and, above all, they give in a public discourse in which CACIF and other associations are assumed to be better than the State in managing public tasks like distributing food or medicine during the pandemic.

10.5.2 Honduras: Connections between COHEP and the Executive

In Honduras, the connection between the economic elites and the government has been particularly profitable for the elites. These linkages with the government of Juan Orlando Hernández defined the economic and fiscal solutions proposed through Multisector Roundtables – a negotiation process promoted by the executive branch publicly announced in April 2020. Armed with lawyers, bills, and analysts, COHEP has always found open doors in the Honduran ministries and presidential offices. Thus, far from opposing the closures proposed by the government of Juan Orlando Hernández, COHEP became a valuable resource for the government by lending support to closing the economy and promoting information campaigns on health measures.

In a first statement made on March 17, 2020, COHEP pointed out that two types of urgent economic measures, financial and fiscal, were needed to provide legal certainty and peace of mind to the business sector. In terms of financial measures, it requested the extension of loan payment terms, the interest rate reduction, and the legal reserve to zero. These concrete measures should be considered in light of the critical role played by the Honduran elite in the banking system – probably more so than the elites of other countries (Kasahara 2012). Regarding fiscal measures, COHEP requested the extension of income tax liquidation deadlines for companies and the creation of tax incentives for the tourism, commercial, and industrial sectors.[5]

COHEP's proposals in negotiations with the government were presented as the only responsible option to avoid closing the economy and increasing unemployment. In addition to defining what should be done, the roundtables constantly figured in the associations' public communication, demanding that the government always respect "what was agreed upon at the roundtables". The donations made by the business sector were also repeatedly mentioned, especially those related to creating the Attention, Diagnosis, and Stabilization Center for COVID-19 and the Saint John Paul II Stabilization Center for COVID-19. These were presented as a joint effort between business associations, mayors' offices, and more than 40 companies. They were promoted on social networks with the hashtag #NosLevantaremos (#WeWillRise).

Several public statements also referenced the productive work of Honduras' business sector and the economic damage it suffered, using the hashtag #ApoyoLaEmpresaNacional (Figure 10.5). The business association's publications in social networks called for support of the private sector's efforts, mainly through "We believe in Honduras! We all need each other".

Figure 10.5 Hierarchic proportionality map of "What Should be Done" in Honduras.

Source: Prepared by the authors.

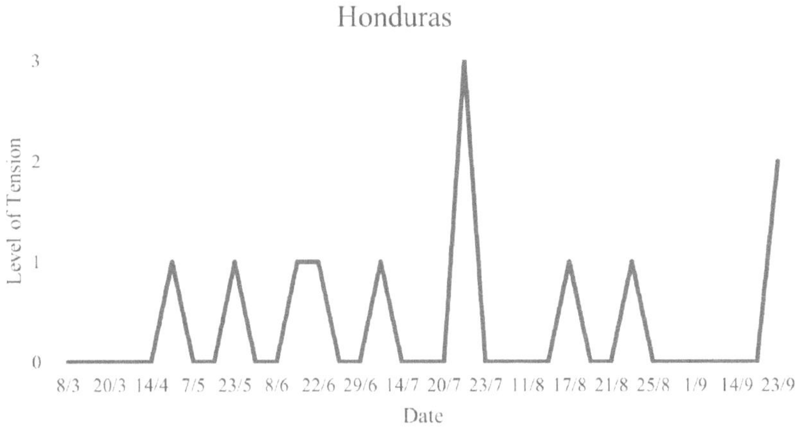

Figure 10.6 Discursive tensions in the case of Honduras.

Source: Prepared by the authors.

On certain occasions, COHEP expressed opposition to some of the governmental measures, which, in its opinion, did not follow what had been agreed upon at the roundtables (see Figure 10.6). Despite this, the levels of discursive tension in the case only remained at the two lowest levels of the indicator (0 and 1). The only two instances of higher tension (3 and 2) were found on July 20, 2020, when COHEP called on the government to reopen the economy, and on September 23, 2020, when the association asked that the income tax and net active tax payments should be postponed.

In the case of Honduras, just as with Guatemala, COHEP possesses a strong discursive power characterized by its capacity to introduce discourses and policies. This is supported by its connections with the executive branch. The sectoral roundtables were the ideal space for the elites to propose their solutions to the crisis and establish the exclusion of other social actors. Furthermore, in this case, the economic and fiscal measures undertaken by the government primarily benefited the elites with tax cuts and fiscal amnesties.

10.5.3 Costa Rica: UCCAEP and Its Roadmap of Pending Policies

In the face of the emergency, and with a government that included important people from the economic elites, the UCCAEP defined potential policies, emphasizing neoliberal structural reforms in its discourse. Compared to the other cases, the economic elites in Costa Rica were the most proactive regarding stating what the government should do, articulating actions and policies, and even confronting the government[6] when they considered it was not doing enough concerning the UCCAEP roadmap.

In the context of the debate, the UCCAEP released a comprehensive document addressing the central economic measures and proposals for dealing with the crisis. Originally published on February 25, 2020, this document is a roadmap centered on austerity policies. Thus, the pandemic provided an opportunity to carry out pending reforms for the neoliberal agenda – for example, measures that address credit supply, the public employment law, and public–private partnerships. In addition, other measures were put back on the table, such as a labor flexibilization law (4/12 hour workdays), the temporary, partial, or total suspension of working hours in the public sector, repealing the School Wage for public employees (*Salario Escolar*), reducing electricity and fuel rates, easing the process for registering agrochemicals and seeds for agricultural technology imports, as well as limiting public spending.

In their speeches, the Costa Rican elites pointed out what the government should do (Figure 10.7). Although there were ideological and political affinities with the executive, through their public participation, the elites sought to define the boundaries of what was possible in a context in which several social groups also sought to influence the response to the crisis. Initially, the business association called for prudence in the face of the health emergency to avoid severe effects on production and labor. However, as of May 2020, the association's demands focused on structural adjustments around the rationalization of public spending, measures that would

Figure 10.7 Hierarchic proportionality map of "What Should be Done" in Costa Rica.

Source: Prepared by the authors.

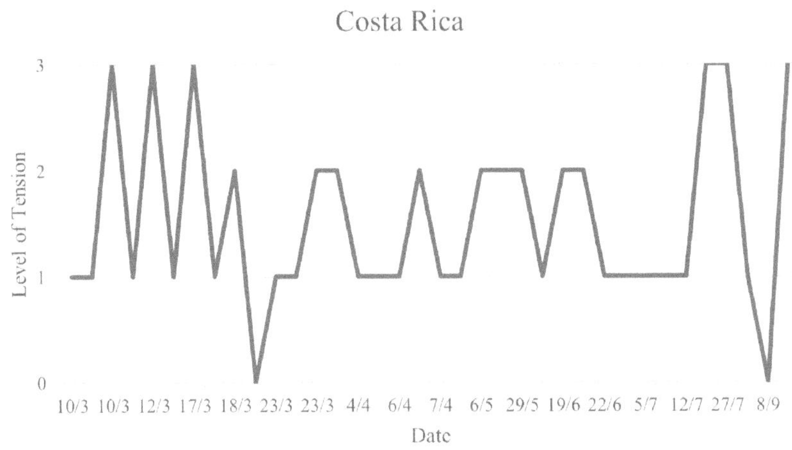

Figure 10.8 Discursive tensions in Costa Rica.

Source: Prepared by the authors.

generate employment, and the participation of the private sector in discussions about the health system, among other issues. It is worth noting that the business association's posts on social networks were significantly reproduced in the press, television news, and radio.

In the case of Costa Rica, variable and inconsistent levels of tension can be observed. It is the second country with the most discursive tensions: of the total number of publications analyzed, 25% are located at level 3 of our scale, 23% at level 2, and 48% at level 1 (Figure 10.8). As noted, during the pandemic, the government and private sector shared ideas and proposals. Thus, the levels of tension observed here seem to be due to pressure from business elites to tilt some policies and actions in their favor. Therefore, in Costa Rica, the creation of a Strategic Liaison Committee "[…]to influence the President of the Republic, Carlos Alvarado, and the deputies in the design and the implementation of measures that will help overcome the COVID-19 health crisis and its structural effects […]" (UCCAEP, 2020) is of particular interest for its discursive power.

In the case of Costa Rica, promoting the roadmap proposed by the UCCAEP gave the elites solid discursive power. This roadmap incorporated a series of policies and actions that, beyond addressing the crisis, sought to clear the way for pending agenda items for the restructuring of the State. The closeness between the States' executive and the elites and the reproduction and socialization of these discourses as the only possible solutions to the crisis in the media helped to promote these policies.

10.5.4 El Salvador: The ANEP in Retreat?

In El Salvador, ANEP has played a hegemonic role in defending the interests of the economic elites since at least the 1980s, alongside political actors (*Alianza Republicana and Nacionalista* – Nationalist Republican Alliance – ARENA), think tanks (*Fundación Salvadoreña para el Desarrollo Social y Económico* – Salvadoran Foundation for Social and Economic Development – FUSADES), and the media (Wolf 2009). However, from the start of the pandemic, their influence was reduced by the urgency of attending to the severe public confrontations between President Bukele and the president of the association, Javier Simán. From his position in the ANEP, Simán, a well-known Salvadoran businessman, led an opposition to the measures implemented by the Salvadoran government. At first, the ANEP called for public–private alliances that would work to contain the spread of the virus and make collective decisions. In a statement made on March 21, 2020, the ANEP advertised the creation of a special fund to support farmers, ranchers, and poultry farmers, but the executive did not heed this call. Five days later, on March 26, the first conflict with Bukele broke out after the president accused ANEP of pocketing US$300 million monthly from the Salvadoran Social Security Institute (ISSS).

In the following months, the presidential decrees, closing the economy and forcing Salvadorans to stay home (Number 593 and subsequent decrees), led to increased conflicts with the elites. From ANEP's point of view, these decrees and the mobility restrictions caused legal insecurity and confusion. Far from supporting the measures, from May 2020 onward, their declarations emphasized the urgency of gradually reopening the economy. Faced with the impossibility of dialogue and joint work with the government, ANEP distanced itself from the Bukele government, pointing out the multiple economic and social costs of the closures and proposing protocols for opening the economy. On the government side, Bukele publicly labeled ANEP a historical obstacle to El Salvador's development.

In the context of the pandemic and in the face of the government's refusal to work with ANEP, these elites mainly oriented their efforts toward information campaigns and defending the association. ANEP's discursive demands emphasized calling for what the government should do (see Figure 10.9). In particular, the request that the government and the private sector should work together was recurrent. Allusions to individual and collective responsibility in the context of the pandemic were accompanied by the hashtags *#JuntosSaldremosAdelante* (#We'llGetAheadTogether) and *#CuidaTuSalud* (#TakeCareofYourHealth), with the slogans: *"No te rindas de esta salimos todos"* ("Don't give up, we'll all get through this") and *"Si te cuidas nos cuidas a todos"* ("If you take care of yourself you take care of everyone").

The allusions to the business sector's actions focused on reiterating that the companies complied with the health protocols and even proposed their own protocols that they voluntarily followed. In addition, as with Guatemala, but to a lesser degree, they evoked medical supplies and food donations for affected families.

Figure 10.9 Hierarchic proportionality map of "What Should be Done" in El Salvador.

Source: Prepared by the authors.

Furthermore, these donations "competed with" government policy that provided unemployed people with subsidies and food bags containing propaganda for the Government of El Salvador.

In the context of the pandemic, discursive tensions varied (0 and 2 – see Figure 10.10). However, three moments of high discursive pressure on the government (level 3) existed. The first was on June 30, when Javier Simán filed a complaint against President Bukele; the second was on July 7, when ANEP urged the government to create an economic reactivation plan; and the third was on September 7, when the business association opposed the government's use of funds from the Salvadoran Social Security Institute (ISSS).

In the case of El Salvador, the confrontation between ANEP and President Bukele weakened the association's ability to produce a unified public discourse around handling the pandemic. As a result of the confrontation around the economic shutdowns, Bukele's accusations of corruption against the association, and the need to defend Javier Simán, the association's responses were limited to these specific issues. In the face of President Bukele's public visibility and popularity, the expression of elite discursive power was diluted between the confrontation with the executive and the information campaigns.

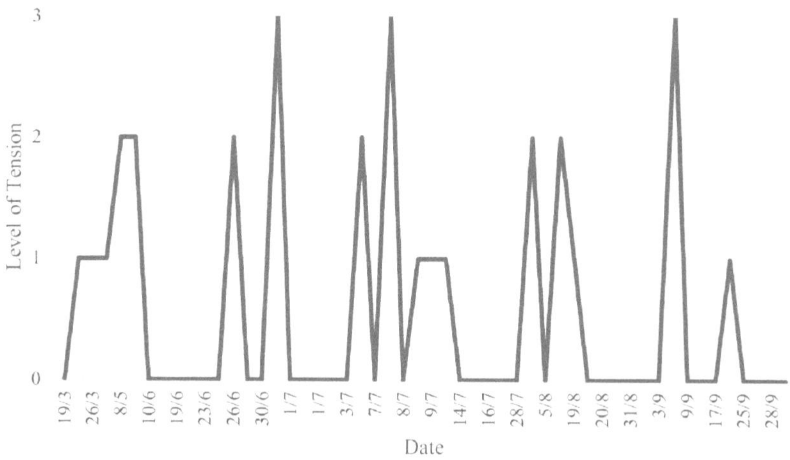

Figure 10.10 Discursive tensions in El Salvador.

Source: Prepared by the authors.

10.5.5 Nicaragua: The End of the COSEP – Ortega Family Model

For nearly a decade, Nicaragua (2007–2018) was the Central American reference for public policy being managed by the economic elites through "the COSEP model" (Chamorro 2018). Since 2007, the linkages between the elites and political power have been arranged through alliances between COSEP, the Ortega family, and the Military Social Welfare Institute – *Instituto de Previsión Social Militar* (Monte and Gómez 2020). The nature of this alliance allowed economic elites to access economic resources and State-linked projects in exchange for being positive global spokespeople on legal security and the business climate in Nicaragua (Spalding 2017).

In Nicaragua, the co-governing pact between the Ortega family and economic elites lasted between 2007 and 2018 (Monte and Gómez 2020). The political crisis unleashed in February 2018 broke this contract and deteriorated the communication channels between economic elites and the executive. Given that the government did not proactively address the economic crisis and health dimensions, the elites' discourses were mainly oriented toward drawing attention to the pandemic. To this end, the economic elites sought to define the agenda around three issues. The first issue was facilitating the process of importing and nationalizing inputs for COVID-19 prevention and organizing support for the supply chains of essential goods. The second was creating a private sector working group to help formulate the measures proposed by the Central American Institute of Business Administration (INCAE), the American Chamber of Commerce of Nicaragua (AMCHAM), and COSEP to address the crisis. The third and final issue was the development of a humanitarian assistance fund, the reduction of fuel and electricity prices, the easing of labor contracts, and the restructuring and financing of credits. These requests continued for several months, and the elite organized a series of conferences and communication materials directed at the general population under the hashtag *#LaVidaEsPrimero* (#LifeComesFirst).

In the first trimester, COSEP repeatedly mentioned that the government needed to take restrictive measures to contain the spread of the virus (Figure 10.11). This was due to the inactivity of the Nicaraguan authorities and the softness of their strategies for containing the pandemic. Responding to this situation, COSEP presented its proposals and requests for the containment and prevention of COVID-19 to the business sector and the population.

The case of Nicaragua presents the highest levels of discursive tension recorded, with 83% of publications reaching level 3 (Figure 10.12). These publications emphasized the urgency for the government to implement health measures to control contagion levels. Another particularity of the Nicaraguan case is that COSEP publications that were critical of the government changed their focus after June when the association issued its last critical commentary on handling the pandemic. From July onward, COSEP's publications focused on electoral reform (July 15), freedom of the press in the face of the embargo of Nicavisión S.A. (September 12), and the controversial Law for the Regulation of Foreign Agents[7] (September 25).

Figure 10.11 Hierarchic proportionality map of "What Should be Done" in Nicaragua.

Source: Prepared by the authors.

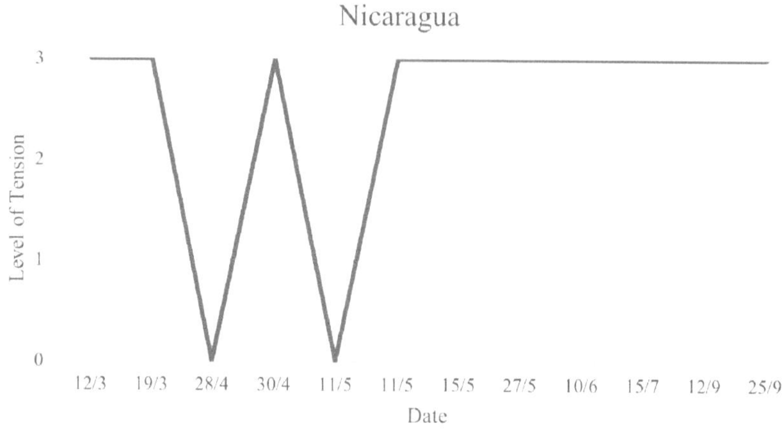

Figure 10.12 Discursive tension levels in Nicaragua.

Source: Prepared by the authors.

In the case of Nicaragua, the confrontation between the Ortega family and the business sector, represented by COSEP, illustrates the end of the public/private co-management model that began in 2007. In the face of the government's inaction in the public management of the pandemic and the breakdown of communication channels between COSEP and the Ortega family, the discursive power of the Nicaraguan elites was limited to information campaigns on COVID-19. Thus, in this case, although the elites sought to propose policies, their influence on politics and politicians was limited or nonexistent.

10.6 Conclusion

The discursive power of the elites is diffuse and difficult to observe. Its specific reproduction in regional contexts such as in Latin America is aided by control over think tanks, teams of lawyers, and unequal access to and close relationships with the media, which, in turn, are highly concentrated in the hands of few families or economic groups. It is a form of power that generates a "social class" identity among the elites and helps circulate and socially legitimize their ideas, norms, and worldviews in virtue of their supposed value for the "collective benefit." We argue that it is a power that precedes collective action (instrumental power) by generating cohesion and providing elites with shared ideas, discourses, and identities.

This comparative study demonstrates the importance and relevance of emphasizing the discourses of the elites to gain insight into the characteristics of their discursive power concerning access to governments and the definition and dissemination of specific programs and policies. Although this study did not focus on tracking State responses to the requests of business elites, we consider that public statements are helpful material for the comparative analysis of discourses of distinct actors in different countries in similar contexts.

Theoretically, this chapter broadens the discussion around the power resources of the elites and their relationship with public policies. The description of the two scenarios presented in this chapter adds to the debate on how economic elites may seek to support or obstruct policy reforms. At the same time, this work allows us to identify differences among economic elites and their relations with political elites. It is not a matter of homogenizing elites and their power, but instead of thinking about them in terms of their own internal ties, trajectories, discourses, and ideas. Moreover, our work shows that the discursive power of elites is not monolithic and can change, both in terms of the historical trajectories of elite influence on public policy and their social and public legitimacy.

In empirical terms, we highlight that, when weighing levels of discursive power, historical trajectories of public activism and unrestricted access to political elites will be critical factors to consider. Likewise, access to the media is fundamental, not only for legitimizing discourses publicly but also for defining and establishing the boundaries of possible public policy. In the face of weak civil societies, the limited dialogue between economic and political elites intensifies the reproduction of discourses that can have direct consequences on the public policy decisions of governments.

In methodological terms, this work sought to innovate in the study of the discourses and ideas of the elites through the construction of databases of the business associations' public statements. The aim is to understand not only the content of the discourses but also the context in which they are produced and the reasons why. Through this approach, we sought to bring into dialogue two parallel theoretical developments (*framing* and *discursive power*) and operationalize them to enrich future studies. Given the limited access to economic elites, we hope this work will encourage new ways of gaining insight into the elites and the public spaces of communication in which they operate. Finally, although it transcends the focus of this study, we considered that the wide diffusion of the measures promoted by the elites in the media, as well as the dissemination of their opinions and speeches during the pandemic, helped define what policies should be approved to deal with the crisis. This poses new questions regarding the relationship between elites and the media in critical times and situations.

Notes

1 March to September 2020.

2 In order to obtain a replicable quantitative result, we first coded the corpus of analysis based on the identification of prescriptive verbs and then proceeded to identify the markers. Besides these four levels, an additional category (miscellaneous) was created for texts in which deontic modal markers could not be identified. In this sense, it is important to note that 56 items were excluded where markers did not appear. The coding was reviewed among the authors for monitoring purposes.

3 Congress used the exemption to the prohibition that Bank of Guatemala give the State credit in the case of catastrophe or public disasters.
4 This law was approved in May 2021.
5 The measures approved by the Honduran Legislature and Executive are four tax amnesties (payments to the Honduran Social Security Institute – IHSS – the Telecommunications, Vehicle and Municipal sectors), postponement of income tax payments, 10% additional incentives to those who do not lay off employees, 10% discounts on the payment of real estate taxes, and the consideration of donations as deductible on income tax.
6 The most complicated moment in this confrontation occurred in August 2020, when the president of the UCCAEP joined other social actors in demanding changes regarding the negotiation of a loan with the International Monetary Fund.
7 The law limits funding to non-governmental organizations and creates a designation (foreign agent) that can lead to disproportionate penalties, such as cancellation of legal personality or fines of hundreds of thousands of dollars.

References

Bell, Stephen. 2012. "The Power of Ideas: The Ideational Shaping of the Structural Power of Business." *International Studies Quarterly* 56 (4), 661–673.
Bernhagen, Patrick. 2008. *The Political Power of Business: Structure and Information in Public Policy-Making*. New York: Routledge.
Bull, Benedicte. 2014. "Towards a Political Economy of Weak Institutions and Strong Elites in Central America." *European Review of Latin American and Caribbean Studies* 97, 117–128.
Bull, Benedicte, and Mariel Aguilar-Støen. 2019. "Peacebuilding and business elites in Guatemala and El Salvador: Explaining the discursive 'institutional turn.'" *Conflict, Security & Development* 19 (1), 121–141.
Cárdenas, Julian, and Francisco Robles-Rivera. 2021. "Corporate Networks and Business Influence in Panama, Costa Rica, and El Salvador." *Colombia Internacional* 107, 87–112.
Carragee, Kevin M., and Wim Roefs. 2004. "The Neglect of Power in Recent Framing Research." *Journal of Communication* 54 (2), 214–233.
CEPAL. 2020. El desafío social en tiempos del COVID-19. CEPAL. www.cepal.org/es/publicaciones/45527-desafio-social-tiempos-covid-19 (March 22, 2023).
Chamorro, Carlos. F. 2018. ¿'Modelo COSEP'o el régimen de Ortega?. *Confidencial*. January 2, 2018. https://confidencial.digital/opinion/modelo-cosep-o-el-regimen-de-ortega/ (March 22, 2023).
Davis, Aeron. 2007. *The mediation of power: A critical introduction*. New York: Routledge.
Entman, Robert M. 1993. "Framing: Toward Clarification of a Fractured Paradigm." *Journal of Communication* 43 (4), 51–58.
———. 2003. "Cascading Activation: Contesting the White House's Frame After 9/11." *Political Communication* 20 (4), 415–432.
Fairfield, Tasha. 2015. *Private Wealth and Public Revenue*. Cambridge: Cambridge University Press.
Freedman, Des. 2014. *The Contradictions of Media Power*. London: Bloomsbury Publishing.
Fuchs, Doris A. 2007. *Business power in global governance*. Boulder: Lynne Rienner.
Fuchs, Doris A., and Kalfagianni, Agni (2009). "Discursive power as a source of legitimation in food retail governance." *The International Review of Retail, Distribution and Consumer Research* 19 (5), 553–570.

Gamson, William A., and Andre Modigliani. 1989. "Media discourse and public opinion on nuclear power: A constructionist approach." *American Journal of Sociology* 95 (1), 1–37.

ICEFI. 2015. Política fiscal: Expresión del poder de las élites centroamericanas—Google Search. https://icefi.org/sites/default/files/pf_expresion_del_poder_de_las_elites_cr_jm190516.pdf (March 22, 2023).

Iyengart, Shanto. 1991. *Is Anyone Responsible? How Television Frames Political Issues*. Chicago: University of Chicago Press.

Kasahara, Yuri. 2012. "Should I stay or should I go? A comparative study of banking sector policies and the strategies of Central American business groups." *Business and Politics* 14 (4), 1–43.

Latinobarómetro. Banco de Datos. 2018. "Latinobarómetro 2018". www.latinobarometro.org/latContents.jsp (March 16, 2023).

Marsh, David, Sadiya Akram, and Holly Birkett. 2015. "The structural power of business: Taking structure, agency, and ideas seriously." *Business and Politics* 17 (3), 577–601.

Mills, C. Wright. 2000. *The power elite*. Oxford: Oxford University Press.

Monte, Antonio, and Juan Pablo Gómez. 2020. "Autoritarismo, violencia y élites en Nicaragua. Reflexiones sobre la crisis (2018–2019)." *Anuario de Estudios Centroamericanos* 46, 1–29.

Pérez Sáinz, Juan. P. 2017. "Imaginarios sociales del empresariado en Centroamérica. Una aproximación a partir de la competitividad y la responsabilidad social." *Anuario de Estudios Centroamericanos* 43, 15–36.

Pérez Sáinz, Juan. P., Rafael Segura Carmona, and Diego Fernández Montero. 2011. *Sociedades fracturadas: La exclusión social en Centroamérica*. San José: Flacso.

Rettberg, Angelika. 2016. "Need, creed, and greed: Understanding why business leaders focus on issues of peace." *Business Horizons* 59 (5), 481–492.

Robles-Rivera, Francisco. 2020. "Élites y estrategias de captura de medios en América Central." *Revista Mexicana de Sociologia* 1 (1), 9–40.

Robles-Rivera, Francisco, and Koen Voorend. 2012. "Los dueños de la palabra en Costa Rica en un contexto de reforma neoliberal." *Revista Rupturas* 1 (2), 144–161.

Rockwell, Rick, and Noreene Janus. 2003. *Media Power in Central America*. Champaign: University of Illinois Press.

Sánchez-Ancochea, Diego, and Juliana Martínez. 2022. *Can COVID-19 prompt more inclusive social policy? A closer look at policy opportunities*. Early Draft.

Sánchez-Ancochea, Diego, Juliana Martínez, and Salvador Martí. 2015. La incorporación social en Centroamérica: Trayectorias, obstáculos y oportunidades. http://repository.eclac.org/handle/11362/39657 (March 16, 2023).

Sandoval García, Carlos. 2008. "The media in Costa Rica: Many media, scarce communication." In *The Media in Latin America,* edited by Lugo, Jairo. 100–115. New York: Open University Press.

Schneider, Aaron. 2012. *State-Building and Tax Regimes in Central America*. Cambridge: Cambridge University Press.

Spalding, Rose. J. 2017. "Los empresarios y el estado posrevolucionario: El reordenamiento de las élites y la nueva estrategia de colaboración en Nicaragua". *Anuario de Estudios Centroamericanos* 43, 149–188.

UCCAEP. March 27, 2020. Cámaras empresariales crearon Grupo de Enlace Sector Privado con Gobierno. https://uccaep.or.cr/index.php/comunicados-prensa/60-comunicados-de-prensa/597-camaras-empresariales-crearon-grupo-de-enlace-sector-privado-con-gobierno.html?fbclid=IwAR13elY5STev5XUHLPF84jEL5XHCS4_pPOQuYq1JSvuBsPfHpQHDnUdmhLs (March 14, 2023).

Van Dijk, Teun. 1989. "Structures of Discourse and Structures of Power". *Communication Yearbook* 12, 18–59.

Vogel, David. 1987. "Political Science and the Study of Corporate Power: A Dissent from the New Conventional Wisdom". *British Journal of Political Science* 17 (4), 385–408.

Weber, Max. 1978. *Economy and Society*. Berkeley: University of California Press.

Wolf, Sonja. 2009. "Subverting democracy: Elite rule and the limits to political participation in post-war El Salvador." *Journal of Latin American Studies* 41 (03), 429–465.

11 Wealth Concentration in Latin America

The Role of Direct Taxation

Juan Pablo Jiménez, Fernando Lorenzo, James Mahon and Gustavo Viñales

11.1 Introduction

After a long period of absence from the public debate, there has been a renewed academic and political interest in the concentration of wealth in recent years. Various trends account for this interest—new historical and theoretical academic works (Piketty 2014; Saez and Zucman 2019), public disgust at flagrant and persistent inequalities, and fiscal shortfalls worsened by the COVID pandemic.

At the same time, there is a growing recognition that income is an insufficient measure of the economic well-being of households (Stiglitz, Sen, and Fitoussi 2009). Wealth allows people to smooth consumption over time and protect it from unexpected changes in income. Households with reserves of wealth can benefit from capital income streams that support a higher material standard of living, even if the wealth is held in assets that are not easily converted into money. Pledged as collateral, they facilitate borrowing to finance expenses. By the same token, severe inequity in the distribution of wealth can increase economic vulnerability and translate into lost opportunities, reductions in social mobility, and political inequality (see Hills 2015; Piketty 2014; Stiglitz 2012).

Recent schollars confirm the importance of wealth concentration. Studies have shown that a high concentration of wealth hurts the economic growth of countries (Bagchi and Svejnar 2013; Brueckner and Lederman 2018; Davies et al. 2008; Morck et al. 2000); on citizen suspicion and mistrust of elites and institutions (Bagchi and Svejnar 2013; Freund and Oliver 2016); as well as on democratic practices (Islam and Islam 2018; Brzezinski, Sałach, and Wroński2019). In addition, reducing the concentration of wealth can lead to environmental benefits, including a decline in carbon emissions (Hailemariam et al. 2020).

This topic acquires particular relevance in Latin America. According to the World Inequality Database (WID), in 2019, the wealthiest 1% of the population of Latin America obtained 31.7% of total national income and around 46% of the wealth. The last figure is higher than the world average, which is 38%, and also higher than that recorded for other regions of the world, such as the European Union (24%), Asia (36%) or sub-Saharan Africa (37%). The pandemic probably made this inequality worse.

DOI: 10.4324/9781032636764-14

This brings us to taxation for two reasons. First, the growth and reproduction of the region's wealth concentration can be blamed not only on its weak taxation of assets (stock) but also on its inadequate taxation of income (flow), historically aimed at easy-to-tax salary income and away from capital. Second, adequate taxation of the richest could expand revenue collection while enhancing the legitimacy of the tax system (Jiménez and Solimano 2011).

This chapter argues that Latin American governments need to strengthen the measurement of wealth concentration at the same time as they more adequately tax concentrated wealth and the high incomes that create it. Although further study is needed on the optimal wealth tax in the regional context, in the near term, an expansion of real estate (*predial*) taxes appears most applicable, with other wealth taxes expanded later, perhaps in tandem with reforms to capital income taxation.

The chapter proceeds as follows. The first section describes several changes in the policy context that have favored a reconsideration of wealth taxation: advances in the measurement of household wealth, new academic and theoretical support for wealth taxes, a more congenial attitude among international organizations, and an increase in international cooperation with regard to tax information and assessment. The next segment turns to Latin America, showing why there is ample room for stronger wealth and income taxation across the region. It is followed by a section on the policy options to reduce wealth concentration in Latin America and another on the distinctive challenges to these efforts in the region. The chapter concludes by considering the role of direct taxation in the broader policy context of Latin America.

11.2 Recent Developments Favorable to a Revival of Wealth Taxation

Several global trends now favor a reconsideration of tax policy as a response to wealth concentration: advances in wealth and income measurement, changes in optimal taxation theory; related to this, a new openness to wealth taxation among international financial institutions; and a notable increase in international cooperation around tax information.

11.2.1 Advances in Measuring Wealth and Income

In the past ten years, more and better data on household wealth have become available. International compilations include the OECD's Wealth Distribution Database (WDD) (Balestra and Tonkin 2018); the Credit Suisse Global Wealth Report and Databook (Davies, Lluberas, and Shorrocks 2017); and the WID, which was used for the World Inequality Report 2018 (Alvaredo, Garbinti, and Piketty 2017). Taken together, these studies begin to provide a more complete picture of the distribution of wealth around the world. However, it should be noted that several methodological differences may hamper comparisons of the results of these studies.

To make meaningful comparisons of wealth inequality across countries and over time, it is essential to adopt a consistent definition of wealth (Saez and Zucman 2019). Following the definition codified in the System of National Accounts

(UN 2009), household net worth includes all non-financial assets (real estate, land, buildings) and financial assets (stocks, bonds, bank deposits, life insurance, pensions), over which people can assert real property rights.

Compared to the measurement of income, measuring wealth brings us face-to-face with the economic structure of a society. Wealth is less sensitive to changes in the labor market than income, and it is more permanent over time (ECLAC 2022). Positions of affluence tend to be inherited from one generation to another. Recent studies suggest that large sums are transferred yearly through inheritance and succession (OECD 2021). The annual flow of inheritance was estimated to be between 8% and 15% of Gross National Income (GNI) in some European countries (Piketty and Zucman 2014). Recent academic analyses comparing income and wealth inequality show that wealth is distributed more unequally than income in the world and the region (IMF 2014; ECLAC 2019).

11.2.2 The Conceptual Framework

For decades, economic theory has questioned whether wealth taxes should be part of an optimal tax model. The dominant perspective questioned the advisability of taxing wealth accumulation, expressing doubts about both the adequacy of criteria for defining the tax base and the setting of tax rates in case such a tax were to be implemented. However, over the past few years, a growing body of literature has begun to incorporate more realistic assumptions about the functioning of labor markets into traditional models of optimal fiscal policy (Scheuer and Slemrod 2021). This line of research has focused on labor income taxes in static models that capture recent trends in occupational classification and wage inequality. Since a growing concentration of profits can affect, through savings, the degree of wealth inequality in the future, it is worth asking whether these trends, too, alter the general criteria of optimal taxation on capital and wealth.

Theoretical analysis has traditionally assumed that all wealth inequality is driven by inequality in labor income (Scheuer and Slemrod 2021). In this case, the Atkinson-Stiglitz theorem (Atkinson and Stiglitz 1976) provides a classic reference, which states that if there is a (non-linear) tax on labor income, any distortion on saving is Pareto-inefficient. The conclusion derived from this approach is that there could be no well-founded reason for taxing income from capital or wealth.

Various works developed over the last few years have questioned the realism of the underlying assumptions in this theoretical approach. Sáez (2002), for example, has provided evidence on the positive correlation between labor productivity and the propensity to save, which would defy the second condition of the Atkinson-Stiglitz theorem to the extent that individuals would have different discount rates, depending on their ability to generate profits.

At the same time, we should acknowledge that in reality, those responsible for designing policies do not face a blank piece of paper. They must make decisions in a context dominated by an existing inequality of wealth, where nothing indicates that the differences they observe could be attributed to disparate levels of productivity. People might differ in the wealth they possess, either because they have inherited it from previous generations or because they themselves have saved in the past.

Recognizing these developments, the contemporary theory of optimal taxation supports taxing the accumulation of wealth, although the literature has not settled on the most appropriate instruments for doing so (Scheuer and Slemrod 2021). It is worth bearing in mind that in the traditional models, a wealth tax is equivalent to a tax on capital income—so the discussion remains open between progressive taxes on income generated by capital (flows) and a tax on accumulated wealth (stock).

As far as inherited wealth is concerned, various models have been proposed to define optimal taxation. In Piketty and Saez (2013), the authors show that optimal inheritance tax formulas can be expressed in terms of estimable "sufficient statistics" constructed from the elasticities that determine the behavior of individuals, the parameters that characterize distribution, and social preferences for redistribution. In short, the taxation of capital, accumulated wealth, and inherited wealth have returned to the toolbox of optimal taxation after years of being left aside. The old conventional advice that an ideal tax system should not include this type of tax today appears severely questioned.

11.2.3 Changes within International Organizations

Influenced by the conceptual developments mentioned above, as well as by the distributive and fiscal effects of the crises of the last decade, international organizations have come to accept the importance of direct taxation, especially property taxation. The IMF's *Fiscal Monitor 2021* (IMF 2021) concludes that countries should consider closing existing gaps in direct taxation by applying more progressive personal income taxes (PITs) and strengthening underused property and inheritance taxes. In the event that reforms are insufficient to achieve their objectives, governments could consider taxing wealth directly, addressing the challenges involved in the design and implementation of this type of tax.

Granted, these taxes are often unpopular with taxpayers. In a study carried out by Ahmad, Brosio, and Jiménez (2018), the authors attribute the unpopularity of the property tax to several factors. These include the determination of the tax base, which for most taxpayers means the assessment of home values (Slack and Bird 2014); taxpayers' lack of participation in the asset valuation process (Sheffrin 2010); the lack of correspondence between "capacity to pay" and the rates applied; and the high visibility of the payment process, which generates animosity and opposition in taxpayers (Cabral and Hoxby 2012).

However, we can see another side of the story from recent surveys. The referred IMF publication of 2021 presents the results of a multi-country survey in which most respondents thought that the tax burden on low and middle incomes was too high while the burden on the rich was too low. It also shows that in most economies, a higher proportion of respondents would support more progressive taxation. This balance of opinion holds across all income levels, for both advanced and emerging economies, and for respondents with high and low confidence in public officials.

It is fair to say that the overall direction of reform has changed. Whereas two decades ago, the main policy objective among international financial institutions was the harmonization of tax agreements to avoid "double taxation." Today, guided by the OECD and the current administration of the United States, discussions within the same forums have shifted toward the implementation of a global minimum tax rate to bypass "double tax avoidance."

11.2.4 Increased International Cooperation and Coordination

The most formidable barrier to significant taxation of mobile assets has been the lack of international cooperation. In his book *Capital in the 21st Century*, Piketty (2014) proposed an annual and progressive tax on individual holdings of capital as the net value of the assets each person controls (see Viñales et al. 2021). Yet he admitted that the main obstacle to this tax was the meager progress in the automatic submission of banking information about taxpayers. At the time, his example of progress in this regard was the FATCA (Foreign Account Tax Compliance Act) of the United States, which requires foreign financial institutions to transmit information to the US Tax Administration (the IRS).

This regulation remains in force, but it has been significantly extended and fortified. Since 2017, the system for the automatic exchange of financial information between tax administrations has become global within the framework of the OECD's CRS (Common Reporting Standard). The wide-ranging multilateral application of conventions among tax administrations, promoted after the international financial crisis of 2008, has represented a significant milestone for international coordination in tax matters.

Rich Latin American taxpayers have long kept much of their wealth abroad, especially since the 1982 debt crisis. For many tax experts, this situation has reinforced a position against wealth taxation. At the same time, it has been used to support the reduction of tax rates on capital gains and to maintain exemptions intended to stimulate investment. As pointed out by Viñales et al. (2021), however, this concern may now be exaggerated to the extent that the relevance of this line of argument has been diminishing because of the changes in the international context just described.

11.3 Why There Is Room to Strengthen Wealth Taxation in Latin America

As noted above, estimates of wealth distribution in Latin America place it as the most unequal region in the world. However, detailed information about the disposition of this wealth is uneven.

Leaving aside natural wealth (with which Latin America is well endowed) and real estate, the most important form of wealth in contemporary accounts is financial assets held by companies, governments, households, and institutions that serve households (ECLAC 2019). While only four Latin American countries (Brazil, Chile, Colombia, and Mexico) have published financial account figures as part of their national accounts system, we can get a rough idea of the regional pattern.

Brazil has the largest total, $11 trillion in financial assets (measured in purchasing power parity, PPP, not including debt). It is closely followed by Mexico, with 7.9 billion dollars (PPP); Colombia and Chile have just over 2 billion dollars each (PPP). However, these differences are largely due to the size of the population of each country. If financial capital (not including debt) were divided by the number of inhabitants, Chile would rank first, with 120,000 dollars per capita, followed by Mexico, with 61,000 dollars per capita (ECLAC 2019).

We can provide further insight into the wealthiest households based on global compilations. The largest accumulations of business income in Latin America and the Caribbean are derived to an unusual degree from finance, telecoms, and food and less from technology and real estate. Compared to the rest of the world, 24% of the billionaires in Latin America (citizens and/or residents), who accumulate 22.5% of their total wealth, belong to the Finance and Investment industry, while this figure is approximately 12% in the rest of the world. The opposite occurs with the technology industry, which represents only 3.4% of the wealth of Latin American billionaires (being only 3 people) compared to 15.6% for the rest of the world, although in both groupings, the percentage has recently increased. As for real estate, in the rest of the world, it accounts for 9.3% of the billionaire fortunes, while in Latin America, this figure is only 0.7%. In Latin America, the greatest average wealth among billionaires occurs in telecommunications, with one extremely rich person who nonetheless accounts for 16% of billionaire assets, said value being 1.2% for the rest of the world. Finally, fortunes derived from the food and beverage industry make up 18% of the wealth among Latin American billionaires and 7% in the rest of the world (Jiménez, Lorenzo, Mahon, and Viñales 2021).

Confronted with such accumulations of wealth, fiscal systems in Latin America have historically shown weak redistributive power, especially on the taxation side. In the region, revenue from the PIT represents only 30% of all income tax revenue (the rest is from corporations), while in the OECD countries, this figure reaches 70%. If we compare the regional average weight of PIT revenue (as a percent of GDP) to figures for other world regions, we find that the PIT collects less in Latin America than anywhere else (Mahon 2019, Table 8.1). Moreover, the revenue it generates comes predominantly from formal-sector labor income, where tax is collected via withholding. The highest incomes, dominantly from the capital, escape this net by taking advantage of incentives or by evasion. These characteristics produce a greater concentration of (after-tax) income and, consequently, of wealth.

Table 11.1 presents information on the revenue generated in Latin America and the Caribbean by all property taxes, expressed first as a percentage of GDP and then as a proportion of total public-sector tax revenues. It can be seen that the average of the OECD countries (recently or as of 1990) amounts to more than the average of Latin America (or of the thirteen largest countries), both in terms of GDP and as a proportion of public sector revenues. The total (OECD category 4000) includes these five items: recurring taxes on real estate, recurring taxes on net worth, inheritance and gift taxes, taxes on financial and capital transactions,

Table 11.1 Revenue Totals by Type of Property Tax, and the Same Totals Minus Income from Financial Transaction Taxes, Expressed in Percentages of GDP (Roman Script) and of Total Tax Revenues (*Italics*). Various Comparison Groups over Three Decades

Groups		*Periods*		
		1990–99	*2000–09*	*2010–19*
Current OECD countries (36)	Total revenues from property taxes	1.72/*5.50*	1.75/*5.46*	1.87/*5.69*
	Total minus rev from fin transaction taxes	1.24/*3.88*	1.24/*3.82*	1.46/*4.40*
24 Pre-1990 OECD countries	Total revenues from property taxes	1.93/*6.08*	2.10/*6.46*	2.21/*6.65*
	Total minus rev from fin transaction taxes	1.39/*4.29*	1.46/*4.44*	1.68/*5.04*
Latin America and the Caribbean (25)	Total revenues from property taxes	0.79/*4.57*	0.86/*4.48*	0.84/*3.90*
	Total minus rev from fin transaction taxes	0.31/*1.73*	0.37/*1.82*	0.43/*1.99*
13 largest Latin American countries	Total revenues from property taxes	0.64/*3.65*	0.96/*4.66*	0.91/*3.95*
	Total minus rev from fin transaction taxes	0.39/*2.29*	0.47/*2.32*	0.53/*2.45*

Source: Adapted from Jiménez, Lorenzo, Mahon and Viñales (2021). Current OECD and Latin America include Chile and México. *OECD.stat*.

and non-recurring taxes on property. The transaction taxes—administratively convenient but distortionary and with unclear distributive effects—account for a much greater part of the total in Latin America than elsewhere. Considering all the taxes, Latin America and the Caribbean collect an average of 0.84% of GDP, while the OECD countries average more than double that figure (1.87% of GDP). If taxes on financial and capital transactions are excluded, the regional average falls to 0.43% of GDP, while the OECD countries collect, on average, more than triple this amount (1.46% of GDP).

11.4 Assessing the Varieties of Wealth Taxation for Latin America

As noted above, property or wealth taxes have historically been of little importance in Latin America, to the point of going practically unmentioned in recent fiscal policy debates. It was also noted that all the main types of property tax can be found in the region, but they are not equally common, and in all cases, their revenue contributions are unusually small. (Here, we do not consider the widespread taxes on financial transactions deducted from regional totals in several cells in Table 11.1.) Let us now consider the advantages and disadvantages of these main types—landed property, net wealth, and inheritances—in the Latin American context.

11.4.1 Real Estate Tax

The most widespread property or wealth tax in the region is the real estate tax (*predial*). This tax exists in all countries and mainly contributes to the funding of subnational and municipal governments. However, its revenue collection does not reach an average of 0.5% of GDP, which is far from its potential (Ahmad, Brosio, and Jiménez 2018).

Real estate taxes have many advantages. Their revenue potential exceeds that of inheritance and net wealth taxes. Their effective collection, allocated to the financing of subnational governments, would improve the mobilization of local resources and expand the compensatory components of intergovernmental transfer systems. This would attenuate fiscal imbalances and vertical intergovernmental asymmetries, contributing to the sustainability of fiscal decentralization while improving access to essential public goods. They could also contribute to a more efficient use of real estate as collateral for access to credit, encouraging investment in metropolitan areas and stimulating sustainable employment generation. The tax could be designed with the active participation of taxpayers, who would be asked annually to provide information on the characteristics of their properties. The application of a flat rate would fit the current institutional framework in the countries of the region, relying only on a registry of occupation of the property in question. This design could also facilitate the provision of basic public services (drinking water and health care) in informal settlements.

At the same time, there are a host of reasons that justify an increase in the tax burden on real estate in Latin America: the rapid growth of urbanization, the upward trend in the value of urban property, the high degree of informality in the housing sector; the significant territorial disparities; the overall weakness of direct taxation; significant gaps in road infrastructure; and most important, huge disparities in the access to basic services in the region's main cities. There are political justifications as well: the full use of the taxing powers assigned to subnational governments would increase the flow of their own resources, reducing their dependence on transfers from above while fortifying local accountability in spending the locally derived revenues.

However, there is one important challenge. Values of all assets and liabilities have to be updated continuously to the market. The traditional approach to property valuation, based on cadastral surveys and with the separate treatment of land, buildings, and improvements, has not worked nearly as well in Latin America as it has in other countries. The regional reality, even the case of countries such as Colombia and Argentina that have a long tradition of maintaining cadastral records, shows that updating is done sporadically and, in many cases, involves complex and costly assessment techniques (Ahmad, Brosio and Jiménez 2019).

11.4.2 Net Wealth Tax

Before the pandemic, net wealth taxes were still in force only in Argentina, Colombia, and Uruguay. With the global health crisis and its economic effects, governments in several countries approved taxes on wealth or net worth, such as the Solidarity and Extraordinary Contribution in Argentina and the Tax on Large Fortunes in Bolivia. Taxes on large fortunes have been proposed in Chile and Peru, with differing bases and rates. The estimated revenue contribution in each case does not exceed 0.5% of GDP (Oxfam 2020; Paez and Oglietti 2020; Jiménez, Lorenzo, Mahon, and Viñales 2021).

The advantages of net wealth taxes go well beyond their potential revenue collection. They are eminently progressive in their incidence, which makes them attractive for political, though not opportunistic, reasons. In addition, some experts consider that net worth taxation has second-order effects that could improve the revenue performance of the PIT (Tanabe 1967; Lehner 2000; Benítez and Velayos 2017). Scheuer and Slemrod (2021) argue that the main role of a wealth tax is to make tax policy and resulting inequality more stable so that threats of political and social conflict can be resisted (see Farhi et al. 2012; Piketty 2014). Such threats were important in Europe when deep reforms in fiscal policies were promoted in connection with modern welfare states (Esping-Andersen 1990). These types of motivations seem appropriate in some South American countries. If political instability and social grievances are pressing issues, annual net wealth taxes could help improve wealth distribution more quickly than inheritance or capital income taxes.

The political history of net wealth taxes in Latin America shows a notable pattern. The extraordinary property tax rate approved in December 2020 in Argentina was promoted by a center-left government, publicly justified by a high fiscal deficit and limited access to financing. In Bolivia, the Tax on Great Fortunes was also created in December 2020, as soon as the (leftist) Luis Arce government took office. However, historically, this type of tax has been the creation of conservative governments (Jiménez, Lorenzo, Mahon, and Viñales 2021). In Uruguay, the modern net wealth tax originated in 1964, under the government of the National Party, was confirmed in 1967 by the government of Jorge Pacheco, and its current format was adopted in 1996 on the occasion of a reform promoted by the administration of Julio María Sanguinetti, also belonging to the Colorado Party. In Colombia in 2002, President Álvaro Uribe imposed a temporary tax on capital, justified by national security reasons. President Uribe then extended the tax from 2004 to 2006, which was renewed repeatedly until 2018. In Argentina, the recurrent net wealth tax was created during the administration of Carlos Saúl Menem, in a context marked by a deep economic crisis, large fiscal deficits, and a suite of neoliberal reforms.

To meet their objectives, wealth taxes must be designed carefully, in concert with other property taxes. Vertical and horizontal inequities that could distort savings and investment decisions or negatively impact tax compliance must be avoided. Considering the interactions among the various property taxes, a coherent design would avoid multiple taxation on some assets or zero taxation on others. Applied in this way, the net wealth tax could be considered complementary to the other property taxes.

11.4.3 Inheritance Tax

As for the inheritance tax, while it is collected in seven countries, its revenue importance is marginal, not reaching 0.1 percent of GDP in any of the countries in which it is in force (OECD 2020).

Compared to other taxes on wealth, the inheritance tax has several advantages. For one, equity arguments apply even more clearly to inheritances, which constitute income unearned by their recipients and, for the largest estates, represent a significant contribution to intergenerational inequality. For another, with inheritance taxes, the taxable event corresponds to a necessary administrative encounter with the state, the transfer of ownership to heirs, easing the burden on the tax authorities. Although, like other wealth taxes, this one has to deal with the valuation of seldom-marketed assets (e.g., art, jewelry), it also brings into the net those assets that appreciated without being taxed during the life of the deceased (Díaz de Sarralde 2023, 183–84).

The disadvantages of inheritance taxation are broadly similar to other wealth taxes. From the standpoint of the eventual donor, they might have little effect on total saving, but they do prompt significant planning regarding the form of saving, introducing distortions to capital investment. In particular, because they are a one-time but often relatively large liability, they can exhaust household liquidity and threaten the continuity of family businesses. The last, along with the argument of double taxation, may be why they are generally unpopular (*ibid.*, 184–86).

Ultimately, the persistence and deepening of wealth inequality will drive political demand for some reform of wealth and income taxation. Adopting international standards in inheritance taxation is essential if the aim is to minimize aggressive tax planning that favors owners of great fortunes. International cooperation is an important resource for ensuring that wealth transfers between generations do not continue to perpetuate extreme inequality of opportunity.

11.5 Obstacles to a Greater Role for Wealth Taxes in Latin America

Many countries have made significant efforts to quantify wealth inequality, using information from tax records or special surveys of the holding of assets and debts. These types of surveys, called "family finance" surveys, provide information on accumulated assets and household debts, as well as income and expenses. Longstanding examples are the Survey of Consumer Finance (SCF) carried out in the United States and the Family Financial Survey (EFF) in the case of Spain. Their design often includes oversampling of higher income households.

In many countries, this procedure has been carried out with the help of national tax authorities, which provide information on taxpayers' incomes. This makes it possible to build a more precise sampling frame of households with higher incomes while respecting tax secrecy. With this type of information, it is possible to analyze the distribution of wealth, going beyond inequality of income or consumption. It should be noted that, in the countries for which information exists, studies indicate that the distribution of wealth is considerably more unequal than that of income (Davies and Shorrocks 2000; IMF 2014, ECLAC 2019).

This type of survey is rare in Latin America. Three efforts explicitly sought to survey household wealth: the National Survey on Household Living Standards (ENNViH) in Mexico, carried out in 2002, 2005–2006, and 2009–2012; the Household Financial Survey (EFH) in Chile, carried out in 2007, 2011–2012, 2014, and 2017; and the Financial Survey of Uruguayan Households (EFHU), for the periods 2012–2014 and 2015–2017.

Household surveys from Latin American countries are also insufficient for analyzing the transmission of wealth in the region. An important limitation is the scarcity of long-period panel data, which would make it possible to determine the trajectory of individuals and households and measure intra- or intergenerational mobility. For the first, the analysis considers two moments in the life of a certain person. In contrast, for the second, it considers trajectories between generations of the same family (from parents to children). In some countries of the region (Argentina, Chile, Mexico, Brazil, Venezuela, and Peru), rotating panels of household surveys are available, from which a set of households can be monitored over many periods. It should be noted, however, that this type of data is more useful for analyzing labor mobility than for examining different forms of intergenerational wealth transmission (see Amarante and Jiménez 2015).

While extensive literature estimates the relationship between labor supply and taxable income, as well as the impact of income taxes on income distribution (Saez and Zucman 2020), much less is known about how taxes affect the concentration of wealth. It is still difficult to answer questions such as: How would wealth taxes affect the savings and consumption decisions of the rich? How would wealth taxes affect tax avoidance and evasion? Would they reduce wealth inequality, and by how much? Recent work on developed countries, such as Denmark (Jakobsen et al. 2020), seeks to answer these questions. Because wealth is always highly concentrated, it is crucial to estimate behavioral responses for wealthier individuals—yet plausible sources of exogenous variation at the top of the wealth distribution have so far been elusive. To assess the desirability of wealth taxes, it is important to obtain estimates of their long-term effects. While the design of taxes always depends on such effects, this is more of a challenge for capital taxes than for labor taxes due to the slow and variable nature of capital accumulation.

Empirical work on the real concentration of wealth is lacking in the region. In the developed world, there is a growing availability of data on wealth inequality, such as the OECD's WDD; the WID; the publications of *Forbes*, UBS, and Credit Suisse; and financial surveys by national government agencies (e.g., the SCFs in the United States); not to mention tax records.[1] Estimates such as those of *Forbes* or *Fortune* use published statistics on the asset holdings of certain individuals or families, in which Latin America is clearly underrepresented.

In addition to these problems, it is worth noting that comparing the results of these studies is hampered by differences in methodology and sources. A key problem is that most countries do not carry out a detailed follow-up of the capital stock accounts for the national economies. Hence, the aforementioned estimates must rely on sources such as household surveys in which asset and debt holdings are recorded. These, however, are unreliable due to their well-known sampling and underreporting problems. Other sources include information from wealth tax records or imputed via multipliers, although these sources may fail to consider some kinds of wealth, such as durable consumer goods or jewelry. They might also provide undervalued estimates for some assets, a more serious problem in the region due to its weak cadastral records.

11.6 Conclusions and Final Considerations

Investigating the mechanisms that generate wealth inequality is especially important in Latin America. Beyond frequent references to the region as an extreme case of economic inequality, up to now the analysis of wealth concentration has presented notorious weaknesses, lacking a quantitative foundation that would allow us to understand how this inequality is reproduced. Instead of rigorous and systematic studies highlighting the role of public policies in this process, we frequently hear rhetoric that makes inequality both the cause and consequence of inequitable politics and economics. However, the absence of good information, in turn, hampers the design of tax instruments that might tax high incomes and extreme wealth more effectively.

Although we benefit from new wealth and income estimates, they are less useful because of methodological differences. We see this also in the absence of consistent records on the ownership structure of companies, movable assets, and real estate.

Hence, the regressivity of current tax structures is hard to remedy. While the taxation of property and wealth is very insignificant in the regional average and almost absent in several countries of the region, the taxation of personal income is biased toward salary income, taxing capital income only weakly. It thereby accentuates the regressive character of the tax system while increasing the accumulation of wealth in the richest deciles. With better information, we could compare, say, the distributive impact of a wealth tax to that of expanding the base of the income tax.

Despite the challenges, several factors now favor a resurgence of property and wealth taxation. Chief among these is the significant improvements in information on the distribution of income and wealth in developed countries, which has created a more favorable context for progressive taxation. In the academy, new theoretical arguments have also supported the incorporation of taxes on wealth into the models of optimal taxation. Meanwhile, direct taxes on wealth and inheritance are less unpopular with the public than they once were.

We have noted a few policy guidelines. With regard to inheritance and net wealth taxation, it is possible to identify actions that would contribute to improving their collection, facilitate audit, expand their coverage, and maximize their distributive incidence. The key is to ensure internal consistency between the different forms of wealth taxation and adapt the new tax instruments to achieve synergies with income taxation, especially PITs. Here, it is useful to note the proposal from Díaz de Sarralde (2023) to integrate the personal tax on capital income with income imputed from an assessment of capital value (like an annual net wealth tax) while limiting the inheritance tax to the very largest estates (188–193).

However, it must be emphasized that strengthening property taxation in Latin America will not suffice to cover most governments' fiscal gaps or reverse the ongoing concentration of wealth. The fiscal effort necessary to overcome recent crises and their associated debt loads will require recourse to other tax instruments. In this context, wealth taxation would make only a minor revenue contribution, but this should not be an argument against it. Its importance lies in its effect on distribution and public opinion. It would lend additional legitimacy and political support to those other tax reforms aimed more directly at closing the fiscal deficit. This is particularly important at the moment, as the fitful exit from the COVID emergency has combined with new social mobilizations demanding improvements in the quality of public services and expansion of social welfare coverage.

Hence, the agenda must include the improvement of other taxes as well, ideally through a comprehensive reform. This should involve consumption taxes (VAT and excises), PIT, corporate income tax, and various schemes of special contributions to finance the region's social security systems. Only with such an expansive view, emphasizing distributive equity and environmental sustainability will tax reform gain the social legitimacy and political support necessary to make durable and progressive changes. It follows that the specific reform guidelines, already identified a few years ago in many countries, are still useful.

With regard to the PIT, its strengthening, especially with regard to capital income, is the main challenge for every Latin American government. This requires effectively monitoring all income flows, whether from labor, business, finance, or mixed activity. As an intermediate step, some countries have already adopted a dual scheme, with progressive rates for labor income and proportional rates for capital income. Knowing how hard it is to tax the richest individuals, reformers should consider surcharges or higher rates, whether temporary or permanent.

With the corporate income tax, the main problem is not the current rates or revenues, which are in line with international averages, but the proliferation of poorly designed incentives and loopholes. For example, tax-advantaged promotional zones often have little economic justification, as companies use them mainly for tax avoidance. If these incentives could be rationalized, this could raise more revenue—and it would do so more equitably and efficiently.

The region has a long way to go in controlling tax evasion. However, the next steps are obvious. It is necessary to continue and advance the technical and operational strengthening of tax administration, following an approach that is segmented by groups of taxpayers with differentiated examination and audit strategies. The expansion of electronic invoicing should also continue. It brings benefits in terms of tax management, audit, and, ultimately, revenue collection.

As noted above, international tax coordination has advanced (CEPAL 2020; Jiménez, Ocampo, Valdés and Podestá 2020). It is gratifying to see vigorous initiatives taken by the United States, the OECD, the G20, and the G7: the proposed global minimum rate of 15% on corporate income; measures to combat tax avoidance and jurisdiction shopping; and related to this, the gathering of information necessary to determine wealth. Many Latin American governments have already adhered to the key initiatives, such as the BEPS Project (Base Erosion and Profit Sharing) promoted by the OECD.

Despite this, the problem of harmful tax competition, as businesses divert profits to locations with low or no taxation, continues to have significant effects in the region. By taking advantage of synergies between international cooperation and national policy measures, governments could recover their ability to choose the effective level of their tax revenues, expenditures, and redistribution autonomously while respecting the right of other governments to exercise these powers.

Note

1 Definitions of wealth also differ. While the World Bank (World Bank 2021) uses information related to asset values along with diverse macroeconomic data to estimate capital stock, Credit Suisse (Credit Suisse 2019) measures wealth as net worth, that is, the commercial value of financial assets and non-financial assets, minus liabilities.

References

Ahmad, Ehtisham, Giorgio Brosio, and Juan Pablo Jiménez. 2019. "Options for retooling property taxation in Latin America." *Macroeconomics of Development Series 202*. Santiago de Chile: ECLAC.

Ahmad, Ehtisham, Giorgio Brosio, and Jelle Gerbrandy. 2018. *Property taxation, Economic features, revenue potential and administrative issues in a development context*. Brussels: European Commission.

Alvaredo, Facundo, Bertrand Garbinti, and Thomas Piketty. 2017. "On the Share of Inheritance in Aggregate Wealth: Europe and the USA, 1900–2010." *Economica* 334 (84), 239–260.

Amarante, Verónica, and Juan Pablo Jiménez. 2015. "Desigualdad, concentración y altas rentas en América Latina." In *Desigualdad, concentración del ingreso y tributación sobre las altas rentas en América Latina*, edited by Jiménez, Juan Pablo, 13–48. Santiago de Chile: Libros de CEPAL.

Atkinson, Anthony, and Joseph E. Stiglitz. 1976. "The Design of Tax Structure: Direct versus Indirect Taxation." *Journal of Public Economics* 6, 55–75.

Bagchi, Sutirtha, and Jan Svejnar. 2013. "Does wealth inequality matter for growth? The effect of billionaire wealth, income distribution, and poverty." *IZA DP* 7733.

Balestra, Carlotta, and Richard Tonkin. 2018. "Inequalities in household wealth across OECD countries: Evidence from the OECD Wealth Distribution Database." *OECD Statistics Working Papers* 2018/01, Paris: OECD Publishing.

Benitez, Juan Carlos, and Fernando Velayos. 2017. *Impuestos a la Riqueza o al Patrimonio de las Personas Físicas con especial mención a América Latina y El Caribe*. Centro Interamericano de Administraciones Tributarias (CIAT).

Brueckner, Markus, Daniel Lederman. 2018. "Inequality and Economic Growth: The Role of Initial Income." *Policy Research Working Paper; No. 8467*. Washington, DC: World Bank.

Brzezinski, Michal, Katarzyna Sałach, and Marcin Wroński. 2019. "Wealth Inequality in Central and Eastern Europe: Evidence From Joined Household Survey and Rich Lists". Available at SSRN: https://ssrn.com/abstract=3497399 or http://dx.doi.org/10.2139/ssrn.3497399 (June 23, 2023).

Cabral, Marika, and Caroline Hoxby. 2012. "The hated property tax: salience, tax rates, and tax revolts." Working Paper 18514 Cambridge: NBER (National Bureau of Economic Research).

CEPAL. 2020. *Panorama Fiscal de América Latina y el Caribe, 2020: la política fiscal ante la crisis derivada de la pandemia de la enfermedad por coronavirus (COVID-19).* Santiago de Chile: CEPAL.

Credit Suisse. 2019. *Global Wealth Report 2019*. Zürich: Credit Suisse Research Institute.

Davies, James B., and Anthony F. Shorrocks. 2000. "The distribution of wealth." In *Handbook of Income Distribution, 1,* edited by Atkinson, Anthony B., 605–675. Amsterdam: North Holland.

Davies, James B., Rodrigo Lluberas, and Anthony F. Shorrocks. 2017. "Estimating the level and distribution of Global Wealth, 2000–2014." *Review of Income and Wealth* 63 (4), 731–759.

Davies, James. B., Susanna Sandström, Anthony Shorrocks, and Edward N. Wolff.2008. "The World Distribution of Household Wealth." *Discussion Paper No. 2008/03*. Helsinki, Finland: United Nations University, World Institute for Development Economics Research (UNU-WIDER).

Díaz de Sarralde Miguez, Santiago. 2023. "¿Qué puede aportar la imposición sobre la riqueza (y cómo)?" *Cuadernos Económicos De ICE* 105, 169–195.

ECLAC. 2019. *Social Panorama of Latin America 2019.* (LC/PUB.2019/22-P/Rev.1), Santiago de Chile: ECLAC.

______ 2022. *Economic Survey of Latin America and the Caribbean 2022.* (LC/PUB.2022/9-P/Rev.1), Santiago de Chile: ECLAC.

Esping-Andersen, Gøsta. 1990. *The Three Worlds of Welfare Capitalism*. Princeton: Princeton University Press.

Farhi, Emmanuel, Christopher Sleet, Iván Werning, and Sevin Yeltekin. 2012. "Non-linear capital taxation without commitment." *Review of Economic Studies* 79, 1469–1493.

Freund, Caroline, and Sarah Oliver, Sarah. 2016. "The Origins of the Superrich: The Billionaire Characteristics Database" Peterson Institute for International Economics Working Paper 1–16, Washington, DC: PIIE.

Hailemariam, Abebe, Ratbek Dzhumashev, and Muhammad Shahbaz. 2020. "Carbon Emissions, Income Inequality and Economic Development." *Empirical Economics* 59 (3), 1139–1159.

Hills John. 2015. *Good Times, Bad Times: The Welfare Myth of Them and Us*. Bristol: Policy Press.

IMF. 2014. "Fiscal policy and income inequality." IMF POLICY PAPER January 23, 2014. Washington, DC: IMF.

———.2021. Fiscal Monitor 2021. Washington, DC: IMF.

Islam, Md Nazrul, and Md Saidul Islam. 2018. "Politics and Islamic Revivalism in Bangladesh: The Role of the State and Non-State/Non-Political Actors." *Politics, Religion & Ideology* 19 (3), 326–353.

Jakobsen, Katrine, Kristian Jakobsen, Hentrik Kleven, and Gabriel Zucman. 2020. "Wealth Taxation and Wealth Accumulation: Theory and Evidence from Denmark." *The Quarterly Journal of Economics* 135 (1), 329–388.

Jiménez, Juan Pablo, and Andres Solimano. 2011. *Elites económicas, desigualdad y tributación, Serie Macroeconomía del Desarrollo*. Santiago de Chile: CEPAL.

Jiménez, Juan Pablo, Fernando Lorenzo, James Mahon, and Gustavo Viñales. 2021. Hacia *el fortalecimiento integral de la imposición sobre la riqueza y la propiedad en América Latina: nuevas oportunidades des y viejos desafíos*. Montevideo: Laboratorio Fiscal y Tributario.

Jiménez, Juan Pablo, José Antonio Ocampo, Andrea Podestá, Fernanda Andrea-Valdes. 2020. *Explorando sinergias entre la cooperación tributaria internacional y los desafíos tributarios latinoamericanos en tiempos de COVID-19*. Macroeconomía del Desarrollo. Santiago de Chile: CEPAL.

Lehner, Moris. 2000 "The European experience with wealth tax: Comparative discussion." *Tax Law Review* 53 (4), 615–692.

Mahon, James E. 2019. "Weak liberalism and weak property taxation in Latin America." In *The Political Economy of Taxation in Latin America*, edited by Flores-Macias, Gustavo, 193–218. New York: Cambridge University Press.

Morck, Randall K., David A. Stangeland, and Bernard Yeung. 2000. "Inherited Wealth, Corporate Control, and Economic Growth The Canadian Disease?". In *Concentrated Corporate Ownership*, edited by Morck, Randall, 319–372. Chicago: University of Chicago Press.

OECD 2021. "Inheritance taxation in OECD countries." *Tax Policy Studies* May 2021. Paris: OECD Publishing.

———. 2020. *Revenue Statistics in Latin America and the Caribbean* 2020. Paris: OECD Publishing.

OXFAM. 2020. *¿Quién paga la cuenta? Gravar la riqueza para enfrentar la crisis de la COVID-19 en América Latina y el Caribe*. OXFAM.

Paez, Sergio, and Guillermo Oglietti. 2020. "¿Cuánto podría recaudar el impuesto a las grandes fortunas en América Latina?" *Centro Estratégico Latinoamericano de Geopolítica*. CELAG. www.celag.org/cuanto-podria-recaudar-el-impuesto-a-las-grandes-fortunas-en-america-latina/ (June 22, 2022).

Piketty, Thomas. 2014. *El capital en el siglo XXI*. Madrid: Fondo de Cultura Económica.

Piketty, Thomas, and Gabriel Zucman. 2014. "Capital is back: Wealth-income ratios in rich countries 1700–2010." *The Quarterly Journal of Economics* 129 (3), 1255–1310.

Piketty, Thomas, and Emmanuel Saez. 2013. "A Theory of Optimal Inheritance Taxation." *Econometrica* 81 (5), 1851–1886.

Sáez, Emmanuel. 2002. "The Desirability of Commodity Taxation Under Non-Linear Income Taxation and Heterogeneous Tastes." *Journal of Public Economics* 83 (2), 217–230.

Sáez, Emmanuel, and Gabriel Zucman. 2019. "Progressive Wealth Taxation." *Brookings Papers on Economic Activity* Fall, 437–511.

Saez, Emmanuel, and Gabriel Zucman. 2020. "The Rise of Income and Wealth Inequality in America: Evidence from Distributional Macroeconomic Accounts." *Journal of Economic Perspectives*, 34 (4), 3–26. DOI: 10.1257/jep.34.4.3

Scheuer, Florian, and Joel Slemrod. 2021. "Taxing Our Wealth." *Journal of Economic Perspectives* 35 (1), 207–30.

Sheffrin, Steven M. 2010. "Fairness and Market Value Property Taxation." In *Challenging the conventional wisdom on the property tax*, edited by Bahl, Roy, Jorge Martinez-Vazquez, and Joan Youngman, 241–262. Cambridge: Lincoln Institute of Land Policy.

Slack, Enid, and Richard Bird. 2014. "The Political Economy of Property Tax Reform." *OECD Working Papers on Fiscal Federalism* 18. Paris: OECD Publishing.

Stiglitz, Joseph E. 2012. *The Price of Inequality: How Today's Divided Society Endangers Our Future*. New York: W.W. Norton & Company.
Stiglitz, Joseph E., Amartya Sen, and Jean-Paul Fitoussi. 2009. *Report by the Commission on the Measurement of Economic Performance and Social Progress*. IEP.
Tanabe, Nobor. 1967. "The Taxation of Net Wealth." *IMF Staff Papers* 14 (1), 124–168.
United Nations. 2009. *System of National Accounts, 2008* (2008 SNA). New York: UN.
Viñales, Gustavo; Carlos Grau, and Cecilia Alonso. 2021. *La pandemia COVID-19 y los impuestos a la riqueza*. Montevideo: Laboratorio Fiscal y Tributario CINVE.
World Bank. 2021. The Changing Wealth of Nations 2021: Managing Assets for the Future. Washington, DC: World Bank. doi:10.1596/978-1-4648-1590-4. License: Creative Commons Attribution CC BY 3.0 IGO
World Bank. 2021. "Un impuesto sobre el patrimonio para abordar cinco disrupciones globales." World Bank Blogs.

12 Trusts

Searching for the Hidden Treasure in Ecuador

Jonathan Báez Valencia

12.1 Introduction

Where and how is the wealth of nations hidden? Zucman's (2016) pioneering research on tax havens – and the elites who park their money there – is at the heart of this question. According to his analysis, this process costs Latin America approximately 21 billion US dollars in lost tax resources annually. This money is needed to combat persistent inequalities in the region. From this perspective, for a proper redistributive tax policy to take place, countries must keep a register of actors with companies in tax havens.

In the case of Ecuador, significant progress has been made in this area, and through the compilation of the database "Conformation and Tax Behavior of Economic Groups" made by the country's Internal Revenue Service (SRI),[1] it was found that 90 individuals had connections with 456 companies in tax havens in 2019. However, this figure is even higher if one considers the existence of trusts that, like a matryoshka, cover up these companies and thus distort the actual extent of tax havens. In the mentioned database, trusts nearly double the number of companies in opaque jurisdictions. However, these trusts have not been studied despite making up almost 9% of net assets and serving as a mechanism usually used – though rarely deeply analyzed – by elites to hide wealth.

As a first step, this chapter aims to analyze the ultimate beneficiaries of 942 trusts listed in the above database to find companies in tax havens that have not been registered and, secondly, to estimate the resources lost through them. To this end, different official databases will be studied containing information on the ultimate beneficiaries of the trusts (like Superintendence of Companies, Values, and Insurance) as well as changes in the level of taxes generated (Internal Revenue Service) by these beneficiaries. With this information, the goal is to contribute to an adequate measurement of wealth in Ecuador, with a registry that demonstrates one of the many mechanisms that elites use to avoid paying their share of taxes and revealing the *matryoshka* that trusts represent by searching for the treasure hidden in these fiscal labyrinths.

Some of the most important results include identifying 59 offshore companies hidden in trusts, which comprise 70% of foreign companies. Through this mechanism, it is also estimated that individual members of the elites have not paid

DOI: 10.4324/9781032636764-15

5 million in taxes. The trusts' tax revenue would have nearly doubled if these amounts had not been evaded. Consequently, progress in registering these companies is needed for the adequate measurement of wealth and the possibility of taxation that enables redistribution and thus offers possibilities to combat social inequalities more effectively.

Economic elites in Latin America pay income tax that amounts to less than 4.8% of their income, far below the 21.3% that is paid in countries in the European Union (CEPAL 2018, 56). Ecuador's situation is even more complicated; in 2019, the percentage of tax paid reached 3.3% (Báez 2020a). This demonstrates with more clarity that (economic) elites hardly pay taxes in Ecuador – likewise in the rest of the region. This is due, among other causes, to the elites' use of tax havens to elude taxes. While studies have addressed this subject (Zucman 2016), there are still mechanisms that have not been deeply grappled with and that are necessary to analyze to be able to understand the complex scheme put in place by elites to forgo taxes and which, as a result, affects society at large by creating inequality. Indeed, trusts are among these often-mentioned but little-studied tax avoidance schemes.

The information presented by the SRI- shows that out of the 302 Economic Groups (EGs) in Ecuador[2] identified in 2019 (which are equivalent to the economic elite, as will be shown at a later stage), a total of 90 had 456 members domiciled in tax havens. Approximately 30% of EGs use these jurisdictions to avoid taxes. Yet, a closer examination reveals that 157 EGs possess 942 trusts, almost twice the number of trusts held by other EGs and companies located in tax havens. In other words, 52% of EGs have trusts, and while most trusts are registered in Ecuador, in some instances, the beneficiaries are not, but some are found in tax havens.

Based on this knowledge, it is necessary to ask: How many of the beneficiaries of EG trusts are located in tax havens? Are they individuals or legal companies? In which tax havens are they located? Can their existence be connected to a probable non-payment of taxes in the country? The upcoming chapters seek to address these inquiries. To achieve this, the chapter is divided into three primary segments. The initial section reviews existing literature on trusts, their association with tax havens, and their impact on tax systems. Subsequently, the methodology and the databases used for identifying offshore entities and quantifying their effects on tax revenues are presented. An illustrative example of this process is provided to showcase the analysis outcomes. Finally, the main findings are outlined in the concluding section.

12.2 Literature Review

From the legal studies perspective, analyses of trusts and their relationship with taxes and tax havens offer extensive literature to review. In some cases, this literature aims to observe how a change in regulatory frameworks affects business (Hamilton 1979); in others, to justify the secrecy that trusts provide (Allan 2011). In the same vein, some Authors establish specific parameters that should be met for trusts located in tax havens to be considered legitimate (Ausness 2007). Apart from this, some studies demonstrate how trusts in tax havens enable their beneficiaries to avoid paying taxes (Cockfield 2015). Along the same lines, but from an economic perspective, trusts in tax havens are analyzed in order to "quantify" the opacity of these jurisdictions. Such is the case of the "Financial Secrecy Index," which studies the existence of trusts as a component of the index. (Tax Justice Network [TJN] 2015, 16–18). In addition, balance sheets are beginning to link the use of offshore trusts by the wealthiest individuals:

> *The assets of trusts that are established in tax havens are usually kept thousands of miles away; and neither the grantor nor the beneficiary is normally resident in the tax haven country. [...] Tax haven operations consist fundamentally in establishing within a tax haven country one or more legal entities, such as trusts, personal holding companies, or corporate subsidiaries, and attributing, to them income earned elsewhere in order that it should be taxed at the country's low rates – or perhaps not taxed at all. [...] it is probable that the "clients" of tax havens are increasingly being drawn from higher-income and greater-wealth brackets.*
>
> (Casanegra de Jantscher 1976, 31–33)

In economics, trusts are increasingly being recognized as one of the mechanisms associated with tax havens, highlighting their role in evading tax payments. However, this study does not delve into analyzing this aspect; its primary focus is on quantifying the amount of money concealed in these havens rather than on the evasion mechanisms. Consequently, it is estimated that "[...] the Cayman Islands had about $1.25 trillion in portfolio assets at the end of 2008, of which about $700 billion were U.S. equities and bonds" (Zucman 2013, 17), shedding light on the extent of wealth held in such jurisdictions and demonstrating the magnitude of tax evasion by the ultra-wealthy.

> *Some assets are held through intermediaries such as trusts [...]. Estate tax revenue collected in 2017 from wealthy individuals who died in 2016 was only $20 billion. This is only about 0.13% of the $15 trillion net worth of the top 0.1% wealthiest families in 2016. This demonstrates quantitatively that the estate fails to take much of a bite on the wealthiest (in spite of a reasonably high 40% nominal tax rate above the $5 million exemption threshold, set to increase to $10 million in 2018). Tax avoidance is the main factor driving such low tax revenue.*
>
> (Zucman and Saez 2019, 20)

A similar trend is observed in Ecuador, but even more alarming. The literature primarily focuses on the legal aspects (Mayorga 2017; Álvarez 2019). However, in economics, there is a notable lack of literature concerning trusts in tax havens and their connection to high-net-worth individuals. References to trusts typically acknowledge their existence without delving into detailed analysis regarding their prevalence, beneficiaries, geographical locations, etc. (Ordóñez 2017). This holds true for other studies that aim to quantify the relationships between tax havens, wealthy individuals, and non-payment of taxes (Báez 2017). Hence, it becomes imperative for other studies to explore the mechanisms facilitating the transfer of resources to tax havens, their retention in these opaque territories, and how tax evasion and avoidance are facilitated in this process. The contribution of this chapter is to specifically focus on trusts, and therefore, advancing the study of these structures is crucial for informing public policies aimed at addressing inequalities through progressive taxation-based redistribution. The chapter seeks to demonstrate the presence of trusts in tax havens utilized by Ecuador's wealthiest individuals, referred to hereafter as the economic elites. Additionally, it seeks to quantify the amount of tax revenue lost by the country due to the utilization of trusts. Such endeavors represent a significant contribution to the literature on trusts and their ramifications.[3]

12.3 Methodology and Data

One of the initial challenges in investigating the trusts used by economic elites in Ecuador is the scarcity of information. It appears that opacity is a fundamental characteristic of elites, prevalent not only in Ecuador but throughout Latin America. This lack of transparency extends beyond fiscal matters, with fewer databases available to study economic elites in the region compared to other parts of the world, which further leads to a dearth of empirical research on the topic (Báez Valencia 2021).[4]

In relation to the ongoing challenge of identifying economic elites, in the context of Ecuador, the closest information comes from the "Conformation and tax behavior of Economic Groups" report produced by the SRI in 2019. This administrative dataset, which contrasts the existing literature on the formation of elites in Latin America as EGs (Cárdenas 2016), serves as the primary source for this chapter. Accordingly, it outlines the methodology for identifying elites and their companies, including trusts. In this regard, the terms economic elites and EGs are used interchangeably. Based on this framework, a total of 942 trusts owned by 157 elites were analyzed. After identifying the trusts used by elites, the next "dilemma" is examining the beneficiaries to gather their social characteristics. This presents a challenging endeavor as opacity and secrecy are the trusts' raison d'être. In fact, Escario (2011) points out that:

> *the real problem with trusts is the availability of information. Since trusts are based on a simple contract and do not have a legal personality, they do not need to be registered in certain jurisdictions, which renders their identification extremely difficult. Even if it is known who the trustee is, the identity of the settlors and beneficiaries may remain unknown by virtue of a confidentiality agreement signed between the three parties. In fact, in tax havens, the trustee will typically be an anonymous trust company that specializes in acting as trustee for many thousands of trusts. […] The issue is further complicated by the creation of new legal tools to protect the identity of beneficiaries. Many tax havens allow re-domiciliation or "flight clauses," which require trustees to*

> *transfer assets to a different jurisdiction (normally another tax haven) in the event of an imminent preliminary inquiry by tax authorities.*
>
> (Escario 2011, 45)

Nevertheless, in the Ecuadorian context, it is feasible to carry out an analysis using databases and tools provided by the Superintendency of Companies, Securities, and Insurance (known as SCVS in Spanish), enabling the observation of trust beneficiaries, their domiciles, and even the duration and dates of their operation. With this information at hand, it becomes feasible to address the posed questions. Moreover, by using the available dates, it is possible to gain insight into the time frames during which businesses in tax havens were active. Consequently, a clearer understanding emerges regarding how these enterprises likely managed to evade tax payments owed to other beneficiaries of the trust.

Thus, in order to detect businesses in tax havens, this chapter follows the SRI categorization of tax havens as well as of low-tax regimes and of preferential tax regimes (SRI 2012), even drawing from historical archives according to the date of operation of these companies. In this list assembled by the SRI, 88 territories were recognized as tax havens and 11 as preferential regimes. Falling in the latter category are jurisdictions in the United States referred to as companies under Limited Liability Company (LLC) and other jurisdictions like England, the Netherlands, Costa Rica, and New Zealand.[5] In reality, the businesses in those territories hide the final beneficiary; generally, they are the same beneficiaries as the trust. Thus:

> *Using and registering shell companies in low-tax secrecy jurisdictions is another way to conceal wealth and beneficial ownership information. Such companies do not perform any productive activity in the tax haven territory. They are false legal structures, with the tax haven allowing investors to establish an additional domicile that allows them to exploit what amounts in practice to a virtually zero-tax regime. The companies registered are no less than fronts-desks serving as mailboxes for parent companies operating in high-tax jurisdictions.*
>
> (Escario Díaz-Berrio 2011, 46)

The disclosures made by the International Consortium of Investigative Journalists (ICIJ) regarding trust beneficiaries in tax havens, such as the Panama Papers (2016), Paradise Papers (2017), and Pandora Papers (2021), corroborate the aforementioned.[6] From this perspective, the current study confines itself to revealing the beneficiary companies located in tax havens, acknowledging the considerable challenge in accessing information regarding the ultimate beneficiaries of these companies, with many not featured in the mentioned leaks. Nevertheless, it's crucial to note the likelihood that the ultimate beneficiaries correspond to those uncovered in the trusts but concealed, as previously explained. Therefore, in estimating tax avoidance, it is assumed that the trust beneficiaries align with the offshore beneficiaries. Therefore, in order to analyze the effects of possible tax avoidance, the time in which the company located in the tax haven was extant is taken into consideration, as well as whether this caused a drop in income tax payments for the beneficiaries in comparison with the immediately preceding or following years. As such, businesses will not be considered due to limited information. In short, an estimate is made of what trust beneficiaries with companies in tax havens stop paying thanks to them. To this end, the following formula is proposed to evaluate this amount:

$$\hat{E} = \sum \left(I_t - \left(I_{t+1} + I_{t-1} \right) \right)$$

where:

$\hat{E}$ = *Estimated tax avoidance*
I_t = *Income tax during the offshore company's operation*
I_{t+1} = *Income tax the year after the offshore company's operation.*
I_t = *Income tax the year before the offshore company's operation.*

In order to elucidate this study's research process and proposed methodology, one of the economic elites mentioned in the Pandora Papers, President Guillermo Lasso, will be used as an example.[7] According to the SRI's database of EGs, President Guillermo Lasso was linked to the EG "Banco de Guayaquil." This group has two registered companies residing in tax havens. However, it also has 49 registered trusts. Among these, the one with the highest income on record is the "Fideicomiso Mercantil de Administración GLM," with 13 million dollars in 2019 and assets of more than 34 million dollars. However, no income tax has been generated. In an analysis of the SCVS's database of the beneficiaries of said trust, the president and his children appear, as well as a company called "Positano Trade LLC" based in the United States (Table 12.1). The Pandora Papers leaks reveal

Table 12.1 Beneficiaries of the GLM Trust that Belongs to the EG Banco de Guayaquil

Last and first name/business name	*Nationality*	*Date of designation*	*Sector*	*Transfer of fiduciary rights*
LASSO MENDOZA GUILLERMO ALBERTO SANTIAGO	Ecuador	18/2/2013		
LASSO ALCIVAR GUILLERMO ENRIQUE	Ecuador	15/3/2011		
LASSO ALCIVAR JUAN EMILIO	Ecuador	15/3/2011		
LASSO ALCIVAR SANTIAGO XAVIER	Ecuador	15/3/2011		
LASSO ALCIVAR MARIA DE LOURDES	Ecuador	15/3/2011		
LASSO ALCIVAR MARIA MERCEDES	Ecuador	15/3/2011		
POSITANO TRADE LLC	**United States of America**	**31/1/2012**	**PRIVATE**	**18/2/2013**

Source: SCVS, prepared by the author.

that this company is based explicitly in Delaware, a recognized tax haven in the United States where "billionaires pay millions to hide trillions" (Collins 2021). This same leak also showed that the ultimate beneficiary of this shell company was President Guillermo Lasso himself. In effect, there is a chain of "shields" that act as matryoshkas to prevent the final beneficiary from being observed, and the case of the company Banco de Guayaquil, the main member of the EG of the same name, shows this clearly, as shown in Figure 12.1. A structure that other MEs have, including Banco de Guayaquil itself with other trusts.

Thus, the offshore company, beneficiary of a trust registered in Ecuador with President Lasso as the ultimate beneficiary, was operational in 2012 and transferred its rights in 2013. When analyzing the income taxes paid by President Lasso in 2011, a year before the offshore company's operation, his income tax

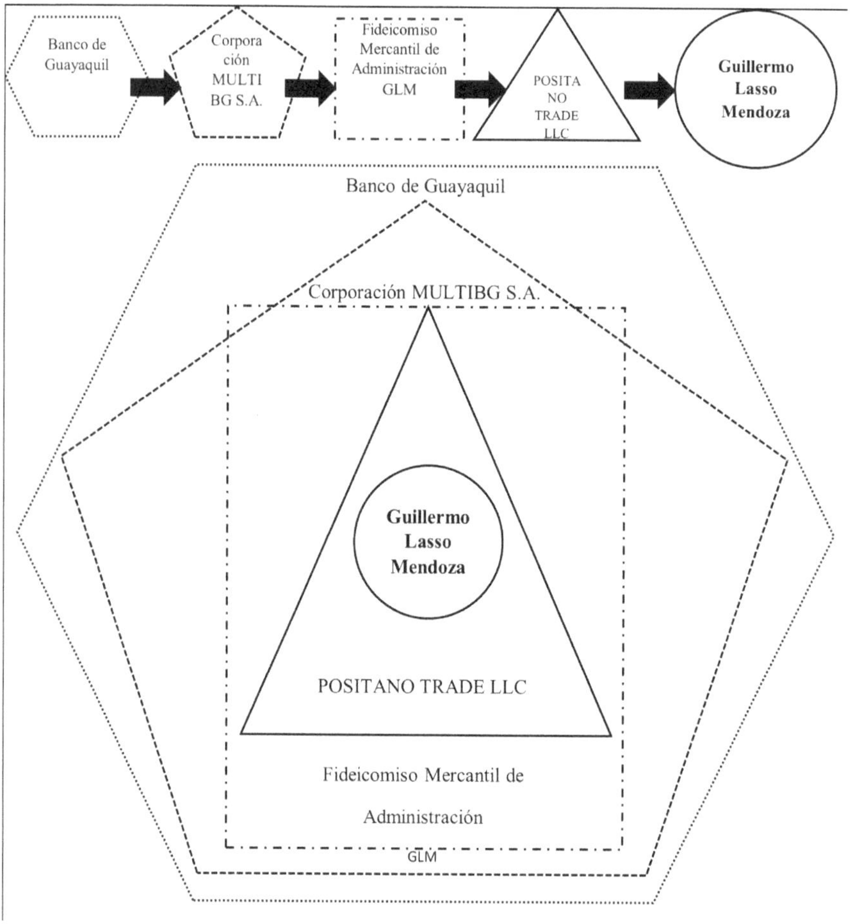

Figure 12.1 Matryoshka of the company Banco de Guayaquil.

Source: SCVS, prepared by the author.

Table 12.2 Guillermo Lasso Mendoza's Income Tax 2011–2013

Tax year	*Income tax expenses*
2013	$2,041,323.29
2012	$200,765.70
2011	$2,609,649.44

Source: SCVS, prepared by the author.

amounted to 2.6 million dollars (see Table 12.2). In contrast, in 2012, when the company was active, his taxes only amounted to 200,000 dollars, a 92% decrease. In 2013, when the offshore company in the United States transferred its rights and ceased operations, the president's tax payment rose again to two million dollars. This suggests that the offshore company allowed for a reduction in income tax payment, averaging the years immediately before and after the offshore company's operations, which would have amounted to 2.3 million dollars annually, resulting in the evasion of 2.1 million dollars in taxes to the Ecuadorian state.

These results reveal how a single trust represents a whole scheme that enables the final beneficiary to have a significant tax reduction in the EG Banco de Guayaquil case. In the same manner and accordingly, this study presents the results of the 942 trusts that were analyzed.

12.4 Results[8]

The analysis reveals that the 942 trusts scrutinized amass assets exceeding 7 billion dollars, constituting approximately 5.46% of the EG's total assets (see Table 12.3). In terms of net worth, these trusts represent nearly 9.66% of the elites' aggregate wealth, equivalent to over 4.6 billion dollars (see Table 12.3). Conversely, concerning income, the tax contribution comprises less than 0.50% of the total taxes collected. Moreover, the Effective Tax Rate, which juxtaposes the tax burden with income, stands at less than 2.25% for income tax and less than 6% for total taxes, underscoring the minimal taxation on trusts. Notably, no taxes on assets held abroad have been collected, highlighting the necessity for an in-depth analysis of trust beneficiaries, particularly those in tax havens.

An in-depth analysis of beneficiaries reveals three types of beneficiaries (see Table 12.4): private companies figure among those with the most importance, making up 60% (1431), followed by individuals, 39% (935), and public companies, 1% (20). Out of the total number of individuals, the vast majority, 96.5%, is from Ecuador, and a smaller number are from other countries, some of which are recognized in the country as tax havens: Switzerland and the Bermudas (see Table 12.5). In other territories, regulations do not necessarily apply as they do with the private companies presented below.

Among the private companies' domiciles, those registered in Ecuador also predominate, but to a lesser extent than individuals: they represent 86%. They are

Table 12.3 Economic Indicators of Trusts of the Economic Elite in Ecuador, 2019 (N=942)

Values	*Trusts*	*Total*	*Percentage*
	-in millions of dollars-		
Total assets	7,117.20	130,327.33	5.46
Total net worth	4,658.35	48,214.44	9.66
Total income	329.54	71,743.11	0.46
Total amount collected	18.35	6,120.83	0.30
Total income tax levied	7.39	1,771.63	0.42
Tax on overseas assets	0.00	21.93	0.00

Source: SRI-SCVS, prepared by the author.

Table 12.4 Economic Elite Trust Beneficiaries in Ecuador, 2019 (N=942)

Type of beneficiary	*N*	*Percentage*
Private companies	1,431	60
Individuals	935	39
Public companies	20	1
Total	2,386	100

Source: SRI-SCVS, prepared by the author.

Table 12.5 Domicile of the Economic Elite Trust Beneficiaries in Ecuador, 2019 (N=942)

Country	*N*	*Percentage*
Ecuador	902	96.5
Venezuela	10	1.1
Switzerland	7	0.7
Colombia	5	0.5
Argentina	2	0.2
China	2	0.2
Costa Rica	2	0.2
Lebanon	2	0.2
Belgium	1	0.1
Bermudas	1	0.1
USA	1	0.1
Total	935	100.0

Source: SRI-SCVS, prepared by the author.

followed by those registered in the United States, 5%, from Uruguay, 3%, and from Panama, 2% (see Table 12.6). Panama is a recognized tax haven. In turn, it is crucial to remember that, up until 2009, Uruguay was considered a tax haven, according to Resolution No. NAC-DGERCGC09-00704 (Jarrín Sevilla 2011), which makes its level of beneficiaries noteworthy. Moreover, regarding the leading non-Ecuadorian

Table 12.6 Domicile of the Private Company Beneficiaries of Economic Elite Trusts in Ecuador, 2019 (N=942)

Country	*N*	*Percentage*
Ecuador	1,237	86.4%
USA	76	5.3%
Uruguay	44	3.1%
Panama	29	2.0%
Spain	7	0.5%
Costa Rica	6	0.4%
Holland	6	0.4%
Canada	5	0.3%
England	4	0.3%
Norway	4	0.3%
Colombia	2	0.1%
Hong Kong	2	0.1%
British Virgin Islands	2	0.1%
Peru	2	0.1%
Germany	1	0.1%
Bahamas	1	0.1%
Belgium	1	0.1%
France	1	0.1%
Italy	1	0.1%
Total	1431	100.0%

Source: SRI-SCVS, prepared by the author.

country, the United States, while it depends on the type of private company, the fact that it is the most recurrent case calls for an analysis that considers the country's preferential regimes. Likewise, other regimes are shown in lower percentages like Holland, England, and Costa Rica, tax havens like Hong Kong, the British Virgin Islands, and the Bahamas, as well as other countries that are not considered tax havens or low-tax regimes.[9]

At this stage, it is necessary to clarify two aspects. First, analyzing each private company from the preferential regimes is essential. For example, the case of the United States suggests that the LLC private companies offer similar benefits to those of a tax haven, which is the case with other regimes recognized by the SRI. From this perspective, not all companies in this territory can be considered offshore businesses. As such, it is necessary to consider the conditions of each regime. Secondly, while the data indicates 1,431 companies, different trusts have the same company as their beneficiary. In other words, companies are counted more than once, leading to an inaccurate quantification of the foremost jurisdictions that enable tax avoidance.

Enhancing the analysis to provide an overview of the private companies and main territories considered tax havens in Ecuador is necessary. To simplify these results, each preferential regime's characteristics were considered, and the number

Table 12.7 External Beneficiary Companies of Trusts Held by Economic Elites in Ecuador, 2019 (N=942)[a]

Country	*Offshore*
United States	*21*
Panama	*21*
Uruguay	7
Spain	7
Costa Rica	*5*
England	*4*
Holland	*3*
Canada	2
Norway	2
Colombia	2
Hong Kong	*2*
British Virgin Islands	*2*
Peru	1
Germany	1
Bahamas	*1*
Belgium	1
France	1
Italy	1
Total	84

Source: SRI-SCVS, prepared by the author.

Note

[a] The residences considered tax havens and preferential regimes appear in italics.

of companies was presented without repetitions to observe recurrences. The same was done with companies in tax havens.

Eighty-four foreign beneficiaries (private companies) from trusts were identified. Fifty-nine private companies were located in eight tax havens and preferential regimes used by economic elites (see Table 12.7; for more details, see Annex). This means that, out of the total number of foreign businesses, 70% are located in jurisdictions that allow for the non-payment of taxes. As such, 59 companies can be added to the 456 that make up the tax havens, an increase of approximately 12.94%.

In this manner, the LLCs in the United States and Panama become the leading offshore jurisdictions used by the Ecuadorian economic elites through trusts. While Panama holds an ample lead in the standard count of companies in tax havens (SRI 2020), when it comes to trusts, the United States catches up, showing similar numbers. This demonstrates the importance of combatting practices detrimental to tax collection in certain states in this country. Other regimes that appear include Costa Rica with five companies, England with four, Holland with three, and finally, Hong Kong, the British Virgin Islands, and the Bahamas, each with one.

Based on these results, an estimate of the possible tax avoidance carried out by these economic elites can be made (see Table 12.8). By collecting all available

Table 12.8 Estimated Evasion by Elite Beneficiaries of Trust Companies Domiciled in Tax Havens, in Millions of Dollars

Indicator	*IR t−1*	*IR t+1*	*Average*	*IR t*	*Estimated avoidance*
	(a)	*(b)*	*(c)=(a)+(b)/2*	*(d)*	*(e)=(d)−(c)*
Total $	6.41	8.84	7.63	2.35	−5.28

Source: SRI-SCVS, prepared by the author.

information, it was possible to identify 21 elite individuals who were beneficiaries of 59 companies in tax havens. The results indicate that while offshore companies were not operating, these elites paid approximately 7.63 million dollars in income tax. By contrast, the amount paid dropped significantly while they were in operation, only amounting to 2.35 million dollars. In effect, 5.28 million dollars were left unpaid by elites with offshore companies in trusts. This value makes up 71% of the total income tax expenses of the trusts in 2019, which amounted to 7.39 million dollars. This means that, with this amount, income tax collection from trusts could nearly double.

12.5 Conclusions

These results indicate that using an offshore company makes it possible for economic elites to reduce their tax burden significantly, in the case at hand, through trusts that work as *matryoshkas*, concealing various layers and, consequently, the ownership of their beneficiaries: the economic elites of Ecuador. This corroborates the theses and findings of the literature discussed earlier and diverges from authors attempting to justify the use of trusts through technocratic reasoning. It's important to note that the analysis presented here is confined to the amounts evaded by individuals. Nonetheless, this study represents a significant step forward that ideally will spur discussions on the necessity for further research exploring tax havens and the myriad schemes employed, including trusts. Such studies are vital to moving toward a society committed to tackling prevailing inequalities through progressive tax policies.

Finally, this issue is essential in Latin America, considering that economic elites have shaped their businesses on the basis of opacity, which has had a palpable effect on public policies, shaping neoliberal states where decisions are made to strengthen market-oriented logic. In these circumstances, constructing institutions that confront this logic is necessary to avoid decisions that benefit the few at the expense of the many. This has only been an approach to the case of Ecuador. Still, for there to be a systematic advance, it is necessary to undertake a global fight against tax evasion and sanction the elites who use these and similar schemes. From this point of view, one of the first steps is to expose these dark labyrinths, and it is hoped that this and other studies will contribute to this end.

Notes

1 Government institution in charge of tax processes in Ecuador.
2 Article 5 of the Regulation for the application of the Internal Tax Regime Law in Ecuador, for tax purposes, defines an economic group as "the combination of parties, made up of both national and foreign legal persons and companies, where one or several of them directly or indirectly hold 40% of shareholdings or more in other companies."
3 This contribution focuses on quantifying trusts and showing which parts of the elites use them. The current work will not analyze the concrete devices deployed through trusts, such as transfer pricing. For more on this topic, works by Grondona (2015) and Zanotti and Gaggero (2021) are recommended.
4 An overview of the anatomy of the Ecuadorian elites is found in the work of Báez (2020b).
5 Among other existing lists, one notable contains an index of corporate tax sanctuaries of 70 territories and was updated in 2021 (Tax Justice Network [TJN], 2021). Others include those within the index of financial secrecy, which covers 133 jurisdictions in its most recent update (TJN 2020).
6 See: www.icij.org/ (June 23, 2022).
7 The main shareholders are considered to build the figure and represent the mechanism, to observe in detail see: www.bancoguayaquil.com/conocenos/accionistas/ (June 23, 2022). See: www.icij.org/investigations/pandora-papers/power-players/
8 Special thanks to Estefanía Chicaiza for her collaboration in gathering information.
9 Nonetheless, all the countries observed are found on the aforementioned lists created by the Tax Justice Network, with different levels of opacity.

References

Allan, Gregory W. 2011. "The Secret Is Out There: Searching for the Legal Justification for the Doctrine of Secret Trusts through Analysis of the Case Law." *Common Law World Review* 40 (4): 311–344.

Álvarez González, Diana P. 2019. *Normas anti-paraísos fiscales incorporadas con la Ley Orgánica de Incentivos a la Producción y Prevención del Fraude Fiscal y su efecto tributario en el contribuyente* [Masterthesis]. Quito: Universidad Andina Simón Bolívar.

Ausness, Richard C. 2007. "The Offshore Asset Protection Trust: A Prudent Financial Planning Device or the Last Refuge of a Scoundrel?" *Duquesne Law Review* 45 (2), 147–193.

Báez, Jonathan. 2017. "Hilando la desigualdad: Grupos económicos y paraísos fiscales en Ecuador." *Revista Economía* 69 (110), 13–24.

———. 2020a. "¿Cuánto pagan por impuestos las élites económicas en Ecuador?" *UNIDAD DE ANÁLISIS Y ESTUDIOS DE COYUNTURA*. https://coyunturauceiie.org/2020/10/18/cuanto-pagan-por-impuestos-las-elites-economicas-en-ecuador/ (June 23, 2022).

———. 2020b. *Desigualdad de ingresos: Élites económicas empresariales ecuatorianas, multiposicionalidad y política fiscal (2016)*. Quito: FLACSO.

———. 2021. "En las sombras: Investigando a la élite económica en América Latina." *UNIDAD DE ANÁLISIS Y ESTUDIOS DE COYUNTURA*. https://coyunturauceiie.org/2021/04/21/en-las-sombras-investigando-a-la-elite-economica-en-america-latina/ (June 23, 2022).

Cárdenas, Julian. 2016. "Enredando a las elites empresariales en América Latina: Análisis de redes de interlocking directorates y propiedad en México, Chile, Perú y Brasil." *América Latina Hoy* 73, 15–44.

Casanegra de Jantscher, Milka. 1976. "Tax Havens Explained: The Advantages and Disadvantages of Tax Havens and How They Operate." *Finance & Development* 13 (001), 31–34.

CEPAL. 2018. *Panorama Fiscal de América Latina y el Caribe 2018: Los desafíos de las políticas públicas en el marco de la Agenda 2030*. Santiago de Chile: CEPAL.

Cockfield, Arthur J. 2015. "Big Data and Tax Haven Secrecy." *SSRN Scholarly Paper 2670156*. Social Science Research Network. https://papers.ssrn.com/abstract=2670156 (June 23, 2022).

Collins, Chuck. 2021. *The Wealth Hoarders: How Billionaires Pay Millions to Hide Trillions*. Cambridge: Polity Press.

Escario Díaz-Berrio, José. L. 2011. *The Fight against Tax Havens and Tax Evasion: Progress since the London G20 Summit and the Challenges Ahead*. Madrid: OPEX.

Grondona, Verónica. 2015. "La Manipulación De Los "Precios De Transferencia" Y La Fuga De Capitales En Argentina, 2014." *ROF* 8 (20), 175–196.

Hamilton, Roger 1979. "Book Review: Modern Trusts and Taxation." *Federal Law Review* 10 (2), 203–206.

Jarrín Sevilla, Jeannette K. 2011. *Parámetros del servicio de rentas internas para determinar paraísos fiscales, y su aplicación al caso de la República Oriental de Uruguay* [Masterthesis]. Quito: Pontificia Universidad Católica del Ecuador. http://repositorio.puce.edu.ec:80/xmlui/handle/22000/4840 (June 23, 2022).

Mayorga Imbaquingo, Iván E. 2017. *Sociedades instrumentales y su vinculación con los paraísos fiscales, como elemento de elusión y evasión para el pago de impuesto a la renta en el caso ecuatoriano* [Masterthesis]. Quito: Universidad Andina Simón Bolívar.

Ordóñez, Michelle C. 2017. "Lucha contra paraísos fiscales: Una mirada crítica" *Notas de Reflexión* 44, Centro de Estudios Fiscales, 1–14. https://docplayer.es/56080464-No-44-junio-2017-lucha-contra-paraisos-fiscales-una-mirada-critica.html (June 23, 2022).

SRI. 2012. *Regímenes fiscales preferentes* (Circular No. NAC-DGECCGC12-00013). Quito: SRI.

———. 2020. *Grupos Económicos y su relación con paraísos fiscales y Panama Papers*. Quito: SRI. www.sri.gob.ec/grupos-economicos1 (June 23, 2022).

Tax Justice Network (TJN). 2015. *Financial Secrecy Index 2015. Methodology*. Bristol: TJN.

———. 2020. "*Financial Secrecy Index 2020 reports progress on global transparency – but backsliding from US, Cayman and UK prompts call for sanctions*". Bristol: Tax Justice Network. https://taxjustice.net/press/financial-secrecy-index-2020-reports-progress-on-global-transparency-but-backsliding-from-us-cayman-and-uk-prompts-call-for-sanctions/ (June 23, 2022).

———. 2021. *Índice de Guaridas Fiscales Corporativos 2021*. Bristol: Tax Justice Network. https://cthi.taxjustice.net/es/ (June 23, 2022).

Zanotti, Gustavo García, and Alejandro Javier Gaggero. 2021. "Precios de transferencia en el comercio exterior del complejo sojero argentino (2004–2020)." *Revista Economía* 73 (117), 29–44.

Zucman, Gabriel. 2013. "The Missing Wealth of Nations: Are Europe and the U.S. Net Debtors or Net Creditors?" *The Quarterly Journal of Economics* 128 (3), 1321–1364.

———. 2016. *The Hidden Wealth of Nations: The Scourge of Tax Havens*. Chicago: University of Chicago Press.

Zucman, Gabriel, and Saez, Emmanuel. 2019. *How would a progressive wealth tax work? Evidence from the economics literature* [Independent Commission for the Reform of International Corporate Taxation]. www.icrict.com/you-should-also-read/2019/6/17/how-would-a-progressive-wealth-tax-work-evidence-from-the-economics-literature (June 23, 2022).

Annex

Table A12.1 Offshore Companies in Economic Group Trusts 2019

Economic group name	*Trust*	*Offshore company*	*Nationality*
BANCO PICHINCHA	DOS	PICHINCHA HOLDINGS LLC	USA
BANCO PICHINCHA	TARDCE	TARDCE HOLDINGS LLC	USA
ALMACENES JUAN ELJURI	HOTEL PROYECTO CUENCA	PREMIER ROYAL C.A.	HOLLAND
ALMACENES JUAN ELJURI	HOTEL PROYECTO CUENCA	ROYAL BLUE BRISTOL S.A.	COSTA RICA
ALMACENES JUAN ELJURI	MERCANTIL HOSPITAL UNIVERSITARIO DEL RIO	FINANCIERA UNION DEL SUR S.A.	PANAMA
ALMACENES JUAN ELJURI	MERCANTIL BOULEVARD ORELLANA	EMPRONORTE OVERSEAS INC.	ENGLAND
ALMACENES JUAN ELJURI	MERCANTIL BOULEVARD ORELLANA	ALAMO INVESTMENTS INC	ENGLAND
ALMACENES JUAN ELJURI	DE ADMINISTRACION ACCIONES AUSTRO TF-C-518	SOUTHERN OHIO GROUP LLC	USA
ALMACENES JUAN ELJURI	GE CAPITAL-HOSPITAL DEL RIO	GE HFS LLC	USA
ALMACENES JUAN ELJURI	GENTE TF-G-01-03-04-099	AUSTROBANK OVERSEAS PANAMA	PANAMA
CORPORACIÓN FAVORITA	CITY MALL	AUHACHAPAN INVESTMENT CORPORATION LTD.	ENGLAND
CORPORACIÓN FAVORITA	CITY MALL	VUDSE INVESTMENT S.A	ENGLAND
CORPORACIÓN FAVORITA	INMOBILIARIO LOS CEIBOS	CEIBOS HOLDING LLC	USA
BANCO DE GUAYAQUIL	MERCANTIL DE ADMINISTRACION GLM	POSITANO TRADE LLC	USA
BANCO DE GUAYAQUIL	MERCANTIL DE ADMINISTRACION MELM	GRANADA INTERNATIONAL LLC	USA
BANCO DE GUAYAQUIL	MERCANTIL DE ADMINISTRACION CLM-MMS	MONTPELLIER LLC	USA
BANCO DE GUAYAQUIL	MERCANTIL DE ADMINISTRACION DCD-UNO	BERLIN TRADE LLC	USA
BANCO DE GUAYAQUIL	MERCANTIL DE ADMINISTRACION DCD-DOS	CAMBRIDGE TRADE LLC	USA
PRODUBANCO	MEGAPLAZA	ACROBUSINESS INC	PANAMA
PRODUBANCO	MEGAPLAZA	IVECO FINANCIAL INC	PANAMA

DINADEC	MERCANTIL DE ADMINISTRACION USUFRUCTO AB INBEV	AB INBEV SOUTHERN INVESTMENTS LIMITED	ENGLAND
KFC	HIDRONORMANDIA FLUJOS	NEDERLANDSE FINANCIERINGS-MAATSCHAPPIJ VOOR ONTWIKKELINGSLANDEN N.V.	HOLLAND
EXPORTADORA BANANERA	DE GARANTIA – CAMIONES LGCH	BANISI	PANAMA
SOCIEDAD AGRÍCOLA E INDUSTRIAL SAN CARLOS	DESARROLLO INMOBILIARIO MOCOLI	PROMOTORA DE CIUDADES CENTRALES S.A.	COSTA RICA
LA FABRIL	LA FAVORITA	AUSTROBANK S.A.	PANAMA
CONSENSOCORP	MERCANTIL M-CERO TRES – CERO VEINTE – DOS MIL UNO INDURAMA	BANCO PICHINCHA PANAMA, S.A.	PANAMA
N.I.R.S.A.	GAMMA	SHALVEX HOLDINGS INC.	PANAMA
N.I.R.S.A.	ALFA		
TELCONET	BOSQUES DE LOS CEIBOS	OMNIGLOBAL LIMITED	BAHAMAS
CORPORACIÓN CIPAL	MERCANTIL ACCIONES ICP	SIA PRODUCTS LLC	USA
SURPAPEL	MERCANTIL PROEXPO-IIG CAPITAL	IIG Capital LLC	USA
EDIMCA	GARANTIA GEM	COMPAÑIA ANTLER ASSOCIATES LLC	USA
		NEDERLANDSE FINANCIERINGS-MAATSCHAPPIJ VOOR ONTWIKKELINGSLANDEN N.V.	HOLLAND
EXPALSA	MERCANTIL DE GARANTIA DON ISIDRO	CARGANI HOLDING LLC	USA
		CYBER FINANCIAL OVERSEAS INC.	PANAMA
		DUMMORE ASSETS CORP	PANAMA
PICA PLÁSTICOS INDUSTRIALES	BOYACA	MALVINA INVEST & TRADE INC.	PANAMA
PICA PLÁSTICOS INDUSTRIALES	SAN MARTIN.	NADINA MANAGEMENT CORP.	PANAMA
TECOPESCA	DE GARANTIA MARINA VISION	BANCO INTERNACIONAL DE COSTA RICA S.A.	PANAMA

(Continued)

Table A12.1 (Continued)

Economic group name	*Trust*	*Offshore company*	*Nationality*
IMBAUTO	ASSET MANAGEMENT	ADMC ASSET MANAGEMENT & DEVELOPMENT CORPORATION S.A.	PANAMA
IMBAUTO	VASA	DESARROLLOS INTERNACIONALES SIGNO INVESTMENTS S.A	COSTA RICA
CENTROS COMERCIALES DEL ECUADOR	MADISON II	LA CUADRA RAYES, SOCIEDAD ANONIMA	COSTA RICA
CENTROS COMERCIALES DEL ECUADOR	LA CUADRA		
NUEVO RANCHO NURANSA	MERCANTIL RIOLAGO	PACIFIC COAST REAL PROPERTY LLC	USA
	PLAZA LAGOS II		
	MERCANTIL ISLALAGO		
	MERCANTIL CASALAGO DOS		
	MERCANTIL PLAZA LAGOS		
	MERCANTIL CONDOMINIOS PLAZA LAGOS		
	DE GARANTIA ELEVEN GLOBAL – GLIDE MASTER I	GLIDE MASTER FUND SPC LTD. – AV ALTERNATIVE FUND II – (MASTER) SEGREGATED PORTAFOLIO	BRITISH VIRGIN ISLANDS
ENVASES DEL LITORAL	CULVER	NEWELL BUSINESS CORP.	PANAMA
BANCO AMAZONAS	BOSQUE REAL	ZEUDI ENTERPRISES S.A.	PANAMA
CARTIMEX	MERCANTIL EN GARANTIA FUROIANI CERO CERO UNO	SANTA DANIELA S.A	PANAMA
DELCORP	GARANTIA ECUAGRAN CARGILL	CAI Trading LLC	USA
ICESA	GARANTIA PLASMA	TULIP ELECTRONICS MANAGEMENT C.V.	HOLLAND
		BRIGHT EXPORT LIMITED	HONG KONG
		SUNIL KAMUR RAMCHANDANI	HONG KONG
		SMILESTAR LTD.	PANAMA
		NASIM BEKHAR	PANAMA

ANDINAMOTORS	CAROLINA IV	CARMAR INTERNATIONAL LLC	USA
	CAROLINA II	MARCAR DF LLC	USA
	CAROLINA GUAYAQUIL		
	DIANA IX		
	MERCANTIL CAROLINA III		
ASISERVY	DE GARANTIA ASISERVY-BICSA	BANCO INTERNACIONAL DE COSTA RICA S.A.[a]	PANAMA
	DE GARANTIA N&H		
CONDUTO ECUADOR	EN GARANTIA HIDROSIERRA	CIFI LATAM S. A.	PANAMA
	FLUJOS CIFI – HIDROSIERRA		
ORTEGA ABOGADOS & ASOCIADOS EJOMOT	DE ADMINISTRACION Y PAGO ANGLO – TERCEROS	ESTRELLAMAR INVERSIONES S.A.	PANAMA
	DE PAGO FDP-POL		
	DE PAGO FDP-SALDO		
	DE PAGO FDP-SALDO TERCEROS		
	MERCANTIL DE GARANTIA TERRABIENES – STARVILLE	STARVILLE CORPORATION	BRITISH VIRGIN ISLANDS
TALLERES Y SERVICIOS TASESA	MARGATE	GRANDERSON RESOURCES LLC	USA
TOTEM	GAMBELI	WAKEFIELD ENTERPRISES LLC	USA

Source: SRI-SCVS, prepared by the author.

Note

[a] This company is also used by another EG. It is used as a reference, but it amounts to 59 companies.

Index

FSC
www.fsc.org
MIX
Papier | Fördert gute Waldnutzung
FSC® C083411

Kolibri 360 GmbH
Ferdinand-Jühlke-Straße 7
99095 Erfurt, Deutschland
produktsicherheit@kolibri360.de